FAILURE IS IMPOSSIBLE

FOAL

ALSO BY LYNN SHERR
Susan B. Anthony Slept Here
(with Jurate Kazickas)

Failure Is Impossible

SUSAN B. ANTHONY
IN HER OWN WORDS

LYNN SHERR

TIMES 𝕿 BOOKS

RANDOM HOUSE

Yours Sincerely
Susan B. Anthony

Copyright © 1995 by Lynn Sherr

All rights reserved under International and Pan-American Copyright Conventions.
Published in the United States by Times Books, a division of Random House, Inc., New
York, and simultaneously in Canada by Random House of Canada Limited, Toronto.

This work was originally published in hardcover by Times Books, a division of Random
House, Inc., in 1995.

LIBRARY OF CONGRESS CATALOGING-IN-PUBLICATION DATA

Sherr, Lynn.
   Failure is impossible : Susan B. Anthony in her own words / Lynn
Sherr.
     p.   cm.
   ISBN 0-8129-2718-4
   1. Anthony, Susan B. (Susan Brownell), 1820–1906. 2. Feminists—
United States—Biography. 3. Suffragists—United States—
Biography. I. Anthony, Susan B. (Susan Brownell), 1820–1906.
II. Title.
HQ1413.A55S48   1995
324.6'23'092—dc20
[B]   94-29913

DESIGNED BY BETH TONDREAU DESIGN
Manufactured in the United States of America
LSI 001

COVER: SUSAN B. ANTHONY, 1899. IN HER BIOGRAPHY,
IDA HUSTED HARPER CAPTIONED THIS PHOTOGRAPH,
"MISS ANTHONY MAKING AN UNANSWERABLE ARGUMENT."

FRONTISPIECE: ANTHONY STAINED GLASS WINDOW,
MEMORIAL A.M.E. ZION CHURCH, ROCHESTER, NEW YORK.
THE FIRST MEMORIAL ERECTED TO ANTHONY
AFTER HER DEATH, IT WAS DONATED BY MEMBERS OF
THE AFRICAN-AMERICAN COMMUNITY IN ROCHESTER.

TITLE PAGE: ILLUSTRATION FROM A
PHOTOGRAPH OF ANTHONY IN HER FIFTIES

THIS BOOK IS FOR THE HILFORD MEN—
Jeffrey, Andrew, and James—
with love.

CONTENTS

INTRODUCTION

Ffebruary 15, 1894: Susan B. Anthony was spending her seventy-fourth birthday the way she knew best. She was in Washington, D.C., where neither slush nor icy winds had kept her from the meeting at the opera house at the corner of Twelfth and F Streets. As usual, Anthony wore a black silk dress, with her thick hair—mostly gray now—pulled back in a knot, her blue eyes flashing behind gold-rimmed spectacles. As usual, she was presiding over the annual convention of the National American Woman Suffrage Association and talking about getting the right to vote. And as she had done throughout her long and productive life, she was zeroing in on a fundamental truth, one that resonates a century later. Reminding an audience filled with an unusual number of younger women delegates that she and her colleagues were now in their fifth decade of seeking votes for women, she predicted with stunning accuracy:

We shall some day be heeded, and when we shall have our amendment to the Constitution of the United States, everybody will think it was always so, just exactly as many young people believe that all the privileges, all the freedom, all the enjoyments which woman now possesses always were hers. They have no idea of how every single inch of ground that she stands upon today has been gained by the hard work of some little handful of women of the past.

A year earlier, she had used even blunter language:

[S]o many of these young people know nothing of the past; they are apt to think they have sprung up like somebody's gourd, and that nothing ever was done until they came.

I used to think that myself. Back in the late 1960s, as a young reporter covering the first public outbursts of the new wave of feminism, I was skeptical, then intrigued, and finally committed to the phenomenon known as the women's movement. It was an exciting and confusing time: wildly energizing to those of us who understood that we, too, had been trapped in Betty Friedan's "feminine mystique"; plainly frightening to those who were unprepared for the upheaval of traditional social behavior. But we were convinced, and with the arrogance of the converted, we also believed we had just invented this new revolution.

And why not? Like most Americans who had been taught history as a succession of wars and dates, I was unacquainted with the notion of foremothers. If pressed, I might have identified Susan B. Anthony as a stern spinster who ran around in bloomers getting women the right to vote—a right I had never, ever questioned. I knew we had gotten full suffrage in 1920, thanks to the Nineteenth Amendment to the Constitution. But I had no idea of the struggle that had preceded it, not a clue about the hatred it engendered and the ugly tactics used to prevent it.

Fortunately, a new crop of books by female historians, restoring women to their rightful place in our past—as well as my own discovery of original sources with their rich, unfiltered details—made me realize how much I had missed. I learned that Anthony and her colleagues had not only gotten there first, and said it better, but that they had carefully, wittily, and sometimes painfully laid the groundwork for virtually every right we were either demanding or already took for granted. And they had done it precisely so that future generations might enjoy the freedom denied them. We were their beneficiaries, and we barely remembered them. Inspired by my new knowledge, I hastened to help spread the word.

As I dug into the research, I realized that the brightest star of all was Susan B. Anthony. She not only helped create the first women's movement in this country, she led it, brilliantly, for more than fifty years. Indeed, it was her tireless dedication to The Cause—the drive for the most crucial political right of all, the vote—and her astounding skill at organization that not only changed laws and attitudes, but also helped introduce the entire realm of equal rights to a very reluctant nation. Neither the first nor the only woman to seek justice for women, she was by far the best known and least expendable link in a long chain of committed feminists. She broke every rule that didn't suit her, charmed almost every reporter who ever met her. And she was smart and funny, as well. Although she died in 1906, fourteen years before the Nineteenth Amendment was ratified, her last public words—"Failure is impossible"—reflected her unflagging optimism and became a battle cry that inspired the final push for the ballot. She became my hero, too.

Today the world has taken notice of the roles of women in shaping our civilization. But for all the new consciousness, for all the new courses in classrooms, it is hard to find anyone who appreciates the power and personality of this extraordinary woman. Of the five full-fledged Anthony biographies, only one is recent and only two are in print. On the shelves of women's history books, few make the connection between what she did then and what we still face today. As a result, modern feminists, whatever they call themselves, tend to believe that every problem they face is a new one, that every issue needs a new solution. In short, they are still trying to reinvent the wheel without realizing that the instruction manual has already been written.

This book is intended to reclaim Susan B. Anthony's place in our lives. She was so prescient, she wrote much of it herself.

My dinner-party description of the work in progress was "Susan B. Anthony in Sound Bites," which is not meant to disparage either her life time of reform or my own career in television news. Rather, it is meant to make her more accessible in modern terms; to capture, from a rich body of letters, speeches, and writings, both her character and her passionate pursuit of justice. As a journalist, I rely on words—specifically, one's own words— to define an individual. And I spend a good deal of my professional life trying to get them down accurately. So I wanted to let Anthony speak for herself, without the intrusion of biographers and revisionists, who have on occasion tended to smooth over her delightfully candid comments or disregard her very personal observations. Just for example, after hearing a Sunday sermon in 1901, she informed the minister of her disappointment that he had neglected to speak out against lynching—the horrid practice then spreading through the South. Her official biographer, Ida Husted Harper, wrote that Anthony recorded her polite protest in her diary: "I waited and told him so." Not bad, and the kind of attitude I wanted to communicate. But when I returned to the original source, I found that Anthony had written simply, "I told him so." She would not have waited to convey such an important message. It may seem minor, but that is vintage Susan B. Anthony—sharp, precise, uncompromising. That is the person I wanted to capture.

My goal was attainable only because she left such a long, lush stream of words: on the podium, in print, and especially in the fine ink-penned lines that cover countless thousands of sheets of stationery. Anthony was an inces-

sant letter writer and a devoted diarist, and the collections of those most intimate thoughts reveal a thoughtful, caring, and determined friend. Her lectures, even as captured piecemeal by the newspaper reporters of the day, without benefit of tape recorders, still make their points logically and forcefully. And her frequent interviews with some of the top journalists of her time give us valuable eyewitness accounts of a political leader in action. The challenge was to limit the words to fit between two covers. While many of the quotes I've selected will be familiar to students of women's history, many more have never before appeared in print, at least not in our era. I believe they prove definitively that this woman of the nineteenth century, who made us more equal in the twentieth, now effortlessly joins us on the brink of the twenty-first; that she is as relevant to our lives today—and to those of our children tomorrow—as she was to the enormous following she finally enjoyed in her own lifetime.

Back then, she was a very important person. At first ridiculed by politicians and dismissed by the press, she was ultimately welcomed into the White House, cheered in Congress, and revered in print as the "dominant mind that guided the destinies of the greatest women's movement of the century." She was so famous that headlines identified her only as "Susan B.," and her autograph was marketed as aggressively as modern baseball cards.

She was so beloved as a national leader that in 1896 a colleague from Utah sent along a proposal to make her birthday a national holiday. It would be celebrated "throughout civilized lands" as "Woman's Day," with speeches, songs, and other exercises to commemorate "the betterment of woman"—in short, "a grand woman's holiday." The letter went on to suggest that "every woman in the land . . . white or black, rich or poor . . . no matter who or what she may be . . . gratefully drop into her ward contribution box a dime or nickel for the cause of woman . . . it being a privilege to donate so small and yet so potent a sum for the onward progress of her sex."

It is a measure of her modesty that Susan B. Anthony herself immediately amended the proposal to suggest that the birthdays of all such pioneers be honored; it is indicative of her charisma that the letter writer was a Mormon (one of Brigham Young's daughters), who had become Anthony's close friend and ardent admirer even though her polygamous heritage enraged the great agitator for women's independence. And it is a telling sign of the times—then and now—that the purpose of the event was to raise money for the eternally underfunded campaign to get women the right to vote; and that, after all, nothing was ever done to implement the suggestion.

Amazingly, you can't blame this one on the federal government. At least five times since her death in 1906, U.S. officials have done their part to make Susan B. Anthony a household name. There is the marble statue in the crypt of the U.S. Capitol of Anthony and her women's rights colleagues, Lucretia Mott and Elizabeth Cady Stanton, dedicated in 1921. There are the two postage stamps with her picture—the three-cent purple, issued in 1936, and the fifty-cent in deeper purple in 1955. There is her home in Rochester, New York, a national historic landmark since 1966. (Not to mention the nearby street, airport wing, university building, and stained-glass church window named for her by local supporters.) And of course there is the Anthony dollar coin, introduced in 1979 with great fanfare and now gathering dust in government vaults. Ironically, it suffered much the same fate as Susan B. Anthony herself, with ridicule and then neglect leading to today's near obscurity.

You could make the case that the coin just didn't work; that the stamps have been bypassed by modern society. You cannot say that about the woman. Susan B. Anthony faced many of today's predicaments herself and addressed them with eloquence and wisdom.

She dealt not only with the vote, but with most of the same issues confronting modern women—domestic violence, the frustration of being single, the value of female friendship, the victimization of prostitutes, the battle for equal pay. She also published a newspaper edited by and for women, cautioned workers to beware of sexual harassment, and railed against the use of tobacco.

A spinster, she was one of the first in the nation to call for the legal rights of married women.

Childless, she approved of a young colleague who adopted a baby without benefit of marriage.

Politically a nonperson, she was arrested in 1872 for daring to vote (but never paid a penny of what she called "your unjust penalty").

Accused of anarchy for upsetting the relations between women and men, she thought of herself as a homebody and casually greeted one reporter while dusting the rug on her front stoop.

Hooted down at her first public meeting (to which, she was told, the women had been invited to listen, not to speak), the young schoolmarm became one of the nation's most popular lecturers, crisscrossing the country at a breathtaking pace, giving speeches and leading rallies for state suffrage organizations until she was well into her eighties.

In fact, she did much of her best and most lasting work after she turned fifty years old, an occasion marked by reverent editorials in the nation's largest newspapers. In what may have been the first documented party of its kind, Susan B. Anthony celebrated her fiftieth birthday at a glittering gathering of prominent women and men in a townhouse at 49 East Twenty-third Street in New York City. At a time when most ladies either ignored or lied about their ages, Anthony, according to the New York Sun, *"had the courage to acknowledge"* hers. *Their headline:* A BRAVE OLD MAID. *The New York* World *called her "the Moses of her sex":*

> She has perpetrated a daring innovation in regard to that subject which has hitherto been with women the most sacred and inviolate. No more talk of women of certain or uncertain age. Susan squarely owns up to fifty; and henceforth the sterner sex need have no compunction in discussing the ages of their female friends. This act of Susan's marks an era in the woman's movement more singular and portentous than any that has preceded it.

The truth is, birthdays played such a public part of her life that Anthony couldn't have hidden her age if she'd wanted to. Her half-century gala—complete with poetry, presents, refreshments, and cake—was merely the first of a series of progressively grander events hosted regularly and very openly by adoring colleagues.
Little wonder. Listen to her diary on the occasion:

> Fiftieth birthday! One half-century done, one score of it hard labor for bettering humanity—temperance—emancipation—enfranchisment—oh, such a struggle!

Who was this woman? The earliest descriptions varied only slightly, from the downright hostile to the vaguely amused. One editor thought he was paying her a compliment by writing "She is an elderly maiden lady, quite different from the vinegar-faced virago whom we had been led to look for . . ." But cut through the drivel from those threatened by her boldness, and you wind up with a towering presence. Working from the outside in, here is the report of her physical examination for a life insurance policy when she was thirty-five:

> Height, 5 ft. 5 in.; figure, full; chest, measure 38 in.; weight, 156 lbs.; complexion, fair; habits, healthy and active; nervous affections, none; character of respiration, clear, resonant, murmur perfect; heart, normal in rhythm and valvular sound; pulse 66 per minute; disease, none. The life is a very good one.

Her only impediment was a slightly crossed right eye that was made worse by surgery—an affront to her vanity that led her to pose mostly in left profile for photographers. From pictures and descriptions we know of her strong chin, erect bearing, trim (for the period) figure, and firm handshake. She had a clear, sturdy voice that made its points logically. And, like so many other victims of nineteenth-century dental care, she had to get false teeth.

As for her manner, here are some of the words used over and over again to depict this most scrutinized figure: selfless, diplomatic, elegant, charming, generous, friendly, determined, polite, curious, open, amusing, self-possessed, and, once again, selfless. As a leader, she was compared to Napoleon and Bismarck—male icons being the only ones considered worthy of emulation. As a friend, she combined the worldly wisdom of a woman with the playful spirit of a girl. She had an irrepressible optimism that gave way only rarely to moods of depression. And she was so focused on her mission, she raced through life—living and writing with dashes, not periods—no time for full stops; making her points by underlining important words in her letters (sometimes twice) and stamping her right foot on the stage for emphasis. Above all, she was a commonsense pragmatist whose lack of pretension reflected deep pride in her Quaker roots. "Sentiment never was and never can be a guarantee for justice," she once said. Another time, requesting a California colleague to send personal information for a book of biographical sketches of suffrage women, Anthony cautioned her to send "no puffs—just bare facts." She could have been describing her own life.

I do not mean to suggest that she was perfect. To her colleagues in the suffrage wars and her adversaries in politics, Susan B. Anthony could be overly forceful, stubborn, and exasperating in her single-minded goal. At her seventieth birthday party in 1890, yet another public ceremony, her close friend Elizabeth Cady Stanton good-naturedly recalled sailing to Europe after years of productive but often strained collaboration between the two suffrage pioneers.

With an ocean between us, I said, now I shall enjoy a course of light reading . . . and write no more calls, resolutions, or speeches for conventions—when, lo! one day I met Susan face to face in the streets of London with a new light in her eyes. Lo! there were more worlds to conquer. She had decided on an International Council in Washington, so I had to return with her to the scenes of our conflict. . . .

Well, as all women are supposed to be under the thumb of some man, I prefer a tyrant of my own sex, so I shall not deny the patent fact of my subjection; for I do believe that I have developed into much more of a woman under Susan's jurisdiction.

Susan B. Anthony was very, very wise. Many of the things she said a hundred or so years ago still sound familiar, starting with her remarks to a sellout crowd at a lecture in Michigan:

We hear it said that the woman's cause is dead. This does not look like it. This does not look as though no interest was being taken on this subject.

There was never in the history of the world such a period of transition as the one through which we are now passing, and it is natural that the institution of marriage should be included in the general shaking up.

The women of this nation must be awakened to a sense of their degradation—political—or at least *we who are awake*—must make an effort to awaken those who are dead asleep.

Susan Brownell Anthony was born on February 15, 1820, in the upstairs bedroom of the house her father had built in Adams, Massachusetts, a rural enclave in the Berkshire Mountains imbued with Revolutionary spirit. It would later be pointed out by her disciples that a radical from another century—the astronomer Galileo, who dared to declare that the earth was not the center of the universe—shared her birthdate, and that at the time she actually appeared on this planet, Ralph Waldo Emerson was seventeen, Abraham Lincoln was eleven, Harriet Beecher Stowe was six, and Elizabeth Cady Stanton was four. The young nation would need them all.

There were only twenty-three states then, but their union was threatened by the practice sanctioned in the South: slavery. And all states—including those in the South—were ruled by what Anthony saw as another type of bondage. Just as slaves belong to their masters, she pointed out, wives belong to their husbands. That's the way the law read—Blackstone's old English common law, which bluntly stated, "The husband and wife are one, and that one is the husband." It meant that a married woman in Amer-

ica had no legal right to any aspect of her relationship with her husband: she could not own property, earn money, make contracts, sue or be sued, or be guardian of her own children. When enforced—which was often—it meant that wives could be seized if they ran away, and beaten; that they had to beg their husbands for spending money; that they lost custody of their children if the father chose to spirit them away.

All women—married or not—were bound by additional restrictions: they could not attend college (there were none for females), could work comfortably in only a handful of professions (housework, sewing, teaching, and factories), and, when they did, generally took home a mere fraction of the pay of their male coworkers. There were no licensed women doctors, ordained ministers, lawyers, or elected senators.

And of course no woman could vote. Not for school board, not for mayor, and certainly not for President of the United States.

But there was no bias in taxation. Single or widowed women who did own property had to pay their dues to a government that would not let them participate in running it.

Luckily for young Susan (who abbreviated her middle name to the famous initial in her teen years), her family and surroundings nourished a far freer spirit. Her father, Daniel, a Quaker, had married Lucy Read, a Baptist, and their relative prosperity formed a solid background in which she and her two brothers and three sisters (another sister died in infancy) grew up. "I had all the freedom I wanted from the time I was a child," she later said of her background, constantly pointing out that at the Friends' Meeting House, men and women were treated as equals. In the mid-1800s, that was unique.

The letters and memories recall a deeply loving family, genuinely close and respectful of one another. Once, when Susan and her sisters persuaded their father to stay in town to hear a concert with them, he told them on the drive home, "Never again ask me to do such a thing; I suffered more in thinking of your mother at home alone than any enjoyment could possibly contemplate." Susan remembered her mother as a kindly soul who "never asked me to stop at home when she was living, not even after she became feeble, but always said, 'Go and do all the good you can.' "

Until her own death, Susan B. Anthony would annually record in her diary the anniversaries of the days her mother and father had died—tender, aching tributes to the very foundations of her life.

Her father proved the stronger influence on her career. Although his Quaker convictions against a government that went to war kept him from voting until 1860 (when the evils of slavery drove him to the polls), he early urged his very headstrong daughter to follow her own instincts and was often ahead of her in the path to social justice.

In 1845 Daniel Anthony moved his family to Rochester, then a center of political activism with a strong emphasis on the need to abolish slavery. Every Sunday at the Anthony farm, a dozen or more abolitionists, including the esteemed ex-slave Frederick Douglass, would meet to discuss the latest news and plan ways to end human bondage. Susan participated fully in the discussions and served as an engineer on the underground railroad that helped escort fugitive slaves to freedom. All her life she would retain close African-American friends and champion their cause.

She also joined the temperance movement—that distinctively nineteenth-century crusade to stem the flow of alcoholic beverages. Today it may seem amusing or even quaint, but public drunkenness was a serious problem in the unregulated society of the early 1800s. In 1875 Anthony claimed that 1 in 17 Americans were alcoholics, by which she meant American men. Other estimates say 1 in 5 people were affected by an alcoholic, with abused and abandoned wives and children highest on the list of victims. Susan B. Anthony never touched liquor in her life and never forgot unpleasant encounters like the one at an early military ball:

> My fancy for attending dances is fully satiated. I certainly shall not attend another unless I can have a total abstinence man to accompany me, and not one whose highest delight is to make a fool of himself.

As happened with many women, temperance and abolition became the training grounds for her even greater commitment to a more widespread problem. On the road, delivering lectures, she recognized woman's utter helplessness when faced with an alcoholic husband. She also experienced for the first time the hostility of some men toward women in public life. Records exist of downright ugliness toward Anthony, like other women, as she spoke her mind. At the age of seventy-five, in a newspaper interview, she gave this sentimental summary of how it affected her—a reminiscence that may describe the general time rather than a specific event. She said she had told her father of one temperance convention she had worked hard to organize:

> . . . and at the close they drafted a resolution of thanks to various people, and my name was included. When the resolutions were introduced, a man rose and moved that my name be stricken out, as it was unbecoming in a convention to thank a woman, and, if she were modest, she would be offended by such publicity, and, therefore, my name was stricken out. I went home to my old Quaker father and said I had resolved that from that

time on I would work for the cause of woman, and, throwing myself upon my knees, I, sobbing, laid my head in my father's lap. He placed his hand on my head and gently said: "If thee must, Susan, thee must."

She had not been present at the creation of the women's rights movement—the historic Seneca Falls Convention of 1848, the first public convention in the world to focus on women's issues. There was delivered the unprecedented Declaration of Sentiments and Resolutions, a feminist version of the Declaration of Independence that proclaimed "all men and women are created equal." Anthony was teaching school at the time and was actually amused to read about the event in the paper—until she learned that her parents and sister Mary had attended the second session of the convention in Rochester. Nor did she attend the first national women's rights convention at Worcester, Massachusetts, in 1850. But she was getting interested—particularly over the custom discussed there of describing deceased wives solely as the "relict," or remnant, of their spouse.

I did read the New York *Tribune,* and I was converted by the report . . . Among the speeches was one by Lucy Stone, whom I then had never seen, in which she said the married woman's epitaph was the "relict" of John Smith, or some other man, who had owned her. I then made up my mind that I would be the relict of no man.

It began to come together for her in 1851, when she met the woman with whom she would form the friendship that fashioned a revolution. Elizabeth Cady Stanton was four years older and already a veteran of a broad range of reform activities. In 1840 she and Lucretia Mott, the forward-thinking Quaker from Philadelphia, had attended the World's Antislavery Convention in London—where the men were so unsettled by the presence of female delegates, they forced them to sit through the entire meeting in a separate section. That inspired Stanton and Mott to call the Seneca Falls Convention, in Stanton's hometown, eight years later. In Stanton, Anthony gained not only a friend and partner, but a new cause. She was an eager pupil and a quick-learning collaborator. Anthony and Stanton would write, plot, and revolutionize together for more than half a century.

Susan B. Anthony attended her first women's rights convention in 1852, in Syracuse, and almost immediately made the connection that would drive her life's work: women needed the ballot to get power. The vote would be her goal. Once again, her father was there early. During her 1853 women's rights lecture tour, Daniel Anthony wrote that he had read news-

paper reports of her meetings, all "in a rejoicing mood that woman at last has taken hold in earnest to aid in the reformation of the mighty evils of the day. Yet with all this 'rejoicing,' " he went on, "probably not one of these papers would advocate placing the ballot in the hands of woman as the easiest, quickest and most efficient way of enabling her to secure not only this but other 'reforms.' "

She would later talk about becoming more famous than he.

I remember once a man who had just met my father asked him if he was the father of Susan B. "There was a time, Susan," said my father, "when a daughter might shine by reflected light from her father, but things seem to have changed considerably."

What made her so famous so fast was evident, in 1856, to Frances D. Gage, her traveling companion on the trail for women's rights. In the bitter (twelve degrees below zero) winter, while they traipsed about New York State "talking to the people all about Woman's Rights, which means woman's wrongs, you know," a star was born.

I wish you could hear Susan, as she stands before her audience, setting forth the necessity of woman's taking hold of industrial employments; of living an independent living; of working because it is right to work, and a disgrace to be idle. And she reads off her list of trades for women—shoemakers, jewelers, machinists, moulders of small wares, tellers in bank, book-keepers, postmasters, copyers, lighthouse and toll-gate keepers, sellers of tickets at railroad depots, grocery keepers, engravers, drafters of buildings, machinery, inventions, and the like, artists, doctors, lawyers, ministers (not of doctrine, but of truth), gardeners, managers of shops, printers, publishers, &c, &c. . . .

If they don't take her advice, it will not be because she does not tell her story well, or fails to give it all the force of her earnest and unselfish womanly interest. . . .

Susan is not, perhaps, the most eloquent speaker in the world. But her earnestness and truthfulness make her eloquent to me. Her labors in her own State are wonderful; and the time will come when her sex will reap the fruit from the seeds of her planting, whether they recognize the hand that strewed them or no.

The women they met responded enthusiastically. The men, then as now, were more appreciative if they had girls of their own. "How men thank us for words of encouragement to their daughters! (whatever they may think of our talk to wives)," Gage continued. But elsewhere, Susan B. Anthony encountered the ridicule that would persist for decades. When she and Stanton tried to rewrite state law by presenting their petition for property rights for married women to the New York Senate Judiciary Committee later that year, the entire chamber fell into roars of laughter. It was all a joke to them, and they didn't even try to disguise their scorn. Their condescending report fueled Anthony's anger for decades:

The Committee is composed of married and single gentlemen. The bachelors on the Committee, with becoming diffidence, have left the subject pretty much up to the married gentlemen. They have considered it with the aid of the light they have before them and the experience married life has given them. Thus aided, they are enabled to state that the ladies always have the best place and choicest tidbit at the table. They always have the best seat in the cars, carriages and sleighs; the warmest place in the winter and the coolest place in the summer. They have their choice on which side of the bed they will lie, front or back. A lady's dress costs three times as much as that of a gentleman; and, at the present time, with the prevailing fashion, one lady occupies three times as much space in the world as a gentleman. It has thus appeared to the married gentlemen of your Committee, being a majority (the bachelors being silent for the reason mentioned and also probably for the further reason that they are still suitors for the favors of the gentler sex) that, if there is any inequity or oppression in the case, the gentlemen are the sufferers. They, however, have presented no petition for redress; having, doubtless, made up their minds to yield to an inevitable destiny.

On the whole, the Committee have concluded to recommend no measure, except as they have observed several instances in which husband and wife have signed the same petition. In such cases, they would recommend the parties to apply for a law authorizing them to change dresses, that the husband may wear petticoats and the wife the breeches, and thus indicate to their neighbors and the public the true relation in which they stand to each other.

The humiliation was only a brief deterrence. Anthony understood that if men wouldn't listen, women might. She found her strength in awakening women to the problem and organizing them into action. She helped form a giant political sisterhood, an enviably affectionate and savvy group of women whose very actions invented the concept, if not the term, of net-

working. The names of her cohorts form an honor roll of women's history: Stanton, Mott, Lucy Stone (her predecessor in temperance and abolition), Antoinette Brown Blackwell (the nation's first ordained female minister), Harriet Beecher Stowe and her sister Isabella Beecher Hooker, Julia Ward Howe (author of "The Battle Hymn of the Republic"), and on and on.

They were not without their differences. One notable split pitted Stanton and Anthony's New York–based National Woman Suffrage Association against Stone and Howe's more conservative, Boston-based American Woman Suffrage Association, for more than twenty years. When they reunited, they worked together, lobbying Congress, stumping the states, rallying other women. In 1888 they expanded into an international organization; in 1893 they got their own pavilion at the Chicago World's Fair. And through it all, Susan B. Anthony slipped in suffrage whenever she could. Her friend, the Reverend Anna Howard Shaw, revealed the leader's creative approach to mailing out suffrage literature:

> She does not wait to be asked for it. She just sends it out in every letter she posts. When she pays her grocer's bill into the envelope go all the leaflets that one cent will carry. Uncle Sam never makes a fraction of a cent off of Miss Anthony. A letter of congratulations to the mother of a new baby has its freight of suffrage documents. Because, if it is a boy, his education on the suffrage question should begin early; if a girl, she should know from the beginning just what she will have to contend with.

The first federal proposals for woman suffrage were presented to Congress in 1868. The first time a formal amendment was submitted was January 1878. It is worth noting that at the time it was called the Sixteenth Amendment. More than four decades later, when it was finally passed, it was the Nineteenth Amendment. Not a word of the original proposal had been changed. Anthony, who did not live to see it happen, was nonetheless optimistic about its inevitability, thanks to incremental victories.

Starting with Kansas in 1861, some two dozen states let women vote in school elections by 1900; another handful gave women suffrage in municipal and other matters. The first big breakthrough came in 1869, when the territory of Wyoming voted its women full suffrage—the first in the world. It would be followed by Utah, Colorado, and Idaho by 1896.

There was more progress in other areas. By the end of the century, married women had most of their legal rights, all women could attend a wide number of colleges and universities, and most professions had at least a few female employees. In 1900 Susan B. Anthony proudly reeled off a list from the last census that included

219 women coal miners, 32 women woodchoppers, 30 quarry-women, 59 women blacksmiths, 129 women butchers, 191 women carpenters, 24 women hostlers, 4 women locomotive engineers and firemen, 1 woman pilot, 83 women undertakers, 48 women livery-stable keepers, 2 women auctioneers, 237 women hackmen and teamsters, 1 woman wheelwright, 42 women brick and stone masons, 147 women bartenders, 30 women sextons, 21 women hunters and guides, 47 women engineers and firemen (not locomotive), 5315 women hotel-keepers, 2 women veterinary surgeons, 4555 women doctors, 208 women lawyers, 1235 women clergymen, 22 women architects, 337 women dentists, 888 women journalists and 10,810 women artists. . . . It is beyond a doubt that before long women will be sent to Congress as Representatives by some of the States . . . and who knows but that within the next century they may be appointed to the Supreme Bench? Indeed, it is not at all beyond the bounds of possibility that a woman may be elected President some day.

Virtually every demand that had been made at Seneca Falls had been won — with a single exception. Anthony knew that without the vote, there would be no further progress.

I do not wish to be understood for a moment . . . as maintaining that woman stands on a perfect equality with man in any of the above-mentioned departments—in the industries, education, organization, public speaking or the laws. She simply has made immense gains in all, and her standing has been completely revolutionized . . . Woman will never have equality of rights anywhere, she never will hold those she now has by an absolute tenure, until she possesses the fundamental right of self-representation. This fact is so obvious as to need no argument.

Which was why she never stopped working for that most elusive right of all.

Because granting to men the right to give these blessings to women concedes the power to take them away. All is on an insecure basis till woman holds in her own hand the ballot—that little piece of paper which can make or unmake laws and legislators, and which compels respectful consideration from the representatives.

Today, as we celebrate seventy-five years of female suffrage, we know that the ballot alone did not bring full equality. But Susan B. Anthony understood that it was the critical first step. "The world never has witnessed a greater revolution than in the sphere of woman during this fifty years," she said in 1904, eager to get on with the next fifty, and the fifties after that, to attain even greater goals. In a magazine article she said she often asked herself the question "How long must the greatest brains, the most commanding ability, of the women of this country continue to be absorbed in this struggle to secure their own freedom, the power to do the work which the nation needs, and which waits for them?"

Carrie Chapman Catt, the woman who succeeded Anthony as president of the suffrage association and presided over the amendment's final ratification in 1920, provided the answer much later:

To get the word male . . . out of the constitution cost the women of the country fifty-two years of pauseless campaign thereafter. During that time they were forced to conduct 480 campaigns to urge Legislatures to submit suffrage amendments to voters; 47 campaigns to induce State constitutional conventions to write woman suffrage into State constitutions; 277 campaigns to persuade State party conventions to include woman suffrage planks; 30 campaigns to urge presidential party conventions to adopt woman suffrage planks in party platforms, and 19 campaigns with 19 successive congresses. Millions of dollars were raised, mainly in small sums, and expended with economic care. Hundreds of women gave the accumulated possibilities of an entire lifetime, thousands gave years of their lives, hundreds of thousands gave constant interest and such aid as they could. It was a continuous, seemingly endless chain of activity. Young suffragists who helped forge the last links of that chain were not born when it began. Old suffragists who forged the first links were dead when it ended.

How you use this book is entirely up to you. Since it is not a proper biography, you don't have to read it in sequence, although the chapters do proceed in a rough chronology, as do most of the quotes within individual chapters. Feel free to dip in and out, to get a sense of this amazing woman. Or, as my English professor used to do when I was in college, shut your eyes, open the book, and start where you land. She always delights. A warning: Not everything about her life is included here, nor is this meant to be the only book you ever read about Susan B. Anthony. It is neither a political history nor a complete picture of the period. Rather, it is meant to illuminate her life—to inform, to inspire, or perhaps to provide favorite quotes to pass on to others.

With some exceptions, the words in italics are mine; most of the rest belong to Susan B. Anthony. When quoted accurately, hers reveal some charming and quirky mannerisms. I have already noted her tendency to underline words for emphasis; *always in a hurry, she also tended to abbreviate. Thus, "W.R." is "women's rights"; "con." is "convention"; and "com." is "committee," to point out some of the common concerns of the suffrage lobbyist. In addition, for Anthony, "race" means "human" race, and capital letters and punctuation mean very little. Ironically for someone whose statements and ideas changed the world, she was never comfortable with the written word, lamenting to her diary in 1883, "It has been the bane of my life work—that I was powerless to catch & put into form & on to paper the glimpses of thoughts that come & go as flashes of lightning—" But it is precisely those "glimpses" that make her so engaging. Elizabeth Cady Stanton perfectly captured her style:*

> Verb or substantive is often wanting, but you can always catch the thought, and will ever find it clear and suggestive. It is a strikingly strange dialect, but one that touches, at times, the deepest chords of pathos and humor, and, when stirred by some great event, is highly eloquent.

Her writings and remarks are also full of asides—clever little comments that perked up her letters and enlivened the suffrage meetings.

I have further tried to illustrate her life with pictures of her artifacts—the inkwell she used for her writings, the glasses that became her trademark, the posters announcing her lectures—to round out the words. To me, they make her much more human than the stiff, awkward poses required by photographers in the days before fast film and short shutter speeds.

There are also a number of quotes here from Susan B. Anthony's contemporaries. For while this is her story, it is as much the story of all the women of her era, and many of the men, too. You will hear a number of voices in these pages: the strong, supportive, and often reverent tones of the women and men who worked with her and the strangers who were converted by her; the discordant, often carping tones of those who were threatened by her radical ideas and attacked her personally. There are unheard voices here, too—the women and children and African Americans who silently waved their handkerchiefs in applause and who later wept in gratitude. And there is my own voice—a frankly awed and appreciative gasp that one woman could figure out how to do so much. As a newspaper columnist wrote after her death in 1906, "Her career illustrates again what a life devoted to a single idea can accomplish—how much of dynamics there is in actually knowing, not merely believing, that you are right."

In which case, failure is, of course, impossible.

FAILURE IS IMPOSSIBLE

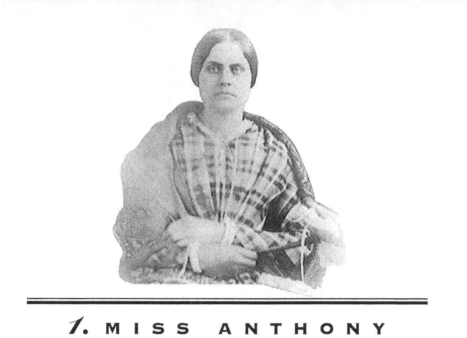

1. MISS ANTHONY

*S*he didn't set out to be an old maid. Nor did she hate men. Indeed, as a young schoolteacher in upstate New York, Susan B. Anthony had a number of gentlemen callers, as well as several proposals of marriage. And at least one letter home reflects the self-assurance of an elegant young woman so pleased with her own allure—clad in a new purple plaid dress with buttoned cuffs, her hair done up in braids—that she seemed flattered at the possibility of being snapped up:

> All say the schoolmarm looks beautiful and I heard some of the scholars expressing fear that some one might be smitten and they thus deprived of their teacher.

But somehow none of her beaux ever quite made the grade, and by the time she had embarked on her life's work, it was clear Anthony was not going to settle for another of society's conventions.

Today we might be tempted to conclude that she was too smart, too single-minded, too revolutionary to marry. All we know for sure is that she does not seem to have regretted her decision to remain single—which did not stop others from questioning, teasing, or attacking her for it all her life. As an unmarried, outspoken woman, Anthony made a particularly vulnerable target for hostile newspaper articles and was called everything from "a

---

slab-sided spinster [who] . . . failed to get a whole man" to a "grim Old Gal with manly air." Even one of her closest friends, Antoinette Brown Black-well, the nation's first female minister, advised Anthony, "Get a good hus-band—that's all, dear." Since Susan was thirty-eight years old at the time, the prospects were slim.

Blackwell was no doubt reacting to one of Anthony's most irritating fixations: a constant harangue to her suffrage colleagues that having too many babies would hamper their ability to get the job done. After An-toinette Brown Blackwell's first two deliveries, Anthony wrote:

Now, Nette, *not another baby,* is *my peremptory command—*

Later she was more adamant:

I *say stop now,* once & for all. Your life work will be arduous enough with *two.*

"Nette" went on to bear five more children. Anthony also accused Lucy Stone of letting down The Cause as a "baby tender" and "maid of all work." She had already scolded Stone for canceling out of an upcoming woman's rights convention because she was pregnant:

Lucy, *neither* of us have *time*—for such *personal* matters—

And she despaired that her closest colleague, Elizabeth Cady Stanton, had to drop off the lecture circuit to bear yet another baby—her seventh:

I only *scold now* that for a *moment's pleasure* to herself or her husband, she should thus increase the *load* of *cares* under which she already groans—but there is no remedy now—

Susan B. Anthony did not dislike children. To the contrary, she adored the young and spent so much time at the Stanton home that she actually helped raise the Stanton brood, bouncing a child on her knee and stirring the pudding while Elizabeth finished a suffrage speech.

And despite her rather uncharitable view of most marital situations— largely due to a wife's dismal legal position and her lack of rights as a spouse—she actually considered the marriage act itself sacred and deeply re-spected those rare couples who seemed to have worked out an egalitarian re-lationship. Ultimately, she accepted the inevitability of romance and marriage with the commonsense Quaker ethic that marked her entire life. "Lucy Dear," she wrote Lucy Stone, after questioning whether Henry Blackwell—her intended—"was good enough for" her:

"Be sure you are *right, Lucy,* & then go ahead," that is all I have to say.

She maintained a similar no-nonsense view about sex. She wrote to Stanton:

If it is fact there it is, to me it is not coarse or gross, it is simply the answering of the highest & holiest function of the physical organism—that is that of *reproduction.*

Unfortunately for contemporary curiosity, we can explore her feelings and actions about sex no further. Perhaps because of the times—perhaps because it did not exist—there is no record of any romantic liaisons with either women or men. What we do know is that with all her friends, mostly the women, she seems to have enjoyed deeply satisfying—loving—relationships that clearly sustained her.

After her famous fiftieth birthday party in 1870, she wrote one favorite companion, Anna Dickinson, that it had been a "grand reception":

Oh Anna—I am so glad of it all because it will help teach the young girls that to be true to principle—to live to an idea—th[ough] an unpopular one—that to live single—*without any man's name*—may be honorable—

Ultimately, the skeptical public grew to accept her situation, as the general disdain for those choosing "single blessedness" seemed to lessen. By the turn of the century, the nation's most famous old maid was even asked to write articles about the ideal husband and the marriage of the future. How did she presume to know so much about a condition she'd never personally experienced? She told a newspaper reporter:

I have been in thousands of homes, and in each I have heard a story that I have added to my stock of knowledge. Oh! the stories that I have heard. Oh! the sights that I have seen. Oh! the miseries of unprofitable marriage.

In 1903 her biographer Ida Husted Harper wrote a worshipful magazine profile of the great leader. It concluded:

Had Miss Anthony married, she would have been a devoted wife, an efficient mother, but the world would have missed its strongest reformer and womankind their greatest benefactor.

It will be of far more value to posterity that she gave to all the qualities which in marriage would have been absorbed by the few.

Anthony herself put it this way:

I'm sure no man could have made me any happier than I have been.

═══════

These old Bachelors are nothing but perfect nuisances to society but an Old Maid is the cleverest creature I ever saw.
—*Letter, 1839*

It is almost an impossibility for a man and a woman to have a close sympathetic friendship without the tendrils of one soul becoming fastened around the other, with the result of infinite pain and anguish.
—*Diary, 1874*

While living with her cousin Margaret, who had just given birth, Susan, not yet thirty years old, wrote her mother about one of the incidents that may well have shaped her harsh view of marriage. Joseph was Margaret's husband:

Joseph had a headache the other day and Margaret remarked that she had had one for weeks. "Oh," said the husband, "mine is the real headache, genuine pain, yours is a sort of natural consequence."
—*Letter, 1849*

Margaret died shortly thereafter, leaving four small children.

For a woman to marry a man for support is a demoralizing condition. And for a man to marry a woman merely because she has a beautiful figure is a degradation.
—*Interview, 1896*

While at school in Philadelphia, eighteen-year-old Susan received a letter from home about a friend who had married an old widower with five children. Her diary entry summed up her feelings:

I think any female would rather live and die an old maid.
—*Diary, 1838*

This idea that a young girl should look forward to marriage as the chief aim in life, that the day after she lets her skirts down to her shoe tops she must look out for a husband, is all wrong. Likewise it is worse than wrong to teach the youth with a budding moustache that some girl in the world is sighing for him, and that it is his duty to marry on nothing a year and with no definite aim in life.

We see the sad consequences of this haphazard sort of marital contract every day of our lives. We see the fruits in discouraged men, broken down, physically wrecked women, sickly, poorly-reared children and wretched homes. For man is a selfish creature, and in the majority of instances where there is not money enough for all he spends what there is on himself, in drink and disgraceful dissipation, as like as not.
—*Interview, 1903*

I would not object to marriage if it were not that women throw away every plan and purpose of their own life, to conform to the plans and purposes of the man's life. I wonder if it is woman's real, true nature always to abnegate self.
—*Letter, 1888*

Those of you who have the *talent* to do honor to poor—oh! how poor—womanhood, have all given yourselves over to *baby* making and left poor brainless *me* to do battle alone—it is a shame, such a body as *I might* be *spared* to *rock cradles,* but it is a *crime* for *you* & Lucy [Stone] & Nette [Brown].
—*Letter to Elizabeth Cady Stanton, caring for six children, in 1856*

Stanton would later bear one more and then write Anthony, "Courage Susan this is my last baby."

I feel *discouraged* when I think of holding a Convention *without Lucy* or *Antoinette*—but they are bound to give themselves over to the *ineffable* joys of *Maternity,* so we must *either* abandon Conventions *altogether,* or learn to do without them—
—*Letter, 1856*

Where are the women to fill the places of those who are (at least temporarily) withdrawn from the public service?—Echo answers, *Where?*
—*Letter, 1857*

There is not one woman left who may be relied on, all have "first to please their husband," after which there is but little time or energy left to spend in any other direction. I am not complaining or despairing, but facts are stern realities. The twain become one flesh, the woman, "we"; henceforth she has no separate work, and how soon the last standing monuments (yourself and myself, Lydia), will lay down the individual "shovel and de hoe" and with proper zeal and spirit grasp those of some masculine hand, the mercies and the spirits only know. I declare to you that I distrust the power of any woman, even of myself, to withstand the mighty matrimonial maelstrom!
—*Letter, 1858(?)*

Mrs. Stanton is jogging around Ohio somewhere and writes me her newly married daughter Maggie is very ill in her new home at the West & she is greatly anxious about her—& may feel compelled to throw up her engagements to go to her—so it is—Marrying daughters but carries mothers back to live over their lives in anxiety for their children & children's children.
—*Letter, 1878*

But so it is; every wife and mother must devote herself wholly to home duties, washing and cleaning, baking and mending—these are the must be's; the culture of the soul, the enlargement of the faculties, the thought of anything or anybody beyond the home and family are the may be's. When society is rightly organized, the wife and mother will have time, wish and will to grow intellectually, and will know that the limits of her sphere, the extent of her duties, are prescribed only by the measure of her ability.
—*Remarks, 1853*

Nette, I don't really want to be a *downright scold,* but I can't help looking after the married sheep of the flock—a wee bit—I am sure it is folly for any human being to attempt to follow too many professions at the same time.
—*Letter, 1858*

Nette, Institutions, among them marriage, are justly chargeable with social & individual ills—but after all the *whole man* or

woman can & *will* rise above them—I am sure my *"True Woman"* will never be dwarfed by them—Woman must take to her soul a *purpose,* & then *make* circumstances to meet that purpose—instead of this *lacadasicial* [sic] way of doing & going, if, & *if* & if—
—*Letter, 1858*

There was another way to look at marriage and motherhood, which Anthony finally recognized after spending weeks taking care of a baby niece:

Oh this babydom, what a constant, never-ending, all-consuming strain! We should never ask anything else of the woman who has to endure it. I realize more and more that rearing children should be looked upon as a profession which, like any other, must be made the primary work of those engaged in it. It cannot be properly done if other aims and duties are pressing upon the mother.
—*Letter, 1861*

Her brother Jacob Merritt's daughter, Lucy, would later help her understand why mothers were so willing to forgo all for the children:

The dear little Lucy engrosses most of my time and thoughts. A child one loves is a constant benediction to the soul, whether or not it helps to the accomplishment of great intellectual feats.
—*Date unknown, ca. 1861*

[T]o be a *Mother* to be a *Father* is the last, highest wish of any human being—to *re-produce himself* or *herself*—the accomplish[ment] of this purpose is only through the meeting of the sexes—and when we come into the presence of one of the opposite sex, who embodies, what to us seems the true & the noble, & the beautiful, our souls are stirred, and whether we realize it or not,—it is a thrill of joy that such qualities are so reproducible, *and* that we may be the *agents,* the *artists* in such re-production.

It is the *knowledge* that the two together may be the instruments . . . that shall execute a work so *God like*—
—*Letter, 1857*

And so she found it possible to praise marriage—provided it was undertaken in the right spirit. In her diary for 1855, in the section reserved for important quotations, Anthony copied down the following words from

Lucretia Mott: "In the true marriage relation, the independence of the hus-
band & wife is equal, their dependence mutual and their obligation recipro-
cal." She adopted the message for her own congratulatory wishes.

May your independence be equal, your dependence mutual,
your obligations reciprocal.
— *Telegram to nephew and his bride on their wedding day, 1897*

My Dear Friends, Mr. and Mrs. Bloomer:—
. . . your lives have been side by side for a whole half-century,
and this, too, when the wife has been one of the public advocates
of the equality of rights, civil and political, for women. I hardly
believe another twain made one, where the wife belonged to the
school of equal rights for women, have lived more happily, more
truly one.

Your celebration of your fiftieth wedding day is one of the
strongest proofs of the falseness of the charge brought against our
movement for the enfranchisement of women, viz., that the condition of equality of political rights for the wife will cause inhar-
mony and disruption of the marriage bond. To the contrary, such
conditions of perfect equality are the best helps to make for peace
and harmony and elevation in all true and noble directions.
— *Letter to Amelia and Dexter Bloomer congratulating them on*
their golden wedding anniversary, 1890

In 1869 Anthony attended a dinner at Delmonico's in New York City,
sponsored by the New York Press Club. It was a rare chance for women to
join men at a business function, and she noted with satisfaction that the very
pleasant meal was accompanied by "No cigars, no spittoons, no drunken-
ness, no profane words, no impolite jests." Partway through the meal, the
prominent women in attendance were asked to respond to certain provoca-
tive questions in the form of toasts. Here was Anthony's impromptu re-
sponse:

TOAST—: Why don't the men propose?
MISS ANTHONY—: Precisely the question, gentlemen, that has
puzzled my brain for the last quarter of a century. My private
opinion, however, is that it is not that men do not propose, but
that it is not the *right* ones who do. But, gentlemen, we "strong-
minded" are working hard to relieve you from this embarrassing

question, and so soon as you give women equal chance in money-getting, we shall make our own fortunes, build our own brown stone fronts, and invite the grandest of you to share them with us.
—*Dinner speech, 1869*

Men want for wives the intelligent, educated and in every way well-developed woman, and at the same time they want to keep her the same, old-fashioned, meek, submissive, willing reflection of the man who marries her. The two cannot be combined. The woman of the past, who was but an echo of her husband's wish and will, can be duplicated in the woman of the present only by keeping her ignorant and dependent.

As a matter of fact the modern, progressive man would not be satisfied with the old-style wife: she would pall upon him—he would be ashamed of her. The college-bred man of to-day wants an educated, up-to-date wife, who can "hold her own" in conversation with his friends, who belongs to a good club, who is a recognized influence in the community. He will have to learn, however, that the very qualifications which fit her for all this make it impossible for her to take a subordinate place in the household, and that her equality must be recognized. But he will find, also, that this education, this discipline, this knowledge of the world will render her a much more capable housekeeper and an infinitely better mother. . . .

This new order of womanhood will finally result in a superior type of manhood. This modern woman will not be averse to marriage, but she will insist upon a manhood which will be worthy of her love and respect, and she never will rest until she brings men up to her standard. We then will have not only a better motherhood, but a nobler fatherhood.
—*Letter to the Editor, 1896*

The ideal husband is the one who does not take advantage of the power which the law confers upon him. . . .

Our foremothers kept no record of their ideal man, not even on the faded pages of their little worn diaries. Whenever their brief, practical entries go beyond the details of the household expenses and the family illnesses, into the realm of aspiration, it is always in regard to the heavenly life. The conditions of this one they considered beyond remedy. But, understanding the nature of woman, and knowing that her dearest hopes, her fondest desires, are concentrated in the future of her children, we may well believe that these old-time mothers did dream of an ideal husband for their daughters and that, if interpreted, it would have read: "A man who will lift women up to a plane with himself."

For the past two generations men have been approaching this ideal . . .

The man of to-day does not find his equanimity very rudely disturbed when his blushing bride declines to promise at the altar "to obey." He has rather more respect for her for not doing it. The old attitude of sovereignty on one hand and obedience on the other has largely disappeared. Enlightened men no longer marry for the purpose of getting a housekeeper or with the sole object of raising a family of children, but through the desire of congenial companionship and with the intention of stimulating the development of the wife along the lines for which she is best fitted. Thus far we have the ideal husband, not universally, but in sufficient numbers to offer much hope for the future.

An ideal husband will not come into the presence of wife and children exhaling the odor of liquor and tobacco. In olden times it is doubtful if women would have dared form such an ideal as this, but already it is partly reached. Then, liquor was on every sideboard, and ladies withdrew from the dinner table in order that gentlemen (!) might get drunk. Now the gentleman who gets drunk carefully conceals that fact from the ladies of his acquaintance. Where formerly the woman endured the intemperate husband as her inevitable lot, the law now steps in and sets her free. The abolition of the tobacco habit forms a part of the future ideal.

The woman of to-day has a moral ideal. She dreams of a time when there shall be but one standard of virtue for the two sexes. . . . The attitude of society toward the immoral man is gradually changing. Like the drunkard he is beginning to cover his tracks. His lapses are no longer a matter of pride. The new self-respect of women is protesting against man's defiance of the moral code and he is commencing to feel the effects of social ostracism, which will increase as women grow stronger in self-reliance. And here again the revised statutes come to the rescue of the wife and relieve her from that body of living death—a husband who is unfaithful to his marriage vows.

—*Newspaper article, "The Ideal Husband," 1901*

The subject of marriage as it related personally to Susan B. Anthony was a source of endless fascination for newspaper reporters and their editors.

One entire article in the June 28, 1896, San Francisco Chronicle *is dedicated to the topic and headlined* THE EARLY COURTSHIPS OF SUSAN B. ANTHONY: Offers of Marriage Which She Has Received; Why the Apostle of Woman's Suffrage Is Unmarried. *Every interviewer tried a different approach, there was only one question: Miss Anthony, why did you never marry? Her answer seemed to depend on her mood.*

I never cared for little boys. I was much too serious. And I am sure they were not interested in me. Why, I wouldn't have left my book for one of them. . . . I was altogether so discreet that when I got well into my teens and used to go to parties with my sisters, my mother would commission me to act as dragon and drag the others home. And I never failed her.
—*Interview, 1899*

It always happened that the men I wanted were those I could not get, and those who wanted me I wouldn't have.
—*Interview, 1897*

There were all kinds among them, except ministers. Being a Quakeress set me apart, and I think that no one even thought that I, with my tongue, would make a good mistress for a manse.
—*Interview, 1896*

[T]he man who sent you couldn't conceive that a woman who had received an offer of marriage could possibly have remained single. Now, I believe that a woman's loves and griefs are her own—even a public woman's. It's no business of the public who asked me to marry or who did not, but for the benefit of all men who think we old maids are always single from necessity, I'll say that a good many men have done me the honor to ask me to marry them.

Why did I refuse them all? Why, child, it was simply that I never met a man whom I thought I loved well enough to live with all my life, and for that matter, I never met one whom I thought loved me well enough to live with me all his life. That marriage proposition has two sides. Probably I'd have been very trying to live with.

. . . I was never engaged—never accepted any one provisionally—though I never said I would not marry. Simply this, I never found the man who was necessary to my happiness. I was very well as I was.
—*Interview, 1896*

I have not yet had a man ask me to be his companion. He has asked me to let him love; and he has said his home needed a housekeeper, and that his children—oh! so many widowers have said this—needed some one to guide their growing minds. I have also had men tell me that together we could be very happy, I at home and he at work. But I have never, and shall never, accept such a proposal. When a man says to me, "Let us work together in the great cause you have undertaken, and let me be your companion and aid, for I admire you more than I have ever admired any other woman," then I shall say, "I am yours truly;" but he must ask me to be his equal, not his slave. As for support! I think a woman should be ashamed to have her husband support her.
—Interview, 1895

[I]n those days no man wanted to marry a woman who had "views." For any woman to allow it to be known that she cherished "views" was to condemn her to a single estate for the rest of her days; and this I knew, but still I dared the situation and I have taken the consequences.
—Speech, 1894

I never felt I could give up my life of freedom to become a man's housekeeper. When I was young, if a girl married poor, she became a housekeeper and a drudge. If she married wealth she became a pet and a doll. Just think, had I married at twenty, I would have been a drudge or a doll for fifty-five years. Think of it!
—Interview, 1896

Anthony had one other explanation for why she wasn't married, one that she used while campaigning for legal and property rights for married women. As she told the story, she once ran into a minister who gave her a hard time:

He said: "Miss Anthony, you are a fine young woman, and with your grand physique and intelligence I think it is a pity you are not a wife and mother of a large family." "I told him," said Miss Anthony, "I thought it was much better for me to devote my life to amending the State law which denied mothers the right of guardianship of their own children, than for me to be the mother of a half dozen children who were not legally my own."
—Speech, 1891

Which is not to say that she did not occasionally suffer for her choice. The following entry from her diary during a winter sojourn at Riggs House in Washington, D.C., illustrates that this apparently fearless public figure could be very vulnerable in private.

> At Home—Riggs
> The Postmaster General & Mrs. Wanamakers at Home—from 9 to 10—this evening Didn't go to their reception—hadn't the courage to go alone
> —*Diary, 1890*

Marriage wasn't anathema to Anthony; it just didn't happen. But even she could imagine. In 1897 a prominent lawyer and former suffrage colleague named Phoebe Couzins renounced the movement, attacking Anthony and others in a newspaper interview. Anthony, citing the "poor, unjointed body and mind of that once-brilliant girl," noted that Couzins had become ill and refused to respond to the criticisms in print. But she did write to her friend Frances E. Willard, head of the Woman's Christian Temperance Union:

> As to her advice to young women to marry, they will all do exactly what she would have done—i.e., marry the first man whom they really love and think really loves them. Phoebe never failed to manifest her desire to marry . . . and I don't think it was her devotion to oratory, to the law, to her home, or to any sort of public work, that holds back any woman from marrying, not even F.E.W. or S.B.A. Had either of us, in our young womanhood, loved a man so much that we thought we couldn't live without him, and made ourselves believe that he loved us so much that he couldn't live without us, we should have been Willard-Jones and Anthony-Smith all these years instead of plain little Willard and Anthony. So I do not think that anything Phoebe, or you, or I, or all the other wise heads put together, can say about girls marrying will have one particle of effect. Human nature, like all bird and animal nature, runs in the direction of marrying, and Phoebe might as well attempt to stem the tide as to turn the current of the girl-nature from its bent toward marriage.
> —*Letter, 1897*

A Singular Wit

She was a quick study and early on figured out that the best way to defuse assaults on her marital status was to joke about it. She even learned to use it as a weapon. When her bold support of the very controversial notion of divorce reform outraged some male colleagues, one of them—abolitionist Reverend A. D. Mayo of Albany, New York—said accusingly, "You are not married, you have no business to be discussing marriage." To which Anthony replied smoothly, "Well, Mr. Mayo, you are not a slave, suppose you quit lecturing on slavery."

2. SCHOOL DAYS

Teaching was the first profession she knew, so it was not surprising that the neglect of women at an education conference set off one of her earliest public protests. The year was 1853; there were more than 500 teachers—mostly women—at the annual New York State Teachers' Association meeting in Rochester. Anthony "listened in vain for one word of recognition for women . . . no speaker even intimated that women had any part or lot in the great question of Education."

My heart was filled with grief and honest indignation, thus to see the minority of the Convention, simply because they were men, presuming that in them, was rooted all wisdom and knowledge . . . And what was most humiliating of all was to look into the faces of those women and see that by far the larger proportion were perfectly satisfied with the position assigned them.

She was well aware of the limitations that she and most other American girls faced. In 1837 there was only one regular college (Oberlin) and one women's "seminary" (Mount Holyoke) providing higher education for female students. So at age nineteen, when a reversal of her father's financial success forced her to quit school and go to work, she wrote, "I probably shall never go to school again and so . . . all the advancement which we hereafter

make must be by our own exertion and desire to gain useful knowledge."
But her father had also seen to it that she was trained to earn a living, and
her first salary—$1.00, then $2.50 per week—plus board, kept her in fine
clothes, although it rankled that men doing the same job got several times
that. Still, with so much else going on in the world, teaching soon bored this
most restless of agitators. She wrote her mother in 1849:

> Dr. Dewitt Rile leaves for the Gold mines in about two weeks.
> I wish I had about $100,000 of the precious dust, I would no
> longer be school marm. I was a man would'nt [*sic*] I be off.

Her views on education were totally democratic and characteristically
progressive. A product of a private Quaker boarding school herself, she was
firmly committed to the public school system. Long before the Civil War,
she fought racial segregation, once offering a resolution at the teachers' con-
vention that "the exclusion of colored youth from our public schools, acade-
mies, colleges and universities is the result of a wicked prejudice." The
delegates insisted that was "not a proper subject for discussion."

And at a time when separate schools for female students were catching
on, she remained a relentless advocate of coeducation. Her low opinion of
women's colleges was reflected in one letter to a university professor friend,
lamenting the fate of students at Radcliffe College, then known as the Fe-
male Annex to Harvard:

> Is there any near prospect of old Harvard's opening *his doors* to
> the Sisters? What a shame for them to be doomed to the
> 'Annex'!!

An entry in her diary during her first trip to Europe, in 1883, indicates
that even as a tourist, Susan B. Anthony was on the job:

> Oct. 4.—In Oxford—visited Baliol [*sic*], St. Margaret's & ever
> so many of the colleges— . . . and as I saw all the millions of dol-
> lars expended for the education of *boys* only—I groaned in
> spirit—and betook me to Somerville Hall for girls—where 20
> were *boarded* last year . . . then there is St. Margaret's Hall—for 20
> more or so—while there are 2,000 boys in [other] Oxford colleges.

She was so convinced of the value of coeducation, she often claimed
that it led to the best marriages.

Her closest target was the University of Rochester, where she started
an all-out drive to admit female students around 1881. It nearly failed some

two decades later when, with the deadline only hours away, the $50,000 fund demanded by the trustees was still not met. Susan B. Anthony herself—who had scraped for money all her life—made up the difference by pledging the final $2,000 on her own life insurance. This, she confided to her diary, when "not a trustee—has given anything—though there are several millionaires among them—"

The University was not the only Rochester institution to change under her influence. She also helped get women on its school board, an innovation so unsettling to one man in 1899, he felt the "same way all the lady school teachers feel about having a woman principal over them—that a woman is not for the place."

Which was exactly the way her colleagues at the 1853 teachers' convention felt about Susan B. Anthony's bold move that August afternoon. It was the end of the second day's session; the men were debating the lack of respect enjoyed by teaching as a profession—a profession dominated by women. Remember—of the 300 or so women present, none had uttered a peep or had even been invited to comment by the 200 men. Suddenly, the thirty-three-year-old Quaker rose from her seat in the rear (only the men sat up front) and said, "Mr. President." As Anthony and her colleagues later described the scene, "If all the witches that had been drowned, burned, and hung in the Old World and the New had suddenly appeared on the platform, threatening vengeance for their wrongs, the officers of that convention could not have been thrown into greater consternation . . . those frightened men could not decide what to do; how to receive this audacious invader of their sphere of action." The hall went silent. Then the head of the group—one Charles Davies, an esteemed but arrogant math professor from West Point, who was presiding in full dress and gilt buttons—stepped in and asked scornfully, "What will the lady have?" Again Anthony dared: "I wish, sir, to speak to the question under discussion." For half an hour the convention debated her request; finally she was given permission. In a clear voice with unarguable logic, Susan B. Anthony made her first memorable public speech:

It seems to me, gentlemen, that none of you quite comprehend the cause of the disrespect of which you complain. Do you not see that so long as society says a woman is incompetent to be a lawyer, minister, or doctor, but has ample ability to be a teacher, that every man of you who chooses this profession tacitly acknowledges that he has no more brains than a woman? And this, too, is the reason that teaching is a less lucrative position, as here men must compete with the cheap labor of woman. Would you exalt your profession, exalt those who labor with you. Would you make it more lucrative, increase the salaries of the women en-

gaged in the noble work of educating our future Presidents, Senators, and Congressmen.
—*Speech, 1853*

Eyewitness accounts report that Anthony sat down in "the profoundest silence, broken at last by three gentlemen . . . walking down the broad aisle to congratulate the speaker on her pluck and perseverance, and the pertinency of her remarks." The local newspaper wrote, "whatever the schoolmasters might think of Miss Anthony, it was evident that she hit the nail on the head." But many of the women were shocked, some later remarking, "I was actually ashamed of my sex" or "I felt so mortified I really wished the floor would open and swallow me up" or "Who can that creature be?" "She must be a dreadful woman to get up that way and speak in public." One woman understood exactly what had happened: "I was so mad at those three men making such a parade to shake hands with her; that will just encourage her to speak again." So it did.

In this State there are eleven thousand teachers, and of these four-fifths are women. By the reports it will be seen that, of the annual State fund of $800,000, two-thirds are paid to men, and one-third to women; that is to say, two-thirds are paid to one-fifth of the laborers in the cause of education, while four-fifths of these laborers are paid with one-third of the fund!
—*Speech, 1853*

For the next nine years, she would attend every state teachers' convention, insisting that women should speak, hold offices, serve on committees, exercise free speech, and, of course, get equal pay. Her tirades and pleas exasperated the delegates. How much of a pain was she? Here's how Teacher, *a professional journal, wrote up one effort to add women to a committee:*

Miss Anthony moved an amendment, that Miss Mary C. Vosburgh of Rochester, and Miss Mary A. Booth, be added to the Committee on Editors of the *Teacher,* and that the same number of women be added to the Committee on Location of Next Annual Meeting.

Mr. Cruikshank asked if it was competent to add to the committee now. . . .

Miss Anthony made a few explanations. She would not trouble the Convention unless a question of principle was at stake. She did not care a straw who acted on committees. But she did care whether the women who composed three-fourths of this body be ignored. They should be represented upon all committees; there was no justice in shutting women's mouths in this convention.

Mr. Danforth rose to a point of order.

Miss Anthony resumed, appealing to the women in the Convention to vote upon the question, and demand their rights. She had hopes, from what she had heard of Lockport, that the result on such questions as these would be different from what it had been heretofore. She attributed the motion of Mr. Bulkley, in the resolution inviting Messrs. Reid and Patterson to act as the Committee on Music, to a determination, on his part, to disregard the claims and courtesies due to the ladies of the Association, and thought women should also have been named on the committee.

Mr. Bulkley arose to vindicate himself . . .

Mr. Heffron of Utica thought this discussion was foreign to the business of the Association . . .

Miss Anthony wanted to ask a question. Suppose that our President had placed five women on each of these committees, wouldn't four out of five of the men have felt aggrieved? It was a poor rule that would not work both ways. Men flatter women when they wish them to add to their enjoyment in the small talk and frivolities of life; but when it comes to the question of practical life, involving the rights of women, they talk differently.

Mr. Bulkley rose to a question of order. The lady was not talking to the question.

Miss Anthony wished to be thoroughly understood.

The Chair hoped Miss Anthony would confine herself to the question before the house.

Miss Anthony had a suspicion that an effort was making [*sic*] to put down the rights of women.

The . . . motion to increase the number of the two committees named, was lost.

—*Convention, 1858*

Teachers should not be regarded as missionaries. It takes years to prepare for their work and their labors should be properly recognized.

—*Interview on teachers' salaries, 1903*

Her official quest for coeducation was documented in detail in 1856, as she prepared for the upcoming teachers' convention. It began with her typical insecurity over writing the speech:

Oh, that I had the requisite power to do credit to woman hood [*sic*] in this emergency—why is nature so *sparing* of her gifts—
—*Letter, 1856*

As ever in those days, she counted on Elizabeth Cady Stanton to prepare the lecture—and scolded her for again letting mere babies get in the way.

And Mrs. Stanton, not a *word written* on that Address for *Teachers* Con.—...& the Mercy only knows when I can get a moment—& what is *worse*, as the Lord *knows full well*, is, that if I *get all the time* the *world has*—I *cant get up a decent document*. So for the love of me, & for the saving of the *reputation* of *Womanhood*, I beg you with one baby on your knee & another at your feet & four boys whistling buzzing hallooing *Ma Ma* set your self about the work—it is of but small moment *who writes* the Address, but of *vast moment* that it be *well done*—I promise you to work hard, oh, how hard, & *pay you* ... for your *time & brains*—but oh Mrs. Stanton *don't* say *No,* nor *don't delay* it a moment, for I must have it all done & *almost commit* it to Memory.
—*Letter, 1856*

Anthony enclosed some talking points in her letter to Stanton, and the speech that resulted illustrates that her lack of self-confidence was certainly misplaced.

Why the Sexes should be Educated together

Because their life work is so nearly identical
By such education they get true ideas of each other—
The College Student associates with only two classes of Women; the kitchen drudge & parlor doll—The Seminary girl ... gets her idea of man mostly from works of fiction—
Because the endowment of Educational Institutions by both public & private ... is ever for those for the Male Sex—while all Seminaries & Boarding Schools for Females are left to Maintain themselves as best they may by means of their Tuition Fees—consequently cannot afford a faculty of 1st class professors—
Because there are already colleges enough established for all of both sexes—*Economy* favors it—...
The grand thing that is needed, is to give the sexes *like motives* for acquirement—...

That man may learn from his boyhood that woman is his *intellectual equal* & no longer look upon her as his inferior——oh, dear dear, there is so much to say & I am so without *constructive power* to put in symetrical [*sic*] order——

Because separation & restraint stimulates the desires & passions——

——*Notes on speech for Teachers' meeting, Why the Sexes should be Educated together*

Both sexes eat, sleep, hate, love and desire alike. Everything which relates to the operations of the mind is common to both sexes. . . . If they are allowed to attend picnics together, and balls, and dancing schools, and the opera, it certainly will not injure them to use chalk at the same blackboard.

——*Speech, 1856*

The Colleges of Oberlin, Antioch & Lima claim to place all their pupils on equal grounds,——yet the girls are restricted as the boys are not, both in body & soul.——whilst the boys are free to ramble over hill, dale,——whilst they are free to think & talk, & speak & write, & do whatever they have the capacity to do, there are in all these institutions . . . some special restraints & limits for girls——Why is this so?——If they are afraid in the literary discussions, that the girls will *out do* the boys, some teacher should prepare the *dear fellows* beforehand.——If they are afraid the girls will molest the boys in their solitary rambles, they ought to send some Professor to protect them;——or imprison the boys, at least, one *half* the time.——Common justice demands that the girls, however dangerous, should sometimes enjoy a little freedom.

——*Speech, 1856*

Resolved, That since the true and harmonious development of the race demands that the sexes be associated together in every department of life; therefore

Resolved, That it is the duty of all our schools, colleges and universities to open their doors to woman and to give her equal and identical educational advantages side by side with her brother man.

——*Motions for coeducation presented to state teachers' convention, 1857*

Professor Davies, her old foe from 1853, called it "a vast social evil . . . the first step in the school which seeks to abolish marriage, and behind this picture I see a monster of social deformity." The state Superintendent of

Public Instruction gasped, "Do you mean to say you want the boys and girls to room side by side in dormitories? To educate them together can have but one result." The resolution was defeated. Elizabeth Cady Stanton wrote her friend, "I did indeed see by the papers that you had once more stirred that pool of intellectual stagnation, the educational convention."

[T]he women's colleges of today don't teach a girl anything regarding her social and economic responsibilities. As far as these matters are concerned she goes out into the world as ignorant as a child. . . . Now the only objection raised against co-education is that the girls and boys divert each others' minds from their work and that too many romances develop. But to my mind that is the greatest advantage of co-education. If I had a family of boys and girls I would send them to co-education colleges if for no other purpose than to get well married. Such marriages are the happiest that there are.
—*Interview, 1899*

The husband of the future should receive his education in schools and colleges which admit both sexes upon exactly the same terms. It is only in this way that he can get a just sense of the proportion of his own mental ability. Whether by inheritance or from hearing the statement so often made, the average boy starts out with the belief that a man has more brains than a woman, and, naturally, that a boy has more than a girl. If this mistaken idea is not corrected while he is young he is very apt to make life unpleasant for the women with whom he comes in contact with. There is no corrective so efficient as co-education.
—*Article, 1901*

Her drive for coeducation ran into a number of obstacles. There was the time she spoke at the all-female Pembroke Hall, then an affiliate of Brown University. She wrote to a friend about her remarks:

"But," I said, "I suppose the girls at Pembroke Hall must make the best of the opportunities they have and keep on hoping that by-and-by old Brown will open wide its doors and give them equal chances with the boys." They clapped heartily at this, but some one told me afterwards that the dean [Miss Anna Crosby Emery, who had invited her to speak] looked rather serious.
—*Letter, 1901*

And then there was the time furious female students at the University of Chicago wrote her for help after their president segregated freshmen and sophomore women from men in the classroom:

Yes, we women have to fight continually for our rights and after we get them we have to watch constantly for fear they will be taken away while our backs are turned, or just as we begin to feel safe and comfortable. . . . When they can't keep the girls out of college they resort to separate recitations, and it's plain enough on the face of it why this is done. The girls stand so much higher in their studies than the boys that it reflects anything but credit on the latter. No, we don't want the sexes separated in the class room. Half the stimulus is competition, and if the boys and girls are given separate recitations and examinations how are we going to tell which stands higher? The girls compete for the same prizes with the boys, that's where the fun comes in.
— *Interview, 1902*

If there is a *fear* that *more women than men* will be the result— or that women will take all the prizes— then there should go to college *more men*—and they should study the harder and come out ahead—that will be the final result
— *Autograph message, 1902*

The real reason that men don't want girls in their colleges is this: They are ashamed to be beaten by them. As a little boy told me once, it makes him feel so darn mean.
— *Interview, 1891*

Curiously, it wasn't just men who stood in the way. In this long and heartfelt letter written upon her arrival in London, Anthony chided one of her good friends, Jane Stanford (who, with her husband, the late railroad mogul and U.S. Senator Leland Stanford, had founded Stanford University):

Before sailing I had read of your magnificent gift to the university and rejoiced in you exceedingly in having excelled all other women; and here in old England I have handed me a special telegram to the New York *Tribune* which contains the following: "Mrs. Stanford specifies that she wishes to have the number of women students limited to 500, as she sees a possible danger to the institution in the rapid increase of the percentage of girls—

which has grown from 25 to 41—and there are now 450 women. Many of the alumni feel that the college spirit is injured—that it cannot hold its own in athletics, oratorical contests, etc." This sends a chill over me—that this limitation should come through a woman and that one my dear Mrs. Stanford to whom I had looked for the fulfillment of our dream of perfect equality for women in her university. Who are the alumni that are thus afraid? The men, of course. And what do they think is endangered? Physical prowess—sports—not high intellectual attainments. I know full well that the men in co-educational universities have to suffer contempt from the shallow-pated of colleges for men only, but Stanford's splendid work hitherto has been to teach its men to stand up bravely and demolish those false ideas. You have done as much as any other human being to educate men to respect women and I cannot bear to have you destroy this work. Had you provided that, when the number of students had reached its maximum, care should be taken that the proportion of the sexes should be the same—that for the well-being of all, there should not be any great preponderance of either—it would have seemed fair and just. But to limit the women to 500 and set no bounds to the number of men makes you virtually say that the presence of women is deteriorating to a university to such an extent that not more than 500 of them can be allowed without jeopardizing its best interests.

Suppose all of the co-educational universities throughout the country should follow your example, where would the thousands and thousands of women find chances for education but the girls' colleges, seminaries and boarding schools, which would mean a return to the old-time methods. Indeed your proposed limitation is a most fatal step backward. Do you think your dear husband would have yielded to the fears of the male alumni? And if not, why should the wife to whom he intrusted all? I wish I could see you and talk it over. I am sure you would change it to half-and-half of the sexes, for the highest good of the students, the home and the university. Lovingly and trustingly yours.
—*Letter, 1899*

She did not hesitate to write her women friends about one of her strongest crusades: public education. Stanton, for instance, had hired a teacher to educate her children at home:

I am still of the opinion that whatever the short-comings of the public schools your children would be vastly more profited in them, side by side with the very multitude with whom they must mingle as soon as school days are over. Any and every private education is a blunder, it seems to me. I believe those persons stronger and nobler who have from childhood breasted the commonalty. If children have not the innate strength to resist evil, keeping them apart from what they must inevitably one day meet, only increases their incompetency.
— *Letter to Elizabeth Cady Stanton, 1862*

I am glad to know that Bishop McQuaid uses his influence to make the Catholic schools as good as possible, but I deprecate more and more all sorts of private and sectarian schools. A republican government should be based on free and equal education among the people. While we have class and sectarian schools the parties supporting them will not give their fullest aid toward building up the public school system. If all of the rich and all of the church people should send their children to the public schools they would feel bound to concentrate their money and energies on improving these schools until they met the highest ideals. To be a success a republic must have a homogeneous people, and to do this it must have homogeneous schools. You may grow more and more in favor of sectarian schools, as you say, but I grow more and more opposed to them.
— *Letter, 1900*

Well they let the girls in—said there was no alternative—
— *Diary, 1900, after the University of Rochester agreed to become coeducational*

The Education of a Judge

When a Connecticut Supreme Court Justice ruled that "no woman must feel she knows more than her husband" and that "girls would make better wives, mothers and housekeepers if they finished school at from fourteen to sixteen years of age," Susan B. Anthony responded in kind. "That is another absurdity, and it convinces me that a little learning has been a pitfall for Justice Baldwin. If happiness in wedded life depended on the mental superiority of the husband in this age of progress, I fear that the divorce courts would be overworked."

3. OH SLAVERY, HATEFUL THING

He was the most famous former slave in nineteenth-century Amer-ica — a six-foot-tall, lion-maned leader who would become a re-spected statesman and diplomat. His name was Frederick Douglass, and he was also one of Susan B. Anthony's closest friends.

As a young woman in her twenties, she had grown used to Douglass' presence at the family farm in Rochester, where local antislavery Quakers gathered on Sunday afternoons to discuss the evil practice gripping the na-tion. Susan listened eagerly and read copies of his publication, North Star.

Not that she had to be taught to hate slavery. Equal rights came natu-rally to Susan B. Anthony, thanks to the teachings of the Quakers and the convictions of her family. While away from home as a schoolteacher in 1839 she wrote an angry letter to her sister about an incident after a Sunday meeting with less liberal Friends:

> The people around here are hot headed Antiabolitionists & anti everything thats good *I* believe; they the Friends raised quite a fuss last summer about a colored man sitting in the meeting house & some left the meeting on the account. The man was rich, well-dressed and very polite, but still the pretended *meek follow-*

FREDERICK DOUGLASS

ers of *Christ* could not worship their God and have *this* sable companion with them what a lack of Christianity is this.

In her mid-thirties, she was invited to join the antislavery lecture circuit and willingly interrupted her growing concerns for women's rights to concentrate on what was—for the moment—the more pressing need. It was a decisive period in American history. Uncle Tom's Cabin, *written by Harriet Beecher Stowe and published in 1852, had awakened hundreds of thousands to the inhuman conditions in the South. The Fugitive Slave Law, a political concession to southerners, infuriated more northerners by requiring blacks who had escaped from their masters to be forced back into bondage. And the pending Kansas-Nebraska Act in Congress (which left the decision about slavery up to territorial legislatures, thus setting off bloody battles) incensed the abolitionists. In a letter to Lucy Stone, Susan B. Anthony expressed her outrage and made it clear she believed she and her sisters had a special calling:*

> I feel that woman should in the very Capitol of the nation, lift her voice against that abominable measure. It is not enough that H. B. Stowe should write.

Anthony lifted her voice wherever she could find an audience, no matter how ugly the bias. She even took on Abraham Lincoln, whose concessions to the South offended the harder line taken by Anthony and other abolitionists. "No Compromise with Slaveholders," she demanded, as she appeared throughout New York State in early 1861. It was a chapter in her life she would later call "The Winter of the Mobs." Starting in Buffalo on the third day of the new year, she took her message to increasingly hostile crowds, who tried to keep her from speaking by dousing the gas lamps to leave her in the dark, tossing pepper onto the stove that heated the hall, or jeering and stamping and calling her ugly names. "Miss Susan B. Anthony & Co. were looked upon as a fatal species of small pox, London plague, or Montreal ship fever," wrote one reporter who didn't try to disguise his own sympathy with the mobs. Anthony faced up valiantly to the worst of them, refusing one mayor's pleas that she postpone the meeting to prevent a full-scale riot. But she would never again face the hatred of one cold January night in Syracuse. Along with her colecturer, Reverend Samuel May, Susan B. Anthony was burned in effigy, the "body" dragged through the streets.

Still, she never softened her demand for racial equality—not even when, after the Civil War was over, she was forsaken by the very men she had championed. In one of the most painful episodes of Anthony's life, she was forced to stand aside while most of her abolitionist friends — Frederick Douglass included — worked for citizenship and the vote for black men. That was the priority, they insisted, unapologetically calling the moment "the Negro's Hour." They didn't need to specify that they meant "the Negro man's hour." It was an agonizing and maddening betrayal, especially since Douglass had delivered the eulogy at Anthony's father's funeral some years earlier. And it would take some years to heal the wounds and restore their very important friendship.

As her own career progressed, Susan B. Anthony made some of her own political compromises, rendering a few tactical decisions that have lately been judged too considerate of southern white sensibilities. For example, she urged the suffrage convention not to adopt a resolution condemning segregated railroad cars because "We women are a helpless, disfranchised class. Our hands are tied." And she talked Elizabeth Cady Stanton out of writing an open letter to the press congratulating Douglass on his new, second marriage — to a white woman — because "it has no place on our platform . . . Your sympathy has run away with your judgment." Her candid explanation was that she wanted nothing to interfere with the demand for the vote. She even blamed the defeat of suffrage campaigns in certain states, she said, on "ignorant foreigners" — Italians, Russians, anyone who was afraid of change. The fact is, she didn't care what color their skin was or what their ethnic background. If they stood in the way of getting women the vote, they were simply wrong. Anyway, she knew what she believed, and she knew that she understood the double prejudice black women felt.

Sojourner [Truth] combined in herself the two most hated elements of humanity. She was black and she was a woman, and all the insults that could be cast upon color and sex were together hurled at her.

In the end she was true to her principles, and to her old friend, whose photograph hung on the wall of her Rochester home. He had, after all, been with them from the beginning. On February 20, 1895, Frederick Douglass, then in his late seventies, was greeted with a standing ovation at a National Council of Women meeting in Washington, D.C. As Susan B. Anthony wrote in that day's diary, she escorted him to the platform, where he

bowed most graciously & gracefully—but declined to say a word—then sat there through the session—& again returned at the P.M. session—& sat till near its close—I chatted with him a half-hour—on returning to his home in Anacostia—he dropped dead as he was telling his wife of that wonderful women's meeting—

At his funeral, Anthony read a eulogy from American women.

═══════

It is the Legalized, Systematic *robbery* of the *bodies* and *souls* of nearly *four millions* of men, women, & children. It is the Legalized *traffic* in *God's* Image.
—*Speech, "What is American Slavery?," 1857(?)*

Anthony's first real encounter with slaves at work came in 1854, during a lecture tour of border cities. She was served by a slave chambermaid at a Baltimore boardinghouse and heard of other slaveholders, and she was stunned to realize the history of Mount Vernon, Virginia, home of George Washington:

[T]he mark of slavery o'ershadows the whole, Oh, the thought that it was here, that he whose name is the pride of this Nation was the *Slave Master* . . .
—*Diary, 1854*

The next day she continued:

This noon I ate my dinner without once asking myself, are these human beings who minister to my wants *Slaves* who can be bought & sold & hired out at the will of a master? And when the thought first entered my mind, I said, even I am getting *accustomed* to *Slavery,* so much so that I have ceased continually to be made to feel its blighting, cursing influence, so much so that I can sit down and calmly eat from the hands of the bondman, without being once mindful of the fact that he is such—

Oh Slavery, hateful thing that thou art, thus to blunt the keen edge of mens conscience, even while they strive to shun thy poisonous touch.
—*Diary, 1854*

Anthony's life was so entwined with abolitionism that acts of heroism we would deem awesome were casually noted in her diary. Unfortunately, we know little more than this offhand reference to her work on the underground railroad with its famed conductor, Harriet Tubman.

[S]uperintended the plowing of the orchard . . . The last load of hay is in the barn; all in capital order. Fitted out a fugitive slave for Canada with the help of Harriet Tubman.
—*Diary, 1861*

Object of meeting; to consider the fact of 4,000,000 slaves in a Christian and republican government. . . . Our mission is to deepen sympathy and convert it into right action, to show that the men and women of the North are slave-holders, those of the South slave-owners. The guilt rests on the North equally with the South, therefore our work is to rouse the sleeping consciences of the North. . . . We demand the abolition of slavery because the slave is a human being, and because man should not hold property in his fellowman. The politician demands it because its existence produces poverty and discord in the nation and imposes taxes on free labor for its support, since the government is dominated by southern rule. . . . We preach revolution; the politicians reform.
—*Notes for Speech, 1857*

Can the thousands of Northern soldiers, who in their march through Rebel States have found faithful friends and generous allies in the slaves, ever consent to hurl them back into the hell of slavery, either by word, or vote, or sword?

Slaves have sought shelter in the Northern army and have tasted the forbidden fruit from the *tree of Liberty*. Will they return quietly to the plantation, and patiently endure the old life of bondage, with all its degradation, its cruelties, and wrong? . . .

What will you do with the Negroes? Do with them precisely what you would do with the Irish, the Scotch, and the Germans—Educate them. Welcome them to all the blessings of our free institutions; —to our schools & churches, to every department of industry, trade & art. Do with the Negroes? What arrogance in *us* to put the question, what shall *we* do with a race of men and women who have fed, clothed and supported both themselves and their oppressors for centuries.
—*Speech, 1862*

In 1863 Susan B. Anthony, along with Elizabeth Cady Stanton, Lucy Stone, and other dedicated abolitionists, formed the Women's Loyal National League to press for an amendment to the Constitution to abolish slavery. Anthony, who had organized the group, addressed the opening meeting, telling women they had a special role to play.

[T]here is great fear expressed on all sides lest this war shall be made a war for the negro. I am willing that it shall be; I am ready to admit that it is a war for the negro. It is a war to found an empire on the negro in slavery, and shame on us if we do not make it a war to establish the negro in freedom! It is a war for the elevation of humanity. And the negro, the portion of humanity most down-trodden in this country—the negro, against whom the whole nation, North and South, East and West, in one mighty conspiracy, has combined from the beginning—must now be made the exponent of the war. There is no name given under heaven wherewith to break, and forever crush out this wicked conspiracy, save that of the negro.

Great care has been taken, ever since the war began, to keep the negro and slavery out of sight and hearing. But my position has ever been, that instead of suppressing the real cause of the war, it should have been proclaimed, not only by the people, but by the President, Congress, Cabinet, and every military commander. And when the Government, military and civil, and the people, acknowledged slavery to be the cause of the war, they should have simultaneously, one and all, decreed its total overthow. Instead of President Lincoln's waiting two long years before calling into the field and to the side of the Government the four millions of allies whom we have had within the territory of rebeldom, it was the first duty of the first decree he sent forth. Every hour's delay has been a sin and a shame registered against him, and every life sacrified . . . to the proclamation that called the slave to freedom and to arms, was nothing less than downright murder by the Government.

. . . We talk about returning to the old Union—"the Union as it was," and "the Constitution as it is"—about "restoring our country to peace and prosperity—to the blessed conditions that existed before the war!" I ask you what sort of peace, what sort of prosperity, have we had? Since the first slave-ship sailed up the James River with its human cargo, and there, on the soil of the *Old* Dominion, it was sold to the highest bidder, we have had nothing but war. When that pirate captain landed on the shores of Africa, and there kidnapped the first stalwart negro, and fastened the first manacle, the struggle between that captain and that negro was the commencement of the terrible war in the midst of which we are to-day. Between the slave and the master there has been war, and war only, from the beginning. This is only a new form of the war. No, no; we ask for no return to the *old* conditions. We ask for something better than the old. We want a Union that is a Union in fact, a Union in spirit, not a sham Union. [*Applause.*]

By the Constitution as it is—that is, as it has been interpreted and executed from the beginning—the North has stood pledged to protect slavery in the States where it existed. We have been bound, in case of slave insurrections, to go to the aid, not of those struggling for liberty, but of the oppressors. It was politicians who made this pledge at the beginning, and who have renewed it from year to year to this day. These same politicians have had control of the churches, the Sabbath-schools, and all religious influences; and the women have been a party in complicity with slavery....

... the hour is fully come, when woman shall no longer be the passive recipient of whatever morals and religion the trade and politics of the nation may decree; but that she shall now assume her God-given responsibilities and make herself what she is clearly designed to be, the educator of the race. Let her no longer be the mere reflector, the echo of the wordly pride and ambition of the other half of the race. [*Applause.*] Had the women of the North studied to know and to teach their sons the law of justice to the black man, as the white, regardless of the frown or the smile of pro-slavery priest and politician, they would not now be called upon to offer the loved of their households to the bloody Moloch of war. And now, women of the North, I ask you to rise up with earnest, honest purpose, to speak the true word and do the just work, in season and out of season. I ask you to forget that you are women, and go forward in the way of right, fearlessly, as independent human beings, responsible to God alone for the discharge of every duty, for the faithful use of every gift, for the multiplying tenfold every talent the good Father has given you. Forget conventionalisms; forget what the world will say, whether you are in your place or out of your place; think your best thoughts, speak your best words, do your best works, looking only to suffering humanity, your own conscience, and God for approval.

—*Speech, 1863*

At an 1864 meeting of the Women's Loyal National League, Anthony read a resolution whose anti-Lincoln sentiment did not please everyone:

Resolved, That a Government which upholds slavery, both by military and civil power, is itself a daring rebellion against the God before whom Jefferson trembled, and whose exterminating thunders he warned us would be our destruction, unless by the diffusion of light and liberty we use every effort to eradicate it from the land.

THE CHAIR.—This resolution declares this Government a Rebellion against God. Are you all prepared to say that?

A MEMBER.—I don't exactly undertand it that way. The resolution says "a Government" without particularizing.

ANOTHER.—Well, it means the same thing. Let us adopt it. It is true any how.

MRS GAGE.—I move to amend it by making it affirm that this Government is a rebellion against God. The resolution is not explicit enough for me.

MISS ANTHONY.—It would suit me better if it read as suggested by the amendment. If this Government does not uphold slavery, both by military and civil power, I know of none that does. The lady then suggested that there could be no question of its character in that respect to the past, anyhow. She went on to excoriate the Administration for nullifying Fremont's proclamation of emancipation in Missouri.

A VOICE.—The intention of the President is to emancipate the slaves.

Miss Anthony didn't care a fig for his intentions. It was an old saying that Hell is paved with good intentions. Without action intentions were worthless. What she wanted now was action—immediate action. Before the war this was a slaveholding Government, and to all intents and purposes it is yet. The President is only drifting in the course of events, but saw fit to come out of the current when Fremont's emancipation event came along. . . .

—*Meeting, 1864*

[After much discussion, the resolution passed]

When Lincoln was assassinated in 1865, Susan B. Anthony suffered very mixed emotions. Horrified at the human loss, she could not forget that the President was supporting the readmission of Louisiana into the union without giving blacks the vote.

Was there ever a more terrific command to a Nation to "stand still and know that I am God" since the world began— —The Old Book's terrible exhibitions of Gods wrath sink into nothingness. And this blow fell just at the very hour he was declaring his willingness to consign those five million faithful brave, and loving loyal people of the south to the tender mercies of the ex slave lords of the lash—. . . .

The Church folks called a Union meeting . . . last Sunday P.M. for *general expression* of *all the people*—but alas *Priests* took the platform, read the Bible, gave out the hymn, said the prayer and called out one man to speak . . . My soul was full, but the flesh was not equal to stemming the awful current, to do what the people have called make an exhibition of myself. So quenched the spirit and came home ashamed of myself.
—*Letter, April 19, 1865*

I was reading the President's last speech when the stunning telegram of his assassination reached me. . . .

So far the interpretation of this awful tragedy, by press and pulpit, is only to visit the whole penalty of the law upon the heads of the traitor chiefs. Not one leading influential voice has yet cried out against the awful crime of building up the Union on the disfranchisement of a whole loyal race—a crime, in view of the light and knowledge of this day, and the faithful heroic service of the race to the nation; vastly more black and damning, than was that of the Fathers in permitting their enslavement one hundred years ago. God's one great purpose, is that this nation shall establish and practice His law of the perfectly equal humanity of all races, nations and colors. . . .
—*Speech, April 23, 1865*

In this City there are Four thousand ex–Missouri slaves—who have sought refuge here . . . —I make it a point to enter into conversation with every one I meet—I want to see the real genuine *"niggers"* that loves [sic] Slavery better than freedom—the ignorant, stupid ones—but so far every man woman & child of them, is brimful of good common sense, & knows more than any ten of the same class of Irish population . . .
—*Letter from Leavenworth, Kansas, 1865*

Anthony was in Kansas because her brothers Daniel and Merritt had traveled there when the battles over slavery in the territory began. They supported John Brown, the fiery abolitionist who brought his guns and himself for the bloody raid on Osawatomie to avenge the deaths of early antislavery settlers. Many years later, when Susan B. Anthony visited the John Brown Farm in Lake Placid, New York, she left this inscription in the visitors' register:

> With the above three—Rev. Anna H. Shaw—who was ordained by the Protestant Methodist Church in 1880—and Mr. & Mrs. Banker—On this beautiful June day—came to this home of Old John Brown—Susan B. Anthony of Rochester—N.Y. whose youngest brother J. Merritt Anthony moved to Kansas in the spring of 1856—in whose cabin John Brown slept—the night before the famous Osawatomie Battle in August of that year 1856— Both of my brothers—D. R. & J. M. Anthony were with John Brown in every way of his Kansas enterprizes—They were perilous days—& no one did so much to give the history to freedom—as did John Brown & the handful of men who stood with him—at least—in the opinion of Susan B. Anthony . . .
> *—Inscription, 1891*

It is not clear who first used the term, but newspaper editor Horace Greeley is quoted early in 1867 as saying to the suffrage women, "This is a critical period for the Republican party and the life of the Nation. The word 'white' in our Constitution at this hour has a significance which 'male' has not. It would be wise and magnanimous in you to hold your claims, though just and imperative, I grant, in abeyance until the negro is safe beyond peradventure, and your turn will come next. I conjure you to remember that this is 'the negro's hour,' and your first duty now is to go through the State and plead his claims." Susan B. Anthony was not prepared to wait.

> The real fact is that we have so long held Woman's claims in abeyance to the Negro's that the naming them now is rec[k]oned an impertinence—I deem no evidence of discretion or good sense that we have thus done for the past four years, and now hope we shall learn the lesson that the price of *asking*—even for liberty, is *eternal vigilance*—so that we shall hereafter keep our demand fre[quently?] before the public—
> *—Letter, 1866*

Anthony was doubly frustrated by the fact that some of the women had also deserted The Cause for the black man. Civil War lecturer Anna Dickinson had long since turned the corner.

On Cars Louisville to Cincinnati

Dear Anna:—The enclosed slips will indicate *my alarm* lest *you,* the Anna Dick, are *off the track*— . . . For I see your speech is not *The New Republic*—is not *Woman*—but only the *black man,* whom, as I told you they would—The Republicans *have thrown overboard*—I tell you *Anna rats*—that is, *female rats*—ought to know enough to leave a sinking ship— . . . . The position of the Republican Party & all men who go only *manhood suffrage* (how I hate the term) is *terribly insulting* to you & me and every woman of us—and, to see you *piping for it*—is sad, *sad*—How do the Republicans expect women & Negroes to work for them . . . I tell you—the *Kansas Republican treatment* of *our movement* disgusted me—and would you—*not one leading politician—living one*— stood by us in the *deadly breach*—& the same is true of *the Nation*—they all mean to delude us into silence . . . *to* serve *party ends*—who can trust the Republican leaders after this—

—*Letter, 1867*

My Dear Olympia

. . . Oh dear a me, Olympia—I got so *soul sick* of the *icy faces* of Boston that I felt I could not stop another minute— . . . Not one of the *old leaders* in *Anti Slavery* now *puts himself* or *herself* in the *front ranks for Woman*—

—*Letter, 1868*

The final blow for Anthony and Stanton came at a meeting of the American Equal Rights Association, the group they formed to gain the vote for everyone—blacks and women. During an 1869 debate over the Fifteenth Amendment—giving black males citizenship, and thus guaranteeing the vote only to them—Frederick Douglass led the fight.

MR. DOUGLASS—I must say that I do not see how any one can pretend that there is the same urgency in giving the ballot to woman as to the negro. With us, the matter is a question of life and death, at least in fifteen States of the Union. When women, because they are women, are hunted down through the cities of New York and New Orleans; when they are dragged from their houses and hung upon lamp-posts; when their children are torn from their arms, and their brains dashed out upon the pavement; when they are objects of insult and outrage at every turn; when they are in danger of having their homes burnt down over their heads; when their children are not allowed to enter schools; then they will have an urgency to obtain the ballot equal to our own. [*Great applause.*]

A VOICE—Is that not all true about black women?

MR. DOUGLASS—Yes, yes, yes; it is true of the black woman, but not because she is a woman, but because she is black. [*Applause.*] Julia Ward Howe at the conclusion of her great speech delivered at the convention in Boston last year, said: "I am willing that the negro shall get the ballot before me." [*Applause.*] Woman! why, she has 10,000 modes of grappling with her difficulties. I believe that all the virtue of the world can take care of all the evil. I believe that all the intelligence can take care of all the ignorance. [*Applause.*] I am in favor of woman's suffrage in order that we shall have all the virtue and vice confronted. Let me tell you that when there were few houses in which the black man could have put his head, this woolly head of mine found refuge in the house of Mrs. Elizabeth Cady Stanton, and if I had been blacker than sixteen midnights, without a single star, it would have been the same. [*Applause.*]

MISS ANTHONY—The question of precedence has no place on an equal rights platform. The only reason why it ever found a place here was that there were some who insisted that woman must stand back and wait until another class should be enfranchised. In answer to that, my friend Mrs. Stanton & others of us have said, If you will not give the whole loaf of justice to the entire people, if you are determined to give it to us piece by piece, than give it first to women, to the most intelligent & capable portion of the women at least, because in the present state of government it is intelligence, it is morality which is needed. We have never thought the question upon the platform, whether women should be enfranchised first or last . . . .

If Mr. Douglass had noticed who clapped [for] him when he said "black men first & white women afterwards," he would have seen that they were all men. The women did not clap [for] him. The proof is that the men cannot understand us women. They think of us as some of the slaveholders used to think of their slaves, all love & compassion, with no malice in their hearts; but they thought "The Negro is a poor lovable creature, kind, docile, unable to take care of himself, & dependent on our compassion to keep them"; & so they consented to do it for the good of the slaves. Men feel the divine today, Douglass, Tilton & Phillips think that women are perfectly contented to let men earn the money & dole it out to us. We feel with Alexander Hamilton, "Give a man power over my substance & he has power over my whole being." There is not a woman born, whose bread is earned by another, it does not matter whether that other is husband, mother, father, or friend, not one who consents to eat the bread earned by other hands, but her whole moral being is in the power of that person. [*Applause.*]

When Mr. Douglass tells us that the cause of the black man is so perilous I tell him that wronged & outraged as they are by this hateful & mean prejudice against color, he would not today exchange his sex & color, wronged as he is, with Elizabeth Cady Stanton. [*Laughter and applause.*]

MR. DOUGLASS—Will you allow me a question?

MISS ANTHONY—Yes; anything for a fight today.

MR. DOUGLASS—I want to inquire whether granting to woman the right of suffrage will change anything—in respect to the nature of our sexes? [*Great laughter.*]

MISS ANTHONY—It will change the nature of one thing very much, & that is the pecuniary position of woman. It will place her in a position in which she can earn her own bread, so that she can go out into the world on equal competition in the struggle for life, so that she shall not be compelled to take such positions as men choose to accord . . . & then take such pay as men choose to give her. . . .

What we demand is that woman shall have the ballot, for she will never get her other rights until she demands them with the ballot in her hand. It is not a question of precedence between women & black men. Neither has a claim to precedence upon an Equal Rights platform. But the business of this association is to demand for every man black or white, & for every woman, black or white, that they shall be this instant enfranchised & admitted into the body politic with equal rights & privileges. . . .

MISS ANTHONY protested against the XVth amendment because it wasn't Equal Rights. It put two million more men in position of tyrants over two million women who had until now been the equals of the men at their side.

—*Debate, 1869*

After that exchange, Anthony, Stanton, and other women walked out of the AERA and formed a new organization with a single purpose: the National Woman Suffrage Association. But Anthony, who understood that the

Fourteenth and Fifteenth Amendments were about politics, not equality, never abandoned her demand for racial justice. When the General Federation of Women's Clubs instituted segregation, she spoke out again:

> The color line cannot be drawn. It would be as sensible to bar women because of the shade of their eyes. If a woman is intellectual, of good faith and character and stands for the progress of women in the largest sense, it makes no difference what her color or nationality may be. Colored women should be given an equal footing with white women when they are working for the same end. . . .
>
> Not many years ago there was a great outcry against admitting Jewish women to conventions. That has all passed away, and it will be the same with the negro.
>
> — *Interview, 1900*

One of her most unyielding hatreds was the lynching of blacks in the South. Articles on the barbaric practice were clipped and pasted into her scrapbooks. And waiting in vain for a minister to speak out ruined an otherwise "splendid" sermon.

> It was splendid—he lacked only the mention of Lynching of negroes . . . the worst, cruelest of all—I told him so—it seemed too bad to make a criticism—but it was too great a mistake not to call his attention to it.
>
> — *Diary, 1901*

One Sunday evening in 1895, she had the great pleasure of hearing Ida Wells (soon to marry and become Ida Wells-Barnett), the black activist and journalist who helped expose lynching, at a church in Rochester. A young man in the audience, a theological student, rudely asked Wells, "If the Negroes don't like it in the South, why don't they leave and go North?" Anthony sprang to her feet:

> [I will tell you why.] It is because they get no better treatment in the North than they do in the South. That is why they don't come here. I will relate an incident that occurred in our city only last week that will serve to illustrate what I mean. A dance was to be given in No. 3 School for the benefit of the children of the seventh grade, and tickets were issued to the children for ten cents apiece. Now it happened that there was a colored girl in that grade who wanted to go to the dance as well as the white children

and so she asked her mother for the money to buy a ticket. But when she went to her teacher, Miss Agnes M. Stewart, she was told that if she insisted on going to the dance, none of the white children would attend and that the affair would be given up; so the poor child was turned away. I consider that the outrage on the feelings of that colored girl was the result of the same spirit that inspire[s] the lynchings of the South. [*Outburst of approval from audience.*]
—*Remarks, 1895*

Anthony took Wells home with her to Madison Street, where she encountered yet another opportunity to act on her convictions. At the time, a young woman named Anna Dorsey was serving as her secretary.

Ida B. Wells of Memphis—guest—went to see Mrs. Fullam about dresses for California trip—told typewriter Anna Dorsey—to ask Miss Wells if she would like to dictate her letters & have them written on the typewriter—when I returned—I found Miss Wells scribbling away—& said "couldn't you dictate & let Anny type write for you"—["]Oh yes—if I had had a chance"—then I went to my room & said—"you didn't understand me did you . . ."—["]Yes—she said—but I didn't choose to write for a colored woman—I engaged to work for *you*." Well—when I ask an employee to do a favor to a guest—I expect her to comply—so the little fatherless & homeless girl of 20—left—The presbyterian ministers this A.M. passed a resolution against lynching.
—*Diary, 1895*

In the end, Anthony's deep respect for people of all colors and backgrounds intersected with her demand for political rights. When southern politicians started denying their Constitutional guarantees, Susan B. Anthony lent her support to mass meetings on the issue. She was eighty-three years old.

To refuse to qualified women and colored men the right of suffrage and still count them in the basis of representation is to add insult to injury and is as unjust as it is unreasonable. The trouble, however, is farther back and deeper than the disfranchisement of the negro. When men deliberately refused to include women in the Fourteenth and Fifteenth Amendments to the national constitution they left the way open for all forms of injustice to other and weaker men and peoples. Men who fail to be just to their mothers cannot be expected to be just to each other. The whole evil comes from the failure to apply equal justice to all mankind, male and female alike, therefore I am glad to join with those who are like sufferers with my sex in a protest against counting in the basis of representation in Congress or the United States, or in the state Legislatures, any class or sex who are disfranchised.

—Letter read during mass meeting, 1903

[T]he only way to solve the race question is to educate both races, the blacks to be equal to their opportunities, the whites to be willing to share their privileges.

—Diary, 1905

The Winning Ticket

In 1865 the Rochester *Union and Advertiser* published the following proposal about its two hometown heroes: "Susan B. Anthony and Fred. Douglass [sic] have more brains than the majority of radical leaders who, being less honest, figure higher. When universal suffrage and negro equality render this country the paradise proposed, we shall expect to see Mr. Douglass President and Miss Anthony Vice President of the United States. They would make a strong ticket."

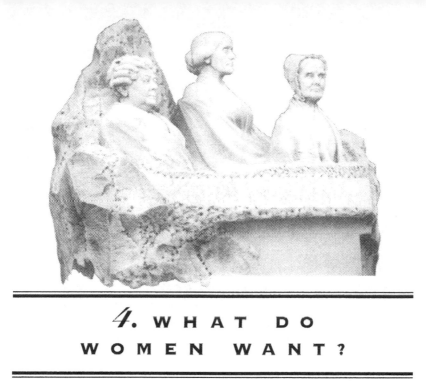

4. WHAT DO WOMEN WANT?

*T*he three-page entry in one encyclopedia begins like this:

> **Wo´man's Rights,** a term used in the U.S. to designate the movement for woman's equal social, civil, political, industrial, religious, and educational rights with man.

It was written in 1878 by Susan B. Anthony, three decades after the first sweeping goals of feminism were declared.

Today, we take those conditions—and the movement to gain them—for granted, with little understanding of how thoroughly outrageous such appeals were to many in the mid–nineteenth century. It was a time when the world believed in "woman's sphere," which generally meant confinement to what Anthony called the "delicately flavored soup" of domestic and charity work. Her own modest mutiny against such restraints began with the temperance movement. She circulated a petition for a law to prohibit the sale of alcohol, whose abuse, she said, led to "shiftless, drunken, precarious, unjust, cruel, libertine husbands." Susan B. Anthony saw temperance

---

SUFFRAGE MONUMENT, U.S. CAPITOL.
LEFT TO RIGHT, ELIZABETH CADY STANTON,
SUSAN B. ANTHONY, LUCRETIA MOTT.

as a legitimate concern of women, its most likely and least powerful victims. But while temperance was gradually becoming acceptable woman's work, the idea of a single woman speaking her mind was still repugnant to many. Preparing to attend the upcoming World's Temperance Society meeting in New York in 1853, Anthony predicted to Lucy Stone, "the brothers will feel very much disturbed at our presence." *It was worse than that. For a full hour and a half, the men in the audience hissed and howled to keep Antoinette Brown from lecturing. The New York* Tribune *summed up the sessions of the convention this way: "First day—Crowding a woman off the platform; second day—Gagging her; third day—Voting that she shall stay gagged."*

But it was Anthony's next crusade that really stunned the public. On the road for temperance she discovered the source of the problem: wives would not contribute to her campaign because they didn't have any money; they didn't have money because, even if they worked, their husbands controlled all the family finances. Click! Without a "purse of her own," woman was helpless.

And it went far beyond economic freedom. At a time when women gave up virtually every legal right after entering into marriage, Anthony believed they were entitled to full equality: specifically, to have custody of their own children, to own property in their own name, to work, and even to divorce. In short, women should not be mere assets in a husband's portfolio. Thus did a thirty-three-year-old spinster devote much of her life to securing legal rights for married women. The idea had been percolating for some years already, but Anthony helped focus the issue by organizing women—in meetings that turned into conventions—to apply their full force to the men in power. She also understood the value of going out among the people, once again taking to the road, for a trip that remains astonishing a century and a half later.

Starting on the day after Christmas in 1854, she braved blizzards, ice storms, miserable accommodations, and vicious crowds during a four-month tour of fifty-four (of the sixty) counties of New York State. Traveling mostly by herself, on trains and sleighs, she sold tracts and collected signatures from Rochester to Riverhead, from Buffalo to White Plains, covering a vast expanse under wretched winter circumstances. Her trip was both trying and revealing. Here is an example of what she saw while accompanied by another woman lecturer:

We stopped at a little tavern where the landlady was not yet twenty and had a baby fifteen months old. Her supper dishes were not washed and her baby was crying, but she was equal to the occasion. She rocked the little thing to sleep, washed the dishes and got our supper; beautiful white bread, butter, cheese, pickles, apple and mince pie, and excellent peach preserves. She gave us her warm bedroom to sleep in, and on a row of pegs hung the loveliest embroidered petticoat and baby clothes, all the work of that young woman's fingers, while on a rack was her ironing perfectly done, wrought undersleeves, baby dresses, embroidered underwear, etc. She prepared a 6 o'clock breakfast for us, fried pork, mashed potatoes, mince pie, and for me, at my especial request, a plate of delicious baked sweet apples and a pitcher of rich milk. Now for the moral of this story: When we came to pay our bill, the dolt of a husband took the money and put it in his pocket. He had not lifted a hand to lighten that woman's burdens, but had sat and talked with the men in the bar room, not even caring for the baby, yet the law gives him the right to every dollar she earns, and when she needs two cents to buy a darning needle she has to ask him and explain what she wants it for.

The purpose of the trip was to get enough signatures to convince the New York State Legislature. A year later, she and Elizabeth Cady Stanton presented one of many petitions to change the state law. The sarcastic response from the lawmakers did not deter them, and after numerous other appeals they won their case. In March 1860, New York State passed a Married Women's Property Rights Law, granting everything they had asked for but the vote. It was a delicious echo of a similar triumph in Ohio several years earlier, as announced by Lucy Stone:

Hurrah Susan! Last week this State Legislature passed a law giving wives equal property rights, and to mothers equal baby rights, with the fathers—So much is gained ... The world moves! Hurrah!

Unfortunately, just a few years later, while the women's attention was directed at other targets, the New York law was rescinded, a double cross which led Anthony to remark, "Well, well; while the old guard sleep the young 'devils' are wide-awake, and we deserve to suffer for our confidence in 'man's sense of justice,' and to have all we have gained thus snatched from us."

It would serve as a warning of the constant danger of backlash—a reminder to seek all rights, all the time. It also helped Anthony realize that women's rights might come more easily if women themselves had a voice in making the laws. That would be her next and most all-encompassing crusade.

———————

Susan B. Anthony's commitment to women's rights, like her work in temperance and abolition, was rooted in her training as a reformer.

I am tired of theory. I want to hear how we must act to have a happier & more glorious world. . . . reform, reform needs to be the watch word. And somebody must preach it, who does not depend on the popular nod for his dinner.
—*Letter, 1848*

Cautious, careful people, always casting about to preserve their reputation and social standing, never can bring about a reform. Those who are really in earnest must be willing to be anything or nothing in the world's estimation, and publicly and privately, in season and out, avow their sympathy with despised and persecuted ideas and their advocates, and bear the consequences.
—*Remarks, 1860*

. . . it is only through a wholesome discontent with things as they are, that we ever try to make them any better.
—*Letter, 1883*

She always credited her temperance work with turning her into a feminist.

In those early days it was considered gentlemanly to use wine to excess; it was customary and was the law for a husband to take all of his wife's property and use it as he pleased. There were cases, not one or two nor twenty nor thirty, but hundreds in which designing men would marry innocent girls for their money, and almost as soon as the marriage vow was uttered, would waste their wives' dowry in riotous living. If a man failed his creditors attached his wife's property, and frequently took away from her everything she had, even down to little ornaments

for her children or family keepsakes that had been transmitted to her by her parents and grandparents. There were cases where women with lazy or dissipated husbands would try to work and support themselves and their little ones, and when it came around to the weekly or monthly pay day a creditor of the husband or the wretched man himself would appear upon the scene, collect the proceeds of her toil and let her go home penniless to, it might be, a starving household. And stranger still, the father had the right of custody over the children at the expense of the mother. These facts will illustrate a condition in which women had no rights and no privileges; where, in fact, they hardly had a soul to call their own. The thing struck me so forcibly that in my youth I determined to enter public life and battle for my sex.
—*Interview, 1895*

I want to ask, and try to answer, why when women combine and make a demand they are always laughed at? Women always begin on temperance. Whiskey is the subject thought of by the ladies. . . . In New York we got up a petition signed by over 2,800. It was presented to the Legislature. It was read and laughed at and laid on the table. A young man who opposed the measure, took up the petition and said: "Who are these people that have signed this petition? Nothing but women and children." It fell to the floor and he kicked it. Why are not women's names as good as men's? Because they had no votes. If they had had the power to cast ballots for or against these legislators it would never have entered his brain to ask the question. He would have thought women's names as good as men's. I then resolved to use my life to make women as good as men.
—*Speech, 1887*

Thus as I passed from town to town was I made to feel the great evil of woman's utter dependency upon man, for the necessary means to aid on any and every reform movement. Though I had long admitted the wrongs, I never until this time, so fully took in the grand idea of pecuniary & personal independence.

It matters not how overflowing with benevolence towards suffering humanity may be the heart of woman, it avails nothing so long as she possesses not the power to act in accordance with those prompting[s]. Woman must have a *purse* of her own, & how can this be, so long as the *wife* is denied the right to her *individual & joint earnings*. Reflections like these, caused me to see & really feel that there was no *true freedom* for woman without the posses-

sion of all her property rights, and that these rights could be obtained through *legislation* only, & if so, the sooner the demand was made of the Legislature, the sooner would we be likely to obtain them—This demand must be made by Petitions to the Legislature, & that, too, at its very next session—How could the work be started, Why, by first holding a Convention & adopting some plan of united action.
—*Diary, 1853*

Friends, when we come before you to advocate the Cause popularly termed "Woman's Rights," we simply ask that woman be not wronged. We ask for her justice & equality—not favor & superiority—the rights and privileges her humanity charters to her equally with man, not arbitrary power & selfish dominion . . .

I am not ignorant of the fact, that great fears are entertained, on all sides, lest the enlargement of woman's area of freedom,—the granting to her perfect liberty to decide for herself, what is proper, & what improper for her to do, or not to do, will have the effect to take from her, her *feminine* nature, & in its stead give to her, that of the *masculine*—

. . . allow me to say that I feel fully assured that woman will be woman, still, be her position what it may, whether she be Mother, wife, daughter, sister, teacher, seamstress, domestic; President, Legislator, Judge, Juror, Lawyer, Doctor, Minister, Astronomer, Sea Captain, Artisan; still, will she be woman. . .

Why is it that the public is *willing* thus to pay *man* twice or three times the sum, for the performance of a certain amount of labor, that it does to woman?—To me, the reason is obvious.—It is the direct result of the *legislation* of the Country— . . . *Society,* taking the law as its precedent, says, a *man* has a wife & family to support, *therefore he must* be *liberally* remunerated for his time & services, that he may meet the *heavy demand* upon him,—While of the *woman,* it says, *she* has no one to support but *herself,* therefore a much smaller remuneration will enable her to meet her individual wants. . . .

Create a public sentiment, that shall open wide to woman, the doors of all our mechanic shops, stores, & offices, & bid her go in & work side by side with her brother man, paying to her equal wages for equal services rendered, & you do more to relieve the suffering, and save the last, of our sex, than all the moral reform societies, Sisters of Charity, Homes for the Friendless & the thou-

sands of other benevolent institutions, that now act as ministering angels to these wretched children of poverty & vice—
— *Speech, 1854*

Men may prate on, but we women are beginning to know that the life and happiness of a *woman* is of equal value with that of a *man;* and that for a woman to sacrifice her health, happiness and perchance her earthly existence in the hope of reclaiming a drunken, sensualized man, avails but little. In nine cases out of ten, if the man *ever* reforms, it is not until after the wife sinks into an untimely grave; or if not in her *grave,* is physically and mentally unnerved, and unfitted for any earthly enjoyment.
— *Letter, 1852*

The issue of divorce, first raised by Elizabeth Cady Stanton in 1852, was a hot topic for many, and Susan B. Anthony spent considerable time convincing not only the men, but otherwise progressive women as well, how important it was to keep it in their women's rights ("W.R.") agenda.

I have thought with you until of late that the *Social* question must be kept *separate* from W.R.—but we have *always claimed* that *our movement* was *Human Rights*—not *Woman's* Rights—therefore we need not confine ourselves to the evils that woman suffers *alone*—but enlarge our borders, as the truth shall be revealed.
— *Letter to Lucy Stone, 1857*

Lucy, I want this convention to strike deeper than any of its predecessors. It seems to me we have played on the *surface* of things quite long enough. Getting the right to hold property, to vote, to wear what dress we please, &c&c, are all good—but Social Freedom, after all, lies at the bottom of all—& until woman gets that, she must continue the slave of man in all other things. . . .

The world, even the *religious* part of it, is ready to grant woman her property rights—her Industrial & almost her Political—But in an *indissoluble* marriage she bows to man's passions.

When woman can be educated to assert her right to control her own person & affections—not only assert but *act* the traitor—then comes the *rub*—then comes the time for opposition. . . .
— *Letter to Lucy Stone, 1857*

Marriage has ever been a one-sided matter, resting most unequally upon the sexes. By it, man gains all—woman loses all;

tyrant law and lust reign supreme with him—meek submission and ready obedience alone befit her. Woman has never been consulted; her wish has never been taken into consideration as regards the terms of the marriage compact. By law, public sentiment and religion, from the time of Moses down to the present day, woman has never been thought of other than as a piece of property, to be disposed of at the will and pleasure of man. And this very hour, by our statute-books, by our (so-called) enlightened Christian civilization, she has no voice whatever in saying what shall be the basis of the relation. She must accept marriage as man proffers it, or not at all.

. . . the discussion is perfectly in order, since nearly all the wrongs of which we complain grow out of the inequality, the injustice of the marriage laws, that rob the wife of the right to herself and her children—that make her the slave of the man she marries.

—*Speech, 1860, in defense of discussing divorce at a women's rights convention*

Some of the men wanted to strike the speeches and resolutions from the record.

I do not believe that divorce always brings evil. It is just as much a refuge for women married to brutal men as Canada once was a refuge from brutal masters.

—*Speech, 1905*

U.S. REPRESENTATIVE A. G. RIDDLE: Now, ladies, what is really the legal status of marriage, so far as the condition of the wife is concerned?

SUSAN B. ANTHONY: One of servitude, and of the hardest kind, and just for board and clothes, at that, too. [*Laughter and applause.*]

—*House Judiciary Committee Meeting, 1871*

Anthony used many examples to rally audiences—particularly audiences of women—to the cause of married women's property rights. One of her most effective illustrations concerned the unfortunate lady from Illinois with the ill-fitting false teeth:

A married woman can not testify in the courts in cases of joint interest with her husband. A good farmer's wife near Earlville,

Ill., who had all the rights she wanted, went to the dentist of the village, who made her a full set of false teeth, both upper and under. The dentist pronounced them an admirable fit, and the wife declared they gave her fits to wear them; that she could neither chew nor talk with them in her mouth. The dentist sued the husband; his counsel brought the wife as witness; the judge ruled her off the stand, saying:

> A married woman can not be a witness in matters of joint interest between herself and her husband.

Think of it, ye good wives, the false teeth in your mouths a joint interest with your husbands, about which you are legally incompetent to speak!
—*Speech, 1873*

Don't trust to the chivalry of man. . . . For 10 years we labored in New York state to secure to women the right to their own wages and the guardianship of their own children and property. A small clique of lawyers went up to Albany and by one stroke of the pen all this reform was obliterated. . . .

Of course it is very different now, but women have no idea how barbarous even the present laws are. I sometimes wish that every husband would persecute his wife just as far as the law allows him in order that married women might know how few rights they have. If they do not know they may charge it to the indulgence of mankind.
—*Speech, 1889*

Primarily I want to say that the object of our movement is not a reversal of the relations existing between the sexes, but only a radical revision of them. I want to elevate the home by making the wife a full partner in the establishment instead of the slave and vassal that she now is. Under the present conditions women marry for a livelihood. The man who gets a wife because the poor thing needs somebody to support her certainly ought not to feel that he has any of the element of a Don Juan in his composition. But liberate woman, give her the same opportunity as man to have her opinion counted, and see how quick the law of natural selection will assert itself and the divorce mills will go out of business.
—*Interview, 1894*

The Men, even the *best* of them, seem to think the Women's Rights question should be waived for the present. So let us do our own work, and in our own way. Ours will eventually become a *political* question; in that day it will always be in order.
—*Letter, 1856*

The following letter to Elizabeth Cady Stanton illustrates the passion with which Anthony embraced women's rights, even as a new convert. She was writing from Collins, New York, where a reformer named Andrew J. Davis was speaking at a packed meeting of Progressive Friends about women's rights:

... he set forth his idea of the nature of the sexes & their relation to each [other]—spoke truthfully & nobly of re-production—of the *abuses* in marriage &c&c—but to his ideas of the sexes—he said woman's inherent nature is Love & man's Wisdom—that Love reaches out to Wisdom man—and Wisdom reaches out to Love—woman—& the two meet & make a beautiful blending of the two principles—In other words, woman *starts* with the *Love* Principle predominant—& grows up into Wisdom—and man starts with Wisdom & grows up into Love—...

My soul was on fire—this is but a *revamp* of the world's idea from the beginning—the very same doctrine that consigned woman from the beginning to the sphere of the affections, that subjugated her to man's wisdom.... the *question* was *called for*—I... said Mr. President I must say a word—and I did say a word—I said *Women,* if you accept the theory given you by Davis, you may give up all talk of change for woman—she is now where god & nature intended she should be—If it be a fact—that the principle of Wisdom is indigenous in man, & Love an exotic, then must Wisdom *prevail*—& so with woman must *Love prevail*—

Therefore woman must look to *man* for *Wisdom*—must ever feel it impossible for her to attain Wisdom equal to him—such a doctrine makes my heart *sink* within me, said I—and did I accept it—I would return to my own Fathers [*sic*] house and never again raise my voice for woman's right to control of her own person, the ownership of her own earnings—the guardianship of her own children—

For if this be true, she ought not to possess those rights—She ought to make final appeal to the wisdom of her husband father &

brother—My word stirred the waters—and brought Davis to his
feet again, but he failed to extricate himself from the conclusions
to which his premises philosophically lean— —Well Sunday,
there were more than a *thousand* people congregated, hundreds
more *out* than in doors—

. . . that evening until 10 . . . o'clock & all day yesterday, the
likeness & unlikeness of the sexes has been topic of discussion. . . .
the discussion has been loud & long . . . I tell you, Mrs. Stanton
after all, it is very *precious* to the soul of man that he *shall reign
Supreme in intellect*—and it will take Centuries if not ages to dis-
posses him of the fancy that he is born to do so. . . .

But I have wearied you already, I fear, and surely have ex-
hausted my moment of time—I must add that many women
came to me & thanked me for the word I uttered in opposition to
Davis said they, had you not spoken we should have gone home
burdened in soul—

— *Letter, 1857*

You blunder on this question of woman's rights just where
thousands of others do. You believe woman unlike man in her
nature; that conditions of life which any man of spirit would
sooner die than accept are not only endurable to woman but are
needful to her fullest enjoyment. Make her position in church,
State, marriage, your own; everywhere your equality ignored,
everywhere made to feel another empowered by law and time-
honored custom to prescribe the privileges to be enjoyed and the
duties to be discharged by you; and then if you can imagine yourself to be content and happy, judge your mother and sisters and
all women to be.

It was not because the three-penny tax on tea was so exorbitant
that our Revolutionary fathers fought and died, but to establish
the principle that such taxation was unjust. It is the same with
this woman's revolution; though every law were as just to woman
as to man, the principle that one class may usurp the power to legislate for another is unjust, and all who are now in the struggle
from love of principle would still work on until the establishment
of the grand and immutable truth, "All governments derive their
just powers from the consent of the governed."

— *Letter to her brother Daniel, 1859*

We want to show womanhood first; we want to show how
wifehood and motherhood are accidental thereto; we want to

show that not every woman is designed and ordained for house-keeping; we want to show that woman should be directed toward or permitted to choose the life work for which she is designed, and thereby help to save many a man from being sacrificed to sour bread and like ills.
— *Remarks, 1893*

The best of men don't see how abject a thing woman is under her present environments. Figs don't come of thorns.
— *Letter, 1883*

That women are subjects—is too true—but I see no way for them to grow into the virtues of freedom except—in *first* giving them freedom & equality—Women cant swim as a rule—& never will be able to do so—unless thrown into the water to learn the art—
— *Letter, 1883*

What every woman who marries ought to insist on . . . is that she does not enter the marriage contract penniless. That is not easy to arrange, because men love to have dependent wives, and it is the greatest pleasure of their lives . . . to feel that they are the purse-holders and to dole out money more or less sparingly. A woman, for instance, who has the ability to command an income before marriage should insist that her wage-earning ability is a definite contribution to the marriage compact, and should de-mand a money equivalent for it from her partner in the contract. If this were done there would be fewer divorces.
— *Interview, 1899*

In the first place I want women to have all the rights that it is possible to give them, for the sake of men. Every man drops down to the level of the woman at his side; every boy drops down to his mother's level. We want to make women companions of men in the most complete sense of the word. . . .

. . . men do not hesitate to enter woman's sphere and take to themselves any advantages possible. They feel perfectly free to be cooks, but when they do so must have a big salary, not one dollar a week, but ten. Men took it into their heads that they would make women's dresses, but when they did so it became a great en-terprise, and Worth, of Paris, is a millionaire. They do not think that women have any rights they are bound to respect, although we women have had so few occupations that one might think that the "boasted chivalry" of men would have led them to say, "We will not intrude on woman's sphere." But no, that was far from their idea,—they wanted to keep all they had and get what they could, and they have done so. Do not misunderstand me, I am not blaming men. If they had not acted in precisely this way we women should not have come to a place (as we have now) where, instead of seven occupations being open to us, as we had some years ago, there are hardly seven that are not open to us. So man's desire to do well for himself has really led him to do well for us although he did not mean it. Nor do I blame him on the merits of the case; he wanted to succeed and make for himself a wider world. He had a right to do so, but the point I want to make is that we have just as good a right, and intend to exercise it.

— *Speech, 1894*

From time immemorial the rule has been not to punish the male offender, but to get the victim out of his way. If a little girl is bullied and abused by a little boy while out in the yard at play the girl is taken into the house while the boy is left in full possession of the yard. If women are insulted on the street at night the authorities, instead of making the streets safe for them, insist that they remain indoors. Some places have gone so far as to make it a finable offense for women to be out after a certain hour. Even in the matter of woman's dress men have arrogated to themselves authority, and whether it was a Mother Hubbard wrapper or a bloomer costume, have taken legislative action prohibiting it. At Huntington, Long Island, the School Board forbade the women teachers to ride to school on bicycles "as it produced immorality among the pupils," but the men teachers were not interfered with. In many places school boards have forbidden women teachers to ride a bicycle, and a number of ministers . . . have preached against it. These are but the expressions of the old idea that the man has dominion over the woman and that she should be subject to his authority in all things.

— *Article, 1896*

The tap-root of our social upas [poison] lies deep down at the very foundation of society. It is woman's dependence. It is woman's subjection. Hence the first and only efficient work must be to emancipate woman from her enslavement.

The wife must no longer echo the poet Milton's ideal Eve, when she adoringly said to Adam, "God, thy law; thou mine."

She must feel herself accountable to God alone for every act, fearing and obeying no man save where his will is in line with her own highest ideal of divine law.

—*Speech, 1898*

We women have been taught that the object of a woman's life is to help a man. No one seems to have suspected that any man was ever born for any purpose except his own happiness and self-development. Now, after forty years of agitation, the idea is beginning to prevail that women were created for themselves, for their own happiness, and for the welfare of the world.

—*Speech, 1889*

A Menu of One's Own

In 1859 Susan B. Anthony sat down to breakfast in an upstate New York hotel with her friend Rev. Antoinette Brown Blackwell and abolitionist Aaron Powell. The waiter pointedly gave Powell the menu. As Blackwell recalled, "Miss Anthony glanced at it and began to give her order, not to Powell in ladylike modesty, but promptly and energetically to the waiter. He turned a grandiloquent, deaf ear; Powell fidgeted and studied his newspaper; she persisted, determined that no man should come between her and her own order for coffee, cornbread and beefsteak. 'What do I understand is the full order, sir, for your party?' demanded the waiter, doggedly and suggestively. Powell tried to repeat her wishes, but stumbled and stammered and grew red in the face . . . while she, coolly unconscious of everything except that there was no occasion for a 'middleman,' since she was entirely competent to look after her own breakfast, repeated her order, and the waiter, looking intensely disgusted, concluded to bring something, right or wrong."

February 15ᵗ 1900.

My dear friend

*Political equality
of rights for women—
civil and political — is
to-day, and has been for
the past half-century the
one demand of*

Yours Sincerely

Susan B. Anthony

Rochester — N.Y.

5. THE CAUSE

*W*hich brings us to the vote. What distinguished Susan B. Anthony from so many others working for women's rights was her uncompromising insistence that no other right was more central, no other need more pressing. Despite her passionate concern for just marriage laws, for equal pay, for coeducation, she lectured time and time again that the key was suffrage; that without the vote, none of the others would last; that with the vote, all others would flow. It was an amazingly prescient understanding of the power of politics.

She also believed in universal suffrage—that is, the right of all citizens to vote for all offices. No educational or property qualifications, no limits like municipal or school suffrage. Only then, she would say, could women be individuals, not echoes.

Anthony liked to point out that she first demanded the vote for women in 1852, while working for temperance. "Women, and mothers in particular," she urged then, should instruct their menfolk to vote against liquor interests; if the men objected, women should

march to the ballot-box and deposit a vote indicative of her highest ideas of practical temperance.... This was my first declaration for woman suffrage, which I have since repeated in

season and out of season at every possible opportunity for fifty
years.

*In Anthony's view, the vote was the solution to everything. To one
woman seeking encouragement for a new hospital for unwed mothers, she
advised that only the ballot would help women control their own conditions. To WCTU members desperate to do away with demon rum, she said,
get the vote first. She was utterly committed—obsessed, one might fairly
say—and she expected no less of everyone she met. After hearing a sermon
on coeducation at her regular church in Rochester, she wrote in her diary
that the minister had preached on the need for coeducation in "the home,
the school & everywhere save in the Government—I told him of his failure
& he looked so sad I felt sorry for doing it."*

*She also refused to be distracted by other causes—however noble.
"Woman and her disfranchisement is all I know," she often said, which was
a statement about her goal, not her very open mind. To Susan B. Anthony,
getting the vote was so personally meaningful that state petitions for suffrage became her "jewels"; every spare dollar went into the suffrage treasury; and her first trip to Europe paled in comparison to fighting for the
ballot. "I am weary of mere sight-seeing," she wrote from Paris. "Amidst it
all my head and heart turn to our battle for women at home." She summed
up her feelings about suffrage to a reporter in 1895: "It is my life, all that I
live for."*

*On rare occasions the usually optimistic leader despaired over the
"long, hard fight" along such a "dark, discouraging road"—a road littered
with obstacles and absurdities. In 1887 a newspaper reporter actually asked
Anthony, "Would woman suffrage require the establishment of separate
voting places for male and female?" Her response had more to do with alcoholism than feminism: "Not necessarily. It is true that the polls are fre-
quented by men who are often in a drunken condition. We can only hope to
eradicate this evil and purify the political atmosphere by introducing
women before whom men will be ashamed to appear as they otherwise do at
the polls."*

*Like many reformers of her time, Anthony claimed that women
would exert a refining influence on both the election process and the government, and cited as proof glowing accounts from the tiny handful of states
where women were already voting. And in the true spirit of an inventive
politician who would try anything to succeed, she once advocated a most
unlikely tactic. A newspaper reported the suggestion:*

It was that the ladies in each election district should go to the
polling places, the day before the election, and decorate the rooms

with flowers and evergreens that the men may see what attractive surroundings the ballot box will have when women come to vote. Such a decoration of the polls would have a silent but a telling effect upon the votes of the men upon the question of admitting their wives, mothers and sisters to equal political privileges with themselves. Try it, ladies.

Disfranchisement means inability to make, shape or control one's own circumstances. The disfranchised must always do the work, accept the wages, occupy the position the enfranchised assign to them. The disfranchised are in the position of the pauper. . . .

If a business man should advertise for a book-keeper and ten young men, equally well qualified, should present themselves and, after looking them over, he should say, "To you who have red hair, we will pay full wages, while to you with black hair we will pay half the regular price"; that would not be a more flagrant violation of the law of supply and demand than is that now perpetrated upon women because of their sex. . . . It is in order to lift the millions of our wage-earning women into a position of as much power over their own labor as men possess that they should be invested with the franchise.
—*Speech, 1860s–1870s*

Disfranchisement *in a republic* is as great an anomaly, if not cruelty, as slavery itself.
—*Resolutions at convention, 1866*

The Chairman of the committee asked Miss Anthony, the other evening, whether, if suffrage was a natural right, it could be denied to children. Her answer seemed to me perfectly satisfactory. She said simply, "All that we ask is an equal and not an arbitrary regulation. If *you* have the right, *we* have it."
—*George William Curtis during legislative debate, 1867*

Anthony spent a good deal of time refuting arguments against the ballot for women. One of her finer performances came in Portland, Oregon, in

1871, where she spent two and one-half hours answering questions and objections sent to her ahead of time. One local paper said she "answered with much ready ingenuity and plausibility, if not with conclusive reason." The objections themselves reveal the bias of the times.

"WOMEN ALREADY HAVE THE VOTE, SINCE THEIR HUSBANDS VOTE FOR THEM."

[W]hat of the women who have no husbands? The women who are . . . the wives of men incapable of properly representing anybody? There are in the United States 300,000 common drunkards. . . . No individual can represent another, as that other would do for himself or herself.

"WOMEN NOW INFLUENCE MEN'S VOTES."

But that is an influence without responsibility and therefore dangerous. Irresponsible power is always dangerous. So far as women now influence men in public life, courtesans exert more power than the combined numbers of all the virtuous and pure women.

"THE BALLOT WILL DEGRADE WOMEN."

Gentlemen, you don't believe it. Good, pure and noble women meet vile men every day; they hold the most intimate family relations with them, being their wives, sisters, daughters. . . . Will woman's meeting vile men on the place of equal powers to control circumstances, make her more the victim of their lusts and tyrannies than now? The ballot would not degrade, but elevate woman morally, intellectually, and therefore, socially. . . . Women would be as refined and pure with power as without it.

"WHO WILL TAKE CARE OF THE BABIES?"

Who takes care of the babies of fashonable women now? Do they not trust their children to irresponsible hirelings, while they flirt and dissipate at fashionable watering places, at balls, parties and receptions? . . . Good women, educated as they ought to be, will take care of their own babies. . . . Let woman have her proper share of the means to live, of the government offices, places of profit and trust, equal wages with men, and she will be able to provide for the *proper* care of her children.

"WOMEN DO NOT WANT TO VOTE."

I don't believe it. . . . Then why do men put the words "white males" into their Constitutions? . . . Men don't fence a corn field because the pigs don't want the corn, but because they, themselves, do. They fence the field to keep the pigs out.

—*Speech, 1871*

A dear and noble friend, one who aided our work most efficiently in the early days, said to me, "Why do you say the emancipation of women?" I replied, "Because women are political
slaves!" Is it not strange that men cannot comprehend? . . . Why
cannot men put themselves in women's place, and feel and act for
us, as they would have us feel and act for them, if we possessed all
the powers of government, and denied all to them?
— *Speech, 1884*

Yesterday's paper brings the news that the governor of California is threatening the mutinous convicts in the state prison at San
Quentin with "a cruel and unusual punishment"—so cruel, so
unusual, that perhaps some man who can feel for the degradation
of his fellow man may rise to declare that such a punishment is
forbidden by the constitution of the United States. Not to keep
the reader in suspense, let me hasten to state that this threat,
adopted as a last resort to quell men who have held out against
the fear of being shot, is that no convict who does not submit at
once shall ever be restored to his citizen's right of voting. . . .

This one little incident shows more eloquently than many lectures the value men place on the ballot, and what they really
think it is worth to a citizen. Actions speak louder than words.
Women are too good to vote, men say; and then the thief, the
murderer, the ravisher, is frequently pardoned, even if only a day
or two before the end of his sentence, expressly so that he may not
lose his vote and thereby be degraded to the legal level of the best
of women. Women do not need the ballot, we are told; but every
effort must be made to prevent any man whatever from losing it.
Voting is a heavy burden, which it would be cruel to place on
women; and yet to deprive a mutinous convict of his chance of
again having to carry this heavy burden is threatened as a last extreme of punishment.
— *Article, 1897*

What is this little thing that we are asking for? It seems so little; it is yet everything. . . . What does your right to vote in this
country, men and brethren, say to you? What does that right say
to every possible man, native and foreign, black and white, rich
and poor, educated and ignorant, drunk and sober, to every possible man outside the State prison, the idiot and the lunatic asylums? What does it everywhere under the shadow of the
American flag say to every man? It says, "Your judgment is
sound, your opinion is worthy to be counted." That is it. And

now, on the other hand, what does it say to every possible woman, native and foreign, black and white, rich and poor, educated and ignorant, virtuous and vicious, to every possible woman under the shadow of our flag? It says, "Your judgment is not sound, your opinion is not worthy to be counted." Do you not see how this fact that every possible man's opinion the moment he arrives at the age of twenty one is thus respected, and thus counted, educates all men into the knowledge that they possess the political authority of every other man? The poorest ditch-digger's opinion counts for just as much as does the opinion of the proudest millionaire. It is a good thing; I believe in it. I would not take from the most ignorant man under the shadow of the flag the right to vote, but I do want to make you understand the difference in our position. I want to say to you what all of you know, that if there was still left under the shadow of the flag any class of men who are still disfranchised, that class would rise in rebellion against the government before it would submit to the outrage. We women cannot rise in open rebellion. Men are our fathers and brothers and husbands and sons. But we shall stand and plead and demand the right to be heard, and not only to be heard, but to have our votes counted and coined into law, until the very crack of doom, if need be. [*Applause.*]
—*Speech, 1888*

Politically her opinion is worth no more than an idiot's.
—*Remarks, 1900, during applause for Clara Barton*

The vote was so indispensable, Anthony said, it superseded questions of personal growth, political reform, and everything else, including war. The brutal Spanish-American War was no exception.

It does seem very strange to me that you should be "more interested in peace and arbitration between nations" than in the enfranchisement of the women of this so-called republic. It is so evident that if the women of our nation had been counted among the constituencies of every State Legislature and of the Congress of the United States, the butchery of the Spanish-American War would never have been perpetrated. There is no possible hope of justice among the nations of the world while there is such gross injustice inside of the highest and best government of them all. Peace and arbitration are the outgrowth of justice, and while one-half of the people of the United States are robbed of their inherent right of personal representation in this freest country on the face of the globe, it is idle for us to expect that the men who thus rob women will not rob each other as individuals, corporations and Government.

—*Letter, 1900*

[U]ntil women are made a balance of power—to be consulted, catered to, and *bargained with,* if you please—My *one article of party creed*—shall be that of *woman suffrage*—All other articles of party creeds shall be with me as a drop in the bucket—as compared with this *vital one*—hence I make it *my whole party creed!!*

I am as deeply and keenly interested in the many reforms in city, state & National government as any one can possibly be—but knowing that no right solution of any great question can be reached until the whole people have a voice in it—I give all of myself to the getting the whole people inside the body politic, so as to be able to begin making even the first equation of any of the problems.

—*Letter, 1894*

Women, we might as well be great Newfoundland dogs out baying to the moon as to be petitioning for the passage of bills without the power to vote. [*Great applause.*] So long as women are a disfranchised class the women can do nothing. Now, women, if you haven't any self-respect for yourselves, you should at least take pity on the men associated with you in your good works. [*Applause.*] So long as the constitutors of New York and Ohio say that all may vote when twenty-one years of age, save idiots, lunatics, and convicts, women are brought down to the level of those disfranchised. This discrimination is a relic of the dark ages. The most ignorant and degraded man who walks to the polls feels himself superior to the most intelligent woman.

—*Speech, 1894*

Woman's progress has been differently managed from that of any other class desiring enfranchisement. With the negroes and the poor of England, the work was taken up by political parties and, after they became entitled to vote, they were also furnished the means of education. Not so with women. We are educating ourselves first, and studying up good government in our clubs and will move on the question in a determined and intelligent manner. We will get what we are after, too.

—*Interview, 1895*

If there is one thing more than another that I am heartily sick and tired of it is listening to women berate the action of a Common Council or the Mayor. It is illogical and unphilosophical to complain of the conduct of men who are acting the will of the people who have elected them to the office they hold. All questions of reform of any kind are settled at the ballot box.

Women, I implore you, stop hunting for an occasional black bottle or a man who has stubbed his toe morally and work the tool with which we can reach the root of all evil and cease imagining that you can do any lasting good without it.
—*Speech, 1897*

The chief danger, socially and politically, that confronts the coming century lies in man's ignoring woman in the making and executing of the laws that govern the world—in man's egotism, which causes him to think he can run the government machine alone. Not until he calls to his aid the woman at his side, counting her opinion at the ballot-box in the election of every officer so that from President to policeman all must reckon with her, will the world be redeemed from the social and political corruption which are now sapping and undermining the very foundations of our Republic. Yours, not for the millennium but the beginning of its possibility.

 Susan B. Anthony
—*Response to December 30, 1900,* New York World *question*
"What is the chief danger, social or political, that confronts the new century?"

You may pet us and worship us, and all that; but if you don't recognize our womanhood, you have done nothing.
—*Speech, 1905*

On a visit to London in 1899, Anthony—received as a heroine and accorded the respect of a world leader—was asked by a reporter for the Sunday Times *to comment on a proposed housing plan for local women.*

I care very little for these palliatives. It seems to me a very poor plan simply to make women comfortable in their poverty. The real aim should be to pay them better, give them the value of their work. It is to the advantage of men, too, that this should be done, for as long as women will take less pay than men for the same work, men will be driven out of their places. You see it all comes back to enfranchisement. Negroes never got the value of their work until they were enfranchised. When the Irish emigrated to the United States they were paid less than native-born men until they were naturalized, and then their pay become equal. They declared that the ballot was worth fifty cents a day to them.

AND DO YOU THINK IT WOULD BE WORTH THAT TO WOM-ANKIND?

I don't pretend to assess the value precisely, but I do say that when women get the ballot they will be on fighting ground. At present they have not arrived. When men know that women can vote their heads off, then officials and office-seekers will attend to women's wants.

— *Interview, 1899*

Now, I appeal to you gentlemen of the committee that you will present your report in favor of this amendment to the Senate at the earliest possible opportunity; that you will do it because you feel and see with us that there is no hope of solving this problem except by the enfranchisement of the women of this country, and I pray you, sir, that you will give this matter your serious consideration. I pray you to think of it as you would if one-half of the people who are disfranchised were men; if we women had absolute power to control every condition in this country and you were obliged to obey the laws and submit to whatever arrangements we made. I want you to speak and act and report on this question exactly as if your half of the people were the ones who were deprived of this right to a vote and voice in governmental affairs. You would not be long in knowing how you would bring in your report if you were the ones who were disfranchised and denied voice in this Government. I say to you if instead of these being the women, the mothers, sisters, wives, and daughters of the men who compose the Government of this nation; if it had not been women, but any class of men; if it had been the farmers of this country, the manufacturing class, or any class of men who had been robbed of their inalienable rights, then, sir, we would have seen that class of men rising in rebellion and the Government, perhaps, shaken to its very foundation; but being women, being the mothers, daughters, wives, and sisters of the men who make the aristocracy we have to accept.

— *Speech to Senate Committee, 1900*

We are utterly sick and tired of being pushed back and insulted. Sick and tired of it.... I am tired of having every little stripling of 21, half drunk, half nothing, look me in the face and feel that he is my superior and feel that he knows more than the best woman that ever lived.

—*Speech, 1893*

Casualties of The Cause

The only bodies strewn on the suffrage battle-fields of America tended to be those of men. During an 1867 hearing on adding woman suffrage to the New York State Constitution, newspaper publisher Horace Greeley, chairman of the committee, smugly asked Susan B. Anthony and Elizabeth Cady Stanton, "Ladies, you will please remember that the bullet and ballot go together. If you vote, are you ready to fight?" Anthony was quick: "Certainly, Mr. Greeley, just as you fought in the late war—at the point of a goose quill." Greeley's humiliation was not yet complete. As he was about to present the committee's adverse report on woman suffrage, Anthony's coconspirator in the Legislature presented a suffrage petition that included the name of Horace Greeley's wife. It would take a long time for Anthony and Stanton to be treated very kindly in Greeley's New York *Tribune.*

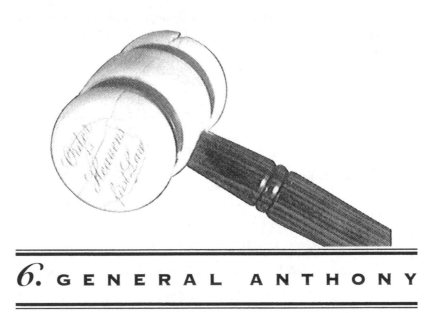

6. GENERAL ANTHONY

*I*t was one thing to want the vote; it was quite another to go out and *get it.* With no experience and absolutely no chance to acquire it, the women's rights agitators of the nineteenth century launched one of the most successful on-the-job training programs in American history. Operating by instinct, imitation, and pure grit, they found their voice in the eloquent pleas of women who refused to obey the rules. They found their leader in Susan B. Anthony.

She did not seek authority for herself. Indeed, she consistently pointed out that others had gotten there first. But her fierce commitment and dynamic appeal were so spellbinding that Anthony inevitably assumed leadership of the newly focused woman suffrage movement, ultimately commanding a giant army that reached across the continent and the ocean.

"I was elected secretary of a woman suffrage society in 1852, and from that day to this have always held an office," she said proudly at her retirement ceremony in 1900, as if that explained everything. Hardly. The challenge was immense: convince women they needed the vote, persuade men to

GAVEL PRESENTED TO ANTHONY
BY ICW REPRESENTATIVES, 1888.
IT WAS ENGRAVED BY STANTON
—"ORDER IS HEAVEN'S FIRST LAW"—
AS A TONGUE-IN-CHEEK MESSAGE TO
HER FREQUENTLY MESSY PARTNER.

grant it, organize the soldiers, and outflank the enemy. The strategy had two distinct phases. First the suffragists approached individual states, seeking to win the right to vote region by region, legislature by legislature. When that seemed to doom suffragists to untold decades of campaigning, the group led by Anthony turned to Plan B: appeal to Congress for a federal ruling—initially with a law, then with an amendment to the Constitution.

Implementing the plan was something else again, something Susan B. Anthony executed with awesome initiative. She was the driving force behind nearly forty years of annual suffrage conventions; she led a constant stream of speakers into the field to stump for The Cause; she petitioned politicians and lobbied legislators; she cajoled, charmed, and convinced members of Congress. She was an exceptional administrator. And in her spare time, she arranged everything from flowers to furniture on the suffrage programs; personally raised huge amounts of money; wrote hundreds, sometimes thousands of letters a year with suggestions, requests, and outright orders to both friends and strangers; in short, almost single-handedly maintained a sprawling army of very diverse women who were united only in their desire for the vote.

Her influence was so profound that one colleague in the suffrage wars took to addressing her in letters, "Dear General." Or even "My dear general."

Ever modest, Anthony once described her lifelong work as "subsoil plowing," insisting that she had merely prepared the field for her more accomplished coworkers. True, she tended to step back and make the introductions at congressional hearings so that younger colleagues might address the members; and she always made sure other women were properly honored for their contributions. But Anthony herself could provide whatever was needed for any aspect of her beloved Cause. There is really only one way to sum up her personal formula for getting the vote: Do Everything.

———

All we can do is to agitate, agitate, agitate.
—*Interview, 1890*

The Anthony approach to agitation was exhausting. The following excerpts illustrate orders from the General for campaigns in two key states, South Dakota and California:

The one work for the winter before our good friends in South Dakota, should be that of visiting every farm house of every school district of every county of the State, talking and reading over the question at every fireside these long winter evenings; enrolling the names of all who believe in woman suffrage; leaving papers and tracts to be read, and circulating, and organizing equal suffrage committees in every district and village. With this done by each of the county committees, the entire State will be in splendid trim for the opening of the regular campaign early in the spring of 1890.

— *Letter, 1889*

I am glad to see so many present. Monday is wash day in the East and meetings on the morning of that day are not well attended. But in California that is not the case. [*Laughter.*] . . .

You must attend every convention that will be held in your State. Appoint committees for the purpose. Let them appear before the Board of Supervisors, Board of Education, political convention, fraternal organizations and industrial societies, and have them pass resolutions favoring the franchise for women. Bring every influence to bear to secure this result. The work in other States is conducted on this plan, and you will soon see the result. If you do this preliminary work so far in advance of the election of 1896, and do your duty faithfully, you will not be required to do any campaign work after that time, for a suffrage plank will be in every platform. [*Applause.*] We cannot expect voters to vote yes on any proposition that is not embraced by the platform of their party. It is to secure a suffrage plank in these platforms that our best efforts must now be directed.

— *Speech, 1895*

First, your local clubs should cover the respective *townships,* and the officers should not only hold meetings of their own to discuss questions pertaining to their work, but should have the men, when they go into their *town meetings* for any and every purpose pertaining to local affairs—especially into the meetings which nominate delegates to county conventions—pledged to present a resolution in favor of the enfranchisement of women. By this means you will secure the discussion of the question by the men who compose the different political parties in each township—an educational work that can not be done through any distinctively woman suffrage meeting, because so few of the rank and file of voters ever attend these.

Then, when the time comes for the county convention to elect delegates to the State nominating convention, let every town meeting see to it that they are instructed to vote for a resolution favoring the submission and indorsement of a proposition to strike the word "male" from your constitution. If the State conventions of the several parties are to put indorsement planks in their platforms, the demand for these must come from the townships composing the counties sending delegates thereto. Women going before a committee and asking a resolution indorsing equal suffrage, are sure to be met with the statement that *they have heard nothing of any such demand among their constituents.* This has been the response on the many different occasions when this request has been made of State conventions. From this repeated and sad experience we have learned that *we must begin with the constituents* in each township and have the demand start there.

— *Letter to South Dakota suffragists, 1895*

The spring campaign is now ended. Its object was to organize the State, to secure political recognition, to awaken public sentiment and to create an active and efficient corps of workers. All this has been accomplished ... The work for the summer now devolves upon those who have been enrolled in this State corps. Every woman, every man, must feel an individual responsibility. They must talk suffrage in season and out of season, wherever two or three are gathered together. They must introduce the subject and secure a discussion at every picnic, farmers' meeting, debating society, social gathering, whenever and wherever they can obtain a hearing. They must occupy all the space that the ever-accommodating newspapers will permit. They must send to headquarters for literature, which may be obtained in quantities, treating upon the question in all its phases, by the most distinguished writers of the present time. These advocates must be willing to sink all other interests, put them aside until after this great issue is settled.

So much for the summer campaign. The fall campaign will be conducted in direct line with that of the political parties. ...

— *Article, 1896*

Occasionally she took some liberties with her instructions, only to find her dry wit unappreciated by a solemn male electorate. When the suffrage amendment lost in Kansas in 1895, Anthony urged the adoption of this resolution announced at a suffrage picnic in Topeka:

Whereas, 117,000 Kansas men declared themselves against female suffrage at the late election and 31,000 showed their opposition by remaining silent; be it

Resolved that it is the duty of every self-respecting woman in the state of Kansas to fold her hands and refuse to help any religious, charitable, moral reform or any political association, until the men shall strike the adjective "male" from the suffrage clause of the constitution and thereby declare that woman's opinion shall be respected and counted at the ballot box.

The reaction to this modern Lysistrata *was predictable: male newspaper editors called it "startling," "unworthy," and "spiteful." Anthony herself was most amused by the commotion:*

I must just say how I laughed over the men's howling over the idea that the women might possibly take our advice and sit down with folded hands refusing to do another thing to help them until the right of self government was accorded. Their agony over the bare suggestion of such a dilemma only proves it to be the true thing to do. Remember that Napoleon said: "Watch your enemy. Learn what he wants you not to do and do it."

Wouldn't it be fun if the women of every household, of which the men voted against their rights would just say, "Run your house alone then;" and the church women say to Dr. Buckley and Bishop Vincent, "Then run your church alone."

But alas, women have too much of the spaniel nature I fear to do other than lick the hand that smites them.

I did not expect to be connected with the resolution but it proves just the word to stir up the lions.

What did the Republican party do to carry the amendment? Absolutely nothing. But by their silence in their platform virtually said to every man, "better not." Well, after this wind blows over you must all begin to work again. It is no use letting the amendment go to the voters until at least two of the larger parties have endorsed it and endorsed it so that they can't go back on their word when the crucial convention comes just before the election.

Lovingly yours,
Susan B. Anthony
—*Letter, 1895*

Her advice was always shrewd. Before an upcoming Atlanta conven-
tion—the first national convention to take place in the South—Anthony
cautioned her colleague Clara Colby, whose newspaper print shop was pro-
viding materials for the meeting, that the audience was far more conserva-
tive than the usual delegates.

But be careful & send only what might be called *"milk for*
babes"—but don't say it out loud—only words of cheer & encouragement must be sent to these people—the rank & file have neither thought, read, or heard of our gospel—only the very
few—so don't—especially don't send any *anti-Church* things.
—*Letter, 1895*

On another occasion, during a Washington convention, Anthony's
message to Colby demonstrated how a pragmatic leader divided her time.

My Dear Friend:—
I hate to promise you the evening of Feb. 3rd, because I am sure
it will turn out just as it did the last time, that I shall be invited
among the gentiles, and I shall feel that it is really my duty to go
among those who are not converted rather than to your house to
meet suffrage saints. While I always love to call on you, and I believe that, notwithstanding there might being [*sic*] an opening on
the outside, I will say to you, that I will spend the hour between 8
and 9 at your house on the evening of Feb. 3rd. Now mark, I say
an *hour,* then if I should have a place to go among the *unconverted,*
I shall be able to make that call after I get through with the one
with you. Now this is not because I *love* you *less* but that I *love con-*
verting the *indifferent* or the *absolutely opposing more.*
—*Letter, 1900*

Susan B. Anthony could be obsessive about her instructions. In this
letter to an obviously efficient worker, she laments Colby's failure to do ex-
actly as she'd been told:

Mrs. Colby writes me she did send out a copy of the Tribune with the Senate Hearing speeches in—to such of the Contributors to the treasury this year—as were not subscribers to her
paper—And that she didn't mark the speeches with red or blue
pencil as I asked her to do—it is queer!—I of course had a special
reason for buying the papers—& having a marked copy sent to
each of our annual contributors to the treasury—so she lost me

my two special points—by doing it her own way—since no one knew the particular point for which the paper came to them!! but so it goes—
—*Letter, 1892*

She even did it to her closest friend. In 1888, planning for the first session of the International Council of Women in Washington—Anthony's brainstorm—she was dismayed to learn that her "co-adjutor," Elizabeth Cady Stanton, was planning to stay in England with her family rather than cross the ocean for the meeting. That was unacceptable to the General. Her diary reveals her talent for leadership.

February 1—Received Postal from Mrs. Stanton saying it was doubtful if she came to Council—Was too incensed to write—so waited—

February 2—Received Mrs. Stanton's letter to Rachel [Foster, who was making the arrangements] bidding her to get *Susan* ready to make the opening speech & get along without her—I was more on fire than ever—

February 3—At 9:30—this eve.—mailed most terific [*sic*] letter to Mrs. Stanton—in response to her Postal to me & letter to Rachel Foster— . . . she might *not* come to Council—

February 14—Wash., D.C. Riggs House.—Got cable-gram from Mrs. Stanton this P.M. saying simply—"Coming"—showing that she had received mine of the 3rd—So my heart was relieved—sent word immediately to Miss Foster & Mrs. Sewall—& ran downstairs to tell news to Mrs. Spofford.

But the drama was not yet over. When Stanton showed up unprepared, Anthony confined her to her hotel room until she had composed a fine speech. Once again the General had organized a winning campaign.

Susan B. Anthony asked nothing of her colleagues that she would not do herself. As her presence guaranteed a good turnout and larger contributions, she rarely declined a speaking invitation—even after she turned seventy, and suffered a bout of ill health.

Better lose me than lose a State.
—*On the way to South Dakota, 1890*

[N]ow comes Colorado with a woman suffrage amendment to be voted upon at the same time with New York and Kansas. Well, we must buckle on our armor for a *triple fight* at the ballot box, and we must shout more loudly than ever to our friends all over the country for money to help these States. Although Kansas is the most certain to carry the question, we must, nevertheless, organize every school district of every county of each of the three States ... in which the battles of the ballot for women's suffrage are to be fought. *Organize! Agitate! Educate!* must be our war-cry from this on to the day of election.
—*Letter, 1893*

No potential assistance was ever overlooked. During President Rutherford B. Hayes' administration, Anthony cleverly (and diplomatically) called upon the First Lady—a friend from the temperance wars—to engage in some political pillow talk:

My Dear Mrs. Hayes
May I not address you, and ask you to help your dear husband the President—to *remember not to forget to sign* the bill to admit Women Lawyers to the Supreme Court? I cannot tell you how my heart leaped for joy yesterday morning as I read the report of the splendid Senate vote of 40 to 20 for that bill! I feel sure the President will not fail to sign it—Can you imagine what faith in truth and right must have sustained the little handful of us who for a whole generation have stood before this American people— the target for the jibes [and] jeers of the unthinking multitude demanding the equal recognition of women in all the fundamental rights of our government? And now that the fruitage of the seed sowing of the thirty years begins to appear, it is not, I am sure, asking too much of the woman whose good fortune places her in the highest position in the nation, that she shall give the influence, nay, the prestige & power of that position, to crown the life efforts of the few for the full completion of the experiment of a genuine republic on this continent.

Your firm & womanly stance on the custom of wines & other intoxicating drinks—at the White House dinner parties, commands the respect & admiration of all true women—And that you may declare yourself on the side of the equal recognition &

counting of *all Womens* opinions at the Ballot-Box—not only on the question of the Liquor Traffic, but upon all questions that pertain to the weal or the woe of this Republic,

Is the hope and the prayer of
　　　　Yours Sincerely
　　　　Susan B. Anthony
—*Letter, 1879*

No detail was too insignificant for her attention. Here is Anthony— never a candidate for assertiveness training—at her authoritative best, writing to the gentleman who would arrange the upcoming convention at Lincoln Hall in Washington, D.C. Newspaper accounts indicate that he followed her instructions to the letter:

Dear Sir

I have ordered the Express to leave *two* packages of books with you—Will you please pay the charge on them—& I will settle with you on my arrival on Wednesday—& will also make a payment on the hall rent.

—Now as to the Hall—Please be sure & have it thoroughly *heated*—to go into a cold hall just *chills* & *kills* a meeting—So don't fail to give us a *well warmed room to begin with*—

Then, *without fail*—please—give us a *carpet on the platform*— with a dozzen [*sic*] *easy* chairs & a sofa—if possible—and three or four small tables along the front—*not* that great long one—put that please, on the floor in front of the platform for the Reporters—

Then, can you not give us a flag or two, over the platform—& make the hall *wear a lady-like* appearance generally—for though we are *strong-minded* we do not wish to have things about us look *mannish*—

Especially—do have the hall *floor cleaned* thoroughly—also the *ante rooms*—They were *simply filthy* last year—we had them just after some sort of *tobacco spitting performance*—So please give us every thing clean as silver, and all in real *Woman housekeeping* order—& we will not only pay our rent promptly—but say a thousand thanks beside—

　　　　Respectfully yours
　　　　Susan B. Anthony
—*Letter, 1875*

The Muddy Pool

Anthony's letters home from Europe in 1883 record yet another skirmish between the General and an unsuspecting male. This one took place in Scotland, at Edinburgh University, with one Professor Blackie. "At my reception he had said he did not want to see refined, delicate women going down into the 'muddy pool of politics,' and I asked him if he had ever thought that, since the only places which were too filthy for women were those where men alone went, perhaps they might be so from lack of women."

Later she wrote, "Men have exercised practically the full and limited franchise for a hundred years, and they have made politics so filthy, according to their statement, not ours, that they are not willing for any decent woman to enter. Is this a confession of success or failure? If women were willing to wait another century, can men give us any assurance that they will have this pool purified?"

7. ONE MORE SCREECH FOR FREEDOM

WHAT ARE YOU GOING TO DO ON WEDNESDAY, MISS ANTHONY?

Just give one more screech for freedom! That's what we have been doing for twenty-five years.

The annual meetings of the suffrage association were not ladies' tea parties. Nor were they rowdy political conventions. Think instead of a more stylish hybrid: a dedicated, polite, yet wildly rebellious organization whose sole purpose was to overturn one of society's most entrenched constraints. Founded in 1869 by Elizabeth Cady Stanton and Susan B. Anthony, the National Woman Suffrage Association (NWSA)—later the National American Woman Suffrage Association (NAWSA), after its merger with its rival American Woman Suffrage Association—was one of the oldest women's groups in the United States, usually meeting twice a year to agitate and educate for the vote. Men were welcome, as long as they agreed. But this was primarily woman's work. Susan B. Anthony, who served as correspond-

SUFFRAGE BADGES

*ing secretary, vice president, chairman of the executive committee, and fi-
nally president from 1892–1900, called it simply The National.*

*She wielded a masterful gavel. More than one reporter watched in
awe:*

> Miss Anthony is the ruling spirit of the convention. She
> dominates. She is constantly on the alert and has a keen appre-
> ciation of every point made by a speaker. She lets no point pass
> without emphasizing it and impressing it upon the conven-
> tion. She talks a great deal, but never without having something
> to say. From the woman suffrage standpoint she is a tower of
> strength.

*She certainly made the events more fun. Days before every conven-
tion—whether the National or the innumerable state organizations—reporters would ask for an agenda. She always gave a good answer—and then
made sure the meetings lived up to it. "[T]he woman suffragists love her for
her good works, the audience for her brightness and wit, and the multitude
of press representatives for her frank, plain, open, business-like way," explained a journalist watching her preside over the 1888 International
Council of Women, a worldwide group that grew out of the NWSA experience. Another newspaper put it this way:*

> If ever there was a gay-hearted, good-natured woman it is cer-
> tainly Miss Anthony. From the beginning of this council it is she
> who has kept the fun barometer way up. The gray-headed
> friends of her youth are all "girls" to her, and she is a girl among
> them. Parliamentary rules have been by no means so severe as to
> keep even the regular proceedings free from her lively interpola-
> tion and comment. When Miss Anthony has felt the public pulse
> or looked at her watch and seen that a speech has gone far
> enough, she says under her breath, "Your time's about up, my
> dear." If the speaker continues, the next thing is, "I guess you'll
> have to stop now; it's more than ten minutes." When this fails, she
> usually begins to hang gently on the orator's skirt, and if pluck-
> ings and pullings fail, she then subsides with a quizzical smile, or
> stands erect and uncompromising by the speaker's side. There is
> none of the rude beating of the gavel, nor any paraphrase of "The
> gentleman's time is up," which marks the stiff proceedings of
> men "in congress assembled." To an unprejudiced eye this free-
> and-easy method of procedure might lack symmetry and dignity,

but there is not the slightest doubt that Miss Anthony has been as
wise as a serpent while being as gentle as a dove.

*For decades, the first meeting of the year was held in Washington,
D.C., generally in January or February to afford easy access to the members
and hearings of Congress. It was planned with all the care and attention to
detail of a presidential inauguration or a daughter's wedding. In the months
ahead, Anthony and her lieutenants would rent the hall, devise the schedule,
book the speakers, argue over topics, set the agenda, print the programs, and
start the publicity. Or at least she pretended to involve the lieutenants. In
truth, the General was so used to controlling this organization — the soul of
her life, whose meetings formed the only fixed point in her annual calendar
of travels — that she found it hard to delegate. Thus Anthony herself charmed
the railroad owners into offering discount tickets to the ladies; it was she who
gleefully wrote delegates of the budget price she'd obtained for their hotel
rooms ($2 a night, two to a room); and of course she fussed over everything
from decorations to the order of speakers. In one letter to Rachel Foster
Avery, the official organizer of the upcoming 1898 convention, Anthony dis-
misses her suggestion of one male lecturer because he "is not a magnetic
speaker, and he will not present a single fact that one of our women has not
access to and cannot work up to better advantage." She rejects another because he has no "national reputation." She wants "the right sort of a
woman" to "make a pen-picture of the steady work of the whole fifty years
in appealing to legislatures." And then she dares to say, "Of course, use your
judgment as to changing the order of the topics, but it does seem to me that
philanthropy and reform should not come first in order."*

*Less than two weeks later she writes again to the impossibly patient
Avery:*

> My dear Rachel;—
> . . . I shall trust you to do all the planning of the programme
> and the getting of the women to carry it out, therefore do not pay
> any attention to what I rattled off in my last letter. . . .
> What do you propose to do with lots of women who will not be
> invited to prepare papers but who really ought to be recognised in
> some way, like Olympia Brown, Mrs. [Isabella Beecher] Hooker
> or any of the state women? Can you get up some kind of spectac-
> ular affair that will make everybody from everywhere feel they
> are included—that *they are in it.* . . .
> Would it not be a pretty thing one evening to have a *grand* &
> great-grand children sing, orate or do something to show that we
> have not only transmitted to the present generation our thoughts

on womans rights but that music and oratory and art and culture
have descended also.

Lovingly yours,

Susan B. Anthony

*The conventions themselves, usually two or three days long, set their
own quaint yet spirited style. The stage of the hall would be furnished like a
mini–living room: rugs scattered on the floor, sofa and plump chairs to the
side, tables for papers and, of course, the lectern. And as in any proper parlor, there might be a portrait or even a plaster bust or two of a favorite suffrage leader. Potted palms would soften the scene, along with a flag or two
hanging as backdrop. But these were not ordinary American flags. In place
of the field of blue stars, the suffrage flag held only the stars of those states
that gave women the vote. Thus, in 1891, there was a lone gilt star, for
Wyoming. Later, Colorado, Idaho, and Utah would be added. Along the
walls, or among the seats, yellow banners designated state delegations or
bore inspirational messages ("Taxation without Representation is tyranny.
Women are Taxed to support criminals and paupers, and to feed and clothe
the law-makers who oppress her" or "Women are Voting on All Questions
in Wyoming and Utah. Their Vote redeemed Wyoming from barbarism to
civilization."). Delegates themselves wore badges and ribbons, also of yellow — the official suffrage color, chosen for the sunflower, symbol of Kansas,
where women got the first right to vote in municipal elections in 1887. As
Anthony explained, "woman suffrage follows civilization as the sunflower
on the Western prairies follows the wheel track and the plough."*

*By 1893 there were seven thousand NAWSA members — not a very
large number, to be sure. But the nucleus of several hundred who made the
annual pilgrimage to Washington made enough noise to command national
attention. Dressed in their silks and bonnets, greeting old friends and making new ones, they came from all over the country to pass resolutions and
rally the troops, to collect energy to take home to inspire a new flock of supporters. Delegates and guests would file in and take their seats, with the reporters — always treated with courtesy — right up front. The president
would gavel them to order, then offer a moment of prayer. After an invoca-
tion by a minister (usually female, once they became available), there might
be a hymn or some musical entertainment — "O! Sing of Wyoming, the
First True Republic" being a heavy favorite. Susan B. Anthony always took
an active part in the next event: memorials to suffrage leaders who had died
over the past year. Then the business would begin.*

A resolution was added and adopted declaring that paying Dr. Susan A. Edson for her services as attendant physician to President Garfield $1000 less than was paid for the same service rendered by Dr. Boynton, a more recent graduate of the same college from which she received her diploma, is an unjust discrimination on account of sex.

During the discussion of the resolutions Mrs. Sewall said that men clerks in the Departments were given extra leave of absence each year to go home to vote. She suggested that women clerks be given (until the time comes for them to vote) extra leave to meditate upon the ballot.

Miss Anthony said she had addressed a letter to each Secretary asking that such women clerks as desired be given permission to attend the meetings of this convention without loss of time to them. She had received but one answer, which was from [Treasury] Secretary [Charles J.] Folger, who wrote: "The condition of the public business prevents me from acceding to your request." —*NWSA, 1883*

The speeches of the evening enthused Miss Anthony, and she came to the front and asked, who was not in favor of woman suffrage? "Those who are in favor will say 'aye,'" she called, and there was a loud chorus.

"Those who are opposed, who do not believe women should be free, and who believe things should go on as they have been, will say 'nay.'"

Miss Anthony turned away as though the question was settled by a unanimous affirmative vote; but she stopped, as a dozen "nays" rang out, and looked surprised. So did every one, and some hissed, while others smiled. —*NWSA, 1886*

At one session, Senator Joseph M. Carey of Wyoming addressed the convention on the glories of woman suffrage in his territory, at that moment applying for statehood. Friendly men were always welcome.

Miss Anthony presented Senator Carey with an immense and exquisite basket of roses, the handle garlanded with lilies of the valley, tied with the suffrage colors. It was in token Miss Anthony said of recognition of his great work for the women of America. Amid long continued applause Senator Carey took the basket and acknowledged it with the graceful remarks that women always did beautiful things, all women even (the strong-minded, Miss Anthony said) those who go to conventions love flowers as they do all things that are pure and lovely.

As the applause subsided, Miss Anthony asked the wives of the Senators from Wyoming, both of whom were on the platform, to rise that the audience might see how Senators' wives looked who were voters. They were warmly greeted.
—*NAWSA, 1891*

If you don't want your President to talk you must not have me for President.
—*NAWSA, 1893, exercising her prerogative and interrupting another speech*

Washington, D.C., had been chosen as the site of the annual suffrage convention for a simple reason: the women could easily go up to Capitol Hill to testify before Congress, and members would be more aware of their activities. Susan B. Anthony would move in, taking up winter residence for a dozen years at a hotel called Riggs House at Fifteenth and G streets, thanks to the generous hospitality of its sympathetic owners, Charles W. and Jane Spofford. Riggs House became convention headquarters, and the capital grew to expect the invasion. But in 1893 a debate arose when some members wanted to hold the meetings in other locations to put more pressure on state legislatures. Anthony was adamant, particularly when she arose to speak after a motion had been adopted limiting speeches to three minutes:

MISS ANTHONY: I cannot say anything in three minutes.

It was moved and seconded that Miss Anthony be allowed more time; which motion was adopted by the Convention.

MISS ANTHONY: I want to ask one question. What is the object of having a national organization? The women in the States have one specific thing to do, and that is to create public sentiment in those States in order to influence their legislators to give suffrage to women. That is clear. The question is, Why do we need a national association since the people in each State must do the work in their own State? There must be an object why we unite in a national body. It is not to educate the people in the school districts of the State. The sole object, it seems to me, of this organization is to bring the united influence of all the States combined upon Congress to secure national legislation. The very moment you change the purpose of this great body from National to State work you have defeated its object.

It is the business of the States to do the school district work; their business to make public sentiment; their business to make a national organization possible, so that all together we can bring the power of all the State organizations here and focus it on Congress. Our younger workers necessarily can not appreciate the vast amount of work done here in Washington by the National Association in the last twenty-five years. When the State delegates come here they do not come as individual women; they come here representing the whole State and every particle of sentiment in that State. They bring here their whole State society. . . . We have had these national conventions here for twenty-five years, and every single Congress has given hearings to our best speakers—the ablest women we could bring from every possible section. In olden times the States were not fully organized—they had not money enough to pay their delegates' expenses. We begged and worked and saved the money and the National Association paid the expenses of delegates from Oregon and California in order that they might come and bring the influence of their States to bear upon Congress. . . .

Look at last winter. We had twenty-three States represented by delegates. Think of those twenty-three women going up before the Senate committee, each making her speech, and convincing those Senators of the interest in all these respective States. We have educated between three and four hundred men and their wives and daughters every two years to go home as missionaries in their respective States. I shall feel it a grave mistake if you vote in favor of a movable convention. It will lessen our power, our influence, our might. But come what may, I shall abide by the decision of the majority. I detest bolting parties. I shall belong to you, and be with you all the way through to the end, though you vote down this and every other pet idea of mine.

—NAWSA, 1893

In time Anthony was voted down, and some of the conventions moved to different cities: Des Moines, Portland, Atlanta. It has been pointed out that far less work got done in Congress when the women went out of town. Still, the meetings were just as lively, especially when NAWSA took itself to the South for the first time in 1895. At the crowded De Give's Opera House in Atlanta, Anthony rapped the group to order with the gavel that had convened the Wyoming Legislature in 1869—the one that had first voted for woman suffrage. Newspaper reporters described the décor:

The badges worn by the representatives represent the coat of arms of Georgia in a frightfully mutilated condition. Instead of portraying the constitution as resting upon the three pillars of wisdom, justice and moderation, symbolizing the different branches of the government, only two pillars are visible, the one belonging to wisdom having completely disappeared as it is claimed there can be no wisdom in a government where women are not allowed to vote. The others are represented as being cracked or decayed. The military guard is also removed, showing that woman has no protection under the laws of the state, being wholly unrecognized by the constitution.
— *Newspaper accounts, 1895*

I hope the good men of Atlanta will understand that we do not claim to be the best half of creation, but we do claim to be half. [*Laughter.*] . . . Let us now proceed to business and show the people of Atlanta that women know how to run a convention. [*Laughter and applause.*]
— *NAWSA, 1895*

She held them spellbound for several days, boosting the cause and stirring up the delegates with her usual mix of parliamentary procedure, serious business, and acerbic asides.

MISS ANTHONY: Now I want Mrs. Taylor of Colorado to come to the platform and show us how a woman looks from a State whose men are great and noble enough to admit women to the ballot-box. . . . I want the convention to see how a woman voter looks and to see that exercising the right of suffrage does not deprive a woman of any of her graces. [*Applause and laughter.*]

MRS. TAYLOR [*rising in her place*]: Am I not sufficiently prominent here?

MISS ANTHONY: No, come to the platform. This is an Alabama girl, transplanted to the Rockies—a daughter of Gov. Chapman of Alabama. [*Loud applause.*] . . . Instead of degrading a woman, it makes her feel nobler not to be counted with idiots, lunatics and criminals. It even changes the expression of her face.

VOICE *in the audience:* How many women are there in the Colorado Legislature?

MRS. TAYLOR: Three—Mrs. Holley of Denver, Mrs. Cressingham of Arapahoe Co., and Mrs. Bryan of Pueblo. . . . And they can hold their own with any man in the assembly.

VOICE *in the audience:* Do they work for half price? [*Considerable amusement as the delegates laughed immoderately.*]

MRS. TAYLOR: No, they do not. They receive their per diem just like the men. I believe it would be a good thing if all the legislators were women. It would not only insure good laws, but the women could afford to give more of their time to legislation than the men, who pretend to be always crowded with the cares of business.

MISS ANTHONY: You see now that Colorado has three women in her state legislature. I know there are men who will say it is a shame. But mind you, it is no disgrace for the women to keep the legislative hall in order, to clean the spittoons and to keep the dust from settling on the floor, but for them to sit in the legislature and to vote with the men is simply degradation itself. [*Laughter and applause, mingled with cries of "good!"*] . . .

MRS. TAYLOR: A bookseller in Denver told me that since women were given suffrage, he had sold more books on political economy than he had sold before in eighteen years.

MISS ANTHONY: The bill raising the age of protection for girls shows that suffrage does not make a woman forget her children, and the bookseller's remark shows that she will study the science of government. . . . There is no danger that women will forget their husbands and children after they have suffrage. You might as well expect a fish to swim on dry land, or a bird to fly through the water. Instinct is too strong. . . .

MRS. LOUISA SOUTHWORTH, *Ohio:* This year, with the new income tax, I shall pay in taxes, national, State and municipal, $5,300.

MISS ANTHONY: Yet how could she know enough to vote? Inconsistency is the jewel of the American people.

MRS. LIDE MERIWETHER, *Tennessee:* Tennessee caps the climax in taxation without representation. In Shelby County there are two young women, sisters, who own farms. Both are married, and both were sensible enough to have their farms secured to themselves and their children. In one case at least, it proved a wise precaution. One of these young women asked the other, when she went to town, to pay a few bills for her, and settle for her taxes. Accordingly she went to the tax office; and as she handed in the papers, she noticed written at the foot of her sister's tax bill, "Poll tax, $1.00." She exclaimed, "Oh, when did Mrs. A. become a voter? I am so glad Tennessee has granted suffrage to women!" "Oh, she hasn't, it doesn't," said the young man, with a smile. "That is her husband's poll tax." "And why is she required to pay her husband's poll tax?" "It is the custom," he said. She replied, "Then Tennessee will change its custom this time. I will see the tax-collector dead and very cold before I will pay Mr. A's poll tax out of my sister's property in order that he may vote, while she is not allowed to do so."

MISS ANTHONY: It seems to me that these Southern women are in a state of chronic rebellion.

MRS. MERIWETHER: We are.

—*NAWSA, 1895*

Each convention takes us farther on our road. By this means we educate the public to an extent that they could not be educated otherwise; we reach more people than could in any other way be reached. . . . We have had resolutions before Congress; we have had congressional committees and hearings before them; the papers have published long reports of these hearings and of the speeches made. It has gone everywhere. We could never have got before the people so well in any other way.

—*Interview, 1887*

I think the most beautiful part of our coming together here in the city of Washington for the last 25 years, has been the seeing of each other, and more friendships, more knowledge of each other has come to the friends of the suffrage movement through the hand shakes here, than through almost any other instrumentality, and I shall never cease to be grateful for all the splendid women who have come up to this great center in these 26 conventions, and who have learned that the North was not such an awful cold place as they believed it was, and I have been equally glad when we came down here, all of us, from Maine, from Michigan, from the great West and met the women from the sunny South, that the women from the sunny South were just like ourselves, if not a little better. Nevertheless, we are all one and seeking the same thing . . . we shall know no North, no South, no East, no West, no Kansas, no New York, as above each and every other state in the Union. This has been the pride of this association for 26 years. We have no political party. We have not been Democrats, we have not been Republicans, we have not been any sort of old fashioned party or new fashioned party anywhere; we have not cared what party anybody belonged to, so everybody was in favor of woman's enfranchisement and would work with might and main for it. We have never known any creed. We have never asked a ques-

tion on this platform what anybody's religion was, whether they were Greek or Jew, Gentile or Mohammedan, Ingersoll, or anything else. All we have ever asked of anybody is simply, "Do you believe in perfect equality for women?"
—*NAWSA, 1894*

You Happened

The suffrage conventions became so much a part of her life that Susan B. Anthony was often unable to distinguish between routine and adulation. In 1903, when the meeting was held in New Orleans, she arrived a bit late and entered the hall to a thunderous ovation. The great leader—at eighty-three, now honorary president of this organization she had co-founded—was baffled by the applause. "What has happened, Anna?" she asked Anna Howard Shaw, her able lieutenant. Shaw's reply: "You happened, Aunt Susan."

8. THE YEARS OF
THE WOMEN

*I*n 1837, when Susan B. Anthony was just a teenager, her father
*traveled to Washington, D.C., in the midst of a financial panic to seek
some redress from Congress. His letter home provides an interesting insight
into her understanding of national politics. Physically, the nation's capital
would hardly be recognizable today. Daniel Anthony wrote that the train
trip from Baltimore—just thirty-nine miles away—took two hours,
through "a barren and almost uncultivated country. The public buildings
and one street called Pennsylvania Avenue are all that are worth mention in
this place." But one glance at the "big finery in the town" convinced Susan's
father—her earliest mentor—of a job-related trait that might sound very
familiar today: "Our Congressmen are some like other folks, they look out
first for themselves."*

*With that wisdom implanted early, the seventeen-year-old Susan de-
veloped into an astute politician herself. She understood without instruction
how to deal with elected officials: how to influence, impress, and correspond
with them; how to appeal to their egos and satisfy their partisan needs. For
months at a time each winter, as she took up residence in the capital, she
lobbied, harangued, and charmed members of Congress on behalf of woman
suffrage. She got so proficient, that when one committee reported unfavor-*

ably on The Cause, she polled the absent members to find out how they would have voted, tallied up the score, then reported the results to the press triumphantly to prove they could almost have won. She was such a fixture on the Washington scene, that one sympathetic Senator—Henry W. Blair of New Hampshire—teased her in a letter just before yet another round on suffrage:

I thought just as likely as not you would come fussing round before I got your amendment reported to the Senate. I wish you would go home. [Antisuffrage Senator Francis Marion] Cockrell has agreed to let me know soon whether he won't allow the report to be made right off without any bother, and I have been to him several times before. I don't see what you want to meddle for, anyway. Go off and get married!

One of Anthony's biographers called her "a lobbyist without money" because she took such clever advantage of congressional franking privileges to send official reprints of favorable testimony through the mail. Ever resourceful, she also enlisted friendly senators to publicize her goal. When Wyoming was admitted into the union as a suffrage state after lengthy debate, a letter of applause from English suffrage leaders became part of the official record, thanks to Senator Blair, who wrote Anthony: "The memorial of congratulation which you sent me is not one which I could press for presentation as a matter of right, but fortunately by a pious fraud I succeeded in reading it without interruption, so that it will appear, word for word, in the [Congressional] Record."

Susan B. Anthony's indelible presence on the national political scene began with a single word: "male." In 1865, when a fourteenth amendment to the Constitution was proposed to permit former slaves to vote, Anthony and Elizabeth Cady Stanton—who had worked hard to end slavery—were horrified to read in the newspapers that the right would be granted only to black men. Never before had the word "male" been written into the nation's charter. Dismayed, they transformed their movement from a state-by-state drive to a federal operation, presenting petitions, appeals, and witnesses to the House and Senate over the next four decades. They bolstered their demand every January, when a host of suffrage leaders descended upon Congress to testify before committees on the merits of granting women the vote. Anthony herself addressed every Congress from 1869 on. Although they lost the fight against the Fourteenth Amendment—and the Fifteenth— Anthony knew exactly which buttons to push. A seating chart of all members of Congress is carefully folded into one of her carefully preserved scrapbooks.

The first suffrage amendment was formally introduced into Congress in 1878. In 1882 the movement had its own committee in the Senate; in 1890, its own committee room, complete with new carpet and desks and, as Anthony boasted to a newspaper reporter, " 'woman suffrage' in big gilt letters on the outside of the door. Oh, we are getting along, but it takes a long time to educate public opinion in a matter like this." Occasionally, the signals were misleading. Carrie Chapman Catt, who took over leadership of the suffrage organization in 1900, described one congressional hearing a decade earlier.

Miss Anthony, bearing her threescore years and ten, closed the hearing with a review of the forty years of effort to secure justice for women and made so pathetic an appeal for action that the great room full of women, with faces drawn and tears running down many cheeks, involuntarily turned their eyes upon the chairman from Virginia. He was clearly perturbed and under the control of emotion. What would he say? What would he do? How could he refuse so unanswerable, so appealing a request? Presently they discovered the source of his emotion—he was in need of the spittoon! And no indication of more sympathetic interest did any of these Southern Democratic chairmen ever show.

Just before she turned seventy-six, Anthony expressed her frustration with the nation's lawmakers to a reporter.

She found the greatest trouble was that each time she came to Congress there were a new set of men, who were like a set of school boys to her, for they had, practically, to be educated up to the question of suffrage for women.

A year later, she told the Senate Judiciary Committee of the New York State Legislature (where she also was a fixture) that she would no longer solicit their support; that she had appealed to their fathers and grandfathers, "and she was tired of begging for her liberty from men not half her own age and with not a hundredth part of her knowledge of State and national affairs."

Of course, she never did stop—not as long as there was someone to convince.

Sec. 1.—The right of citizens of the United States to vote shall not be denied or abridged by the United States or by any State on account of sex.

Sec. 2.—Congress shall have power to enforce this article by appropriate legislation.

—*Woman suffrage amendment first proposed in 1878*

There is no point which ought to be so strongly emphasized, no fact which so needs to be impressed upon those women who are now organizing to work for the different political parties, as that of their utter powerlessness to help or to hinder. Senator James H. Lane of Kansas always used to say to those who came begging him to assist their pet measures, "Well, what do you propose to do for me in return?" This was a brutally blunt way of putting into words what every politician says in effect when he ignores the prayers and petitions of women. . . .

This may be placing government on a low plane. It is altruism with a limit; a desire to help others in the proportion that others help us. It is the Golden Rule read backwards—have others do unto you in the precise ratio that you do unto them. Such is the present status—not the fault of the individual, but the result of the system. The electorate governs. It gives and it takes away. All outside of this body are without power to do either.

—*Article, 1900*

Governments never do any great good things from mere principle, from mere love of justice. . . . You expect too much of human nature when you expect that.

—*Speech, 1891*

At the end of hearings before the Senate Committee on Woman Suffrage in 1884, Anthony was asked to explain why the National Woman Suffrage Association didn't appeal to the states, rather than Congress, for the right to vote.

My answer is that I do not wish to see the women of the thirty-eight States of this Union compelled to leave their homes and canvass each State, school district by school district. It is asking too much of a moneyless class of people, disfranchised by the constitution of every State in the Union. . . .

If it was known that we could be driven to the ballot-box like a flock of sheep, and all vote for one party, there would be a bid made for us; but that is not done, because we cannot promise you any such thing; because we stand before you and honestly tell you that the women of this nation are educated equally with the men, and that they, too, have political opinions. There is not a woman on our platform, there is scarcely a woman in this city of Washington, whether the wife of a Senator or a Congressman—I do not believe you can find a score of women in the whole nation—who have not opinions on the pending Presidential election. We all have opinions; we all have parties. Some of us like one party and one candidate and some another.

Therefore we cannot promise you that women will vote as a unit when they are enfranchised. . . . Our women won't toe a mark anywhere; they will think and act for themselves, and when they are enfranchised they will divide upon all political questions, as do intelligent, educated men. . . .

You ask me if we want you to press this question to a vote, provided there is not a majority to carry it. I say yes, because we want the reflex influence of the discussion and of the opinions of Senators to go back into the States to help us to educate the people of the States. . . .

We ask this little attention from Congressmen whose salaries are paid from the taxes, women do their share for the support of this great Government. We think we are entitled to two or three days of each session of Congress in both the Senate and House. . . . There is no reason why the Senate, composed of seventy-six of the most intelligent and liberty-loving men of the nation, shall not pass the resolution by a two-thirds vote. I really believe it will do so if the friends on this committee and on the floor of the Senate will champion the measure as earnestly as if it were to benefit themselves instead of their mothers and sisters.
—*Speech to Senate Committee, 1884*

One reason why so little has been done by Congress is because none of us has remained here to watch our employe[e]s up at the Capitol. Nobody ever gets anything done by Congress or by a State Legislature except by having some one on hand to look out for it. We need a Watching Committee. The women can not expect to get as much done as the railroads, the trusts, the corporations and all the great moneyed concerns. They keep hundreds of agents at the national Capital to further their interests. We have no one here, and yet we expect to get something done, although

we labor under the additional disadvantage of having no ballots
to use as a reward or punishment.
—*Speech to NAWSA, 1900*

*As a one-woman Watching Committee, Anthony applied her not-so-
gentle pressure on everyone who counted, or who lived with someone who
counted. Here are some examples of her lobbying techniques, starting with
a textbook example of how to reword a request to suit two different parties.
The first letter is to a Democrat in Congress, the second to his Republican
counterpart.*

Dear Sir:
I send you the enclosed copy of petition and signatures sent to
Thaddeus Stevens last week. . . .
The Democrats are now in minority. May they drive the Re-
publicans to do good works—not merely to hold the rebel States
in check until negro men shall be guaranteed their right to a voice
in their governments, but to hold the party to a logical consistency
that shall give every responsible citizen in every State equal right
to the ballot. . . .
Respectfully yours,
Susan B. Anthony
—*Letter, January 20, 1866, to a Democrat*

My dear Friend
I send you enclosed petition with but few signatures but
enough to remind Congress that true Republicanism cannot disfranchise any class of intelligent citizens. If you do [not] feel like
presenting it please hand it to some member who will— . . . it
will be weak & cowardly, if not wicked and craven for the *"White
Male Citizens"* to again vote themselves the government of this republic.
The good spirits spare them from so sad a record of themselves— . . . .
Truly your Friend
Susan B. Anthony
—*Letter, January 21, 1866, to a Republican*

*This one is to Republican William D. Kelley of Pennsylvania, a pro-
suffrage congressman who, in Anthony's opinion, didn't push hard enough.
Her best argument: he was the father of a twenty-five-year-old daughter.*

No one shrinks more from making herself obnoxious than I do, and but for the sake of all women, your darling Florence included, I should never again say a word to you on the subject of using your influence to secure the passage of a Sixteenth Amendment proposition. Last winter you put off my appeal for help with, "This is the short session and the tariff question is of momentous importance." Now, since this is the "long session," will you not take hold of this work, and with the same earnestness that you do other questions?

It is cruel for you to leave your daughter, so full of hope and resolve, to suffer the humiliations of disfranchisement she already feels so keenly, and which she will find more and more galling as she grows into the stronger and grander woman she is sure to be. If it were your son who for any cause was denied his right to have his opinion counted, you would compass sea and land to lift the ban from him. And yet the crime of denial in his case would be no greater than in that of your daughter. It is only because men are so accustomed to the ignoring of women's opinions, that they do not believe women suffer from the injustice as would men; precisely as people used to scout the idea that negroes, whose parents before them always had been enslaved, suffered from that cruel bondage as white men would.

Now, will you not set about in good earnest to secure the enfranchisement of woman? Why do not the Republicans push this question?
—*Letter, 1884*

Representative Kelley must have done something right. His daughter Florence would become a respected social reformer and secretary of the National Consumers' League. And in her own memoirs, Florence Kelley made it clear that Susan B. Anthony's nagging was always on target. She recalled a year when her father had to cancel a speech at a suffrage convention to preside over a subcommittee meeting of the Ways and Means Committee, which he chaired. The subject was vinegar taxes. At the suffrage meeting, Anthony singled out Representative Kelley's failure to appear with the acerbic comment, "This is a new and painful illustration of the lack of respect for the vote even among men who are convinced advocates of suffrage. Even Judge Kelley considers the tariff on vinegar of greater importance than votes." Florence wrote about her reaction: "I went home with my heart in my shoes. I foresaw Father's indignation that, after a quarter century's ac-

tive allegiance to a cause still sufficiently unpopular, he was ridiculed by the great leader whom he counted a friend. At breakfast next morning I watched anxiously as he opened the paper. I had not courage to open it my-self. Great was my bewilderment and relief to hear him laugh and say: 'The good old Major! I'm afraid I deserved that.' "

Dear Sir:—

Will you please answer the enclosed questions for the use of the Congressional Committee of the National American Woman Suffrage Association. I enclose a stamped envelope.

1st. Are you willing that women should vote on exactly the same terms as men vote?

2nd. Are you willing to vote for an amendment to the constitution giving the right to vote in 1896 to all citizens, male or female, who can read and write the English language?

3rd. Are you willing that women should vote provided there is for them an educational qualification?

4th. Are you willing that women should vote at municipal elections?

5th. Are you willing that women should vote on all school matters?

6th. Are you unwilling that women should vote under any conditions?

Yours truly,

Susan B. Anthony

— Letter sent to members of Congress, 1892

I want to ask you to inquire of your good husband if he does not think the time has come when the Senate of the United States should take a vote to show themselves and the world where they stand on the question of woman suffrage. . . . Remind your Senator, will you not, that because of the refusal of Congress to lift the arbitrament of this question from populace to representatives, women who love their homes as dearly as any women in the world have been compelled to leave them to canvass their States with petitions, hold meetings, circulate literature and raise money during the whole last half of this nineteenth century. . . .

I know, my dear Mrs. Chandler, you feel with me that it is a great outrage to compel women thus to work and beg for the privilege of getting their rightful inheritance, while those in power thrust the ballot into the hands of foreign men almost the moment they step foot on our shores . . . I beg you to tell me what

we can do to make our representatives in Congress see that woman's right to self government is just as sacred as is man's.
— *Letter to senator's wife, 1900*

I never come here, and this is the seventeenth Congress that I have attended, but with a feeling of injustice which ought not to be borne, because the women, one-half the people, are not able to get a hearing before the Representatives and Senators of the United States. There are five men on this committee, and to-day we have but three of the five to listen to these arguments. How do you expect that we are ever going to be able to reach the members, who have the right and the power to say yea or nay to us, unless we get a hearing before them?
— *Speech to Senate Committee, 1904*

It wasn't just elected officials who received the Anthony treatment. She also went after the candidates for Congress and the White House at every national party convention—which she once called the "great quadrennial bluster." By roots a Republican, she generally favored that party's stronger stand against slavery and briefly found them more sympathetic towards woman suffrage. But Anthony grasped the inherent truth about politics when she insisted that the movement would support whichever party supported it. Here is her answer to a newspaper reporter who asked, "In what direction do you look for assistance?"

You mean to which party. To neither in particular, but to both. We shall identify ourselves with neither as they are now, but whichever party inserts a woman's suffrage plank in their platform we shall work for that. We are not identified with Prohibitionists nor the anti-prohibitionists. We are neither Free Traders nor Protectionists, nor for soft nor hard money. We are for suffrage wherever we find it, and we shall help those who help us. After we get our right to vote we shall use it as we choose individually. There is not much likelihood of all the women voting one way on anything but suffrage questions.
— *Interview, 1884*

For a long time, no party wanted to help. In 1868 the women's request to address the Republican convention in Chicago was ignored. The Democrats, meeting in their new Tammany Hall headquarters in Manhattan, invited them in but treated them atrociously. With Anthony, Stanton, and two female colleagues seated on the platform, the rowdies took over.

THE CHAIRMAN—I have a memorial from the Woman's Suffrage Association, with the request that it be handed to the Committee on Resolutions. [*Laughter, cheers, "Hear, hear," and cries of
"Read."*]

THE CHAIRMAN—I may mention that this document is signed
by Susan B. Anthony. [*Renewed cheers and laughter.*] The communication was then read.
—*Newspaper account of July 4, 1868, Democratic Convention*

*Four years later, the women tried again. They started with the Liber-
als—to no avail.*

You see our cause is just as the anti-slavery cause was for a long
time. It had plenty of friends and supporters three years out of
four, but every fourth year, when a President was to be elected, it
was lost sight of; then the nation was to be saved, and the slave
must be sacrificed. So it is with us women. Politicians are willing
to use us at their gatherings, to fill empty seats, to wave our handkerchiefs and clap our hands when they say smart things, but
when we ask to be allowed to help them in any real substantial
way, by assisting them to choose the best men for our law-makers
and rulers, they generally push us aside, and tell us not to bother
them.
—*Interview, 1872*

*The Democrats would also ignore them, but this time the Republicans
tossed them a bone. Some women said instead of a suffrage plank, they'd
gotten a "splinter."*

What the women wanted:

Gentlemen:
In behalf of the women of this nation—*one half of the entire
people*—I ask you to put a plank in your platform that shall assert
the duty of the National Government to protect women citizens
in the exercise of their right to vote; & thereby make it possible for
women possessed of true self-respect to advocate the claims of the
National Republican party to the suffrages of the people.
Respectfully yours,
Susan B. Anthony
—*Letter to the Committee on Platform and Resolutions of the
National Republican Convention, 1872*

What the Republicans gave them:

The Republican party is mindful of its obligations to the loyal women of America for their noble devotion to the cause of freedom; their admission to wider fields of usefulness is received with satisfaction; and the honest demands of any class of citizens for equal rights should be treated with respectful consideration.
—*Suffrage "splinter" provided by GOP, 1872*

The empty gesture infuriated Anthony. Her "blood was at boiling heat." She was "disgusted with the miserable sop the party had thrown her," and called it a "trifling reward" for her work as a reformist. Then she got practical again.

I am sure we can make a splendid *educational discussion* of this first little mention of woman & that is precisely what we most *need,* just now—
—*Letter, 1872*

Women of the United States, the hour for political action has come. For the first time in the history of our country, woman has been recognized in the platform of a large and dominant party. Philadelphia has spoken and woman is no longer ignored. She is now officially recognized as a part of the body politic. . . . We are told that the plank does not say much, that in fact it is only a "splinter", and our Liberal friends warn us not to rely upon it as a promise of the ballot to women. What it is, we know even better than others. We recognize its meagerness; we see in it the timidity of politicians; but beyond and through all, we see a promise of the future. We see in it the thin edge of the entering wedge which shall break woman's slavery in pieces and make us at last a nation truly free . . .
—*Address, 1872*

As it turned out, the Republicans did nothing for them. Anthony hated the idea of being taken for granted.

I think about all that we can do now—is to roll up the largest petition ever sent into Congress—first—then secure a hearing before our Committee—you remember we have the promise of a special Com—making the most out of our Wash. Con.—and then at our *May.* 1880 Con. at Indianapolis—to appoint strongest

& ablest women on Committees to memorialize the several *National President Nominating Conventions*—and also to *get our best speaker heard* in their Con—as well as a W.S. Plank in their platform—& then after we have alike besieged each & all—*go into the canvas* for the party that *gives us the nearest* to full recognition—If the Repub's *could be made* to *believe* that *every one of our W.S.* public speakers *would take the stump for the Nationals, or the Democrats*—if *either* of *them gave us a W.S. plank*—& the Repub's did not—It would *settle the* question with the Repub's in the twinkling of an eye—a plank would go into their platform & Mrs. Stanton & Mrs. Livermore would both be not only invited but urged to address their National Convention—but, you see, the *Repub's know* or *feel sure* that *nearly* every individual woman of us will do all we can to help them—whether they do, or don't help us—or *promise* to help us—thus you see, while our women will thus allow themselves to be used by and for the Party—while it *ignores our just claims*—we have no *fulcrum* on which to plant our lever—So we must go on—like the boy—trying, *in* vain, to lift our movement by the straps of its boots, into political recognition—I see no chance for us—at present—
— *Letter, 1879*

WHERE DO YOU FIND THE STRONGEST ANTIPATHY TO WOMAN SUFFRAGE?

In the fears of various parties that the institution might be disastrous to their interests. The Protestants fear the enfranchisement of women lest there would result from it a majority of Catholic women to increase the power of their Church; the freethinkers are afraid that, as the majority of the church-members are women, they would put God in the Constitution; the freewhisky man is opposed to it because they know women would vote down his interest; the Republicans would put a woman-suffrage plank in their platform if they knew they could secure the vote of the women, and so would the Democrats, but they both fear it might be otherwise. Thus, you see, we cannot appeal to the self interests of any party, and this is a great source of weakness.
— *Interview, 1879*

Our next movement will be to question each nominee for any office in the State, and ascertain whether he is in favor of giving the ballot to women, and if he is not, we all intend to bring our influence to bear to defeat his election, no matter who he is, or for what office he is nominated. The women of the association are all going to their homes with this determination. We will support any man, or any party, that is in favor of giving us the right of suffrage.

—*Interview, 1880*

Finally, in 1894, one party came through. During a hot June afternoon session of the Populist Party convention in Topeka, Susan B. Anthony pumped up the crowd:

"We shall ask of every possible gathering of men for a resolution saying that the women should have the same rights as the men. I understand that 80 per cent of the People's party are in favor of suffrage and will vote for it. [*Applause.*] I belong to but one party under the shadow of the flag and that is the party of idiots and criminals. We haven't been pardoned yet by the government. Now, I don't like my company. [*Applause.*] Do you blame me for asking this. [*Loud cries, No! No!*] Do you want to leave your wives and daughters in the society of idiots and lunatics. [*Voices—We wont*] No party can live that does not favor new and radical reform ideas. [*Applause.*] I ask you to say that every woman by your side should have the same rights as you have."

When Miss Anthony had concluded, ex–County Attorney W. H. Carpenter of Marion created a great sensation by saying: "Before Miss Anthony leaves I want to ask her a question before this convention, and out of all due respect for her: Miss Anthony, in the event of the Populists putting a woman suffrage plank in their platform, would you work for the success of the Populist party?"

Miss Anthony came forward to answer amidst the wildest cheers. She said:

"For forty years I have been laboring for the success of woman's enfranchisement and I always said that for the party which first endorsed it, whether . . . Republican, Democrat or Populist, I would wave my handkerchief. [*Applause.*] I will go before the people . . . I will try to persuade every man in those meetings to vote for woman suffrage."

"Miss Anthony," said Mr. Carpenter, "we want more than the waving of your handkerchief . . . will you go before the people and tell them that because the Peoples' party has espoused the cause of woman suffrage it deserves the votes of every one who is a supporter of that cause?"

Miss Anthony: "I most certainly shall!"

Immediately upon hearing Miss Anthony's answer, the convention went wild—yelled and cheered and applauded to its very utmost. Hundreds rose to their feet. The cheering lasted for five minutes without intermission.

—*Newspaper article, 1894*

But Anthony's exuberance over the Populists' endorsement was not echoed by some of her colleagues, many of whom were still loyal Republicans. She defended her position:

Lots of the boys have been here this afternoon interviewing me on "going over to the Pops." I told them we had been floundering in the Dead Sea of Disfranchisement all these years begging the great political parties to throw us a plank on which we could swim safely into the harbor of the body politic, and that this of the Populist Party of Kansas was the first time that either of the two dominant parties had ever answered to our cry. . . . I shall make as many speeches as I can in their campaign meetings, talking only on my own plank, knowing nothing of the rest of the platform. . . . Oh, that all of our women could be Women first and then a Republican or a Populist or any sort of a partisan they chose.

—*Letter to Editor, 1894*

BUT IT ALWAYS HAS BEEN UNDERSTOOD THAT YOU ARE A STRONG REPUBLICAN.

. . . I am for woman suffrage and will work with any party of power that will help us. Remember I say "with," not "for."

—*Interview, 1894*

At home—Reporter from *evening* paper came to *interview* me on my going over to the *"Populists"* . . . and this afternoon Post Express, & Union Advertiser—each & all had my *report* of *myself*—one would think I had committed the Sin *against* the Holy Ghost—in thanking the Populists for their good promise—

—*Diary, 1894*

I was born and reared a Quaker, and am that still; I was trained by my father, a cotton manufacturer, in the Henry Clay school of protection to the American products; but today all sectarian creeds and all political policies sink into utter insignificance compared with the essence of all religions and the fundamental principles of all governments—equal rights to all. Wherever, religiously, socially, educationally, politically, justice to woman is preached and practiced, I find a bond of sympathy, and I hope and trust that henceforth I shall be brave enough to express my thanks to every individual and every organization—popular or unpopular—that gives aid and comfort to our great work for the emancipation of woman, and through her the redemption of the world.

—*Letter, 1894*

When the Populists lost, the women were once again without a party. Anthony retreated to her original position. During her lifetime the refusal of any major party to endorse woman suffrage made it impossible to win the vote.

Women can belong to *no party*—in the sense that men belong—we stand *outside* of each and all alike—and plead with the leaders of all alike   to put Suffrage amendment resolutions in their platforms— . . .

What we try to do is to keep our women from saying they'll belong to—or work for—any political party—until after they are enfranchised—Now—we are beggars of each and all—to declare they'll help carry the amendment— . . .

If such men could only believe in *Nature's Laws*—that neither *men* nor *women* can change their sex—that to allow women's opinions to be counted at the ballot-box, will no more interfere with their wifehood and motherhood—than voting now interferes with men's husband-hood or father-hood.

—The great fact of woman-hood is over and under all the *incidents* of [her] life—as manhood is over and above all the incidents of his life—

Isn't it sickening that these old flimsy objections are thrust before us today,—just as they were a half century ago when our claim was first made

—*Letter, 1896*

A Representative Idea

In 1895, a newspaper asked several prominent figures, "If women came to Congress, what would be the result?" A New Jersey congressman predicted "the deterioration of Congress." Susan B. Anthony had a sunnier view: "When women come to Congress, both the men and the women will be put on their best behavior—morally, intellectually, socially—because the sexes together always inspire each other to be and to do their best. The huge cuspidors at every seat will be banished, the heating registers will no longer emit the fumes of burned tobacco juice; the two houses and the corridors will cease to be filled with tobacco smoke thick enough to cut with a knife. The desks will not be used as foot benches; decency and good order will be observed in the discussions, and the proprieties of civilized society will obtain. Then justice, not bargain and sale, will decide legislation. May the good time come speedily!"

United States District Court,

NORTHERN DISTRICT OF NEW YORK.

The United States of America

vs.

Susan B. Anthony

to

INDICTMENT· FOR ILLEGAL VOTING.

Jan 24/73. Pleads not guilty

Richard Crowley

U. S. Attorney.

A TRUE BILL.

Bruce Millard Foreman

9. A FINE AGITATION

id I mention that she was also a convicted criminal?

That dramatic episode began in 1872, when Susan B. Anthony, growing more and more impatient with futile state campaigns and an indifferent Congress, decided to take matters into her own hands. There was a third way to get the vote, she reasoned. Just do it.

She wouldn't be the first to try. In 1870 lawyer Marilla Ricker of Dover, New Hampshire, demanded the right to vote when she paid her taxes but was refused. A year later, she succeeded. Also in 1871, Nannette Gardner of Detroit registered and voted without major incident. Both claimed the right to the franchise under the Fourteenth Amendment—the one specifying that only "male citizens" were eligible. But the first part of the amendment said that "All persons born or naturalized in the United States . . . are citizens," and that "No State shall make or enforce any law which shall abridge the privileges or immunities of citizens." Therein, said the women, lay their Constitutional guarantee.

Susan B. Anthony agreed and urged other women to test the law by going to the polls. In November 1872 she got her own chance. The notice in the Rochester newspaper was enticing:

> Now Register! To-day and to-morrow are the only remaining
> opportunities. If you were not permitted to vote you would fight

---

BILL OF INDICTMENT, 1873

for the right, undergo all privations for it, face death for it. You have it now at the cost of five minutes' time to be spent in seeking your place of registration, and having your name entered. . . . Register now!

Collecting her three sisters and a close Quaker friend, Rhoda De-Garmo, Anthony set out from her red-brick house on Madison Street to a nearby barber shop to register for the upcoming presidential election. Eleven other women in the ward joined them. Inside, the three male regis-trars (two Republicans, one Democrat) were, to put it mildly, bewildered. But after a brief discussion, they saw no way out and allowed the women to sign in.

The effect was stunning. The offended editors of one local newspaper pointed out the federal act specifying "Any person . . . who shall vote with-out having a legal right to vote; or do any unlawful act to secure . . . an op-portunity to vote for himself or any other person, shall be deemed guilty of a crime." It was punishable by a fine of five hundred dollars and/or imprison-ment for up to three years. The paper demanded, "if these women in the eighth ward offer to vote they should be challenged, and if they take the oaths and the Inspectors receive and deposit their ballots, they should all be prosecuted to the full extent of the law."

Anthony pressed on. Showing up bright and early at the barber shop on the morning of November 5—a thoughtful gesture, to avoid a public spectacle—she cast the first and only presidential ballot of her life—for Ulysses Grant, the Republican candidate, and two congressmen. The deed was done. The furor was just beginning.

More than three weeks later—it was Thanksgiving Day—a tall, ner-vous U. S. marshal wearing a high hat and gloves showed up at the Anthony home. Summoned into the parlor, he said, blushing, "The commissioner wishes to arrest you." She was, after all, a very famous lady. Then he sug-gested that she call at the commissioner's office when she had a chance. An-thony gave him no quarter. "Is this your usual method of serving a warrant?" she asked. And after making him cool his heels while she changed her dress, she thrust out her hands and demanded he put her in handcuffs. The poor soul refused but did agree meekly to escort her downtown. Once again Anthony played the martyr. When the streetcar conductor asked for her five-cent fare, she replied—loudly, so everyone on board could hear—"I am traveling at the expense of the government. Ask him for my fare."

The preliminary examinations took place in the same room where, Anthony never tired of pointing out, "in the days of slavery, fugitives escap-ing to Canada had been examined and remanded to bondage." She and *her colleagues, calling themselves victims of political slavery, all pleaded not guilty. Bail was set at $1,000 for the ringleader, half as much for the others.*

Now she worked the public relations angle. For three solid weeks she stumped the county, delivering a lecture in every single village on the subject "Is It a Crime for a Citizen of the U.S. to Vote?" When the prosecutor complained that her speeches would make it impossible for him to get a conviction, the trial was moved to another county. Anthony then took her act there. A colleague, Matilda Joslyn Gage, joined her with the topic "The United States on Trial, Not Susan B. Anthony."

On June 17, 1873, Anthony, the only one of the wayward women to be tried, took her seat in the U.S. Circuit Court in Canandaigua, New York. Twelve white men sat in the jury box. The audience was packed with friends and gawkers, including several friendly U.S. senators and one ex-President (Millard Fillmore). Anthony's lawyer, former Court of Appeals judge Henry R. Selden, was at her side. The thoroughly biased editors of History of Woman Suffrage *described the front of the room:*

> On the bench sat Judge Hunt, a small-brained, pale-faced, prim-looking man, enveloped in a faultless suit of black broadcloth, and a snowy white neck-tie. This was the first criminal case he had been called on to try since his appointment, and with remarkable forethought, he had penned his decision before hearing it.

That is exactly how it happened. The jurors did nothing and said nothing. The judge directed that their verdict declare her guilty. Anthony, forbidden to defend herself until after the verdict, was convicted and fined. Although never forced to pay or imprisoned, she was denied the right to appeal. In her diary that night she called it "The greatest outrage History ever witnessed."

But the trial had made national headlines, and at least people were talking about the issue. It swiftly became a popular feature of Anthony's suffrage repertory. She had thousands of copies of the trial proceedings printed up and distributed and was regularly called upon to describe her ordeal in all its very stressful detail.

As for the election inspectors, two were put in jail when they refused to pay the $25 fine, but their brief stay was considerably cheered by five days of suffrage women bearing home-cooked dinners. Anthony's intercession won them a pardon from the first and last President she ever voted for, Ulysses S. Grant.

Rochester Nov. 5th 1872

Dear Mrs. Stanton

Well I have been & gone & done it!!—positively *voted* the Republican ticket—strait—this A.M. at 7 o'clock—& *swore my vote in, at that*—was registered on Friday & 15 other women followed suit in this ward—then in sundry others some 20 or thirty other women *tried* to *register, but* all save two were refused—all my three sisters voted—*Rhoda* DeGarmo—to[o] . . . Hon Henry R. Selden will be our Counsel—he has read up the law & all of our arguments & is satisfied that we are right & ditto the Judge Samuel Selden—his elder brother—So we are in for a fine agitation in Rochester on the question— . . .

Affectionately—Susan B. Anthony
— *Letter, 1872*

My Dear Mrs. Wright
 . . . I never dreamed of the . . . officers prosecuting *me* for voting—thought only that if I was refused I should bring action against inspectors—But "Uncle Sam" waxes wroth with *holy indignation* at such violation of his laws—!!—
— *Letter, 1873*

Friends and fellow-citizens:—

I stand before you tonight under indictment for the alleged crime of having voted illegally at the last Presidential election. I shall endeavor this evening to prove to you that in voting, I not only committed no crime, but simply exercised my "citizen's right," guaranteed to me and all United States citizens by the National Constitution, beyond the power of any State to deny . . .

The preamble of the Federal Constitution says:

> We, the people of the United States, in order to form a more perfect union, establish justice, insure domestic tranquility, provide for the common defense, promote the general welfare, and secure the blessings of liberty to ourselves and our posterity, do ordain and establish this Constitution for the United States of America.

It was we, the people, not we, the white male citizens, nor yet we, the male citizens, but we, the whole people, who formed this Union. And we formed it, not to give the blessings of liberty, but to secure them; not to the half of ourselves and the half of our posterity, but to the whole people—women as well as men. And it is downright mockery to talk to women of their enjoyment of the blessings of liberty while they are denied the use of the only means of securing them provided by this democratic republican government—the ballot. . . .

The only seeming permission in our constitution for the disfranchisement of women is in section 1st of Article 2nd:

> Every male citizen of the age of twenty-one years, etc., shall be entitled to vote.

But I insist that in view of the explicit assertions of the equal right of the whole people, both in the preamble and previous article of the constitution, this omission of the adjective "female" in the second, should not be construed into a denial; but, instead, counted as of no effect. . . .

For any State to make sex a qualification that must ever result in the disfranchisement of one entire half of the people, is to pass a bill of attainder, or an *ex post facto* law, and is therefore a violation of the supreme law of the land. By it, the blessings of liberty are forever withheld from women and their female posterity. To them, this government has no just powers derived from the consent of the governed. To them this government is not a democracy. It is not a republic. It is an odious aristocracy; a hateful oligarchy; the most hateful ever established on the face of the globe. An oligarchy of wealth, where the rich govern the poor; an oligarchy of learning, where the educated govern the ignorant; or even an oligarchy of race, where the Saxon rules the African, might be endured; but surely this oligarchy of sex, which makes the men of every household sovereigns, masters; the women subjects, slaves; carrying dissension, rebellion in to every home of the Nation, can not be endured. . . .

But, it is urged, the use of the masculine pronouns he, his, and him, in all the constitution and laws, is proof that only men were meant to be included in their provisions. If you insist on this version of the letter of the law, we shall insist that you be consistent, and accept the other horn of the dilemma, which would compel you to exempt women from taxation for the support of the government, and from penalties for the violation of laws. . . .

There is no she, or her, or hers, in the tax laws. . . . The same is true of all the criminal laws. . . . In the law of May 31, 1870, the 19th section of which I am charged with having violated; not only are all the pronouns masculine, but everybody knows that particular section was intended expressly to hinder the rebels from voting. It reads:

> If any person shall knowingly vote without his having a lawful right, etc.

Precisely so with all the papers served on me—the U.S. Marshal's warrant, the bail-bond, the petition for habeas corpus, the bill of indictment—not one of them had a feminine pronoun printed in it; but, to make them applicable to me, the Clerk of the Court made a little carat at the left of "he" and placed an "s" over it, thus making she out of he. Then the two letters "is" were scratched out, the little carat placed under and "er" over, to make her out of his, and I insist if government officials may thus manipulate the pronouns to tax, fine, imprison, and hang women, women may take the same liberty with them to secure to themselves their right to a voice in the government. . . .

But, whatever room there was for a doubt, under the old regime, the adoption of the XIV. Amendment settled that question forever, in its first sentence:

> All persons born or naturalized in the United States and subject to the jurisdiction therof, are citizens of the United States and of the State wherein they reside.

And the second settles the equal status of all persons—all citizens:

> No State shall make or enforce any law which shall abridge the privileges or immunities of citizens; nor shall any State deprive any person of life, liberty or property, without due process of law, nor deny to any person within its jurisdiction the equal protection of the laws.

The only question left to be settled now, is: Are women persons? And I hardly believe any of our opponents will have the hardihood to say they are not. Being persons, then, women are citizens, and no State has a right to make any new law, or to enforce any old law, that shall abridge their privileges or immunities. Hence, every discrimination against women in the constitutions and laws of the several States, is to-day null and void, precisely as is every one against negroes. Is the right to vote one of the privileges or immunities of citizens?

—*Speech, 1873*

THE UNITED STATES OF AMERICA VS.
SUSAN B. ANTHONY

The Prosecution

D.A. RICHARD CROWLEY: May it please the Court and Gentlemen of the Jury: . . . The defendant, Miss Susan B. Anthony . . . voted for a representative in the Congress of the United States, to represent the 29th Congressional District of this State, and also for a representative at large for the State of New York to represent the State in the Congress of the United States. At that time she was a woman. I suppose there will be no question about that . . . whatever Miss Anthony's intentions may have been— whether they were good or otherwise—she did not have a right to vote upon that question, and if she did vote without having a lawful right to vote, then there is no question but what she is guilty of violating a law of the United States. . . .

Conceded, that on the 5th day of November, 1872, Miss Susan B. Anthony was a woman.

The Inspectors' Testimony

Q: Did you see her vote?

A [BEVERLY W. JONES]: Yes, sir . . .

Q: She was not challenged on the day she voted?

A: No, sir.

Cross-examination by Defense Attorney, Judge Henry Selden

Q: Prior to the election, was there a registry of voters in that district made?

A: Yes, sir.

Q: Were you one of the officers engaged in making that registry?

A: Yes, sir.

Q: When the registry was being made did Miss Anthony appear before the Board of Registry and claim to be registered as a voter?

A: She did.

Q: Was there any objection made, or any doubt raised as to her right to vote?

A: There was.

Q. On what ground?

A: On the ground that the Constitution of the State of New York did not allow women to vote.

Q: What was the defect in her right to vote as a citizen?

A: She was not a male citizen.

Q: That she was a woman?

A: Yes, sir ...

Q: Did the Board consider the question of her right to registry, and decide that she was entitled to registry as a voter?

A: Yes, sir.

Q. And she was registered accordingly?

A: Yes, sir ...

Q: Won't you state what Miss Anthony said, if she said anything, when she came there and offered her name for registration?

A: She stated that she did not claim any rights under the Constitution of the State of New York; she claimed her right under the Constitution of the United States.

Q: Did she name any particular amendment?

A: Yes, sir; she cited the XIV amendment.

Q: Under that she claimed her right to vote?

A: Yes, sir. ...

The Defense

ATTORNEY, JUDGE HENRY R. SELDEN: The only alleged ground of illegality of the defendant's vote is that she is a woman. If the same act had been done by her brother under the same circumstances, the act would have been not only innocent, but honorable and laudable; but having been done by a woman it is said to be a crime.... I believe this is the first instance in which a woman has been arraigned in a criminal court merely on account of her sex.... Another objection is, that the right to hold office must attend the right to vote, and that women are not qualified to discharge the duties of responsible offices. I beg leave to answer this objection by asking one or more questions. How many of the male bipeds who do our voting are qualified to hold high offices? ... Another objection is that engaging in political controversies is not consistent with the feminine character. Upon that subject, women themselves are the best judges, and if political duties should be found inconsistent with female delicacy, we may rest assured that women will either effect a change in the character of political contests, or decline to engage in them. ...

The Judge

THE COURT: The question, gentlemen of the jury . . . is wholly a question or questions of law, and I have decided as a question of law, in the first place, that under the XIV Amendment, which Miss Anthony claims protects her, she was not protected in a right to vote. And I have decided also that her belief and the advice which she took do not protect her in the act which she committed. If I am right in this, the result must be a verdict on your part of guilty, and I therefore direct that you find a verdict of guilty.

MR. SELDEN: That is a direction no Court has power to make in a criminal case.

THE COURT: Take the verdict, Mr. Clerk.

THE CLERK: Gentlemen of the jury, hearken to your verdict as the Court has recorded it. You say you find the defendant guilty of the offense whereof she stands indicted, and so say you all? . . .

MR. SELDEN: I don't know whether an exception is available, but I certainly must except to the refusal of the Court to submit those propositions, and especially to the direction of the Court that the jury should find a verdict of guilty. I claim that it is a power that is not given to any Court in a criminal case. Will the Clerk poll the jury?

THE COURT: No. Gentlemen of the jury, you are discharged.

The Next Day

THE COURT: The prisoner will stand up. Has the prisoner anything to say why sentence shall not be pronounced?

MISS ANTHONY: Yes, your honor, I have many things to say; for in your ordered verdict of guilty, you have trampled underfoot every vital principle of our government. My natural rights, my civil rights, my political rights, are all alike ignored. Robbed of the fundamental privilege of citizenship, I am degraded from the status of a citizen to that of a subject; and not only myself individually, but all of my sex, are, by your honor's verdict, doomed to political subjection under this so-called Republican government.

JUDGE HUNT: The Court can not listen to a rehearsal of arguments the prisoner's counsel has already consumed three hours in presenting.

MISS ANTHONY: May it please your honor, I am not arguing the question, but simply stating the reasons why sentence can not, in justice, be pronounced against me. Your denial of my citizen's right to vote is the denial of my right of consent as one of the governed, the denial of my right of representation as one of the taxed, the denial of my right to a trial by a jury of my peers as an offender against the law, therefore, the denial of my sacred rights to life, liberty, property, and—

JUDGE HUNT: The Court can not allow the prisoner to go on.

MISS ANTHONY: But your honor will not deny me this one and only poor privilege of protest against this high-handed outrage upon my citizen's rights. May it please the Court to remember that since the day of my arrest last November, this is the first time that either my self or any person of my disfranchised class has been allowed a word of defense before judge or jury—

JUDGE HUNT: The prisoner must sit down; the Court can not allow it.

MISS ANTHONY: All my prosecutors, from the 8th Ward corner grocery politician, who entered the complaint, to the United States Marshal, Commissioner, District Attorney, District Judge, your honor on the bench, not one is my peer, but each and all are my political sovereigns; and had your honor submitted my case to the jury, as was clearly your duty, even then I should have had just cause of protest, for not one of those men was my peer; but, native or foreign, white or black, rich or poor, educated or ignorant, awake or asleep, sober or drunk, each and every man of them was my political superior; hence, in no sense, my peer. . . .

JUDGE HUNT: The Court must insist—the prisoner has been tried according to the established forms of law.

MISS ANTHONY: Yes, your honor, but by forms of law all made by men, interpreted by men, administered by men, in favor of men, and against women; and hence, your honor's ordered verdict of guilty, against a United States citizen for the exercise of "that citizen's right to vote," simply because that citizen was a woman and not a man. But, yesterday, the same manmade forms of law declared it a crime punishable with $1,000 fine and six months' imprisonment, for you, or me, or any of us, to give a cup of cold water, a crust of bread, or a night's shelter to a panting fugitive as he was tracking his way to Canada. And every man or woman in whose veins coursed a drop of human sympathy violated that wicked law, reckless of consequences, and was justified in so doing. As then the slaves who got their freedom must take it over, or under, or through the unjust forms of law, precisely so now must women, to get their right to a voice in this Government, take it; and I have taken mine, and mean to take it at every possible opportunity.

JUDGE HUNT: The Court orders the prisoner to sit down. It will not allow another word.

MISS ANTHONY: When I was brought before your honor for trial, I hoped for a broad and liberal interpretation of the Constitution and its recent amendments, that should declare all United States citizens under its protecting aegis—that should declare equality of rights the national guarantee to all persons born or naturalized in the United States. But failing to get this justice—failing, even, to get a trial by a jury *not* of my peers—I ask not leniency at your hands—but rather the full rigors of the law.

JUDGE HUNT: The Court must insist—[*Here the prisoner sat down.*] The prisoner will stand up. [*Here Miss Anthony arose again.*] The sentence of the Court is that you pay a fine of one hundred dollars and the costs of the prosecution.

MISS ANTHONY: May it please your honor, I shall never pay a dollar of your unjust penalty. All the stock in trade I possess is a $10,000 debt, incurred by publishing my paper—*The Revolution*—four years ago, the sole object of which was to educate all women to do precisely as I have done, rebel against your manmade, unjust, unconstitutional forms of law, that tax, fine, imprison, and hang women, while they deny them the right of representation in the Government; and I shall work on with might and main to pay every dollar of that honest debt, but not a penny shall go to this unjust claim. And I shall earnestly and persistently continue to urge all women to the practical recognition of the old revolutionary maxim that "Resistance to tyranny is obedience to God."

JUDGE HUNT: Madam, the Court will not order you committed until the fine is paid.
—*Trial, 1873*

If it is a mere question of who has got the best of it, Miss Anthony is still ahead; she has voted and the American constitution has survived the shock. Fining her one hundred dollars does not rub out the fact that fourteen women voted, and went home, and the world jogged on as before.
—*Newspaper editorial, 1873*

Lawless Abroad

Sometimes she broke the law unwittingly, While in Berlin in 1883, Susan B. Anthony whiled away some rainy days writing letters home— letters she posted in the suffrage stationery she'd thriftily brought along. It never occurred to her that the incendiary mottoes on the envelopes—"No just government can be formed without the consent of the governed" and "Taxation without representation is tyranny"—might offend the German monarchy. Sure enough, a government official paid a call on the American legation with all the offending envelopes wrapped up, explaining, "such sentiments cannot pass through the post-office in Germany." Anthony reluctantly mailed the letters in plain, unmarked wrappers. Her friend Elizabeth Cady Stanton later quipped, "It is well for us that she did not experiment in Russia, or we should now be mourning her loss as an exile in Siberia."

10. THE ORIGINAL
FREQUENT FLIER

If credit had been awarded for all the mileage she accumulated on trains, wagons, stagecoaches, ships, streetcars, ferryboats, horses, mules, and sleighs, Susan B. Anthony might have earned a free ticket to Mars—where she would gladly have gone had they been considering the vote for Martian women.

She traveled for two main reasons: first, to promote The Cause; and second, to raise money and repay the $10,000 debt incurred when she gave up sole ownership of her women's rights newspaper, The Revolution, *in 1870. It is staggering to contemplate the vast area she covered throughout the states and territories of this continent, and within the countries of Europe, where she was acclaimed as an international suffrage leader. Anthony first took to the road just before she turned thirty, with a series of temperance lectures that marked her passage from teaching into public life. "Men, women and children all turn out, curious to see the women lecturers, and hear what they may have to say," she wrote after yet another such trip. They were even more curious when she switched to women's rights and began her marathon expeditions throughout New York State: two trips to fifty-four (of the sixty) counties to collect signatures for a petition to the legislature—in the dead of winter. If that seems easy, take a look at the map. New York is a* *very large state, and before airplanes and good roads, it seemed even larger. "Here I am once more in my own Farm Home, where my weary head rests upon my own home pillows," she wrote Lucy Stone after one exhausting journey. "I had been gone* Four Months, *scarcely sleeping the* second *night under the same roof." Incredibly, she repeated the tour in 1894 at the age of seventy-four. This time she hit all sixty counties in just three months.*

As the movement went national, so did Susan B. Anthony, initiating a series of journeys across the Midwest and West that continued until she was eighty-five. The pace would crack even the hardiest of us today. One eight-week swing in 1871 took her through more than a dozen cities in Illinois (Peoria, Earlville, Bloomington, Lincoln, to name a few), sixteen cities in Michigan (Adrian, Jackson, Albion, Kalamazoo, Battle Creek, Lansing) and Ohio (Toledo, Ravenna, Dayton). Traveling to the Northwest in 1871, she estimated that she had logged two thousand miles and delivered sixty speeches. During the 1896 California campaign, she spent eight months navigating the state, speaking up to three times a day in more than thirty different cities—all this at a time of generally slow, dirty conveyances and often worse accommodations. The train trip to Washington from New York (which she took at least once a year) took ten hours in 1873. The eighty-four-mile stagecoach ride from Del Norte to Lake City in Colorado bumped over

mountains and through their various passes, crossing the divide between the waters that flow into the Atlantic and Pacific, at its highest point over 11,000 feet. And the ride down that mountain pass, "Slum Gullion" they call it, was the most fearful rough and tumble I ever experienced . . . even here, in this deep ravine, just wide enough for the Gunnison river and one street on its bank, the height is still 8,500 feet. All that fearfully long, but beautiful, frosty night, the moon shone brightly and on scenery most magnificent. At midnight I alighted at Wagon Wheel Gap, and with tin cup in hand trudged through the sand to the Rio Grande bank, bound to drink fresh from the pure, cold waters from the snow peaks above.

She slogged through the rain and spoke through the storms; she had her pocket picked and slept on straw-filled mattresses; and she learned as much as she taught. Crossing the drought-stricken prairies of South Dakota in an open wagon at the age of seventy, she was deeply affected to hear from her hostesses that the "hardest part of the life for women was 'To sit in our little adobe or sod houses at night and listen to the wolves howl over the graves of our babies.' " Her diaries and letters recorded how her ordeals drained her:

> I have been on tours for four months, sometimes without the luxury of a cup of coffee in a private home. Once I was traveling for six months without a home-cooked meal. One gets very tired of mediocre hotels and stage depot dining rooms.

> Bloomington Ind. . . . Took train at 3 P.M. two hours at Lafayette depot—So tired I actually slept on soft side of bench with no cushion & no pillow. . . .

But while her journeys were exhausting, she always supplied bound-less energy on the platform. And off. After one springtime jaunt through Kansas, she landed back in Rochester at 2 A.M. Leaving her traveling companion sound asleep on the train, Anthony, a sprightly seventy-four, found the front stoop of her home so pleasant in the predawn light that she "sat on the steps & read the morning paper." That trip also marked the end of her only experiment with carry-on luggage. Finding a small folding suitcase called a "Telescope" most unsatisfactory for her needs in the searing summer heat, she wrote, "For the first time in my many trips to Kansas — I took only a satchel a small Telescope — but I suffered more from the need of cool clothing *than all the trouble from a trunk."*

Anthony even took time from her devotion to duty to smell the roses — traveling to Europe three times and twice marveling at the glories of California's Yosemite valley, which she toured on muleback at the age of seventy-five. It was a rare personal luxury for the woman who almost never said no to a chance to change one more mind about suffrage, no matter how far from home.

[T]hey say that women are not physically able to enjoy the right of suffrage. I talked of that point Saturday at Glens Falls. I pointed to myself to contradict the statement. "Here am I," said I, "a woman who has reached the age of three score and ten with four years added, just finishing a tour of the state during which I have spoken five times a week most of the time, while during the

past two weeks I have spoken fourteen times. I have traveled from twenty to one hundred miles a day." I turned to one of the old lawyers of the place after this and asked him if he could have done the work and he unhesitatingly replied that he could not.
—*Interview, 1894*

Slept in my own bed this night—the 2nd in succession—
—*Diary, 1894*

My trips from Albany to New York and back are like the flying of the shuttle in the loom of the weaver.
—*Diary, 1867*

Susan B. Anthony's fame and charm made some of her travels more bearable. Crossing the Atlantic, she was invited to sit at the captain's table. Crossing the country, she enjoyed the private railroad car of Jane Stanford, whose husband, Leland, had built the railroad. But most of the time she toughed it out alone in the bumpy backseats of the grimiest of carriages. Or perched up front with the stagecoach driver for 400 miles in California. There, as usual, Susan B. Anthony was the perfect, sympathetic listener:

He explained the philosophy of fast driving down steep mountains . . . & such a sad domestic history as he gave me.
—*Diary, 1871*

But the beginning of that trip really rattled her. First she took a steamer from Oakland, California, to Portland, Oregon—a week-long nightmare in strong gales on an unforgiving sea. It was Susan B. Anthony's first, and most miserable, ocean voyage. Then she faced the rigors of the Oregon Territory's "corduroy" roads—those early trails made up of logs laid across the mud. She was a trouper.

Ship Idaho
1st day.—I felt sad and forlorn enough to be thus left on ocean bound alone—but was in for it & bound to go through . . . six pm my time came & old ocean received her first installment.
—*Diary, 1871*

I am now over one hundred miles on my stage-route south, and horrible indeed are the roads—miles and miles of corduroy and then twenty miles of "Joe Lane black mud," as they call it, because old Joseph Lane settled right here in the midst of it. It is heavy clay without a particle of loam and rolls up on the wheels until rim, spokes and hub are one solid circle. The wheels cease to turn and actually slide over the ground, and then driver and men passengers jump out and with chisels and shingles cut the clay off the wheels.

— *Letter, 1871*

Another trip, on a similar road aggravated by frozen mud, amazed even her colleagues:

Recently to reach one engagement she rode seventeen miles from the railroad station "over a most horrible road, a great deal of Corduroy turnpike which smashed our wagon, tire flew off and down went the wheel, the driver had to take one span of horses and go back two miles for a lumber wagon," in which Miss A. made the last ten miles of the seventeen; the wagon, too, minus a spring seat. It took six hours to perform the trip. Should not such a woman be called a missionary indeed?

— *Letter and article about Anthony, 1879*

But there was nothing quite like her first trip out West—almost an entire year away from home that took her to California, Oregon, and Washington and, on the way back East, ended in total travel hell. She was on her way to Washington, D.C., for the NWSA convention, on a winter train trip that took twelve days from Ogden, Utah, to Chicago.

December 28.—Eastern bound train arrived on time—at 12 noon. The western bound train arrived—8 days precisely from Omaha—happy sets of people. We started at 3 pm, three packed sleeping cars went on smoothly to Bitter Creek, 248 miles—there waited three or four hours for extra engine to take us up the grade.

December 29.— . . . backed and started then backed and started. Breakfast at 9:20 . . . along to Percy then delayed all night for trains ahead. Here overtook passenger train that left Ogden Monday A.M.

December 30.—Percy to . . . Medicine Bow—here delayed all day and all night—four passenger trains packed into two.

December 31.—Left Medicine Bow near noon—passed on to Look Out—through deep snow cuts *ten* miles in length . . . passed on to Laramie *two* long freights & one *long* passenger train in front of us—reached Laramie at 10 pm. Thus closes 1871—a year *full* of close work—six months on East & six on West Rocky Mts. 63 lectures to June 1st 26 on way in California—82 Sept. 1st to Oct. in Oregon, Wash, in Cal & Nevada—13,000 miles travel—gross receipts $4,318, paid on debts, $2,271.

January 1, 1872.—Laramie City, Wyoming Territory. On Pullman Car—*America*—Union Pacific R.R. . . . we started on reached an immense snow cut—tremendous wind—about 5 miles west of Sherman—on steepest grade . . . over 100 men shovelling in front . . . at dark 5 pm the wind & snow blowing terrifically—bright sky.

January 2.—This is indeed a fearful ordeal—fastened here in these snowbanks *mid way* the continent & at the very highest point of Rocky Mountains—full 8,000 feet above level of the sea—snow melted for Engine Boiler & car water tanks—Passengers furnished with soda crackers & dried fish—a train loaded with *coal* behind us, hence no danger of *actual* suffering— . . . Trains had moved up 4½ miles to Dale Creek Bridge . . . long & frail looking trestle work—here we remained all night—Train drawn under a long snow shed and hence very close—almost suffocating taking smoke of engine & *rare* atmosphere together— The winds lift up most furiously—no hope of getting beyond Sherman tomorrow—

January 3.—Six days out— . . . Wind gone down—perfectly calm & bright sunshine . . . Stood still in the snow shed until noon—moved onto Sherman about 6 pm.—
— *Diary, 1871–2*

Imprisoned in her snowbound train, Anthony took the time to answer a letter from a cousin that she'd been carrying around since she left Portland, Oregon. Consider the scene as the fifty-one-year-old traveler calmly surveyed the chaos and picked up her pen:

> On Union Pacific R.R. near
> Sherman, Wyoming Jan. 2, 1872

Miss Frank Anthony
My Dear Cousin,
Your letter of October 24, 1871 via Leavenworth, Kans. and Rochester N.Y. and thence to Portland, Oregon, has waited reply to this 2nd of the New Year, 1872, and now fastened in the snow banks five miles from the highest point of the whole Rocky Mountain grade—8000 feet above the level of the Sea. We have now been fast here 24 hours—waiting on 200 men shoveling

snow from track in front. When we shall move on, no one can tell—one train ahead of us is 10 days out from Ogden—ours is only 5 days out. The wind blows a perfect gale—filling into the track faster than the shovels can pitch it out. . . .

I am very glad you thought enough of me and my work to write me this pleasant note now laying before me and glad that you—of my name are putting brave shoulder and brain to life's battle and that you will come triumphantly victorious I have not a doubt—for it is the brave and courageous who dare to strike out alone—and it is they (who) will n[o]t surrender to obstacles—not even those so *almost insurmountable* that are everywhere thrown in the pathway of women.

Single handed and alone I have fought life's battle when the 15th day of Feb. 1872 shall come around for Fifty Two years—and feel not a whit the less inclined thus to finish the good fight. (The cars are crawling along a little.) Our good work for the *freedom* the "emancipation of women" as the English women call it and as it really is—goes on grandly—I hope we shall get from Congress this very session a Declaratory Act that shall secure to the women of the entire nation the exercise of their *right to vote,* and *almost* expect we shall. I trust *you* will offer your name to the proper officers to be registered at your next election in your town—the few of you who believe in Suffrage band together and march to the ballot box every time until by continual coming, the officers of the election shall conclude to accept and count your votes. . . .

        Affectionately your Cousin,
        Susan B. Anthony
—*Letter, 1872*

One of the reasons she put in so much time west of the Mississippi was her conviction that women would have better luck getting the vote there than with the "old fogies of the eastern states." She was right about the result. Wyoming was the first territory to grant women suffrage (in 1869), followed shortly by Utah, then Washington, Colorado, and Idaho. However, historians today dispute her logic, pointing out that Wyoming saw woman suffrage not as a leap toward equality but as "free advertising" for the sparsely populated territory "and would attract women to it." The other states had different reasons. Susan B. Anthony did not have access to that information.

The reporter inquired how it was that the suffragists did not concentrate their efforts on the enlightened New England States, say New Hampshire, Vermont, and Massachusetts; that the chances of early success were certainly better there than in the West.

"You are much mistaken," was Miss Anthony's reply. "In the old States there is little progress. The Western States are most liberal. In Massachusetts the question has been voted on time and again during the past fifteen years, and the vote in its favor is little larger now than at the beginning. No, our hope is first in the West."

— Interview, 1884

WHERE ARE YOU MAKING THE MOST PROGRESS?

In the West. The people there seem to be freer in mind and more ready to listen to reason than elsewhere. Wyoming is knocking at the door of the Union, and will be admitted before long. When she comes in, we shall have our first State where women are on an equality with men as electors. After the ice is once broken by that precedent, we shall find our work easier in other quarters.

— Interview, 1890

When she left for her first trip to Europe in 1883, Anthony, age sixty-three, surprised a reporter with her playful candor: "I don't see why I can't have a little fun the same as anyone else." That was also part of her motivation for her first trip to the Pacific in 1871, a journey that left her wide-eyed with wonder at the natural beauties of the Yosemite valley. As these excerpts indicate, she tackled tourism with the same determination that drove her suffrage work. The first describes her horseback ride down into the Yosemite valley, a trip made even more amusing by the sight of her dear, stout friend Elizabeth Cady Stanton, forced to walk to spare her frail mount:

By this time the sun was pouring down and my horse was slowly fastening one foot after another in the rocks and earth and thus carefully easing me down the steeps, while my guide baited me on by saying, "You are doing nicely, that is the worst place on the trail," when the fact was it hardly began to match what was coming.

At half-past two we reached Hutchings', and a more used-up mortal than I could not well exist, save poor Mrs. Stanton, four hours behind in the broiling sun, fairly sliding down the mountain. . . . About six she arrived, pretty nearly jelly. We both had a hot bath and she went supperless to bed, but I took my rations. . . .

The next day Mrs. Stanton kept her bed till nearly noon; but I was up and on my horse at eight and off with the McLean party for the Nevada and Vernal Falls. . . .

Saturday morning . . . I went up the Mariposa trail seven miles to Artist's Point, and there under a big pine tree, on a rock jutting out over the valley, sat and gazed at the wondrous walls with their peaks and spires and domes. . . . We reached the hotel at 7 P.M.—tired—tired. Not a muscle, not one inch of flesh from my heels to my hands that was not sore and lame, but I took a good rub-off with the powerful camphor from the bottle mother so carefully filled for me, and went to bed with orders for my horse at 6 A.M.

Sunday morning's devotion for Minister McLean and the Rochester strong-minded was to ride two and a half miles to Mirror Lake, and there wait and watch the coming of the sun over the rocky spires, reflected in the placid water. Such a glory mortal never beheld elsewhere. The lake was smooth as finest glass; the lofty granite peaks with their trees and shrubs were reflected more perfectly than costliest mirror ever sent back the face of most beautiful woman, and as the sun slowly emerged from behind a point of rock, the thinnest, flakiest white clouds approached or hung round it, and the reflection shaded them with the most delicate, yet most perfect and richest hues of the rainbow. And while we watched and worshipped we trembled lest some rude fish or bubble should break our mirror and forever shatter the picture seemingly wrought for our special eyes that Sunday morning.

Letter, 1871

On Board the British Prince, March 5

My Dear Sister Mary:

At lunch the captain said, "I'll soon show you land! It will be Mizzenhead, the farthest southwest point of Ireland." . . .

Since Thursday the weather has been lovely—bright sun and crisp air. Rachel succumbed one night when the "stiff breeze" first opened upon us, and I felt a little squalmy. The next morning a sudden lurch of the ship took both feet from under me and I was flat on my back. The following day while I was lying on a seat, reading and half-dozing, the first I knew I was in a heap on the floor. Then I learned it wasn't safe to lie down without a board fence in front. Again, in the evening, I had taken the one loose chair in the saloon, drawn it under a lamp and seated myself

very complacently to read, when lo, I was pitched over as if propelled from a ten-pounder! Three times and out—all in rapid succession—taught me to trust not to myself at all, but always to something fast to the ship. I haven't lost a meal during the whole trip.
—*Letter, 1883*

Rome, April 1

Dear Brother D.R.:
We have climbed Vesuvius. . . . One feels richly paid when the puffing and exploding and ascending of the red-hot lava meet the ears and eyes. The mountains, the Bay of Naples, the sail to Capri and the Blue Grotto are fully equal to my expectations. . . .
—*Letter, 1883*

Heidelberg, May 11

Dear Brother D.R.: I have clambered among the ruins of Heidelberg Castle today. I have thought of all my loved ones left in the new world and wished for each in turn to come across old ocean and look upon the remains of ancient civilization—of art and architecture, of bigotry and barbarism. I am enjoying my "flying," ever and ever so much. We have remained a week in only three places, in most cases not over two days, but I would not again make such a rush—it is too tiresome and confusing, seeing so many things so close on the heels of each other. But I am getting a good relish for a more deliberate tour at some later day. All of life should not be running one's work at home, whether that is woman's suffrage, newspaper, or government affairs.
—*Letter, 1883*

Sept 11.—In Dublin—. . . The Professor of Arabic—took me to & through Trinity College—its library has 200,000 volumes— Thence to the old Parliament House—Bank of Ireland now . . . In P.M. . . . met . . . Mr. Harrison—who has served a sentence in Prison for his love of Liberty for Ireland—
Sept. 29.—In Belfast—Went out & engaged berth in Steamer—also purchased 4 night gowns & 3 white shirts—2 flannel shirts—3 £—Don't know but it is all a cheat—but it is done anyway.
Oct. 3.—Stratford on Avon—Shakespeare Hotel—we visited the *new* theatre building—
—*Diary, 1883*

Anthony also made a pilgrimage to Haworth, to visit the former home of authors Charlotte and Emily Brontë. The gloomy setting on "a dreary cloudy showery day" made a powerful impression.

October 27.—It is a bleak enough place now, and must have been even more so fifty years ago when these sensitive plants lived there. A most sad day it was to me as I looked into the little parlor where the sisters walked up and down with their arms around each other and planned their novels, or sat before the fireplace and built air-castles. . . . Think of those delicate women sitting in that fireless, mouldy church, listening to their old father's dry, hard theology, with their feet on the cold, carpetless stones which covered their loved dead. It was too horrible! . . . How much the world of literature has lost because of their short and ill-environed lives, we can only guess from its increased wealth in spite of all their adverse conditions.
—*Diary, 1883*

Old age slowed her down but did not halt her travels. In 1905 Anthony wrote a very understanding letter to a friend in her eighties who had decided not to attend the upcoming NAWSA convention in Portland, Oregon. Anthony, eighty-five, was already packed.

I am sorry you think you cannot go to Portland but each one knows her own limitations. I suppose if I paid much attention to mine I should stay at home altogether, but I feel that it would be just as well if I reached the end on the cars or anywhere else as at home. It would make a little more trouble for others but I cannot give up going about my work through constant fear of that.
—*Letter, 1905*

Miss Anthony's Nerve

That was the headline of an 1871 newspaper article recounting "the nerve and coolness of Miss Susan B. Anthony in the face of danger." It seems a steamer crossing San Francisco Bay struck a rock while "under full headway, and the crash was terrific. Some of the passengers were paralyzed with fear . . . An Irish woman with four children clinging to her, fell on her knees, and with uplifted hands, commenced screaming like the whistle of a steam engine. The mate, who is a stout burly fellow of 250 pounds weight . . . caught hold of her and sought to calm her fears by telling her there was no danger. . . . In less than thirty seconds after the crash, one man had four life preservers tied around his feet and one around his neck. In striking contrast to these cases of inordinate fright, was the conduct of Miss Susan B. Anthony. She was reading a newspaper when the shock occurred, and manifested not the least emotion of fear or anxiety. She merely raised her eyes for an instant, took a glance at the situation, and resumed her reading with the utmost unconcern."

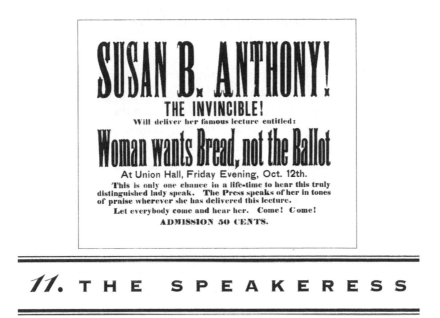

SUSAN B. ANTHONY!
THE INVINCIBLE!
Will deliver her famous lecture entitled:

Woman wants Bread, not the Ballot

At Union Hall, Friday Evening, Oct. 12th.
This is only one chance in a life-time to hear this truly
distinguished lady speak. The Press speaks of her in tones
of praise wherever she has delivered this lecture.
Let everybody come and hear her. Come! Come!
ADMISSION 50 CENTS.

11. THE SPEAKERESS

It always requires a painful effort to enable me to face an audience. I never once felt at perfect ease on the platform.

This blunt admission from one of the most prolific lecturers in America is even more startling when you realize how highly most audiences regarded her. "Miss Anthony's style of speaking is rapid and vehement," wrote her good friend Elizabeth Cady Stanton. "In debate she is ready and keen, and she is always equal to an emergency." Her nephew Daniel Jr. was equally impressed and reported to his parents, "At the beginning of her lecture, Aunt Susan does not do so well; but when she is in the midst of her argument and all her energies brought into play, I think she is a very powerful speaker." Newspaper reporters testified to her very persuasive manner:

Miss Anthony deals in facts. She depends more upon solid and strong argument than elegant diction. She brings an array of illustrations, well propped up by truth, to substantiate the ground she takes that disfranchisement is social, political and industrial degradation for women. . . .

She has something to say, and she says it decidedly, positively;

and her earnestness is stronger than the most conspicuous eloquence.

Miss Anthony evidently lectures not for the purpose of receiving applause, but for the purpose of making people understand and be convinced. She takes her position on the stage in a plain and unassuming manner and speaks extemporaneously and fluently, too, reminding one of an old campaign speaker, who is accustomed to talk simply for the purpose of converting his audience to his political theories. She used plain English and plenty of it . . . She clearly evinced a quality that many politicians lack—sincerity.

Her first trips to the podium required plenty of encouragement. "Dress loose, take a great deal of exercise & be particular about your diet & sleep sound enough, the body has a great effect on the mind," was the sound advice from Stanton, herself a seasoned speaker. "In your meetings, if attacked, be cool and good-natured, for if you are simple and truth-loving no sophistry can confound you." Lucy Stone tried to build her self-esteem:

Why do you say the people won't hear you a bit, when you know you never made a speech that was not *well* listened to? So grandly have you done that you have acquired the name of Napoleon.

Not everyone was convinced. Some of her outings elicited harsh reviews, no doubt largely based on the continuing shock that a woman would actually open her mouth in public. "The speakeress rattled on . . . until a late hour," wrote one offended reporter, "saying nothing new, nothing noble, not a word that would give one maid or mother a purer or better thought." Anthony was equally harsh on herself but, having survived those initial awful outings, occasionally allowed herself approval. "Was happy in a real Patrick Henry speech," she confided to her diary at the age of fifty-one. By the time she was fifty-eight, she noted that she had lectured 148 times in one seventh-month period, to an estimated 42,000 people. Two decades later, she calculated that she had delivered 75 to 100 speeches a year for forty-five years, not counting thirty years of addresses to Congress and the New York State Legislature. She spoke in churches, parlors, town halls, opera houses, and vaulted state capitols; in Colorado, she climbed atop a billiard table for one lecture and a dry-goods box on the courthouse steps for another. She addressed farmers in Kansas, students in New York, townfolk in Iowa (reporting "all converted" in her diary), others in Missouri ("dread-

fully fagged—" but "one of my very best speeches"). She spoke against a background of crying babies, raging thunderstorms, and welcoming applause. And at least once she must have looked exactly like today's orators, giving her talk at an institution for deaf-mutes while their superintendent translated every word into sign language.

For residents of remote areas, the speeches were welcome entertainment in a world unlinked by either radio or television. They paid their ten cents or even fifty cents to hear the news and wisdom of the East. Anthony, one of the biggest draws on the circuit, earned fees up to $150 a night (although usually much less) while under contract to various lecture bureaus—almost all of which went to pay off her debt. When she was not touring under contract—when she did it for The Cause—profits went directly into the suffrage treasury. For Susan B. Anthony, public speaking was not just a source of income—it was her mission.

───────

One of her earliest encounters with the bias against female speakers came in 1852 during her tour for temperance in New York State. A letter to Amelia Bloomer describes her frustration and final vindication after listening first to the men of the society.

Dear Mrs. Bloomer: . . .

According to long established custom, after serving strong meats to the "lords of creation," the lecturers dished up a course of what they doubtless called delicately flavored soup for the Ladies. Barnum [one of the male speakers] said it was a fact, and might as well be owned up, that this nation is under *petticoat* government; that every married man would acknowledge it, and if there were any young men who would not now, it was only necessary for them to have one week's experience as a husband, to compel them to admit that such is indeed the fact;—all of which vulgarity could but have grated harshly upon the ears of every intelligent, right-minded woman present.

At the close of the Mass Meeting, the women, mostly Daughters of Temperance—were invited to meet at the Presbyterian Church, at 3 o'clock P.M., to listen to an address from Susan B. Anthony, of Rochester. The Church was filled,—quite a large number of men (possessed no doubt of their full share of Mother Eve's curiosity,) were in attendance. They were reminded that they ought highly to appreciate the privilege which woman permitted them to enjoy,—that of remaining in the house and being silent lookers on.

It was really hopeful to see those hundreds of women with thoughtful faces—faces that spoke of disquiet within,—of souls dissatisfied, unfed, notwithstanding the soft eloquence which had been that A.M. so bounteously lavished upon *"angel woman."* I talked to them in my plain way,—told them that to merely relieve the suffering wives and children of drunkards, and vainly labor to reform the drunkard was no longer to be called *temperance* work, and showed them that woman's temperance sentiments were not truthfully represented by man at the Ballot Box. . . .

In the evening, . . . [a number of male speakers] addressed a large audience in the Presbyterian Church. Most excellent addresses, all of them, if they had only omitted the closing paragraphs to the *Ladies.* Oh! I am so sick and tired of the senseless, hopeless work that man points out for woman to do. . . .

I again addressed the citizens of [Elmira, New York] . . . While stopping at the Depot . . . a lady addressed me and said: "It is rude to thus speak to a stranger, but I want to say to you, that you have done one thing in Elmira." "And what is that?" "You have convinced me that it is proper for women to talk Temperance in public as well as in private. A gentleman told me that Miss Anthony was going to lecture on Temperance; said I, she had better be home washing dishes. He replied, 'perhaps she does not know how.' Well, said I, let her come to my house, & I will give her a few lessons." . . .
—*Letter, 1852*

No advanced step taken by women has been so bitterly contested as that of speaking in public. For nothing which they have attempted, not even to secure the suffrage, have they been so abused, condemned and antagonized. In this they were defying not only the prejudice of the ages, but also what the world had been taught was a divine command. This was not because they advocated unpopular doctrines, but it extended even to conventions of school teachers and to prayer meetings themselves. "I suffer not a woman to speak in public." This was the law and the gospel enforced by man.

The battle of woman for this right has long since been won. She

is welcomed on every platform the length and breadth of the land, and there is not a question which she is barred from discussing. Indeed, the assertion almost may be justified that the people find more enjoyment in listening to a woman than to a man.
—*Magazine article, 1900*

I haven't gotten over it yet. It is always a little hard for me to face an audience. I have no natural gift for speaking.
—*Interview, 1895*

I have learned to curl myself up in a sort of semi-comatose condition so as to hold my forces in hand for the evening's work. I will not read or write before speaking; it is bad enough to have to be rattled all day on the train without letting those endless shuttles work not only in the body, but among the fine meshes of the brain.
—*Interview, 1897*

Behind the podium, she contended with a number of distractions, including the encumbrance of a dental plate. She took them all in stride.

So difficult to get a plate that does not intercept full enunciation of my words.
—*Remarks, 1880[?]*

A novel spectacle to me, was the almost countless numbers of "Babies" in attendance. It is rarely that we see a baby at meeting in the East, and my risibles would get the better of my gravity, when the little creatures crowing and crying, overtopped the voices of the speakers. But the friends said, "You'll get used to the babies," and doubtless I should.
—*Letter, 1857*

Had a fine crowd—Though the rain fell in torrents the thunder roared & the lightning flashed.
—*Diary, Topeka, 1894*

For all her self-doubt, Anthony took to the platform naturally and wound up guiding the next generation of suffrage speakers. The first very practical advice she gave was delivered at her first women's rights convention, an event marked by very timid voices:

Mrs. President, I move that hereafter the papers shall be given to some one to read who can be heard. It is an imposition on an audience to have to sit quietly through a long speech of which they can not hear a word. We do not stand up here to be seen, but to be heard.

—Remarks, 1852

When a colleague defended the hushed tones by saying, "ladies did not come there to screech; they came to behave like ladies and to speak like ladies," Anthony said it had nothing to do with being ladylike; it had to do with being heard.

The following advice reflects her years of personal experience and still holds true today.

Now—don't stop to think you can't—nor that your *knees will shake*—nor of *yourself in any* way!! Just think the people *must know* of these . . . else they *can't* and won't wake up to help on the great work—You did splendidly with your report at the Wash. Con. last winter & still better with your report at the Salem Convention—all in the world you need is *practice enough* to forget yourself and everything & every body—but just thoughts you want to pound into the heads & hearts of the audience before you—I don't want to make you "get the *big head*"—but I do want you to *believe in yourself*—and your powers to *speak*—as well as write—!! So don't say *"no"* to a single invitation to *speak*—but just prepare yourself—and *read*—if you want to, or when the time comes—drop your paper and talk its contents—*tell the story*!! that is all I have ever done these forty years—just stand up and repeat experiences & facts of things done & to be done!!

—Letter, 1892

Her commitment to The Cause always won over her reluctance to press on, but Anthony's coworkers—like suffrage editor Elizabeth Boynton Harbert in these two letters—had to listen to plenty of complaints.

But I declare to you, that I feel so *restiff* in view of the great & grand work of *organizing* our forces for most efficient coopera- tion, that I should bound out of this mere lecture business, here & there, scattered all over—were it not for the *hungry wolf* that rises before my vision—If I can get $10,000, invested in *good first* mort- gages & 4 per cent bonds—so that I can *go free*—without any- body's saying Susan is reckless—& sure to go back on her friends for support when she gets broken down—then you & the world will see me throw the Bureau's |*sic*| to the winds—and buckle on

the harness for *movement work*—and of course I should do *so* now, *if and if*—*I were sure* of *netting something decent* by *movement work*—but you see—*this Lecture* business *is sure*—and though, with my small $30. fee—not speedy—I am able from it to contribute one & two hundred dollars in cash to the movement work each year—and therefore I feel that I mustn't let drop my little *certainty* of *cash* for an uncertainty—
—*Letter, 1879*

I should vastly prefer *not* to stop off at Chicago—it will so crowd me—& more I have no *new speech* & all my old words have been spoken over & over in Chicago—Still—if you so command—I will stop—& do my very best to be decent—but I enjoy a great deal better—*speaking* in *new places*—where I can feel *all* have not already heard all I know!
—*Letter, 1886*

At first she wrote down every word of her speeches, pacing around the Stanton house while memorizing the words either Stanton or the two of them had put on paper. But starting in 1857, she gave up written addresses, speaking only from scribbled notes. It was far more effective for her quick, energetic style. But it makes historians' work more difficult. With no manuscripts and only scattered newspaper reports as documentation, the only way to read an Anthony speech is to piece together fragments from varying sources. Following are excerpts from such a version of "Woman Wants Bread, Not the Ballot," by all accounts her most successful lecture. She delivered it countless times in the 1870s and '80s, and it generally lasted about two hours.

I am here to answer the popular objection "woman wants bread[,] not the ballot." She wants nothing but a home with her daily needs supplied, and if she gets these, she is happy. I think I shall be able to prove to you that the only possibility of her securing bread and a home for herself is to give her the ballot.

My purpose tonight is to demonstrate the great historical fact that disfranchisement is not only political degradation, but also moral, social, educational and industrial degradation; and that it does not matter whether the disfranchised class live under a monarchial or a republican form of government, or whether it be white workingmen of England, negroes on our southern plantations, serfs of Russia, Chinamen on our Pacific coast or native born, tax-paying women of this republic. Wherever, on the face of the globe or on the page of history, you show me a disfranchised class, I will show you a degraded class of labor. . . . You remember the old adage, "Beggars must not be choosers;" they must take what they can get or nothing! That is exactly the position of women in the world of work today; they can not choose. If they could, do you for a moment believe they would take the subordinate places and the inferior pay? Nor it is a "new thing under the sun" for the disfranchised, the inferior classes weighed down with wrongs, to declare they "do not want to vote." The rank and file are not philosophers, they are not educated to think for themselves, but simply to accept, unquestioned, whatever comes.

Years ago in England when the workingmen, starving in the mines and factories, gathered in mobs and took bread wherever they could get it, their friends tried to educate them into a knowledge of the causes of their poverty and degradation. At one of these "monster bread meetings," held in Manchester, John Bright said to them, "Workingmen, what you need to bring to you cheap bread and plenty of it, is the franchise;" but those ignorant men shouted back to Mr. Bright, precisely as the women of America do to us today, "It is not the vote we want, it is bread;" and they broke up the meeting, refusing to allow him, their best friend, to explain to them the powers of the franchise. The condition of those workingmen was very little above that of slavery. . . .

It is said women do not need the ballot for their protection because they are supported by men. Statistics show that there are 3,000,000 women in this nation supporting themselves. In the crowded cities of the East they are compelled to work in shops, stores and factories for the merest pittance. In New York alone there are over 50,000 of these women receiving less than fifty cents a day. . . .

You say that man protects woman. Let us see. Man holds the keys to everything. . . . In New York there are 50,000 prostitutes. Man refused to each a chance to earn easily an honest living and then offered to her the gilded hand of vice. A few years ago the good sisters of New York opened a foundling hospital and in the first six months 1300 little babies were brought to their doors. All of which shows that 1300 women were not protected. Men may protect their wives and daughters, but they take no care of other men's wives and daughters.

The question with you, as men, is not whether you want your wives and daughters to vote, nor with you, as women, whether you yourselves want to vote; but whether you will help to put this power of the ballot into the hands of the 3,000,000 wage-earning women, so that they may be able to compel politicians to legislate in their favor and employers to grant them justice. . . .

It was cruel, under the old regime, to give rich men the right to rule poor men. It was wicked to allow white men absolute power over black men. It is vastly more cruel, more wicked to give to all men—rich and poor, white and black, native and foreign, educated and ignorant, virtuous and vicious—this absolute control over women. Men talk of the injustice of monopolies. There never was, there never can be a monopoly so fraught with injustice, tyranny and degradation as this monopoly of sex, of all men over all women. Therefore I not only agree with Abraham Lincoln that, "No man is good enough to govern another man without his consent;" but I say also that no man is good enough to govern a woman without her consent, and still further, that all men combined in government are not good enough to govern all women without their consent . . .

I believe that by nature men are no more unjust than women. If from the beginning women had maintained the right to rule not only themselves but men also, the latter today doubtless would be occupying the subordinate places with inferior pay in the world of work; women would be holding the higher positions with the big salaries; widowers would be doomed to a "life interest of one-third of the family estate;" husbands would "owe service" to their wives, so that every one of you men would be begging your good wives, "Please be so kind as to 'give me' ten cents for a cigar." The principle of self-government can not be violated with impunity. The individual's right to it is sacred—regardless of class, caste, race, color, sex or any other accident or incident of birth. What we ask is that you shall cease to imagine that women are outside this law, and that you shall come into the knowledge that disfranchisement means the same degradation to your daughters as to your sons.

Governments can not afford to ignore the rights of those holding the ballot, who make and unmake every law and law-maker. It is not because the members of Congress are tyrants that women receive only half pay and are admitted only to inferior positions in the departments. It is simply in obedience to a law of political economy which makes it impossible for a government to do as much for the disfranchised as for the enfranchised. . . .

Women are today the peers of men in education, in the arts and sciences, in the industries and professions, and there is no escape from the conclusion that the next step must be to make them the peers of men in the government—city, State and national—to give them an equal voice in the framing, interpreting and administering of the codes and constitutions.

We recognize that the ballot is a two-edged, nay, a many-edged sword, which may be made to cut in every direction. If wily politicians and sordid capitalists may wield it for mere party and personal greed; if oppressed wage-earners may invoke it to wring justice from legislators and extort material advantages from employers; if the lowest and most degraded classes of men may use it to open wide the sluice-ways of vice and crime; if it may be the instrumentality by which the narrow, selfish, corrupt and corrupting men . . . rule—it is quite as true that noble-minded statesmen, philanthropists and reformers may make it the weapon with which to reverse the above order of things, as soon as they can have added to their now small numbers the immensely larger ratio of what men so love to call "the better half of the people." When women vote, they will make a new balance of power that must be weighed and measured and calculated in its effect upon every social and moral question which goes to the arbitrament of the ballot-box. Who can doubt that when the representative women of thought and culture, who are today the moral backbone of our nation, sit in counsel with the best men of the country, higher conditions will be the result? . . .

If men possessing the power of the ballot are driven to desperate means to gain their ends, what shall be done by disfranchised women? There are grave questions of moral, as well as of material interest in which women are most deeply concerned. Denied the ballot, the legitimate means with which to exert their influence, and, as a rule, being lovers of peace, they have recourse to prayers and tears, those potent weapons of women and children, and, when they fail, must tamely submit to wrong or rise in rebellion against the powers that be. Women's crusades against saloons, brothels and gambling-dens, emptying kegs and bottles into the streets, breaking doors and windows and burning houses, all go to prove that disfranchisement, the denial of lawful means to gain desired ends, may drive even women to violations of law and order. Hence to secure both national and "domestic tranquility," to "establish justice," to carry out the spirit of our Constitution, put into the hands of all women, as you have into those of all men, the ballot, that symbol of perfect equality, that right protective of all other rights.

—*Speech, 1870s–1880s*

The Heckler

Public speaking had its pitfalls, especially at a time of rampant alcoholism. While campaigning for the vote in frontier South Dakota in 1890, Anthony made her pitch in a half-finished church building with boards laid across nail kegs for seats. One drunken fellow made his way through the crowd and perched on the stage, interrupting her speech with rude comments. When the men in the audience cried, "Put him out, put him out!" Susan B. Anthony retorted, "No, gentlemen, he is a product of man's government, and I want you to see what sort you make."

12. THE ENEMY

he cartoon is one of the more sympathetic portrayals of Susan B. Anthony in print. The year was 1905; the catalyst, an article in Ladies' Home Journal *by former President Grover Cleveland on the so-called "woman question." Taking direct aim at the suffragists, he wrote:*

> To those of us who . . . cling to our faith in the saving grace of simple and unadulterated womanhood, any discontent on the part of woman with her ordained lot, or a restless desire on her part to be and to do something not within the sphere of her appointed ministrations, cannot appear otherwise than as perversions of a gift of God to the human race.

He went on to exalt "the old and natural order of things . . . when Adam was put in the Garden of Eden to dress it and keep it, and Eve was given to him as a helpmeet." Then he attacked Susan B. Anthony and the women's vote.

> The restlessness and discontent to which I have referred is most strongly manifested in a movement which has for a long time been on foot for securing to women the right to vote and

otherwise participate in public affairs. Let it here be distinctly understood that no sensible man has fears of injury to the country on account of such participation. It is its dangerous, undermining effect on the characters of the wives and mothers of our land that we fear. This particular movement is so aggressive, and so extreme in its insistence, that those whom it has fully enlisted may well be considered as incorrigible. At a very recent meeting of these radicals a high priestess of the faith declared: "No matter how bad the crime a woman commits, if she can't vote, and is classed with idiots and criminals and lunatics, she should not be punished by the same laws as those who vote obey." This was said when advocating united action on the part of the assembled body to prevent the execution of a woman proved guilty of the deliberate and aggravated murder of her husband. The speaker is reported to have further announced as apparently the keynote of her address: "If we could vote we'd be willing to be hanged." It is a thousand pities that all the wives found in such company cannot sufficiently open their minds to see the complete fitness of the homely definition which describes a good wife as "a woman who loves her husband and her country with no desire to run either;" and what a blessed thing it would be if every mother, and every woman, whether mother, wife, spinster or maid, who either violently demands or wildly desires for women a greater share in the direction of public affairs, could realize the everlasting truth that "the hand that rocks the cradle is the hand that rules the world."

Cleveland ended by calling the burgeoning woman's club movement "harmful in a way that directly menaces the integrity of our homes."

Reporters couldn't wait to get the response of Susan B. Anthony, by then a widely respected figure. One Rochester newspaperman found her at home and recorded her reaction.

Ridiculous! Pure fol-de-rol!

Well, what does Grover Cleveland know about "sanctity of the home" and "woman's sphere," I should like to know?

Why isn't the woman herself the best judge of what woman's sphere should be? The men have been trying to tell us for years. We have no desire to vote if the men would do their duty. Why are not the laws enforced in regard to saloons, gambling places and houses of ill repute? The women want a chance to see what they can do in making present laws effective.

Mr. Cleveland remarks that the "hand that rocks the cradle is the hand that rules the world." That would be all right if you could keep the boys in the cradle always.

But the minute they are able to go to school temptations beset them on all sides. They have to pass any number of saloons and gambling places on their way to and from school. And all of these places are stretching out their iniquitous arms to call in the boys. The men will do nothing about it and the women can't. How helpless we are is well shown in our own ward, where a saloon may be placed every 200 feet if wished, against the most strenuous objections we can offer. It is no wonder the women demand a vote. . . .

It is from just such men as Grover Cleveland, who writes such "gush" merely because the magazine will pay him well for it, that most of the objections to woman suffrage come.

Mr. Cleveland is inspired to a tirade on women's clubs and organizations. Did he ever stop to think that the men are responsible for these even. Why should a woman settle down to the "hum-drum" as he calls it, of home any more than a man? The men are content to leave their money in some saloon and then go home drunk to abuse their wives and children. In many cases the wife supports the husband. Why then shouldn't the women spend as much time at the clubs as the men?

The few who are married to good husbands are as a rule too well educated to be content with a life of inactivity and of mental stagnation. Besides, present day inventions have so far reduced the woman's work at home that she must needs go somewhere to pass her leisure time.

I think that Mr. Cleveland is a very poor one to attempt to point out the proper conduct of the women.

Anthony was so furious, she tried to get her suffrage colleagues to boycott Ladies' Home Journal, *but the motion didn't pass. The rest of the press, as eager then as now to cash in on a sexy skirmish, played the story big, and public opinion so favored Anthony that a popular jingle at the time went "Susan B. / Anthony, she / Took quite a fall / out of Grover C."*

Which does not explain the ugly cartoon of the suffrage leader as battle-ax with her rolled-up umbrella. That, it seems, was simply a matter of tradition. From the day she entered public life, Anthony was ridiculed for her looks, her clothes, her marital state, her speeches, her voice, and her ideas. The men who opposed suffrage argued that women didn't need the vote because they were either too emotional or too pure; that their husbands or fathers or brothers would take care of that nasty bit of business for them; that voting would ruin family life and dissolve otherwise happy marriages. Anyway, they reasoned, women had their own sphere to run—the home— and should be thankful that men were willing to keep them on their pedestal. Sound familiar?

———————

Our Philadelphia ladies not only possess beauty, but they are celebrated for discretion, modesty, and unfeigned diffidence, as well as wit, vivacity and good nature. Whoever heard of a Philadelphia lady setting up for a reformer, or standing out for woman's rights, or assisting to *man* the election grounds, raise a regiment, command a legion, or address a jury? Our ladies glow with a higher ambition. They soar to rule the hearts of their worshipers, and secure obedience by the sceptre of affection. . . . Our Philadelphia girls object to fighting and holding office. They prefer the baby-jumper . . . Women have enough influence over human affairs without being politicians. Is not everything managed by female influence? Mothers, grandmothers, aunts, and sweethearts manage everything. Men have nothing to do but to listen and obey to the "of course, my dear, you will, and of course, my dear, you won't." Their rule is absolute; their power unbounded. . . .

A woman is nobody. A wife is everything. A pretty girl is equal to ten thousand men, and a mother is, next to God, all powerful. . . . The ladies of Philadelphia, therefore, under the influence of the most serious "sober, second thoughts," are resolved to maintain their rights as Wives, Belles, Virgins, and Mothers, and not as Women.

—*Philadelphia* Public Ledger and Daily Transcript, *1848*

We received a very unfavorable opinion of this *Miss* Anthony when she performed in this city on a former occasion, but we confess that after listening attentively to her discourse last evening, we were inexpressibly disgusted with the impudence and impiety evinced in her lecture. Personally repulsive, she seems to be laboring under feelings of strong hatred towards male men, the effect, we presume, of jealousy and neglect. . . . With a degree of impiety which was both startling and disgusting, this shrewish *maiden* counseled the numerous wives and mothers present to separate from their husbands whenever they become intemperate, *and particularly not to allow the said husbands to add another child to the family;* (probably no *married* advocate of Women's Rights would have made this remark.) Think of such advice given in public by one who claims to be a maiden lady. . . .

Miss Anthony concluded with a flourish of trumpets, that the Women's Rights question could not be put down—that women's souls were beginning to expand, &c., after which she gathered her short skirts around her tight pants, sat down and wiped her spectacles.

— *Utica (N.Y.)* Evening Telegraph, *1853*

We saw, in broad daylight, in a public hall in the city of New York, a gathering of unsexed women—unsexed in mind all of them, and many in habiliments—publicly propounding the doctrine that they should be allowed to step out of their appropriate sphere, and mingle in the busy walks of every-day life, to the neglect of those duties which both human and divine law have assigned to them. We do not stop to argue against so ridiculous a set of ideas. We will only inquire who are to perform those duties which we and our fathers before us have imagined belonged solely to women. Is the world to be depopulated? Are there to be no more children? . . .

It is almost needless for us to say that these women are entirely devoid of personal attractions. They are generally thin maiden ladies, or women who perhaps have been disappointed in their endeavors to appropriate the breeches and the rights of their unlucky lords; the first class having found it utterly impossible to induce any young or old man into the matrimonial noose, have turned out upon the world, and are now endeavoring to revenge themselves upon the sex who have slighted them. The second, having been dethroned from their empire over the hearts of their husbands . . . go vagabonding over the country, boring unfortunate audiences with long essays lacking point or meaning . . . They violate the rules of decency and taste by attiring themselves in eccentric habiliments, which hang loosely and inelegantly upon their forms, making that which we have been educated to respect, to love, and to admire, only an object of aversion and disgust. . . .

— *New York* Herald, *1853*

The farce at Syracuse has been played out. . . . Who are these women? what do they want? . . . Some of them are old maids, whose personal charms were never very attractive, and who have been sadly slighted by the masculine gender in general; some of them women who have been badly mated, whose own temper, or their husbands, has made life anything but agreeable to them, and they are therefore down upon the whole of the opposite sex; some, having so much of the virago in their disposition, that nature appears to have made a mistake in their gender—mannish women, like hens that crow; some of boundless vanity and egotism, who believe that they are superior in intellectual ability to "all the world and the rest of mankind," and delight to see their speeches and addresses in print; and man shall be consigned to his proper sphere—nursing the babies, washing the dishes, mending stockings, and sweeping the house. . . .

What do the leaders of the Woman's Rights Convention want? They want to vote, and to hustle with the rowdies at the polls. They want to be members of Congress, and in the heat of debate to subject themselves to coarse jests and indecent language . . . They want to fill all other posts which men are ambitious to occupy—to be lawyers, doctors, captains of vessels, and generals in the field. How funny it would sound in the newspapers, that Lucy Stone, pleading a cause, took suddenly ill in the pains of parturition, and perhaps gave birth to a fine bouncing boy in court! Or that Rev. Antoinette Brown was arrested in the middle of her sermon in the pulpit from the same cause, and presented a "pledge" to her husband and the congregation; or, that Dr. Harriot K. Hunt, while attending a gentleman patient for a fit of the gout or *flatula in ano,* found it necessary to send for a doctor, there and then, and to be delivered of a man or woman child—perhaps twins. A similar event might happen on the floor of Congress, in a storm at sea, or in the raging tempest of battle, and then what is to become of the woman legislator?
—*Editorial, New York* Herald, *1852*

Susan is lean, cadaverous and intellectual, with the proportions of a file and the voice of a hurdy-gurdy.
—*New York* World, *1866*

In appearance, Miss Anthony typifies the typical old maid, tall, angular and inclined to be vinegar visaged. . . . Miss Anthony's style of speaking is rather stiff and cold. Her forte, very evidently

is disputation, all she needs to fan her into a white flame is for some male biped to say to her, "that's not so."
—*Adrian (Mich.)* Times and Expositor, *1870*

People went there to see Susan B. Anthony, who has achieved an evanescent reputation by her strenuous endeavors to defy nature. Not one woman in a hundred cares to vote, cares aught for the ballot, would take it with the degrading influences it would surely bring. . . . Old, angular, sticking to black stockings, wearing spectacles . . . If all woman's righters look like that, the theory will lose ground like a darkey going through a cornfield in a light night. If she had come out and plainly said: "See here, ladies—see me—I am the result of twenty years of constant howling at man's tyranny," there would never have been another "howl" uttered in Detroit.
—*Detroit* Free Press, *1869*

Some were tall, many medium, several short, some were pretty, a few passable, and many ugly as a mud fence; several looked intelligent, others inquisitive and prying, and several as if they were going just to hear the lectures without caring much for her assertions. The majority of the auditors were married ladies, but not a few maidens, rejoicing in single blessedness, went to list[en] to the oracle recount the horrors of the social evil—an evil which they knew nothing about, and about which it would be better they did not even hear.
—*Portland (Ore.)* Herald, *1871*

We could not help thinking what a fine looking and useful woman she would have been had she got married years ago and would now be sitting in her parlor surrounded by a family of children, grandchildren and perhaps great grandchildren. She would then consider herself the peer of any woman. We wish she had been more fortunate in her younger days.
—*Oregon City (Ore.)* Weekly Enterprise, *1871*

To any who are conversant with the manner in which our system of politics is conducted, the idea of the presence and participation of women therein will be distasteful and abhorrent—out of pure respect for the sex. At such scenes the bold or the bad would attend, perhaps; but we imagine few of the good or the gentle and modest could be brought to engage in the "filthy pool". . . . no unmarried man or woman is competent to fully discuss or to thoroughly understand the question in point in all of its essen-

tial features. And the fact that the vast majority of the married women are the firmest of the opponents of the Woman's Rights movement is in itself a powerful argument against that mischievous late day hobby.
—*Portland (Ore.)* Bulletin, *1871*

To untaught minds she was a wonderful phenomena [*sic*] in the knowledge of the Constitution and Constitutional history,— so glibly did her tongue run in its explanation and exposition. To the well-informed, her history of deductions from the letter of the Federal Constitution was but the balderdash of intense vanity, coupled either with lamentable ignorance or a guilty intention to misrepresent.

Outside of this, her argument was well stated, and her deductions generally logical.
—*Mercer (Pa.)* Western Press, *1873*

The gentlemen of the press were not the only ones threatened by what one called the "gabble [of] the Woman's Righters." Many of the nation's elected representatives and most dignified public figures were equally appalled by the possibility of women's taking part in the democratic process and announced their views on the floor of the House or Senate—vehemently but oh, so politely.

[T]he right of suffrage to women, in my judgment, is not necessary for their protection. . . . Women have not been enslaved. Intelligence has not been denied to them; they have not been degraded; there is no prejudice against them on account of their sex; but, to the contrary, if they deserve to be, they are respected, honored, and loved . . . the sons defend and protect the reputation and rights of their mothers; husbands defend and protect the reputation and rights of their wives; brothers defend and protect the reputation and rights of their sisters; and to honor, cherish, and love the women of this country is the pride and the glory of its sons.

When women ask Congress to extend to them the right of suffrage it will be proper to consider their claims. Not one in a thousand of them at this time wants any such thing, and would not exercise the power if it were granted to them. Some few who are seeking notoriety make a feeble clamor for the right of suffrage, but they do not represent the sex to which they belong, or I am mistaken as to the modesty and delicacy which constitute the

chief attraction of the sex. Do our intelligent and refined women desire to plunge into the vortex of political excitement and agitation? Would that policy in any way conduce to their peace, their purity, and their happiness? . . . Women in this country, by their elevated social position, can exercise more influence upon public affairs than they could coerce by the use of the ballot.
— *Senator George Williams of Oregon, 1866*

I think I am authorized in saying that the women of New Jersey to-day do not desire to vote.
— *Senator F. F. Frelinghuysen of New Jersey, 1866*

Voting is no right; it is a privilege granted . . . There is no wrong done . . . by denying this to certain classes of a community, whether on account of age or sex or any other supposed causes of disqualification. In this country the whole foundation of our institutions has been that the male sex when arrived at years of supposed discretion alone should take part in the political control of the country. . . .

Under the operation of this Amendment, what will become of the family hearthstone around which cluster the very best influences of human education? You will have a family with two heads—a "house divided against itself." You will no longer have that healthful and necessary subordination of wife to husband . . . You will have substituted a system of contention and difference warring against the laws of nature herself, and attempting by these new fangled, petty, puny, and most contemptible contrivances, organized in defiance of the best lessons of human experience, to confuse, impede, and disarrange the palpable will of the Creator of the world.
— *Senator Thomas F. Bayard of Delaware, 1874*

Now it is proposed that all the women of the country shall vote; that all the colored women of the South, who are as much more ignorant than the colored men as it is possible to imagine, shall vote. Not one perhaps in a hundred of them can read or write. The colored men have had the advantages of communication with other men in a variety of forms. Many of them have considerable intelligence; but the colored women have not had equal chances. Take them from their wash-tubs and their household work and they are absolutely ignorant of the new duties of voting citizens. The intelligent ladies of the North and the West and the South cannot vote without extending that privilege to

that class of ignorant colored people. I doubt whether any man will say that it is safe for the republic now, when we are going through the problem we are obliged to solve, to fling in this additional mass of ignorance upon the suffrage of the country. Why, sir, a rich corporation or a body of men of wealth could buy them up for fifty cents apiece, and they would vote without knowing what they were doing for the side that paid most.
—*Senator James B. Beck of Kentucky, 1881*

Society can not be preserved nor can the people be prosperous without good government. . . .

This often requires the assembling of caucuses in the night time, as well as public assemblages in the daytime. It is a laborious task, for which the male sex is infinitely better fitted than the female sex.
—*Senator Joseph E. Brown of Georgia, 1887*

When woman becomes a voter she will be more or less of a politician, and will form political alliances or unite with political parties which will frequently be antagonistic to those to which her husband belongs. This will introduce into the family circle new elements of disagreement and discord which will frequently end in unhappy divisions, if not in separation and divorce. This must frequently occur when she becomes an active politician, identified with a party which is distasteful to her husband. On the other hand, if she unites with her husband in party associations and votes with him on all occasions so as not to disturb the harmony and happiness of the family, then the ballot is of no service, as it simply duplicates the vote of the male on each side of the question and leaves the result the same.
—*Senator Joseph E. Brown of Georgia, 1887*

I am not here to ridicule. My purpose only is to use legitimate argument as to a movement which commands respectful consideration if for no other reason than because it comes from women. But it is impossible to divest ourselves of a certain degree of sentiment when considering this question. I pity the man who can consider any question affecting the influence of woman with the cold, dry logic of business. What man can, without aversion, turn from the blessed memory of that dear old grandmother, or the gentle words and caressing hand of that blessed mother gone to the unknown world, to face in its stead the idea of a female justice of the peace or township constable? For my part, when I go to my home—when I turn from the arena where man contends with man for what we call the prizes of this paltry world—I want to go back not to be received in the masculine embrace of some female ward politician, but to the earnest, loving look and touch of a true woman. I want to go back to the jurisdiction of the wife, the mother; and instead of a lecture upon finance or the tariff or the construction of the Constitution, I want those blessed, loving details of domestic life and domestic love. . . .

The great evil in this country to-day is in emotional suffrage. The great danger to-day is in excitable suffrage. If the voters of this country could think always coolly, and if they could deliberate, if they could go by judgment and not by passion, our institutions would survive forever, eternal as the foundations of the continent itself; but massed together, subject to the excitement of mobs and of those terrible political contests that come upon us from year to year under the autonomy of our government, what would be the result if suffrage were given to the women of the United States?

Women are essentially emotional. It is no disparagement to them they are so. It is no more insulting to say that women are emotional than to say that they are delicately constructed physically and unfitted to become soldiers or workmen under the sterner, harder pursuits of life. What we want in this country is to avoid emotional suffrage, and what we need is to put more logic into public affairs and less feeling. . . .

I would not, and I say it deliberately, degrade woman by giving her the right of suffrage . . . it would destroy her influence. It would take her down from that pedestal where she is today . . .
— *Senator George Vest of Missouri, 1887*

I have always voted against Woman Suffrage & have seen as yet no reason to change my opinion—
— *Letter from Senator Henry Cabot Lodge of Massachusetts in response to a questionnaire from Susan B. Anthony to all members of Congress, 1902*

Kindly do not use my name as a college president in favor of the enfranchisement of women. My attitude on the subject would require more explanation than such a use would justify.
— *Letter from Nicholas Murray Butler, president of Columbia University, in response to a questionnaire from Susan B. Anthony, 1902*

We oppose woman suffrage as tending to destroy the home and family, the true basis of political safety, and express the hope that the helpmeet and guardian of the family sanctuary may not be dragged from the modest purity of self-imposed seclusion to be thrown unwillingly into the unfeminine places of political strife.
—*Resolution adopted by Democratic Party, 1894, after rejecting pleas for a suffrage plank*

The nonstop attacks of the "antis" could be debilitating, but Anthony never gave in. Here is how one sympathetic female journalist described her pluck:

I honor all the old leaders, but I confess I make my lowest *salaam* to Susan B. Anthony. She has dared no more than the others, but she has been compelled to endure more. Lucretia Mott, pure and placid prophetess of reform, disarmed rude opposition by her sweet Quaker serenity, which was after all but a glove of velvet over a grip of steel. Stately Mrs. Stanton has secured much immunity, by a comfortable look of motherliness and a sly benignancy in her smiling eyes, even though her arguments have been bayonet thrusts and her words hot shot; while Miss Anthony, passionate and persistent, with her "undaunted mettle and pure grit," has asked no quarter, and certainly has received none. From first to last she has been the target for "the slings and arrows of outrageous" journalism. Youthful reporters and paragraphists have tried their 'prentice hand on her. When ever the mother-in-law gave out, there was Susan B. Anthony to fall back upon. She has been a boon and a benefaction to these ingenuous young gentlemen. I remember that about ten years ago I said to some of the sauciest of these now in Washington: "For shame boys; not one of you will ever make the man she is."
—*Speech by Grace Greenwood, 1888*

Ladies of the Night

Late one night in 1896 after Susan B. Anthony had appealed to the California Democratic convention to endorse a votes-for-women amendment in the upcoming state election—a plea that was soundly rejected—Anthony and her friends, according to her biographer, "were awakened by loud laughter and women's voices. They arose and went to the window and there in the brilliantly lighted street in front of the hotel were two carriages containing several gaily dressed women. A number of the convention delegates came out and crowded around them, three or four climbed into the carriages, wine bottles were passed and finally, with much talk and laughter, they drove off down the street, the men with their arms about the women's waists. The ladies returned to their slumbers thoroughly convinced that they had not used the correct methods for capturing the delegates of a Democratic convention."

13. GENTLEMEN, TAKE NOTICE

*S*usan B. Anthony has a way of saying the word "male," observed a reporter at a Congressional committee in 1870, "so that it sounds like the snapping of small arms." Indeed, the follies and practices of the men running the government and writing rude reviews about her work provided stores of ammunition for her suffrage wars. And she does seem to have enjoyed entertaining friends and colleagues at the expense of some poor man's ineptitude. In The Revolution, *the newspaper she published, the following item appeared in 1869:*

> Miss Susan B. Anthony considers it her mission to keep the world, or at least her part of it, in hot water. Gentlemen, take notice.

And an Indiana newspaper reporter made these observations after hearing her lecture on The Cause.

> It has become quite the fashion for suffrage lecturers to flatter men until they, the men, leave the audience room with a better opinion of themselves than they had when they entered it. Miss

POLITICAL CARTOON, 1873, "THE WOMAN WHO DARED,"
AFTER ANTHONY VOTED

Anthony is not guilty of any such lobbying. Notwithstanding her unquestioned justice, we doubt if the vanity of the men who hear her is very much inflated. They slink out after the lecture, looking very much as though they had been well whipped.

But she did not hate all men and, more important, did not blame them all for the inequities of the ruling majority. The only thing a man had to do to win Susan B. Anthony's respect—and eternal loyalty—was to be fair. That is, to understand that women were people, too, who deserved equal rights. There were plenty who qualified.

The list begins with her father and includes many of the abolitionists who remained close friends despite their behavior over the Fourteenth Amendment. One of the first men to sign up for The Cause was Henry Blackwell, who cemented his commitment by marrying Lucy Stone. Their daughter, Alice Stone Blackwell, would help lead the second generation to the vote. Anthony introduced Henry at a suffrage convention in 1900 with these teasing, but very grateful, words:

Here is a man who has the virtue of having stood by the woman's cause for nearly fifty years. I can remember him when his hair was not white, and when he was following up our conventions assiduously because a bright, little, red-cheeked woman attracted him. She attracted him so strongly that he still works for woman suffrage, and will do so as long as he lives, not only because of her who was always so true and faithful to the cause— Lucy Stone—but also because he has a daughter, a worthy representative of the twain who were made one.

The honor roll goes on, with special standing reserved for the members of Congress who went out of their way to introduce or support legislation in favor of a suffrage amendment. Representative George W. Julian of Indiana and Senator Samuel C. Pomeroy of Kansas made the first resolutions for proposal in 1868. Senators Henry W. Blair of New Hampshire, Aaron Sargent of California (later ambassador to Germany), and Thomas W. Palmer of Michigan, to name a favored few, remained staunch advocates. At a hearing in 1892, she singled out Senator George F. Hoar of Massachusetts for presenting the first favorable suffrage report to the Senate fifteen years earlier. According to one account, "Laurel wreaths and bouquets would have been Senator Hoar's portion if they had been available."

As a seasoned political operative, Susan B. Anthony perfectly understood how to use her allies. She was quite pleased with her team's ability to turn support into action:

[W]e once induced one of our good friends, ex-Senator Palmer, of Michigan, to deliver a speech on woman suffrage on the floor of the Senate. It was an excellent speech, but no better than I have heard Mrs. Stanton and others of our leading women make. If any of them had made it, nobody would have heard of it again, because everyone would have said, "Oh, it's only a woman's talk." When Senator Palmer spoke, however, the whole country had to listen. The press associations sent off a third of a column or so of condensed abstract; the *Congressional Record* contained the full text of the speech; the daily newspapers of Michigan made copious extracts from it and comments on it; and every weekly paper in that State, except one, published it entire. The same tactics have been used with other public men of note who are friendly to our cause. Speaker [Thomas B.] Reed [of Maine] is one who has made some splendid efforts in our behalf, and what he has said has gone everywhere.

Anthony applauded a wide array of male benefactors and eagerly attended the founding meeting of the Spinner Memorial Association, a group of women honoring General Francis E. Spinner, the first person to hire women for posts in the federal government. She was not aware that his gesture, as U.S. Treasury secretary, was motivated by the realization that female employees would work for less money. But then, everyone has to start somewhere.

I tell you, Mrs. Stanton, after all, it is very *precious* to the soul of man, that he *shall reign supreme in intellect*—and it will take Centuries if not ages to dispossess him of the fancy that he is born to do so.
—*Letter, 1857*

I went to Central Church at evening . . . the same old story— men make & break laws—& women by love & persuasion soften their hearts to abandon their wickedness—not a hint that women should assume ballot & make & execute law[s.]
—*Diary, 1874*

Oh, if men only could know how hard it is for women to be forever snubbed when they attempt to plead for their rights! It is perfectly disheartening that no member [of Congress] feels any especial interest or earnest determination in pushing this question of woman suffrage, to all men only a side issue.
— *Diary, 1883*

Right here I want to say that woman is proving her physical and mental right to equality, at least in the marital state, through a strange compensatory evolution in nature. Vice and dissipation have already begun to tell upon the men. Hence we see, year by year, the physical and intellectual plane of women advancing. Look at the men and women passing in the crowded streets, and note the ever increasing proportion of well-formed, vigorous women—single women—women taller and more athletic than their male escorts. Observe the puny appearance of so many of the men. Man is going backward as an animal.
— *Interview, 1903*

In 1903 the president of Harvard, Charles William Eliot, commented that American families were too small and noted that graduates of his institution tended to have fewer than two children apiece. Susan B. Anthony was sought for a reply:

That is quite enough. Harvard graduates do not always make the best fathers.
— *Interview, 1903*

While she directed her barbs at any man who stood in the way of any progress for women, most of her anger was directed at the men who stood in the way of the suffrage amendment.

[M]en are afraid that if women vote, if they hold office, if they sit in Congressional and Parliamentary halls, they will degrade themselves to the level of men!!
— *Speech, 1899*

. . . every whiskey maker, vendor drinker, every gambler, every Libertine every ignorant besotted man is against us–& then the other extreme—every narrow selfish religious bigot.
— *Diary, 1874, after defeat in Michigan*

In South Dakota there are 70,000 voters, 40,000 American born and 30,000 foreigners. We lost all the foreigners and about half the Americans. History repeated itself in South Dakota. It was the eighth state in which woman suffrage amendments have been submitted. It is an utterly hopeless proceeding to submit such a question to the rank and file of voters. Beside the foreigners we had to fight the whisky interest and what few religious bigots are still left. None of the political parties gave us any help. The democratic state convention declared against us. The Russians went down to that convention wearing badges inscribed "Against Prohibition, Woman Suffrage and Susan B. Anthony." I had been holding a convention in their county. The foreigners always associate woman suffrage with prohibition. The southerners seem to rank it with abolition. No southern congressman has ever helped us in our work.

—*Interview, 1890, after defeat in South Dakota*

The opposition has resolved itself substantially into two classes —the conservative, non-progressive element, who still have lingering doubts as to its effect upon domestic life and upon the women themselves, and the other element who from the very character of their daily lives regard as a menace the granting of any further power to women.

—*Letter, 1896*

It was not in Anthony's nature to be angry all the time. Amazingly, she managed to deal very diplomatically with even the most recalcitrant men. Here is her reply to Edward Rosewater, editor of the Omaha Bee, *who had sent greetings on her eightieth birthday.*

It was indeed kind of you to send your congratulations to me on my eightieth birthday, and then in addition to pray that my life might be prolonged, when you feel from the bottom of your heart that if the end to which I have devoted that life were attained the result would be not good but very bad for the world. I never could quite understand how anyone could love and respect *me* while thinking that what I was working for was absolutely wrong. Nevertheless, Mr. Rosewater, if you cannot believe in the application to women of the underlying principles of our government, I shall have to be grateful that you do believe in me.

—*Letter, 1900*

At the close of the meeting Miss Anthony asked all those who wanted this bill for the 16th amendment to pass Congress to say,

"aye." The ayes rang out in enthusiastic response. Then she asked
all those who wanted things to remain as they are to say "no," and
one man near the door in a rather subdued tone said "no." The
audience began laughing but Miss Anthony told them not to
laugh at the poor man. She sympathized with him, because she
knew what it was to be laughed at for a good many years. With
the singing of the doxology the session adjourned.
— *NWSA Convention, 1886*

*Men were frequent guests at the suffrage conventions, but while Lucy
Stone and others welcomed them as officers of their American Woman Suffrage Association, Anthony did not believe they should hold such positions at
the National.*

As to *men* on our platform—We are always but too glad to
welcome any & all who really have power to help us— . . . *Our
only* difference from the American Society is that *they place men*
in *official positions*—and we do *not*—and it *is* that *little point* of
difference that makes *our Society* a live one—and *theirs* a *dead
one*—in comparison—for men *cannot make Women's* disfranchisement *hurt* them—*as it hurts us*—hence cannot be our guides
& ultimate appeals—as to principles & policies of action— — . . .
For we have invited Statesmen & Ministers of high repute over &
over for these 20 years—and it is only here & there that *one* of
them has or will venture his reputation along side the grandest
women in the grandest movement of the ages—
— *Letter, 1880*

Women are too easily made tools of by the *men who* come into
our movement—& every man of them wants to direct—wants all
of us women to follow his lead—
— *Letter, 1870*

*Among the acceptable men was Henry Blackwell, who called himself
"a true friend of this reform." His position was never in doubt.*

The interests of the sexes are inseparably connected, and in the
elevation of one lies the salvation of the other. . . . I know of but
few movements in history which have gone on successfully without the aid of woman. One of these is war—the work of human
slaughter. Another has been the digging of gold in California. I

have yet to learn what advantages the world has derived from either.
—*Henry Blackwell, Speech, 1853*

In 1885 Senator Thomas W. Palmer of Michigan made a speech on the floor in favor of the proposed woman suffrage amendment. Anthony and her friends called it "a masterly argument which has not been surpassed in the fifteen years that have since elapsed." They had the speech reprinted in huge numbers, and in 1889 Anthony herself sent 50,000 copies—under the senator's free franking privileges—to voters in South Dakota, where a campaign for the vote was in process. Although the campaign lost, Senator Palmer's speech remained a high-water mark in suffrage history.

Like life insurance and the man who carried the first umbrella, the inception of this movement was greeted with derision. Born of an apparently hopeless revolt against unjust discrimination, unequal statutes, and cruel constructions of courts, it has pressed on and over ridicule, malice, indifference and conservatism, until it stands in the gray dawn before the most powerful legislative body on earth and challenges final consideration.

The laws which degraded our wives have been everywhere repealed or modified, and our children may now be born of free women. Our sisters have been recognized as having brains as well as hearts, and as being capable of transacting their own business affairs. New avenues of self-support have been found and profitably entered upon, and the doors of our colleges have ceased to creak their dismay at the approach of women. Twelve states have extended limited suffrage through their Legislatures, and three Territories admit all citizens of suitable age to the ballot-box, while from no single locality in which it has been tried comes any word but that of satisfaction concerning the experiment....

In considering the objections to this extension of the suffrage we are fortunate in finding them grouped in the adverse report of the minority of your committee, and also in confidently assuming, from the acknowledged ability and evident earnestness of the distinguished Senators who prepared it, that all is contained therein in the way of argument or protest which is left to the opponents of this reform after thirty-seven years of discussion. I wish that every Senator would examine this report and note how many of its reasonings are self-refuting and how few even seem to warrant further antagonism.

They cite the physical superiority of man, but offer no amendment to increase the voting power of a Sullivan or to disfranchise the halt, the lame, the blind or the sick. They regard the manly head of the family as its only proper representative, but would not exclude the adult bachelor sons. They urge disability to perform military service as fatal to full citizenship, but would hardly consent to resign their own rights because they have passed the age of conscription; or to question those of Quakers, who will not fight, or of professional men and civic officials, who, like mothers, are regarded as of more use to the State at home.

They are dismayed by a vision of women in attendance at caucuses at late hours of the night, but doubtless enjoy their presence at balls and entertainments until the early dawn. They deprecate the appearance of women at political meetings, but in my State women have attended such meetings for years upon the earnest solicitation of those in charge, and the influence of their presence has been good. Eloquent women are employed by State committees of all parties to canvass in their interests and are highly valued and respected . . .

They object that many women do not desire the suffrage and that some would not exercise it. It is probably true, as often claimed, that many slaves did not desire emancipation in 1863— and there are men in most communities who do not vote, but we hear of no freedmen to-day who asks re-enslavement, and no proposition is offered to disfranchise all men because some neglect their duty. . . .

I share no fears of the degradation of women by the ballot. I believe rather that it will elevate men. I believe the tone of our politics will be higher, that our caucuses will be more jealously guarded and our conventions more orderly and decorous. I believe the polls will be freed from the vulgarity and coarseness which now too often surround them, and that the polling booths, instead of being in the least attractive parts of a ward or town, will be in the most attractive; instead of being in stables, will be in parlors. I believe the character of candidates will be more closely scrutinized and that better officers will be chosen to make and administer the laws. I believe that the casting of the ballot will be invested with a seriousness—I had almost said a sanctity—second only to a religious observance. . . .

. . . Women have exercised the highest civil powers in all ages of the world—from Zenobia to Victoria—and have exhibited statecraft and military capacity of high degree without detracting from their graces as women or their virtues as mothers . . .

Mr. President, I do not ask the submission of this amendment, nor shall I urge its adoption, because it is desired by a portion of the American women, although in intelligence, property and numbers that portion would seem to have every requisite for the enforcement of their demands; neither are we bound to give undue regard to the timidity and hesitation of that possibly larger portion who shrink from additional responsibilities; but I ask and shall urge it because the nation has need of the co-operation of women in all directions. . . .

—*Senator Palmer, Speech in Senate, 1885*

Senator Palmer shared two of Susan B. Anthony's main arguments: that if women were voters they would purify government and in the process make things better for men, too. Anthony always tried to cast the appeal to men in their own interest.

I think one of the first rights a man has is to be well born, and that means to have a good mother as well as a good father. The next right is to have an intelligent companion in his sister. I think he has a right to find in the rest of womankind his peers—women that he can talk to intelligently and not descend to small talk to meet their capacity. I think a man has a right to a wife—a full-fledged woman, not a pet, not a canary bird, not a hothouse plant. Of course, you would not expect anything now from me but to tell you how to get that kind of woman. You California men have the privilege of taking the first step toward bringing to California a really good mother, wife, friend and sister, and that is by going to the ballot box in November, 1896, and striking from the statute that odious adjective "male."

—*Speech, 1895*

A True Gentleman

Susan B. Anthony once received a message from the governor of Wyoming, the first state to grant women full suffrage and thus full equality. The governor was announcing the birth of a child. Anthony sent back her congratulations, adding, "You don't say whether it is a boy or a girl." The governor proved his sympathy with The Cause: "No matter which. We are in Wyoming."

14. **S I S T E R H O O D   I S**
P O W E R F U L

*I*t is a most unusual group photograph. There sits Susan B. Anthony
at her desk, surrounded by her closest friends: Lucretia Mott, top center;
Anna Howard Shaw, just below; Susan's younger sister Mary, two rows
down; and in the spot of honor, front and center, Elizabeth Cady Stanton.
What makes the picture unusual is that the friends are all photographs,
too — hung, placed or perched about her workspace with the care and concern that most people lavish on members of their family.

And that's the point. The women in Susan B. Anthony's life were her
family. She revered the leadership of Lucretia Mott and the legacy of Mary
Wollstonecraft. She wore a ring from pioneering physician Dr. Clemence
Lozier and a dress from Mormon women in Utah. She gazed "in silent, reverential awe" at sculptor Harriet Hosmer's marbles and drew inspiration
from Elizabeth Barrett Browning's poetry. She was befriended by the rich
and defended the poor. She traveled, worked, commiserated, plotted,
planned, and revolutionized with her female friends, transforming the
world with such reformers-in-arms as Lucy Stone, Paulina Wright Davis,
Amelia Bloomer, and Antoinette Brown Blackwell.

Some of them tried to be genuine family. After Lucy Stone married

Henry Blackwell and became in-laws with Antoinette Brown, who had married Henry's brother, Stone wrote Anthony:

I wish he had another brother for you Susan. Would we not have a grand household then?

There was a special place in Anthony's heart for her younger colleagues—a rotating cadre of admiring workers whom she trained, then depended upon, to carry on the job. Known as "Susan's Girls," they were allowed to call her "Aunt Susan" and included such future leaders as Carrie Chapman Catt and the Reverend Anna Howard Shaw, both of whom would succeed Anthony as president of the suffrage association. Her real nieces were even more special: among them her brother Jacob Merritt's daughter, Lucy E. Anthony (who would devote her own life to The Cause), and Susie B. Anthony, her brother Daniel's daughter. It was one of the great tragedies of Susan B. Anthony's life that in 1889 her beloved namesake drowned in an ice-skating accident at the age of sixteen. She was so stunned by the loss of the bright young woman that even the minister took note of the normally undemonstrative leader at Susie B.'s funeral: "As a mother's hopes and ambitions and expectations are bound up in a child of especial promise, so Miss Anthony was waiting for her heart longing to be realized in Susie. . . . A mutual bond, a mutual taste, a mutual sympathy held them as one in loving hands."

But you did not have to be related to Susan B. Anthony to be close to her. Indeed, with all her female friends and "nieces" she enjoyed both an emotional and physical intimacy that is hard to define a century later. They shared passions, convictions, and, often as not, beds. The letters are punctuated with casual references to grown women, married and single, literally sleeping—or staying up all night talking—in each others' beds, apparently a common practice. And they corresponded in the florid language we tend to identify with romance: "Dearest Susan," writes Lucy Stone, and Anthony responds, "My dear . . . Lovingly yours." Anna Dickinson, the renowned public lecturer who captivated audiences with her fiery pro-Union speeches during the Civil War, inspired some of Anthony's most ecstatic outbursts: "Dicky darling Anna" or "My Dear Chicky Dicky Darling . . . I wish this tired hand could grasp yours this very minute."

In a celebrated analysis, historian Carroll Smith-Rosenberg points out that such relationships were common in the nineteenth century—an age that may have tolerated close female friendships far better than our own. The women bonded together out of common needs and understanding. "They valued one another," she writes. "Women, who had little status or power in the larger world of male concerns, possessed status and power in the lives of other women."

For Anthony, the first among equals was Elizabeth Cady Stanton. They became the indivisible odd couple of the American women's rights movement: Stanton, the short, stout mother of seven, with a quick wit and facile pen; Anthony, the tall, slim spinster who tended toward the serious and agonized over setting words on paper. But underneath Stanton's white curls and Anthony's gray bun functioned two brains in search of one goal: women's rights—obtainable only through the vote. For more than half a century they led the charge together, sustaining an enviably fulfilling relationship that survived vast distances and occasional strains but never lessened in intensity. Anthony called Stanton "my oldest and longest tried woman friend."

When they first met in 1851 on a street corner near Stanton's home in Seneca Falls, New York, Anthony was thirty-one. Stanton, thirty-five, was immediately captivated.

There she stood with her good earnest face and genial smile, dressed in gray silk, hat and all the same color, relieved with pale blue ribbons, the perfection of neatness and sobriety. I liked her thoroughly.

Already a veteran of the groundbreaking women's rights convention at Seneca Falls, Stanton crafted most of the early oratory as their work fused into one revolutionary product. Even Stanton's children remembered the customary scene in their parlor: Mother writing a speech on the dining room table while Susan paced the room spouting ideas. Anthony spent so much time with the family (often caring for the offspring to free up Mom to write) that Stanton occasionally called them "our" children. One of her sons, Gerrit ("Gat"), so cherished the memory of their collaboration, he later decorated the wall above his living room sofa with matching lithographs of his mother and her best friend, "looking earnestly at each other. Gat says it reminds him of the time when we used to sit opposite each other and write, write, write calls, petitions, appeals, resolutions, speeches, letters, and newspaper articles."

But while Stanton may have led the way into feminism, Anthony met the challenge herself brilliantly, ultimately writing her own speeches, formulating her own strategy, and more often than not taking charge of Stanton herself. "I am willing to do the appointed work at Albany," Stanton wrote in 1860, acquiescing to yet another of Anthony's urgent appeals. "If Napoleon says cross the Alps, they are crossed." In her autobiography, Stan-

ton described Anthony as the missionary who fired up her own rebellious fervor:

> Thus, whenever I saw that stately Quaker girl coming across my lawn, I knew that some happy convocation of the sons of Adam were to be set by the ears, by one of our appeals or resolutions. . . . We never met without issuing a pronunciamento on some question. In thought and sympathy we were one, and in the division of labor we exactly complemented one another. In writing we did better work than either could do alone. While she is slow and analytical in composition, I am rapid and synthetic. I am the better writer, she the better critic. She supplied the facts and statistics, I the philosophy and rhetoric, and together, we made arguments that have stood unshaken through the storms of long years; arguments that no one has answered.

Henry Stanton, Elizabeth's husband, summarized the team: "You stir up Susan, and she stirs the world."

They had their disagreements, of course, and the two of them also quarreled with other women. The most famous dispute resulted in a split in the movement for two decades. But in the end Anthony and Stanton always made up, and Anthony, who figured out that sisterhood was more powerful when they all worked together, urged her reluctant colleagues to put aside their differences. Their reunification as a large organization encompassing all shades of feminism created a more potent force for the vote — foreshadowing the contemporary women's movement as it tries to embrace, rather than alienate, different points of view.

There is and was no other choice. Once, after a falling out, Elizabeth Cady Stanton teasingly asked Anthony if she wanted "a divorce" from her, then asserted stubbornly, "I shall not allow any such proceedings. I consider our relation for life so make the best of it."

———

To secure "equality of rights, privileges and opportunities" for the women of the world I know of no way but . . . to all join hands, hearts and heads in the demand for the right to vote. . . . But women do *scatter so much*. It seems impossible for all to *unite* to get *one thing* at the *same time* when *all* want it. Take, for instance, the states now. One state is working to get School Suffrage, another Presidential Suffrage, another Municipal Suffrage, another Whiskey Suffrage, etc; and a great many more people are working to secure various things which can never be had until women get the right to vote for them. Women are so like the negroes; that is, the minute one of their own number gets, by perseverance and work elevated, to a little higher position than themselves. Look at the war, for instance, that is waged upon *Clara Barton*. I do not believe there is any other motive with women than a desire to *get her place* and the *honors* she has showered upon her. Then look at Booker T. Washington; negroes are fighting him; it is mainly because they are jealous of his prominence.

But all this does not discourage me; we shall have simply to work on until we are enfranchised, and then work for years after that till we grow into a larger and broader nature.
—*Letter, 1903*

Susan B. Anthony's defense of Clara Barton—under siege for management problems at the Red Cross—was typical of her loyalty to her female buddies. After all, Barton was a pal whose company she truly enjoyed. From her winter headquarters in Washington, D.C., she dropped Barton a line:

Dear Clara Barton
Can you not come round and let us talk over the world in general & the women in Particular—say on Monday evening Dec. 16th . . .
—*Letter, 1889*

The time is past—when the mass of the suffrage women will be compromised by any one person's peculiarities!! We number over 10,000 women—& each one has opinions & rights &c—And we can only hold them together to work for the ballot—by letting alone—their whims & prejudices on other subjects!!
—*Letter, 1897*

No *one* woman in these new days—when there are thousands—when there used to be a hundred . . . can speak for all—there must be a willingness to concede—on the part of each—a little something to the others—who are equally true & earnest with the *each*—But I know you see!! 25 & 20 years ago—Each woman went on her own hook—without thought of any other one's caring what she said or did!! While now—each *one* who

speaks or writes or acts—there is a large constituency of thinking, intelligent, earnest women who feel themselves honored or dis-graced—as the *one's* words or actions—may be judged good or bad!!—strong or weak—discreet or reckless—hence *mutual* un-derstandings & agreements—as the public utterances and actions are vastly important to-day—as never before—
—*Letter, 1885*

We women are all united on one subject and that is the only question which we try to pass upon. In order to belong to our as-sociation, a woman has got to answer in the affirmative this ques-tion: "Do you believe in the perfect equality of women?" No other question is asked of her. Men have tried to involve us in other questions, but we refuse to be involved. We hold different beliefs on marriage, on divorce; we have all kinds of political and religious beliefs in our association; we differ widely on the solu-tion of the liquor problem, but we all agree in working for perfect equality for women.
—*Interview, 1905*

For all her exhortations, Anthony also wanted it clear that women didn't have to leave the home to work for The Cause.

It is not necessary for you to be a public speaker or to go on the platform. Every woman in her own home can be a teacher of this great principle of equality. She can instruct her husband and her children in the ways of justice toward all. But for the good and true women in all the homes, but for the loyalty of these home women, who never speak in public, but who in a quiet way are teaching this gospel in season and out of season, we who stand at the front, could never have stood here. We would have had no constituency but for this silent, magnificent army of women in the homes throughout the nation.
—*Speech, 1897*

Every woman presiding over her table in the homes where I have been has helped to sustain me. It isn't necessary for all to make sacrifices and go to the front. I want them to realize how they have supported and helped me in their own homes.
—*Speech, 1890*

One of Anthony's favorite "nieces" was Rachel Foster, who served as an indispensable aide in suffrage business for many years. But in 1887 their relationship was critically threatened when Rachel, almost thirty and still single, boldly adopted an infant girl. It is interesting to note that Anthony's concern was not about the propriety of single motherhood, but about the baby's impact on Rachel's ability to work! (Rachel would marry the following year and bear two more children.) This letter to the child, Miriam Alice, reflects Anthony's apprehension of, and grudging welcome to, the next generation of Susan's Girls.

Dear Miriam Alice

It is doubtful whether Aunt Susan welcomes your little ladyship to the home of 748 North 19th Str Phila.—!—she is thinking whether you will not divert all the love of the *Foster* Mama's from the greatest work for the emancipation of *woman*—to the little business of caring for the material & moral wants of the one wee one—your little self—

So my dear—if you would wish Aunt Susan's best will—so deport yourself as to help the junior Aunties to be more—to do more—for the *woman general* than ever before you came to them—

So shall it be with
your *Great* Aunt
Susan B. Anthony

—*Letter, 1887*

Anna Dickinson and Susan B. Anthony communicated in their own language. "The sunniest of sunny mornings to you, how are you today?" Dickinson wrote. "I want to see you very much indeed, to hold your hand in mine, to hear your voice, in a word, I want you . . ." "Dear Chick a dee dee," Anthony responded, later eager to give her "one awful long squeeze."

My Dear Chicky Dicky Darling

. . . I wish this tired hand could *grasp* yours this very minute— Well my dear child, doesn't the world move—and don't we all move with it—

I have a world full of things to say—but not a minute to begin—only this to tell you I still love you and believe in you— but this early day want to *engage you* not to *marry a man*—but to speak at our Equal Rights Anniversary next May the 12th or 13th. . . .

Lovingly, lastingly yours
SB Anthony

—*Letter, 1868*

Dear Dicky Darling

... Now when are you coming to New York—Do let it be soon—then do let me see the child—I have *plain quarters*—at 44 Bond St.—*double bed*—and big enough & good enough to take you *in*—So come & see me—or let me know & I'll meet you at Depot—Hotel or any place you shall say—only let me see you—I do so long for the scolding & pinched ears & every thing I know awaits me—

— *Letter, 1868*

While it may appear that Anthony had truly lost her head over the young Dickinson (she was more than twenty years Anthony's junior), Anthony described her affection as "real mother yearnings." And despite a long hiatus, during which Anna seems to have had mental (and money) problems, Anthony reiterated her feelings at the end of Dickinson's troubled life.

My Darling Anna

I'm awfully glad to know you still live—and that I have a chance to tell you that my *motherly love*—my elderly sister's love—has never abated for my *first Anna*. I have had several lovely *Anna* girls—"nieces," they call themselves now-a-day— since my *first Anna*—but none of them—ever has or ever can fill the niche in my heart that you did—my dear.

— *Letter, 1895*

Curiously, for all their closeness, when writing letters Anthony always addressed her closest friend as "Mrs. Stanton." That never mitigated their confidences.

Dear Mrs. Stanton

How I do long to be with you this very minute—to have one look into your very soul & one sound of your soul stirring voice—

I did hope to call on you before embarking on this Western voyage—but ... opportunity came not— ... That Convention has been a heavy burden to me, the last two months—nothing looking promising—nobody seemed to feel any personal responsibility and, *alone,*—feeling utterly incompetent I go forward, unless sure of reliable & effective speakers to sustain the Con.; I could but grope in the dark—but I now hope Lucy will say *amen* to my proposition—

... Mrs. Stanton, I have *very weak* moments—and long to lay my weary head somewhere and nestle my full soul close to that of another in full sympathy—I sometimes fear that *I too* shall faint by the wayside—and drop out of the ranks of the faithful few—

There is so much, amid all that is so hopeful, to discourage & dishearten—and I feel *alone.* Still to know I am *not alone,* but that all the true & the good souls, both in & out of the body, keep me company, and that the good Father more than all is ever a host in every good effort—

But you will see that this is one of my tired moments—so no more, but to the Cause thereof. . . .

—*Letter, 1857*

Like all friendships, theirs was tested and tempted by meaner spirits. When they were on the road together, it was Anthony who generally wound up making the arrangements, renting the hall, and generating the publicity while Stanton napped. Little wonder that Stanton, the more instinctive speaker with the flair for the right phrase, tended to get better press at first. And little wonder, too, that when Anthony left her collaborator for a solo speaking tour in the Pacific Northwest in 1871, she felt somewhat liberated:

I miss Mrs. Stanton, still I can not but enjoy the feeling that the people call on *me,* and the fact that I have an opportunity to sharpen my wits a little by answering questions and doing the chatting, instead of merely sitting a lay figure and listening to the brilliant scintillations as they emanate from her never-exhausted magazine. There is no alternative—whoever goes into a parlor or before an audience with that woman does it at the cost of a fearful overshadowing, a price which I have paid for the last ten years, and that cheerfully, because I felt that our cause was most profited by her being seen and heard, and my best work was making the way clear for her.

—*Letter, 1871*

At her seventieth birthday celebration, Anthony sat through a slew of effusive tributes, capped by one from Stanton, who captured their unique camaraderie with characteristic good humor:

If there is one part of my life that gives me more satisfaction than any other, it is my friendship of forty years' standing with Susan B. Anthony. Her heroism, faithfulness and conscientious devotion to what she thinks her duty has been a constant stimulus to me to thought and action. Ours has been indeed a friendship of hard work and self-denial. . . . *Sub rosa,* dear friends, I have had

no peace for forty years. . . . She has kept me on the war-path at
the point of the bayonet, so long that I have often wished my un-
tiring coadjutor might, like Elijah, be translated, a few years before I was summoned, that I might spend the sunset of my life in
some quiet chimney corner, and lay superfluous on the stage no
longer.
— *Speech by Elizabeth Cady Stanton, 1890*

Anthony responded in kind.

The one thought I wish to express is how little my friend and I
could accomplish alone. What she has said is true; I have been a
thorn in her side, and in that of her family, too, I fear. Mr. Stanton
was never jealous of any one but Susan, and I think my going to
that home many times robbed the children of their rights. But I
used to take their little wagon and draw them round the garden
while Mrs. Stanton wrote speeches, resolutions, petitions, etc.,
and I never expect to know any joy in this world equal to that of
going up and down, getting good editorials written, engaging
halls and advertising Mrs. Stanton's speeches. After that is
through with, I don't expect any more joy. If I have ever had any
inspiration she has given it to me. I want you to understand that I
never could have done the work I have if I had not had that
woman at my right hand.
— *Remarks, 1890*

*It amused — and sometimes frustrated — Anthony that so many people
confused her with Stanton.*

My Dear Mrs. Stanton
I enclose a letter from a dear soul who has cherished your
lovely curls & loving words all these years—as belonging to me—
It is too funny the way peoples [*sic*] memories do carry you and
me—one for the other & both as one.
— *Letter, 1896*

*Anthony was well aware that her dear friend Mrs. Stanton was aging
at a swift and uncomfortable rate. Always plump, she gained even more
weight as she grew older and finally went blind. A letter to Stanton's cousin
characteristically blended concern for her health with dedication to The
Cause:*

It is too cruel that such mental powers must be hampered with such a *clumsy body*. If we could only give her elasticity of limbs—and locomotive powers—but we must be thankful that we still have her marvelous *dear powers* to push along our march for the redemption of the race from *sex slavery*!!

—*Letter, 1892*

In 1902, a few weeks before Stanton's eighty-seventh birthday, Anthony wrote another letter to her dear old friend. Her reference to the possibility of equality in heaven— "the next sphere of existence"— is particularly touching when you realize this was the last letter Anthony would ever write her.

My Dear Mrs. Stanton:—

I shall indeed be happy to spend with you the day on which you round out your four score and seven . . . It is fifty-one years since first we met, and we have been busy through every one of them, stirring up the world to recognize the rights of women. The older we grow, the more keenly we feel the humiliation of disfranchisement, and the more vividly we realize its disadvantages in every department of life, and most of all in the labor market.

We little dreamed when we began this contest, optimistic with the hope and buoyancy of youth, that half a century later we would be compelled to leave the finish of the battle to another generation of women. . . . These strong young women will take our place and complete our work. There is an army of them, where we were but a handful . . .

And we, dear old friend, shall move on the next sphere of existence—higher and larger, we cannot fail to believe, and one where women will not be placed in an inferior position, but will be welcomed on a plane of perfect intellectual and spiritual equality.

Ever lovingly yours,

Susan B. Anthony

—*Letter, 1902*

Just a few days later, on October 26, 1902, Anthony received a stark telegram from one of Stanton's daughters: "Mother passed away today." It was an unimaginable loss to the eighty-two-year-old Anthony. For several hours that Sunday she sat out her grief in shocked silence. Her secretary de-

scribed the heartbreaking aftermath of a life in the public eye: "To see poor Miss A. questioned over and over about her early times with her dead friend and climbing up to the attic to find a picture for the reporter, with her hands shaking so that she could hardly lift the cards, was a piteous thing." A New York newspaper headline acknowledged their unique friendship with the headline ANTHONY LEFT BEHIND. *The next day she boarded the express train to New York for the funeral — a private family event, with a poignant salute to their uncommon union: at the head of Elizabeth Cady Stanton's flower-draped coffin rested a photograph of Susan B. Anthony.*

Well, it is an awful hush—it seems impossible—that the voice is hushed—that I have loved to hear for fifty years—longed to get her opinion of things—before I knew exactly where I stood—It is all at sea—but the Laws of Nature are still going on—with no shadow or turning—What a world it is—it goes right on & on— no matter who lives or who dies!! . . . I can think of nothing—
—*Letter, 1902*

Dear me! how lonesome I do feel, not to have any Mrs. Stanton to write to, to think of going to see, and talking to! It was a great going out of my life when she went, but she is gone not to return and we can only follow, where? and Echo answers, where?
—*Letter, 1903*

The Dinner Party

Lucretia Mott, the wise Quaker preacher and abolitionist who was both mentor and close friend to Susan B. Anthony, taught her more than just women's rights. A description of Mott's method of entertaining gives a rare insight into the Superwomen of the nineteenth century. In 1854, at the end of one vibrant dinner party in Mott's Philadelphia home, with abolitionist William Lloyd Garrison on her left and Anthony on her right, Mott had a cedar tub of hot water brought to the table. While the sparkling conversation on slavery, suffrage, and other affairs of state continued, she washed the crystal, silver, and fine china, then handed them to Anthony to dry with a snowy white towel.

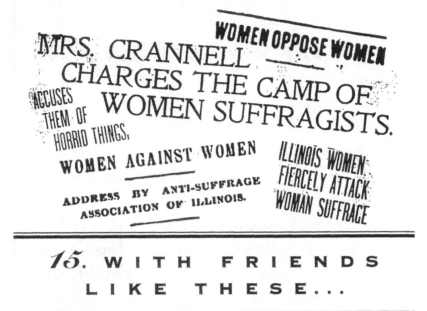

MRS. CRANNELL
CHARGES THE CAMP OF
WOMEN SUFFRAGISTS.

WOMEN OPPOSE WOMEN

ACCUSES
THEM OF
HORRID THINGS,

WOMEN AGAINST WOMEN

ADDRESS BY ANTI-SUFFRAGE
ASSOCIATION OF ILLINOIS.

ILLINOIS WOMEN
FIERCELY ATTACK
WOMAN SUFFRAGE

15. WITH FRIENDS
LIKE THESE...

*I*n the autumn of *1898, a woman identified only as Mrs. W.
Winslow Crannell was interviewed in the San Francisco* Bulletin. *She
was described as "a gracious, dark-haired, dark-eyed, youthful-looking ma-
tron, who reads her own poetry in a low, pleasant voice . . . tall, plump,
fashionably dressed, with diamonds in her ears, a number of pretty rings on
her fingers, and on her breast the order of the Daughters of the American
Revolution . . ." Her title was chairman of the executive committee of the
Anti-Suffrage Association of Albany, New York. Protesting a line of criticism that might sound familiar to modern antifeminists, Crannell told the
reporter that the publicity associated with her antisuffrage work had become very disagreeable.*

"What is the disagreeable side?" I asked.

Mrs. Crannell laughed aloud.

"Oh, you know," she said, "they accuse me of being the newest
of the new women!"

"They?"

"The leaders of the Woman Suffragists, you know. They say
that I leave my husband and my children to go out to lecture

other women upon their duty to stay at home and take care of their families! . . ."

"And what is your answer to the indictment?" I asked.

"Why, this. That my youngest son is just about to enter college, and the two older ones, one of whom is a newspaper man in New York, are able to take care of themselves. But you can understand that the sort of personal criticism is the very thing which deters my associates from doing this work. . . . They accuse me of being sent out by the brewers, by the saloon-keepers. They declare that I am working for pay—which is not true. . . ."

"And Susan B. Anthony?"

"O!" Mrs. Crannell's pleasant voice was distinctly disapproving. "I do not like Miss Anthony. She believes that women should not marry, and that if women do marry they should not bear children."

More than four decades after she had entered the fray, Susan B. Anthony was still being shunned as an old maid—this time, by other women. Crannell's antisuffrage philosophy continued:

Nature puts certain duties upon us women, from which man cannot relieve us. If we fulfill these duties there is no possibility of taking on extra responsibilities of his. It is with us as with the lower animals. Darwin tells us that the wild horses will form a hollow square in which the mares and their colts are placed in crossing a plain, or in facing danger.

Of course, you understand, that I do not consider the responsibility of voting restricted to going to the polls once in two or four years to deposit a ballot. If women are to vote they should go to the caucuses and primaries. And women are doing too much now as it is. . . .

[A]bove all we are opposed to suffrage because we fear that it may ruin the home. Women are emotional creatures. If their vote is not merely a duplicate of their husband's or father's or brother's, there will be terrible dissension in the family. . . .

No, that "taxation without representation" cry is altogether absurd.

The next day, one of the women running the California amendment campaign told the reporter that Mrs. Crannell would "serve only to help us."

It is typical of Susan B. Anthony's boundless curiosity—and toler-
ance—that the article about Mrs. Crannell, including the inaccurate refer-
ence to Anthony's beliefs about marriage, was carefully clipped out and
pasted into the Anthony scrapbooks. She was both appalled and fascinated
by the women who didn't want the vote—women who, according to her
History of Woman Suffrage, *"have dwelt since they were born in well-*
feathered nests and have never needed to do anything but open their soft
beaks for the choicest little grubs to be dropped into them." To her eternal
frustration, most women did not want the right to vote, and their opposi-
tion—or at best, apathy—was a major obstacle in the path of the suffrag-
ists. The organization of the "antis" reached such proportions that an 1897
article in the New York Times *asked, "Do Women Hate Women?" The*
answer was No.

Susan B. Anthony sometimes made excuses for these women, claiming
their husbands had put them up to it. She always tried to convert them,
turning on her most politic charm. But she was simply unable to compre-
hend why anyone would opt for protecting the status quo when social
change was so much more desirable. And she was forever baffled that they
could view her dream of political equality—to which she'd devoted her en-
tire life—as "the burden of the ballot."

We feel that our present duties fill up the whole of our time
and abilities, and that they are such as none but ourselves can perform. . . . Our fathers and brothers love us. Our husbands are our
choice and are one with us. Our sons are what we make them. We
are content that they represent us in the corn field, the battle-
field, at the ballot-box, and the jury box, and we them in the
church, in the school-room, at the fireside, and at the cradle. Believing our representation even at the ballot-box to be thus more
full and impartial than it could possibly be were all women allowed to vote, we do therefore respectfully protest against legislation to establish woman's suffrage in Ohio.
— *1870 protest by 100 women of Lorain County, Ohio*

I never could see how it was that an old maid who had neglected to fill her office in society for which God in his providence

had wisely created her, should essay to lecture married women upon child-bearing, maternity and other kindred topics, when, as a Miss, who was never married, she is supposed to be innocently ignorant of all such matters.
—*A woman who met Anthony in Oregon, 1871*

[Susan B. Anthony is] a shrewish old mischief-maker who, having failed to secure a husband herself, is tramping the continent to make her more fortunate sisters miserable by creating dissensions in their households.
—*Letter to the Editor, from "A Wife and Mother," Victoria, B.C., 1871*

A large majority of American women would regard the gift of the ballot, not as a privilege conferred but as an act of oppression, forcing them to assume responsibilities belonging to a man, for which they are not and cannot be qualified; and consequently, withdrawing attention and interest from the distinctive and more important duties of their sex.
—*Catharine Beecher, 1871*

To the Congress of the United States, Protesting against an Extension of Woman Suffrage:
We, the undersigned, do hereby appeal to your honorable body, and desire respectfully to enter our protest against an extension of suffrage to women; and in the firm belief that our petition represents the sober convictions of the majority of the women of the country.
Although we shrink from the notoriety of the public eye, yet we are too deeply and painfully impressed by the grave perils which threaten our peace and happiness in these proposed changes in our civil and political rights, longer to remain silent.
Because holy scripture inculcates a different, and for us higher sphere, apart from public life,
Because, as women, we find a full measure of duties, cares and responsibilities devolving upon us, and we are therefore unwilling to bear other and heavier burdens, and those unsuited to our physical organization,
Because we hold that an extension of suffrage would be adverse to the interests of the working-women of the country, with whom we heartily sympathize,
Because these changes must introduce a fruitful element of discord in the existing marriage relation, which would tend to the

infinite detriment of children, and increase the already alarming prevalence of divorce throughout the land,

Because no general law, affecting the condition of all women should be framed to meet exceptional discontent,

For these, and many more reasons, do we beg of your wisdom that no law extending suffrage to women may be passed, as the passage of such a law would be fraught with danger so grave to the general order of the country. . . .
— *Presentation to Congress by Catharine Beecher, the wives of*
General William Tecumseh Sherman, Admiral John A. Dahlgren,
and 1,000 other women, 1871

Why has the male sex alone made the laws? Because law, with whatever majesty we may invest it, is will which, to give it effect, must be backed by force; and the force of the community is male. That the tendency of a state governed by women would be to arbitrary and sentimental legislation can hardly be doubted. The women of France some years ago would probably have voted a war for the support of the temporal power of the Pope. The women of England might have voted intervention in favor of the Queen of Naples. In both cases the men would have refused to march or act, and government would have succumbed. . . .

If women were a class without votes, their class interests might suffer. But they are not a class, but a sex. What special interest of women can be named which is in danger of suffering at the hands of a legislature composed of their husbands, sons, and brothers? Not only are the lives, liberties, and properties of American women secure, but they are more secure, if anything, than those of the men. . . .

By their own concession, it is not woman as a sex, but a clamorous minority of women whom they represent.
— The Remonstrance, *antisuffrage publication, special South*
Dakota Edition, 1890
A handwritten note accompanying this clip in Susan B. Anthony's scrapbook reads, "Large mail sacks of this sheet were sent to [South Dakota Senator John A.] Mitchell & a copy placed in seat [sic] of the Republican convention hall & scattered . . ."

We assert that women today are so protected by laws made by men, that they have nothing more to ask for legally. . . . To imagine a government unbacked by the physical power to enforce its laws, is to imagine an anomaly, or something which must of necessity develop into anarchy.

—*Mrs. Winslow Crannell, Address to the Committee for the Republican National Convention, 1896*

Women vote! Never! Have we not made mistakes enough in the political, economic and religious administration of affairs in this country of late without adding on this most pitiful confusion, this vulgar mistake, this arrant folly . . . ?

I am not fit to vote myself because I cannot regard questions dispassionately, because I cannot get over the intense revolt within myself against what seems the unsexing influence of such a proceeding. I cannot give up what is a woman's proudest privilege to unselfishly advise men as to what is the moral, the spiritual, the highest reason for their vote. Had I a vote I could be bought and sold. I fear at least it would be bargained for, and I should be much greater than most men if I had not my price. . . .

Imagine the contradictory elements it would involve.

Respect, tenderness, chivalry from the man toward the woman must cease to exist. She is no longer his wife, the mother of his children, the creature he keeps in the dearest corner of his heart. She is his opponent, his antagonist, the democrat when he is a republican; the mugwump, or to use the old and now forgotten terms, the barn burner when he is a silver gray. Will this tend to the pleasures of the domestic fireside? Not at all; let the man enjoy alone the fascinations of the Silver bill or the amenities of the tariff. Women cannot understand them and are much better off than if they could. What woman wishes to handle the Sugar Trust? All that she wants of that question is two lumps to put in her tea, which the man must earn for her. . . .

Do those women wish to meet all other women? The strife and confusion would not be ended by a separation of the sexes. No class of human creatures are less apt to get along with each other than masses of women. Look at the attempted clubs—the Daughters of the Revolution, who are in perpetual states of rebellion; look at the Colonial Dames, made up of "every creature's best," and consider how long a primary or a female caucus would hold together.

No, our very virtues unfit us for the masculine duties of official and parliamentary law. . . .

The American man is the most chivalrous being in the world.

He is willing to do all the dirty work of political arrangement, and for my part he may do it, his share and mine. . . .

We have a good woman's work to do, and do not let us ask for the vote.

If we hysterically demand more than our rights I hope the chivalrous man will really refuse us the boon.
— *Mrs. M. W. W. Sherwood, 1894*

[T]he glory of womanhood has been her purity, her superiority to men in the possession of a higher moral sense and standard. Why risk this precious certainty for a doubtful good, when the superiority claimed and admitted by all is the result of protection from the temptation which this doubtful good would entail?
— *Anna Robinson Watson, 1895*

The antisuffrage women were also known as "Remonstrants," and Anthony went out of her way to be polite to them. Once she helped them gain access to congressional hearings so they might present their case. She knew their approach was far different from her own — like the time they entertained New York State legislators in low-necked dresses, with champagne suppers, flowers, and music. Anthony's biographer commented, "And the suffrage advocates hoped to offset these political methods by trudging through mud and snow with their petitions and using their scanty funds to send out literature!" Anthony expressed her own opinion on a number of occasions.

This opposition movement is not the work of women, although it has the appearance of having been started by them. There was held in Albany yesterday afternoon a meeting at which resolutions condemning our work were adopted. Listen to the names of the women who were present:

[*Miss Anthony here read a number of the names from an Albany paper*]

Do you see that they are all Mrs. John, and Mrs. George and Mrs. William this and that. There is not a woman's first name in the whole list, and I do not see a Miss, either. This goes to show that the women are simply put forward by their husbands, and that they themselves are not the real movers in the movement.
— *Interview, 1894*

All women who oppose the movement for the enfranchisement of their sex will be proud to be women who are chiefly dominated either by ignorance or selfishness or by both.

In the class of those who oppose their own freedom as a result of ignorance, there are many who pass for highly educated and intelligent women. . . . She who is not for good laws is against good laws. Her apathy and indifference render her a stumbling block in the progress of good, where she should be an active, energetic assistant. . . .

When a so-called educated woman is . . . found protesting against the enfranchisement of her sex, she will invariably be found to be a shallow and thoroughly selfish woman. There are, unhappily, millions of such women in this republic. They are usually the richer women, clothed in purple and fine linen, and who clasp their jeweled fingers complacently over silken robes, simpering, "I have all the rights I want, so long as I have my present privileges." Sometimes they are women so thoroughly trained to let men do all the thinking that they have really come to believe it to be unwomanly to think and express an opinion themselves concerning a public question. Occasionally, they conscientiously believe that it is somehow more creditable to beg a man to vote than it is to show one's appreciation of the dignity of a vote by using the ballot one's self. These are they who are more shallow than selfish.
—*Article, 1894*

Our worst enemies and the greatest hindrance to the progress of our movement are the wives of our legislators. It would be a nice thing if we could only spike these guns.
—*Speech, 1885*

They forget, too, that but for the suffrage movement they would not have had the privilege of coming before men in public to criticize and to ask that we be not given the things we pray for.
–*Interview, 1900*

But for all her anger at antisuffragists, Anthony was even more furious at the apathy among the women who were supposed to be working for the vote. Women, she believed, simply did not do enough for themselves—as if anyone could have done half what she herself did. In 1898 she tried to incite younger colleagues over pending legislation to admit Hawaii as a territory without woman suffrage:

I wonder if when I am under the sod—or cremated and floating in the air—I shall have to stir you and others up. How can you not be all on fire? . . . I really believe I shall explode if some of

you young women don't wake up—and raise your voice in protest against the impending crime of this nation upon the new islands it has clutched from other folks—Do come into the living present & work to save us from any more *barbaric male governments.*
—*Letter, 1898*

While I do not pray for anybody . . . to commit outrages, still, I do pray . . . for some terrific shock to startle the women of this nation into a self-respect which will compel them to see the abject degradation of their present position; which will force them to break their yoke of bondage, and give them faith in themselves . . . The fact is, women are in chains, and their servitude is all the more debasing because they do not realize it. O, to compel them to see and feel, and to give them the courage and conscience to speak and act for their own freedom, though they face the scorn and contempt of all the world for doing it!
—*Letter, 1870*

I have very little hope or faith in *our women rolling up an immense* list of *names* for *their own freedom*—if we wanted them to do the *Herculean task* for Negro *men*—Irish *men* or any *class* of the *superior sex*—they would all, as one earnest woman, rush to the work— . . . All I should fear would be that our *own women speakers* would not be prepared to *shout for freedom* as brilliantly as did Patrick Henry & Sam Otis of old—but for *themselves*— they seem so listless—it is hard to keep in the patience with them. If it *were* possible to rouse, *even* our *woman* suffrage women to take hold of the work of circulating a good address—a *tremendous Centennial growl* of the *women* of the United States, I should be delighted & ready to join in the work . . .
—*Letter, 1875*

[T]his great national suffrage movement that has made this immense revolution in this country . . . probably represents a smaller number of women, and especially represents a smaller amount of money to carry on its work than any organization under the shadow of the American flag. We have known how to make the noise, you see, and how to bring the whole world to our organization in spirit, if not in person. I would philosophize on the reason why. It is because women have been taught always to work for something else than their own personal freedom; and the hardest thing in the world is to organize women for

the one purpose of securing their political liberty and political equality.
—*Speech, 1893*

Oh, if I were but thirty years younger! The plans crowd upon me and everywhere I see new opportunities for pushing this work, but I can't rouse the women to take advantage of them. They are willing, but they don't know how.
—*Remarks, 1900*

It is the disheartening part of all my life work—that so very few women will work for the emancipation of their own half of the race!
—*Letter, 1894*

The Ladies

THE CHAIRMAN: What I want to know is, where do you stand with the ladies?

MISS ANTHONY: I don't care. We have been getting the ladies for fifty years; and we are after the men now. The men have the vote, and it is all nonsense to refer me back to the ladies.

THE CHAIRMAN: It seems to me that there is a decided majority of the ladies against this legislation.

MISS ANTHONY: Suppose there is! The majority of children are against public schools, but we put the children in public schools just the same.

—Congressional hearing, 1897

16. DRESSING FOR SUCCESS

*F*irst you lace up your corset—a stiff, uncomfortable, waist-cinching contrivance with ribs of whalebone. Somewhere along the line you roll on silk stockings and slip into long drawers. Then come the petticoats: layers and layers of heavy, starched cotton that stick out all the way to there. Finally, the dress itself. It might be made of silk, cotton, or wool, its bodice darted and sewn in a manner that constricts breathing and eating, its skirt grazing the tops of your side-laced shoes. Now try to walk. Or get in and out of carriages. Or cross a muddy, unpaved street. Or take to the podium night after night to spread the word about The Cause.

Little wonder that the women of the mid-1800s turned to dress reform. Their most celebrated alternative was the body-freeing outfit known as the Bloomer costume, after temperance advocate Amelia Bloomer, one of the first to show up in public in the scandalous new garb. What, you may ask, was so disgraceful about long, voluminous pantaloons topped with a knee-length skirt for additional modesty? Why the big fuss when not even an inch of ankle showed? You might as soon ask why, more than a century later, so many of us were at first forbidden to wear trousers to work during the mid-1970s. It seems to have something to do with legs. Or, perhaps, wearing the pants.

SUSAN B. ANTHONY'S RED SHAWL

"I admit that we have 'got on the pantaloons,' but I deny that putting them on is going to make us any the less womanly or any the more masculine and immodest," wrote Amelia Bloomer at the time, rebutting one of the most common criticisms. While she stuck with the liberating costume for eight years, most of the other fashion pioneers surrendered much more quickly. It was simply too embarrassing to face the snickers. Listen to Clara Barton's description of what faced another dress reformer when she put on bloomers:

The boys followed her in the streets and shouted; men stared at her. The good dames gathered in their darkened parlors and said, "Shame, the doings of this person." The turkish pantalet that rested on the instep of her neatly fitting boot came six inches—ay, possible [*sic*] eight, below the hem of her pretty gathered skirt. Indeed, "She must be very bad." The heads wagged and the tongues wagged as well.

It has been estimated that no more than a hundred or so women in the entire country dared to don bloomers. Susan B. Anthony held out until sometime late in 1852. "What think you Lucy, I am in short skirts and trousers, and have spoken in Auburn!" she wrote triumphantly to Lucy Stone that December. She had also cut off her long hair. Anthony, then thirty-two, did not yet appreciate the torment of public rejection. Within half a year one newspaper would taunt "her ungainly form rigged out in the bloomer costume," and her closest friends, having retreated to the safety of long skirts, would urge her to do the same. The pain the incident caused her—and the lengthy, passionate correspondence that followed—illustrate the sacrifices demanded by reform.

Susan B. Anthony's resilience enabled her to survive the bloomer wars with few scars. Anyway, she had a bit of a fixation on fashion that seemed to escalate as she aged. She was constantly having her dresses made and remade. And while she anticipated today's fashionable women by preferring to wear black, she acceded to the urging of her aide Rachel Foster and ordered a dark garnet velvet dress in London in 1883. It became her distinctive uniform for future state occasions, like tea at Queen Victoria's palace. Her letters home contain frequent references to her attire: "I want to tell you that with my gray silk I wore a pink bow at my throat and a narrow pink ribbon in my hair!" she writes Elizabeth Cady Stanton while on her Oregon trip. And after an exhausting two-month lecture tour in the Midwest, understandably "ragged and dirty" as she heads for the NWSA convention in Washington, D.C., she asks a good friend, "Please tell the little milliner to have a bonnet picked out for me, and get a dressmaker who will patch me together so I shall be presentable." She always was.

Still, it bothered Anthony that her clothing became a public issue. During nearly fifty years of conventions in the capital, it was a source of both amusement and irritation that reporters covering the annual meetings paid more attention to what the women wore than what they said. A friendly female journalist of the time could have been writing today:

Why cannot these earnest, patriotic women be judged by the facts of their lives, and the dignity and justice of their demands and arguments, rather than by the clothes they wear, their age or personal appearance?

But by the time Anthony chaired the 1898 convention—her third decade of leadership—she had seen such a change in the attitude towards the suffrage women, that she did not seem to mind the attention paid to her clothing, particularly her trademark red shawl. It was described by the Washington Evening Star *as "silk crepe of exquisite fineness, with long, heavy, knotted fringe. . . . Miss Anthony's red shawl has been the oriflamme of suffrage battle. She wears it with the grace of a Spanish belle." Another paper wrote, "Spring is not heralded in Washington by the approach of the robin red-breast but by the appearance of Miss Anthony's red shawl." For the grand old pioneer who was fastidious about her appearance, it was at least an indication that she—and her movement—had arrived.*

The dispute over bloomers went far beyond comfort. Anthony and her friends understood that if woman were confined to "her clothes-prison & her powers crippled by her dress" she would not be able to effect the more important reforms of the day. And they believed on another level that wearing the new outfit struck a blow for independence from the tyranny of fashion. It was an issue that affected their own wardrobes for several years and that engaged Anthony on a broader scale for decades. The following set of letters was written while Anthony was in Albany, New York, for state legislative hearings. She wore her bloomers for the entire meeting, which was more than her friend Elizabeth Cady Stanton did, as reflected in Anthony's first letter, to Lucy Stone.

Dearest Lucy: . . .

[H]er petticoats have assumed their former length, and her wardrobe cleared of every short skirt. I am sorry, but still feel a great deal of sympathy for her. She stood all alone, without Father, Mother, Sister, Brother or Husband. She imagines now that she will be *less persecuted* by them all, but I tell her that the dress is not a matter of trouble to them, her ultraisms will become more obvious to them. Every one who *drops* the dress, makes the task a harder one for the few left.

Lucy there are a thousand things I want to say to you, indeed, I have been so pressed by those who are perhaps better and wiser than myself, to lay aside the short dress, so implored for the sake of the Cause, &c, &c, that for the last ten days my heart has almost failed me, and but for my reliance on my own convictions of right and duty, must have sat down disheartened and discouraged. It is hard to stand alone, but no doubt good discipline for us. . . .

S.B.A.

— *Letter to Lucy Stone, February 9, 1854*

Dear Susan

—About the dress, it is all fudge for anybody to pretend that any Cause that deserves to live is impeded by the length of your skirt. I know from having tried through half the Union, that audiences listen, and assent, just as well to one who speaks truth in a short as in a long dress. Did you see any want of willingness on the part of the people to hear us at Syracuse, New York or Cleveland? No, no, Susan, it is all pretence that the Cause will suffer. I wish the dress gave me no other troubles, but I am annoyed to death by people who recognize me by my clothes, and when I get a seat in the cars, they will get a seat by me and *bore* me for a whole day with the stupidest stuff in the world. Much of that I should escape if I dressed like the others. Then again, when I go to a new city where are many places of interest to see, and from which I could learn much, if I go out a horde of boys pursue me and destroy all comfort. Then too the blowing up by the wind which is so provoking, when people stare and laugh! I have bought me a nice new dress; I have had it a month and it is not made because I can't decide whether to make it long or short. Not that I think any Cause will suffer by a short dress, but simply to save myself from a great deal of annoyance, and so as not to feel when I am a guest at any house, that they are mortified by my dress, if other persons happen to come in.

I was at Lucretia Mott's a few weeks ago, and her daughters took up a regular labor with me to make me abandon the dress. They said they would not go into the street with me, and when Grace Greenwood called, and others like her, I think it would have been a real relief to them if I had not been there! It gave me a most uncomfortable feeling. James and Lucretia defended me most bravely, and none of them knew that I did not feel perfectly at ease with them. In Kentucky and Missouri I was not in the least annoyed. I think I shall have me some long and some short dresses, and then wear (as circumstances vary) the one that will give me the most comfort.——

    Lucy

—*Letter from Lucy Stone, February 13, 1854*

Dearest Lucy,

Your letter of the 13th inst. caused a bursting of the floods long pent up; and I went straight to Mrs. Stanton and read her the out-gushings of your innermost. If I have done wrong to you, pardon me. Mrs. S. had said much to me on the subject. She has passed a most bitter experience in the short dress; says she now feels a mental freedom among her friends, that she has not known for the two years past. But Lucy, if *you waver,* and talk, yea, and re-solve to make a long dress, why then, who may not? If Lucy Stone, with all her reputation, her powers of eloquence, her love-liness of character, that wins all who once hear the sound of her voice, cannot bear the martyrdom of the dress, who, I ask, can? Mrs. Stanton's parting words were, "Let the hem out of your dress *to-day,* before to-morrow night's meeting." (Mrs. Rose speaks again to-morrow night, and we hope Mr. Channing will come up the river in the P.M. and be here too.) I have not obeyed Mrs. S. but have been in the streets and printing offices all the day long; had rude, vulgar men stare me out of countenance, and heard them say as I opened the doors, "There comes my Bloomer!" Oh, hated name!

[*Stanton writes to Stone on the same sheet.*]

Dear Lucy, I have just read your letter to Susan. Would that I could spend a brief time with you. I have but a moment to say, for your own sake, lay aside the shorts. I know what you suf-fer among fashionable people. Not for the sake of the cause, nor for any sake but your own, take it off. We put the dress on for greater freedom, but what is physical freedom compared

with mental bondage? By all means have the new dress made long.
— *Letter to Lucy Stone from Anthony and Stanton, February 16, 1854*

Dear Susan:

I wish to write to Lucy Stone. What is her address? I know what she has suffered and what she must suffer in consenting to bow again to the tyranny of fashion. I hope, Susan, you have let down a dress and a petticoat. The cup of ridicule is greater than you can bear. It is not wise, Susan, to use up so much energy and feeling in that way. You can put them to better use. I speak from experience.

> Your friend,
> E.C Stanton

— *Letter from Stanton, February 19, 1854*

Lucy Stone also advises her to abandon the bloomers. Anthony is in agony:

Here I am known only as one of the women who ape men— coarse, brutal men! Oh, I can not, can not bear it any longer.
— *Letter to Lucy Stone, February 1854*

Dear Susan

Your convention is over and I hope you are resting. I am sure you are worn out or you would not feel so intensely about the dress. I never shed a tear about it in my life, nor came within a thousand ages of martyrdom, on account of it. And to be compelled to travel in rain or snow, in mud and dust in a long dress would cost me more in every respect than the short dress ever did. I don't think that I can abandon the short skirts, but I will have two suits, and hope you did not misunderstand what I said of Mrs. Mott's daughters. The only reason they did not wish to go in the street with me was on account of the staring, and the impertinence, of rude people, and the notoriety and conspicuity. . . . I have not made any long dresses yet, and do not know whether I shall this spring. . . . I have this feeling women are in bondage. Their clothes are a great hindrance to their engaging in any business which will make them primarily independent, and since the soul of womanhood can never be queenly and noble as long as it must beg bread for its body, is it not better, at the expense of a great deal of annoyance even, that they whose life deserves respect and is greater than their garments, should give an example by which woman may more easily work out her own emancipation?

. . . But enough of that. It is a part of the "mint and anise and cummin," and the weightier matter of justice and truth occupy [*sic*] my thoughts more.
—*Letter from Lucy Stone, March 3, 1854*

Lucy is not this a wonderful time—and [*sic*] era long to be remembered? . . .

Lucy I have let down some of my dresses and am dragging around with long skirts. It is humiliating to my good sense of cleanliness and comfort.

In love
—*Letter to Lucy Stone, March 7, 1854*

The dress question I pass over, fully agreeing with you that woman can never compete successfully with men in the various industrial avocations, in long skirts. No one knows their bondage save the few of us who have known the freedom of short skirts.
—*Letter to Lucy Stone, March 12, 1854*

I stand alone in my opinion of the *dress* question. I can see no business avocation, in which woman, in her present dress, *can possibly* earn *equal wages* with man—& feel that it is *folly* for us to make the demand until we adapt our dress to our work—I every day, feel more keenly the terrible bondage of these long skirts—I own that the *want* of *moral courage,* caused *me* to return to them—And I can but doubt my own strength, in that it has failed me in one instance—& why should I marvel that *man* should doubt—I cannot think you meant to say aught that should *discourage* even the most feeble worker—& I thank you for having written that letter, if for no other reason, that it has roused our women from their seeming lethargy & will make them put forth new efforts to prove that they can accomplish great things in long skirts even—
—*Letter to Gerrit Smith, dress reformer, December 25, 1855*

If you are going to act wisely you want a costume to suit the occasion. If a woman goes into a factory with spindles flying, she does not want lace down on her wrists nor flounces on her dress. Yet some men talk as if the world were coming to an end because of this very natural evolution. When women are enfranchised they will cease to live merely to please men, to please conventional fancy. As long as there was no profession for women but to marry, it was about as much as any woman's life was worth to be an old maid. She had to dress and behave so as to be attractive to man, without any regard to the mere intellect. Now, just as soon as woman's influence counts at the ballot box she will have some stock in trade besides her youth and beauty; that is to say, her intellect will count at the ballot box and her judgment on every question.

—*Speech, 1895*

I felt the need of some such garments because I was obliged to be out every day in all kinds of weather, and also because I saw women ruined in health by tight lacing and the weight of their clothing; and I hoped to help establish the principle of rational dress. I found it a physical comfort but a mental crucifixion. It was an intellectual slavery; one never could get rid of thinking of herself, and the important thing is to forget self. The attention of my audience was fixed upon my clothes instead of my words. I learned the lesson then that to be successful a person must attempt but one reform. By urging two, both are injured, as the average mind can grasp and assimilate but one idea at a time. I have felt ever since that experience that if I wished my hearers to consider the suffrage question I must not present the temperance, the religious, the dress, or any other besides, but must confine myself to suffrage.

Remarks, date unknown

In 1895, with bloomers—or at least, divided skirts—far more evident and acceptable, a reporter from St. Louis devoted an entire interview to the subject of dress reform. It concluded by noting that "while Miss Anthony chatted on, one could not help noticing how very far removed from all semblance or suggestion of 'dress reform,' as it is generally understood, was her own costume of soft, black silk net, with its trimmings of little, narrow satin ribbons. About her wrists were the softest and daintiest of white crepe lisse ruffles, and her gray hair was parted in the middle and brushed smoothly down over the tops of her ears. An old-fashioned gold and jet chain was attached to the long brooch she wore at her throat, and fell to her waist, where the tiny gold watch that was fastened to its end was tucked away in a little pocket. . . ." The headline on the story was SUSAN B. ANTHONY DOES NOT PRACTICE HER PREACHING ON DRESS REFORM. *Here is what she preached:*

I am glad to see women asserting themselves in this matter. Not so much because I particularly want them to don bloomers rather than any other style of dress, but because all such movements show that woman is declaring her right to be untrammeled, not only in matters of dress, but opinions as well.

Why, pray tell me, hasn't a woman as much right to dress to suit herself as a man? If he wants to dress in or out of style nobody dares to comment upon it. Certainly the condition of woman is much better today than it was, say, half a century or so ago, but she will never be in her rightful position until she has equal suffrage with man.

We haven't far to look for the reason that prevents many women who advocate just the reform in dress that is causing so much talk now from adopting it, for men must be consulted and pleased in all these matters.

Now, when woman is enfranchised, she will dress as she pleases, and she will dress according to the business that she is engaged in. She won't go in a factory with long sleeves and flowing skirts. She will dress according to good, common sense and her occupation.

Women have been trying to reform their dress for the last 40 years, but they have made a failure of it because they are not free and enfranchised. The first step in the reform of woman's dress is a reform in the ballot.

Now, when a woman goes to a factory or office to work she knows she must be subordinate to man. No matter how elevated and responsible the position she holds may be considered, all the same she is a subordinate. This is why she does not change her style of dress, as well as claim her right to do many other things she feels it should be her privilege to do. Man must be catered to in all this. If woman had a controlling voice in politics she would soon have a controlling voice in business, and, of course, I believe the world would be better for it.

When I speak, though, about the influence men have in the matter of dress for women, I do not mean to say that every man opposes their movement in this direction. There are many men who are noble-minded enough to accord to them the right that is theirs as judge of such matters themselves, and when we talk of the opinion of men in relation to these things we naturally mean the majority—the general rule, and not the exceptions . . . and the stand she is taking in the matter of dress is no small indication that she has realized that she has an equal right with man to control her own movements.

—*Interview, 1895*

I wear corsets, but they are loose and comfortable. I think all women ought to wear them, but not the tight kind such as young girls wear until they grow old enough to know better. You see, the boys like to see the girls have little, trim waists, and the girls think they must have them so. The girls would laugh if the boys strapped themselves up that way. I've heard that some boys do it, but I've never been able to discriminate.
—*Interview, 1899*

The men are hard to please. They protested because the women's skirts dragged on the ground, and now they object because they are too high.
—*Interview, 1895*

All her life Susan B. Anthony received gifts from her friends—including many of the clothes she wore. Shawls were apparently the perfect present.

Dear Friend:—
Your letter of Jan. 4th came in advance of the box containing the beautiful shawl. It is lovely and just what I wanted. A nice Quaker girl who had inherited the shawl from her aunt who wouldn't wear it because it was red, gave me that shawl that has been worn in the interim between Mrs. Spofford's present before I went to Europe. She then gave me a red silk shawl. The one I have now is Canton Crepe, but yours, I think, it is called Chudder, or is it simply an *Indian shawl?* I shall take great pleasure in wearing it and I thank you a thousand times over. You couldn't have hit upon a prettier thing. Then I have a shawl that was given me by Mrs. Gross of Chicago. It is an old fashioned white Paisley, a double shawl and with figures almost all over it. Mrs. Gannett, the Unitarian minister's wife, says she likes to see me wear that shawl. I frequently wear it under my velvet cloak which Mrs. Gross gave me also, so I am rigged out with shawls and cloaks to my heart's content.
—*Letter, January 7, 1904*

Somehow I feel at home in a shawl, and I thank you a thousand times over for sending this one . . .
—*Letter, 1904*

No scene better illustrates her meticulous concern for details than this charming moment from an interview with Olivia Howard Dunbar of the

New York World. *The exchange comes at the end of the article, as Anthony is preparing to sit for the newspaper photographer:*

"I want the best picture that ever was taken of me," she declared.

And then this most valiant reformer of her time—the woman who for years was vilified because of her "strongmindedness"—looked perturbed. It was all because of an extra little fold in her sleeve.

"Please fix it," she said, smilingly. "You know I mustn't be photographed in unfashionable sleeves."

—*Interview, 1899*

The Red Shawl

Her red shawl became such a cherished symbol of the venerable leader that even the usually cynical Washington press corps was swept along. In 1898, when she chose instead a white shawl for one session of the suffrage convention, the newspapermen sent her a note that read "No red shawl, no report." Anthony gamely played along, telling them, "All right, boys, I'll send to the hotel for it." When it arrived and she placed it around her shoulders, the audience burst into applause and the reporters took up their pencils.

17. PUBLISH OR PERISH

*S*he had a reporter's curiosity and a columnist's convictions; a publisher's vision and a publicist's savvy; a sales manager's drive and so
much charisma as a celebrity that the mere mention of her name in the headlines sold papers. At one time or another, Susan B. Anthony played each of
those roles. Acutely aware of the power of the printed word, she was a one-
woman press phenomenon, utilizing every aspect of the media that existed —
daily newspapers, monthly magazines, women's journals — to promote The
Cause with impressive skill. She even had the moxie to get a press pass from
her brother, D.R., publisher of the Leavenworth (Kansas) Times, when denied an official seat at the 1876 Centennial Celebration in Philadelphia.

Her brief publishing career began when George Frances Train, a
flamboyant and wealthy Democrat, offered to finance the newspaper she'd
dreamed about to advocate suffrage. Although Train was condemned by
many as a racist, Anthony and Elizabeth Cady Stanton, smarting from their
betrayal by those who insisted that black men should get the vote first, refused to abandon this loyalist to their Cause. His money and dedication
were welcome. Their new weekly, The Revolution, with its incisive
motto — "Men, Their Rights and Nothing More; Women, Their Rights and

Nothing Less"—debuted on January 8, 1868. The masthead listed Stanton and Parker Pillsbury, an abolitionist friend, as editors, and Susan B. Anthony as proprietor. Among the causes the sixteen-page weekly promised to advocate:

> Educated Suffrage, irrespective of Color or Sex; Equal pay to Women for equal Work; Dignity of Labor with Reduction of its Hours; Abolition of all standing Armies and all party Despotisms. Down with Politicians—Up with People!

The Revolution's columns were crammed with news, nuggets, and propaganda about women's rights, so lively and original in content and style that even on microfilm the paper continues to captivate. Anthony's job was to sell the ads and the newspaper, an assignment she fulfilled admirably from the start. The first edition contained her report to an audience of a visit to the White House to call on President Andrew Johnson:

> Johnson stood at his desk. Said "No," had a thousand such applications every day; more papers than he could read. I told him he was mistaken. That he never had such an application in his life. You recognize, I said, Mr. Johnson, that Mrs. Stanton and myself, for two years, have boldly told the Republican party that they must give ballots to women as well as negroes, and by means of *The Revolution* we are bound to drive the party to logical conclusions, or break it into a thousand pieces as was the old Whig party, unless we get our rights. [*Applause.*] That brought him to his pocket book, and he signed his name Andrew Johnson, with a bold hand, as much to say, anything to get rid of this woman and break the radical party. [*Loud applause and laughter.*]

Some three thousand more households, presumably acquired with less pressure, would subscribe to the radical new journal. Anthony worked inhuman hours, climbing up and down the stairs from her office opposite New York's City Hall to drum up advertising. Readers were offered incredible bargains on the $2 (later $3) annual subscription fee: 15 subscriptions plus $30 brought a washing machine; 12 plus $24, a clothes wringer ("No housewife should be without it."). Other premium items included a clock, a dress pattern (with 15 yards of alpaca), a dozen silver-plated spoons, forks, and butter knives. Unfortunately, none of it was enough. After two years, despite good critical reviews and a devoted readership, Train's money was gone and Anthony was forced to relinquish The Revolution *and assume the remaining $10,000 debt. She was heartbroken. It would take her seven* *years on the road to pay off the money, but she cleared the books and never regretted the experience. As she wrote to a friend:*

> None but the good Father can ever begin to know the terrible struggle of those years. I am not complaining, for mine is but the fate of almost every originator or pioneer who has ever opened up a way. I have the joy of knowing that I showed it to be possible to publish an out-and-out woman's paper, and taught other women to enter in and reap where I have sown.

Anthony never gave up on the idea of a national women's publication. But in the meantime, she tried other approaches. She had copies of suffrage speeches printed up for instant distribution to local newspapers. She arranged most of the advertising and promotion. And her byline, which had first appeared in temperance and women's journals, became a regular feature in many publications. During the California campaign in 1896, while she made speeches and plotted strategy at the age of seventy-six, she wrote a weekly column for two San Francisco papers for seven months, grinding out 1,500 words every Sunday with the help of her biographer, journalist Ida Husted Harper. If you have ever met a deadline, you will appreciate the panic that could be caused by the following telegram Anthony received on a Tuesday in May:

> The Examiner will have an entire page devoted to Womans Suffrage this week. Will you kindly contribute one thousand words by Friday noon.
> The Examiner.

But mostly Susan B. Anthony was in the newspapers, sitting for interview after interview in a concentrated attempt to spread the word about suffrage. After years of sarcasm, journalists considered her a prize subject, and she was regularly greeted in her hotel or on her front steps by eager writers. As the editors of The Papers of Elizabeth Cady Stanton and Susan B. Anthony *point out, "gaining access to Stanton or Anthony could boost a reporter's career."*

It didn't hurt her own needs, either. She learned how to put a good face on a suffrage defeat long before the term "spin" gained popular usage. (For instance, telling one reporter that a recent congressional vote wasn't bad news after all—they'd gotten more than anticipated!) She invented a Press Bureau in the suffrage association precisely to ensure the right take on any given event. She knew when to withhold information so as not to incur nasty headlines. At a symposium in Oregon in 1905 entitled "How Can We

Best Utilize the Press?," the editor of a Portland newspaper conceded, "[I]f the great political organs of the United States knew how well these women have the tricks of the trade at their fingers' ends they would employ special detectives to watch for suffrage literature in disguise." Susan B. Anthony knew exactly how potent an ally—or enemy—the newspaper columns could be. Her advice to her coworkers still holds true a century later:

> Our movement depends greatly on the press. The worst mistake any woman can make is to get crosswise with the newspapers.

———————

At the International Conference of Women meeting in Berlin in 1904, a debate on whether the press should be present was stopped cold when Anthony spoke. It should be noted that her remarks led reporters to clap their hands and bang on the tables in approval. They stayed.

My friends, what are we here for? We have come from many countries, travelled thousands of miles to form an organization for a great international work, and do we want to keep it secret from the public? No; welcome all reporters who want to come, the more the better. Let the people everywhere know that in Berlin women from all parts of the world have banded themselves together to demand political freedom. I rejoice in the presence of these reporters, and instead of excluding them from our meetings, let us help them to all the information we can and ask them to give it the widest possible publicity.

—Remarks, 1904

I remember well the days in New York when we couldn't get any kind of a report in the papers except in the way of a caricature. Things have changed and we are not caricatured now; but it isn't because we look any better than we did thirty or forty years ago. We don't look half so well. They called us cackling hens and other complimentary names. I can see the headlines now as they used to stare us in the face.

—Speech, 1893

The press was as kind as it knew how to be. It meant well and did all for us it knew how to do. We couldn't ask it to do more than it knew how. [*Laughter.*]
—*Speech, 1893*

I had an experience in publishing a paper about twenty-five years ago and I came to grief. I never hear of a woman starting a suffrage paper that my blood does not tingle with agony for what that poor soul will have to endure—the same agony I went through. I feel, however, that we shall never become an immense power in the world until we concentrate all our money and editorial forces upon one great national daily newspaper, so we can sauce back our opponents every day in the year; once a month or once a week is not enough.
—*Speech, 1893*

Women's papers are all right, but it is through the great dailies we must convert the world.
—*Remarks, 1905*

The time has come when women should organize a stock company and run a newpaper on their own basis. When woman has a newspaper which fear and favor cannot touch, then it will be that she can freely write her own thoughts. I do not mean that any individual woman should strive to get a newspaper of her own, but that all should combine. I fancy that Chicago is the place to start such a newspaper in, since Chicago has shown such superiority as a World's Fair city. We must have a great daily paper here edited, printed and controlled by women. Now it is quite generally known, I suppose, that I am somewhat of a woman suffragist myself. [*Laughter.*] But in this daily paper I would not ask for any special phase of woman's ideas. I would ask that the paper be edited from woman's standpoint and not in the interests of any "ism." Let it be from a woman's point of view just as a Republican paper is edited and filled with news from a Republican standpoint, and as a Presbyterian periodical is given its tone from a Presbyterian point of view.

We need a daily paper edited and composed according to woman's own thoughts, and not as a woman thinks a man wants her to think and write. As it is now, the men who control the finances control the paper. As long as we occupy our present position we are mentally and morally in the power of the men who engineer the finances. Horace Greeley once said that women ought not to expect the same pay for work that men received. He advised women to go down into New Jersey, buy a parcel of ground, and go to raising strawberries. Then when they came up to New York with their strawberries, the men wouldn't dare to offer them half price for their produce. I say, my journalistic sisters, that it is high time we were raising our own strawberries on our own land.

—*Speech, 1893*

That speech, from the Columbian Exposition in Chicago in 1893, drew instant attention. A reporter from the Chicago Tribune *followed up with a lengthy interview, published under the headlines:* HER IDEAL JOURNAL: Miss Anthony Tells How She Would Make a Newspaper. WOMEN WOULD RUN IT. *She also took a position that might appeal to today's tabloid-weary readers:* SENSATIONS NOT PLAYED UP.

WHAT IS YOUR IDEA OF A NEWSPAPER MADE BY WOMEN?

What I mean is simply this. Woman could never speak, could never write for the press from the standpoint of woman until women would be the controlling power in the management of the paper; if it be a stock company to have the controlling power in that stock company. That is, women should be the priorities to control and should have the control of the financial department, should have the control of the moral department, should have the control of the political department, etc. The papers are run to make money, of course. If the men own the paper—that is, if the men control the management of the paper—then the women who write for those papers must echo the sentiments of these men, and if they do not . . . they are cut off. . . . Alexander Hamilton very aptly said: "Give to a man the right over my subsistence and he has power over my whole moral being." The position of woman is simply that. A man who employs her has power over her whole moral status, and everybody must read what these people who control the paper wish them to.

HOW WOULD THE MONEY BE RAISED AND WHAT AMOUNT WOULD BE NECESSARY TO ESTABLISH SUCH A NEWSPAPER?

That I do not know. In the first place I wouldn't care whether or not all the stock was owned by women. What I would care is that they should own the controlling part of the stock. . . . What women want is a newspaper that can go into a home, can go before the children, that we can safely bring into a home without

making the children shudder at the murders that are recorded.
. . . Nothing can be done on a newspaper in accordance with the
views and ideas of women until they have that control of the
management of the paper. . . . We may want men to write in these
papers in various departments. The people want the views of men
and they want the views of women, and if we have both then we
can strike the happy medium. . . .

I want a daily newspaper that would report all the news,
would report everything just exactly as *The Tribune* does today.
All I want is that when an editorial is written, on whatever subject it may be written . . . the women who are engaged to write
those editorials are engaged by women and are writing to please
women and not men. . . .

WILL YOU EXPLAIN IN WHAT WAY A CERTAIN CLASS OF
NEWS ARTICLES COULD BE WRITTEN FROM ANY OTHER POINT
OF VIEW THAN THAT IN WHICH THEY ARE NOW WRITTEN—AS
EXAMPLES, MURDERS, EXECUTIONS, ROBBERIES, CONFLAGRA-
TIONS, ACCIDENTS, AND SO ON?

Well, in answering that I should say that I would have them
put in the background. I wouldn't have a whole page blistered
over with murders and criminal assaults and thefts. That sort of
thing is doing more now than anything else to demoralize.

WOULDN'T THAT KEEP IT FROM BEING A GENERAL NEWS-
PAPER?

Well, you would have to mention them, but I mean not to blister them out and make big headlines. I think it is something fearful the way this is done in great newspapers. I would not report a
murder or a theft any more than a news item. Why should an act
of this kind be reported more than an act of an honest man? The
papers of today have got into the habit of bringing it conspicuously before the public every time a man or a woman trips her
toe. For instance, you tell of a bank that fails, but you do not mention others that are doing good right along. One bank failure is
spread all over the country and in that way people become imbued with the idea that Chicago is rotten. We are unduly magni-
fying the exhibition to the world, if the exhibition is not that of an
honest man. It creates an impression upon the young which is
hard to eradicate.

WOULD THE PAPER ADVOCATE WOMAN SUFFRAGE?

It should advocate absolute equality of all human beings and it
would have to advocate equal suffrage.

—*Interview, 1893*

The Anthony Interview was an art form. Sometimes she paced the floor and dictated rapidly; sometimes she made a grand entrance into the hotel parlor or sitting room. But mostly she sat patiently and poised, the courtly leader answering the same questions from Maine to Oregon, beguiling some of the most hardened reporters. One of the most thoughtful sessions was conducted by Nellie Bly, herself a journalist of great renown. She covered many of the same themes that had already become legendary in Anthony's life but elicited some provocative new answers. The interview came at the end of the 1896 suffrage convention. When Anthony, then president of the group, was unable to fit her in during the Washington, D.C., meeting, Bly tracked her to Philadelphia. The story, plus seven pictures, took up an entire page in the Sunday edition of the February 2, 1896, New York World. Following are some excerpts.

CHAMPION OF HER SEX
Miss Susan B. Anthony Tells
the Story of Her Remark-
able Life to "Nellie Bly"
WOMAN SUFFRAGE MUST COME
Interesting Views, Ideas and Opinions
on All the Live Questions
of the Hour
ADVANCED THEORIES ABOUT MARRIAGE
Perfectly Proper for Women to Pro-
pose Now That They Are Inde-
pendent Wage Earners

Susan B. Anthony! She was waiting for me. I stood for an instant in the doorway and looked at her. She made a picture to remember and to cherish.

She sat in a low rocking-chair, an image of repose and restfulness. Her small-shaped head, with its silken snowy hair combed smoothly over her ears, rested against the back of the chair. Her shawl had half-fallen from her shoulders and her soft black silk gown lay in gentle folds about her. Her slender hands lay folded idly in her lap, and her feet, crossed, just peeped from beneath the edge of her skirt. If she had been posed for a picture, it could not have been done more artistically or perfectly. . . .

"Tell me, what was the cause of your being a suffragist? How did you begin?" I asked.

"My being a suffragist resulted from many other things that happened to me early in my life," she answered, unclasping her hands and resting them on the arms of her chair. "I remember the first time I ever heard of suffragists I was bored and complained because my family were so intensely interested in the subject. 'Can't you find anything else to talk about?' I asked my sisters in disgust. That was over fifty years ago." . . .

"But what gave you the idea of becoming a suffrage leader?" I urged.

"Many people will tell you," she answered, smiling, "that from their earliest . . . they cherished the ideas that eventually became their life work. I won't. As a little girl my highest ideal was to be a Quaker minister. I wanted to be inspired by God to speak in church. That was my highest ambition. My father believed in educating his girls so they could be self-supporting if necessary. In olden times there was only one [career] open to women. That was teaching. So every one of us girls took turns at teaching. I began when I was fifteen and taught until I was thirty." . . .

"Tell me about your first school," I pleaded. "Were you frightened?"

Susan B. Anthony leaned on the arm of the chair and smiled at me.

"I wasn't a bit timid," she said frankly. "I was only fifteen, but I thought I was the wisest girl in all the world. I knew it all. No one could make me think anything else. The first time I taught was in 1835. An old Quaker lady came to our house for a teacher for her children and several of her neighbors', making in all a class of eight. I accepted the position. I lived in her family, and for teaching the children three hours before dinner and three hours after, I got $1 a week and my board. . . ."

"Did you ever whip any of your scholars?" I inquired anxiously.

"Oh, my, yes!" she laughed. "I whipped lots of them. I recall one pupil I had. I was very young at the time. I had been warned that he had put the last master out of the window and that he would surely insult me. I went into that school boy when he began on me. I made him take off his coat and I gave him a good whipping with a stout switch. He was twice as large as I, but he behaved after that.

"In those days," she said, "we did not know any other way to control children. We believed in the goodness of not sparing the rod. As I got older I abolished whipping. If I couldn't manage a child I thought it my ignorance, my lack of ability as a teacher. I always felt less the woman when I struck a blow." . . .

"The secret of all my work," she said, "is that when there is something to do, I do it. I rolled up a mammoth temperance petition of 20,000 names and it was presented to the Legislature. When it came up for discussion one man made an eloquent speech against it. 'And who are these,' he asked, 'who signed the petition? Nothing but women and children.' Then I said to myself, 'Why shouldn't women's names be as powerful as men's? They would be if women had the power to vote. Then that man wouldn't have been so eloquent against temperance, for he would have known that the women would vote his head off.' I vowed there and then women should be equal. Women could not respect themselves or get men to respect them as equal until they had the power to vote.

"In the spring of 1853 we held the first annual convention of the Daughters of Temperance. Mrs. Stanton made an address advocating the right of divorce for women whose husbands drank. It raised an awful hubbub. The prejudiced women said Mrs. Stanton was going to violate the Bible. Same old battle, don't you see? It resulted in their saying that Mrs. Stanton was not good enough Christian to be their President. I knew if she wasn't good enough to be their President I wasn't good enough Christian to be their Secretary. So I resigned. 'If Mrs. Stanton was too much of an infidel,' I said, 'I certainly am.' " . . .

"Do you ever lose hope?" I asked the little silvery-haired warrior.

"Never!" she answered stoutly. "I know God never made a woman to be bossed by a man. You know Lincoln said, 'God never made a man good enough to govern other men without their consent.' I said, 'God never made a man good enough to govern any woman without her consent.' " . . .

"What is the main thing the suffrage association is trying to get now?" I asked,

"The Sixteenth Amendment: 'Citizens' right to vote shall not be denied on account of sex,' " was her reply.

"What is your greatest ambition now?"

"Oh, my!" with a laugh. "The right to vote. Not that I care for myself, but I want to see discrimination against women killed. We have three States in which women have the right now to vote, and we hope before '97 to have Oregon and Nevada and perhaps California."

"Do you expect to see women enfranchised?"

"Yes; if I live four years longer. I expect to see it. A tidal wave will sweep us right over. Or it may sweep us back. Our work is exactly like the tide of the ocean. We are swept forward and back."

"Are you superstitious, Miss Anthony?" I asked, for I adore the little peculiarities of people.

"No, never!" she declared, laughing. "But," she added slyly, "I never see the new moon that I don't stop to notice whether I see it over the right or left shoulder. Not that I believe it alters anything. And I never start away on Friday that I don't think of it. Still, I do not change the time of my departure because it is Friday."

"Are you afraid of death?"

"I don't know anything about Heaven or hell," she answered, "or whether I will ever meet my friends again or not. But as no particle of matter is ever lost, I have a feeling that no particle of mind is ever lost. The thought doesn't bother me. I feel that nothing is lost and that the hereafter will be managed as this life is managed now."

"Then you don't find life tiresome?"

"Oh, mercy, no! I don't want to die just as long as I can work. The minute I can't, I want to go. I dread the thought of being enfeebled. I find the older I get the greater power I have to help the world. I am like a snowball—the further I am rolled the more I gain. When my powers begin to lessen, I want to go. But," she added significantly, "I'll have to take it as it comes. I'm just as much in the hands of eternity now as when the breath goes out of my body." . . .

"Do you like flowers?" I asked, leading her into another channel.

"I like roses first and pinks second, and nothing else after," Miss Anthony laughed. "I don't call anything a flower that hasn't a sweet perfume."

"What is your favorite hymn or ballad?"

"The dickens!" she exclaimed, merrily. "I don't know! I can't tell one tune from another. I know there is such a thing as 'Sweet By and By' and 'Old Hundred,' but if I heard them I couldn't tell them apart. All music sounds alike to me, but still if there is the slightest discord it hurts me.

"Neither do I know anything about art," she continued, "yet when I go into a room filled with pictures my friends say I invariably pick out the best. I have sound company, I always say, in my musical ignorance. Wendell Phillips couldn't tell one tune from another. Neither could Anna Dickinson."

"What is your favorite motto, or have you one?"

"For the last thirty years I have written in all albums, 'Perfect equality of rights for women, civil or political.' There is another, one of Charles Sumner's. 'Equal rights for all.' I never write sentimental things. There isn't much sentiment in me. Neither can I read poetry. I cannot make it jingle. I suspect that is also due to my lack of musical ability." . . .

"What would you call woman's best attribute?"

"To have great, good common-sense. She has a great deal of uncommon-sense now, but I want her to be rounded down to a level —not to be gifted overly in one respect and lacking in others."

"What kind of woman do you think succeeds best?"

"The all-around woman. I have noticed that women especially gifted in one respect can never make a living. We want fewer extreme characters and ones more on the level. All abilities should be cultivated, or we lose them, and we are poor creatures when left with but one. It recalls to my mind what Sojourner Truth said. Sojourner Truth was as black as the ace of spades and six feet tall. She had been a slave for forty years, and attending one of our conventions after the war she was called upon to speak. 'I can't, chil'ern,' she said. 'Where the l'arnin' ought to be is all growed up.' That's what becomes of our abilities that we neglect to cultivate—they grow up."

"What [do] you think is woman's greatest forte in life?"

"That she shall be a woman. My point is this, that she must first be a woman—free, trained, above old ideas and prejudices, and afterwards the wife and mother. The old theory of a wife and mother needing only the capacity to cook and scrub is rapidly going to the dark ages."

"Who is the greatest woman of our age?"

"Elizabeth Cady Stanton. She is a philosopher, a statesman and a prophet. She is wonderfully gifted—more gifted than any person I ever knew, man or woman—and had she possessed the privileges of a man her fame would have been world-wide, and she would have been the greatest person of her time." . . .

"And now," I said, approaching a very delicate subject on tiptoes, "tell me one thing more. Were you ever in love?"

"In love?" she laughed, merrily. "Bless you, Nellie, I've been in love a thousand times."

"Really!" I gasped, taken aback by this startling confession.

"Yes, really!" nodding her snowy head. "But I never loved any one so much that I thought it would last." . . .

In disposition Miss Anthony is very lovable. She is always good-natured and sunny tempered. Everybody loves her dearly and she never loses a friend. She has a remarkable memory and in speaking is both eloquent and witty. She keeps an audience laughing during an entire evening.

Miss Anthony enjoys a good joke and can tell one. She never fails to see the funny side of things though it be at her own expense.

Susan Anthony is all that is best and noblest in woman. She is ideal, and if we will have in women who vote what we have in her, let us all help to promote the cause of woman suffrage.

— *Interview, 1896*

The Yellow Dog

As a former publisher and frequent interview subject, Susan B. Anthony understood the press all too well. During an 1887 speaking engagement in Chicago, a stray dog of a distinctly yellow hue wandered across the platform and thrust his nose onto her shoulder. The barking and panting disruption did not amuse Anthony. Later she predicted "that the dog would figure in the press reports more conspicuously than anything that was said and done, and so he did." The impertinent mongrel was mentioned in the headlines and leads of three surviving newspaper stories.

MISS ANTHONY.

A Talk with the Great Woman-Suffrage Leader.

Why Should She Not Sit on Mr. Tilton's Knee?

Her Opinion of Men—They Know Too Much.

She Slept with Mrs. Tilton, But Will Not Tell What She Said.

And Will Testify Only in Court.

Miss Anthony Gets Mad, Pulls Off Her Coat, Rolls Up Her Sleeves, and Wades in.

Victoria C. Woodhull Taken as a Text and Discussed.

MURDERESS AND HER CHAMPION

18. CURRENT AFFAIRS

*L*est you think Susan B. Anthony's world was all suffrage and no spice; lest you wonder whether anything ever happened in the nine-teenth century that might make good tabloid television today, stay tuned. Judging by some of her friends and their exploits, Anthony's life would have been a ratings success.

You can hear the promos now:
HER HUSBAND PUT HER IN AN INSANE ASYLUM!
THEY HAD AN AFFAIR!
DID MISS ANTHONY SIT ON HIS KNEE?
SHE ADVOCATES FREE LOVE!
ACCUSED OF MURDERING HER CHILD!

As usual, such headlines belittle the gravity of most of these cases. But they also indicate the universality of certain themes in our society—and continue to demonstrate that no matter how unlikely the subject, once again, Susan B. Anthony, with her enormous scope of concern, got there first. Long before certain social issues were written into the agenda of today's women's groups, Anthony and her colleagues had not only identified but embraced them.

THE ABUSED WOMAN

Susan B. Anthony was forty years old, in the midst of her series of antislavery lectures in Albany, New York, when she sheltered the battered wife. Her name was recorded only as Mrs. Phelps—or "Mrs. P.," in the protective code of contemporary accounts. But our research indicates that she was Phoebe Harris Phelps. She showed up one wintry night that December of 1860, her face disguised by heavy veils. Anthony and her friend Lydia Mott listened to the stranger's story with horror. She was from a prominent family: the wife of a Massachusetts state senator (Charles Abner Phelps, a physician who had also been Speaker of the state house), the sister of a U.S. senator (Ira Harris), and herself former principal of a girls' academy in Albany. All that success didn't help her. It turned out her husband had been unfaithful to her, and when Phoebe confronted him, Charles threw her down the stairs and continued to abuse her. When she threatened to go to authorities, he had her confined in an insane asylum, "a very easy thing for husbands to do in those days." For eighteen months, Phoebe Phelps languished in confinement, protesting her innocence while barred from any contact with her friends or family, including her three children. Finally released and allowed brief visits with her children, she begged for more time with her daughter. Her own brother refused to help, telling her, "The child belongs by law to the father and it is your place to submit."

Desperate, Phoebe took the thirteen-year-old girl and went into hiding. Then she found Susan B. Anthony. After making some inquiries to determine that the woman's story was true, Anthony, undaunted by the prospect of reprisals from the famous Phelps family, took on the case and escorted mother and child to New York by train. They reached Manhattan at 10 P.M. on Christmas Day. Finding a place to stay was another lesson in injustice. After being turned away from several hotels because they were "unaccompanied by a gentleman," the gutsy Anthony told one proprietor, "You can give us a place to sleep or we will sit in this office all night." When he threatened to call the police, she bluffed, "Very well, we will sit here till they come and take us to the station." He was not the first stunned man to give in to an Anthony ultimatum.

After a miserable night in a room without heat, the frigid trio sought a more permanent refuge. Finally Anthony got them to a friend who gladly took in the runaway wife. Phoebe Phelps was safe—for a time. But Anthony was just beginning to feel the heat. Her abolitionist friends got wind of the story when the Phelps family figured out Anthony's role and tried to make her reveal the woman's new home. Concerned that her part in the seedy drama would taint the antislavery cause, they repeatedly advised her to give up the woman and child. Anthony refused and forever lamented the fact that the same men who felt so strongly for black men in chains could not understand a woman in need.

I can not give you a satisfactory statement on paper, but I feel the strongest assurance that all I have done is wholly right. Had I turned my back upon her I should have scorned myself. In all those hours of aid and sympathy for that outraged woman I remembered only that I was a human being. That I should stop to ask if my act would injure the reputation of any movement never crossed my mind, nor will I allow such a fear to stifle my sympathies or tempt me to expose her to the cruel, inhuman treatment of her own household. Trust me that as I ignore all law to help the slave, so will I ignore it all to protect an enslaved woman.

When she met the men at the antislavery convention, abolitionist William Lloyd Garrison again went at her.

DON'T YOU KNOW THE LAW OF MASSACHUSETTS GIVES THE FATHER THE ENTIRE GUARDIANSHIP AND CONTROL OF THE CHILDREN?

Yes, I know it, and does not the law of the United States give the slaveholder the ownership of the slave? And don't you break it every time you help a slave to Canada?

YES, I DO.

Well, the law which gives the father the sole ownership of the children is just as wicked and I'll break it just as quickly. You would die before you would deliver a slave to his master, and I will die before I will give up that child to its father.

Although Anthony never gave in, poor Phoebe Phelps was tracked down by a detective, her daughter abducted by her father's agents. Mother and child were never reunited.

THE FAIR AFFAIR

Of all her ventures into the seedy underworld, nothing invited so much scorn as Susan B. Anthony's lecture in support of a prostitute named Laura D. Fair.

When Anthony and Elizabeth Cady Stanton arrived for their California suffrage campaign in July 1871, one of their first stops in San Francisco was at a cold, dank cell with an iron-barred window in the county jail. There they visited Fair, who had been tried and convicted of shooting to death her lover, Alexander Crittenden, a prominent local attorney. According to reports, Fair had taken out her pistol when Crittenden abandoned her, pulling the trigger in broad daylight in front of his wife and children. Now she was scheduled to be hanged. The dauntless suffragists defended Fair as a victim of man's uncontrolled sexual appetites. But they hadn't counted on the intensity of anger among San Franciscans. Before twelve hundred people at Platt's Hall (including, in the front row, Fair's mother, who had brought along the prisoner's little daughter), Anthony turned her suffrage speech, "The Power of the Ballot," into a testimonial for Laura Fair. Challenging the popular notion that women are supported and protected by men, she said, "If all men had protected all women as they would have their own wives and daughters protected, you would have no Laura Fair in your jail tonight."

The hisses and boos were overwhelming.

Anthony paused, then repeated her statement: "If all men had protected all women as they would have their own wives and daughters protected, you would have no Laura Fair in your jail tonight."

Again, the hisses—but this time, with a few cheers.

Anthony said it again: "If all men had protected all women as they would have their own wives and daughters protected, you would have no Laura Fair in your jail tonight."

Now the applause drowned out the boos. She had prevailed! Anthony concluded: "I tell you, gentlemen, that wherever there is a woman wanting in self-respect, wanting in dignity of character, wanting in propriety of behavior, not as strong as possible in all the affairs of life, as strong as God can make her, there are twenty vultures in the shape of men willing to clutch her. . . . I don't take sides on the Fair case; I have not read a column about it; I know nothing about it . . . except that so far as the fact is concerned that a woman never gets protection at the hands of man unless she protects herself. There I stand." More applause followed, as Fair's mother was seen to shed a few tears.

"You women who have kind brothers and husbands and sons, I ask you to join with us in this movement, so that woman can protect herself."

Anthony went to bed content, certain she had proven her point:

> S.B.A. spoke Platts Hall—Power of the Ballot—a splendid au-
> dience—& great speech—hisses at allusion to Laura Fair . . . si-
> lenced them & then turned them to cheers—

*But then the press turned against her. Her diary entries for the next
few days illustrate her agony over the reaction.*

> Every paper came out terrifically against me & my speech last
> night—never before got such a raking.

> The shadow of the newspapers hangs over me every minute.

*The adverse reaction almost destroyed her, and it was weeks before she
could get back into gear. Meanwhile, Laura Fair was granted a new trial.
One year later, after deliberating nearly sixty hours, the new jury acquitted
her. Mrs. Fair, as the newspapers called her, fainted at the announcement.*

THE OTHER FALLEN WOMEN

*Laura Fair was only the most prominent of the prostitutes Susan B. An-
thony defended. The fact that she used the term "prostitute" at all is revealing. Based on reports in the popular press, in polite society it was rarely
printed and more rarely spoken. Favorite euphemisms included "the social
evil" or more plainly, "vice." Prostitutes were commonly called "fallen
women." Susan B. Anthony had an entire speech on the subject of "Social
Purity," which encompassed a wide range of evils—including drunken,
abusive husbands. In the speech, she also used the word "prostitute" more
than half a dozen times.*

*Anthony had another speech, on "The Social Evil," and suffered con-
siderable ridicule when she delivered it. The idea of an unmarried woman
discussing sex was just too much for some to bear. But her heart was with
prostitutes—as victims—and when someone asked what to do about "fallen
women" at an upcoming convention, she had a ready answer:*

But alas—alas—*the first thing needful* is to *reform* the *fallen men*—& their name is *legion*—while even the *very elect* of men feel it *no crime* to despoil any woman's virtue they meet—it will be very, very hard work to lift poverty stricken homeless girls above their seductive reach—nothing but to *make woman's work easy, profitable, honorable*—can do it—and that can't be done while no woman even washes her own dishes who can find a man either in or out of marriage to pay for the doing it for them—

If the *ballot* in the hands of women shall fail to do the desired work of elevating women, then I shall not despair—but look in some other direction for help.

She reiterated her position at suffrage conventions:

I should gladly welcome all the infamous women in New York, and sit side by side with them on this platform, if they were willing to make speeches in favor of freedom. [*Applause.*] They shall stand by my side—I will be their champion. I will take by the hand every prostitute I can find who seeks to escape the inequalities of that law which places all womanhood at the mercy of manhood. [*Immense applause.*]

Later, in a newspaper interview, she expanded on her rather ungenerous opinion of the the male gender.

Man is the grosser animal, and it is his money that causes the downfall of poor innocent girls.

And a tantalizing entry in her diary—of which we have no further information—indicates that her attitude was firmly set:

Now comes the Jersey City News—Pomeroy Rv. John S. C. Glendenning—case—perfectly atrocious—Then—too a methodist minister incest with his own daughter—& father of her child—The fact is *man* as *a rule* does not *feel* it a sin & crime to possess the body of woman save only in lawful marriage—his crime is *being exposed* in the act—not in committing it—

THE WORKING WOMAN

Hester Vaughan, a twenty-year-old houseworker, was accused of murdering her baby. She had come to America from England with her husband, who had not bothered to tell her he had another wife. Hester was seduced by another man, who deserted her when he found out she was pregnant with his baby. Alone, untended, and ill, Hester gave birth in a garret. The child was dead when both were discovered. Tried with inadequate defense, convicted by an uninformed court, she was sentenced to die by hanging.

That's when Susan B. Anthony, Elizabeth Cady Stanton, and the Working Woman's Association established by The Revolution *got on the case. They held rallies, raised money, and visited Vaughan in prison outside Philadelphia. Through Stanton's editorials and Anthony's organization, the governor of Pennsylvania pardoned Hester Vaughan, and she was allowed to return home to England. Anthony was jubilant. She had predicted the next case:*

> Miss Anthony wanted it understood that the workingwomen were going to defend the defenceless of their own sex, and act on the doctrine that the crime of women shall be condemned no worse than the same crime by men. [*Applause.*] . . . I want to tell you a secret. As soon as we get Hester Vaughan out of prison we will get somebody else to work for. We intend to keep up the excitement. . . .

THE MURDERESS

Maria Barberi provided another opportunity for Susan B. Anthony to denounce the system that prohibited women from electing the judges who tried them or serving on the juries that convicted them. Like Hester Vaughan, Barberi was a poor immigrant; worse, she spoke no English and could not defend herself. Her sensational crime grew out of her passion for a cad. Barberi, it seems, wanted to marry him. What happened next was reported in a contemporary newspaper: "in the miserable light of a saloon she glanced into the eyes of her faithless lover, Dominico Cataldo, and drew a razor blade across his throat when he sneeringly said, 'Ah! Hogs marry; I don't.' " A jury found Maria Barberi guilty and the judge sentenced her to the electric chair. Susan B. Anthony and Elizabeth Cady Stanton rallied to her side. Anthony's statement:

My opinion is ever and always against murder, whether by the individual or the State, but especially am I opposed to the State's murdering a young woman who cannot understand our language and for a crime that is condoned in a man, young or old, with scarce a reprimand. The law refuses to punish the man who, under promise of marriage, robs the woman of her chastity. When the forsaken creature takes summary vengeance upon her cruel seducer the law consigns her, without judge or jury of her peers, to a most ignominious death; whether by electrocution or hanging for women in the State of New York have no political peer among men save those inside the State prisons, the idiot and lunatic asylums.

All decency, all justice is outraged at the barbarism of judicial murder of man by man in accordance with his own man-made and man-executed laws, but when he proceeds to perpetrate the atrocity upon the defenceless head of woman all nature revolts and cries "Hands off!" at least until women are enfranchised and together with men shall decide what shall be law and who shall execute it. The whole state of affairs, the two moral codes, the foraging upon poor, ignorant girls—a mere harmless pastime for men—and then consigning their victims to shame and death, all cry out for power in the hands of women to make, shape and control their own moral code not only, but that of men also. Things are surely all one sided now.

I hope that the Governor will commute the poor girl's sentence, and that the law for judicial murder will be annulled by the next Legislature.

Anthony's appeal was not isolated. The unfaithful Cataldo, a bootblack, apparently did not enjoy much respect, for tens of thousands—men and women—signed petitions in Barberi's favor, all claiming she had merely acted in self-defense. One added, "the world is not any worse off, but by far the contrary, it is a great deal better for being rid of this good for nothing being Cataldo . . . he had nothing but what he deserved, and . . . if every girl proved a Barberi to her Cataldo, every family over the world would live in peace and harmony." Another wrote that electrocuting Barberi "would be a crime against civilization. It would be besides an encouragement given to all betrayers of women. If a man comes in my house at night and robs me, I have the right to kill him legally, but if a villain robs a woman of what is most precious to her, her virtue, she has no right whatsoever against him! Moreover, she is condemned to death! It is against all principles of morality and common sense."

The campaign worked. In December 1896—more than a year after her conviction—Maria Barberi got a new trial and was acquitted by reason of insanity.

THE SCANDAL

And then there was Victoria Woodhull, the source of a genuine scandal. An alluring divorcée with proven financial prowess at her own Wall Street brokerage firm, she first shocked the citizens of the 1870s by declaring herself a proponent of Free Love. Woodhull defined it as another political right, but in fact she was urging society to abolish its double standard and allow women—as well as men—to make love with whomever they choose, no matter the bonds of matrimony. Such a nontraditional approach was not quite what Susan B. Anthony had in mind, but for a time she defended the outrageous Free Lover for a simple reason: Victoria Woodhull was also a fervent, articulate supporter of women's rights. Despite her reputation, Anthony welcomed her to The Cause and allowed her to address the NWSA convention, answering the objections of coworker Isabella Beecher Hooker with her usual single-mindedness:

Not until we *catechise* and *refuse men*—will I consent to *question women*—And it is *only* that *Mrs. Woodhull is a woman,* & that *we* are *women—all of an enslaved class*—that we ever *dream* of such a thing—I know the *pressure* upon you—and I know more—that so soon as you get breath you will rebound in spirit & say with me—come one, come all—the deeper the gaul [*sic*] of bitterness the poor woman's soul has drank [*sic*]—the more does she need the *saving grace* of absolute freedom from dependence on men for the control of her circumstances— . . . .

I am proud of you every day—& have full faith that in the end, you will stand by the side of *all women* who are struggling into freedom—precisely as Jefferson & Washington stood by *all men*—What would have been thought of those men stopping to trace out every gossip of every Revolutionist & proving clearly that he had never violated the 7th Commandment before admitting him to the Federal Army? or into *Independence Hall*!! You see the *theory* you propose for the *Woodhull Scandal*—applied to *men,* living or dead is simply ridiculous—

She elaborated to another friend, with references to such prominent men as Reverend Henry Ward Beecher, Reverend Thomas W. Higginson, Senator Benjamin Butler, journalist Frank George Carpenter, and Senator Samuel C. Pomeroy:

When we women *begin* to *search individual records* and antecedents of those who bring influence, brains or cash to our work of enfranchising women—we shall *begin* with *the man*—now *I* have *heard gossip* of *undue familiarity* with persons of *the opposite sex* relative to Beecher, Higginson, Butler, Carpenter, Pomeroy— and before I shall consent to an arraignment of *Woodhull* or any other *earnest woman worker* who shall come to our Platform in Washington or elsewhere—I shall insist upon the *closest investigation* into *all* the *scandals* afloat about those men—not one of whom I have heard Mrs. Hooker or any other woman express any fears of accepting whatever they may say or do for us—

When we shall require of the *men,* who shall speak—vote, work for us—to *prove* that they have never been unduly familiar with any woman, never guilty of trifling with or desecrating womanhood—it will be time enough for us to demand of the *women* to *prove* that *no man has ever trifled with* or desecrated them.

And she was even more loyal to her sex in general—Woodhull in particular—at the 1872 suffrage convention, a lively meeting that one newspaper headlined, "WOMEN ON THE WARPATH . . . Miss Anthony Gets Mad, Pulls Off Her Coat, Rolls Up Her Sleeves, and Wades In."

When I heard of a woman on Wall street, I went to see how a woman looked among the bulls and bears. Women have the same right there as men. Who brought Victoria C. Woodhull to the front? I have been asked by many why did you drag her to the front. Now, bless your souls, she was not dragged to the front; she came to Washington from Wall street with a powerful argument and with lots of cash behind her and I bet you cash is a big thing with Congress. [*Uproarious applause.*] She presented her memorial to Congress, and it was a power. I should have been glad to call it . . . the Anthony memorial. It was a mighty effort, and one that any woman might be proud of. She had an interview with the Judiciary Committee; we could never secure that privilege. She is young, handsome, and rich. Now if it takes youth, beauty, and money to capture Congress, Victoria is the woman we are after. [*Laughter and applause.*]

Women have too much false modesty. I was asked by the editors of New York papers if I knew of Mrs. Woodhull's antecedents. I said I didn't, and I did not care any more about them than those of Congress. Her antecedents will compare favorably with any member of Congress. I will not allow any human being, wearing the form of manhood, to ask me to desist working with any woman; for what woman is to-day, is the result of man's handiwork.

I have been asked all along the line of the Pacific coast, What about Woodhull? You make her your leader? Now, we don't make leaders; they make themselves. If any can accomplish a more brilliant effort than Victoria C. Woodhull, let him or her go ahead and they shall be leaders. [*Applause.*]

But Victoria Woodhull went too far for Susan B. Anthony when she tried to co-opt a New York NWSA convention for her own People's Party and her own fanciful run for office. Anthony literally turned out the lights while Woodhull was speaking. She told a friend:

If she were influenced by *women* spirits, either in the body or out of it, in the direction she steers, I might consent to be a mere sail-hoister for her; but as it is, she is wholly owned and dominated by *men* spirits and I spurn the control of the whole lot of them . . .

And Anthony never forgave Woodhull for telling the world about the love affair that rocked the suffrage world. In Woodhull & Claflin's Weekly, *the racy newspaper Woodhull published with her sister, Tennessee Claflin, she disclosed that Henry Ward Beecher, the famed preacher, was having an affair with Elizabeth Tilton, a member of his Brooklyn congregation. What made it so scandalous was that Tilton's husband, Theodore, like Beecher, was the leader of one of the suffrage organizations. Anthony, who was close to all the players, knew all about the sordid story because once, on a visit to the Tilton house, Mrs. Tilton had reportedly confided in her after bolting the bedroom door to keep Mr. Tilton outside. Among the other dirty details: Mrs. Tilton had done it because she found out her husband had had an affair himself; he had arranged for an abortion when the woman he was seeing got pregnant; Reverend Beecher was known for his amorous overtures to other parishioners. The Beecher-Tilton liaison dominated the headlines for several years.*

But Susan B. Anthony wasn't talking. Hounded by reporters, she refused to participate in the public gossip, even when her colleague Elizabeth Cady Stanton gave interviews on Beecher's hypocrisy. At first she told Stanton she was irritated by references to "this kissing & hugging — & putting away old men & getting new ones to hug & kiss emblazoned in print constantly. Your leading *W[oman].S[uffrage]. women, its simply sickening —"*

Anthony wouldn't even speak out to deny rumors of her involvement in the case. During one trial marked by lurid headlines, Tilton's ward Bessie testified that she had seen the esteemed suffrage leader in the house with Mr. Tilton:

> BESSIE: I saw her sitting on his lap on one occasion when I was coming into the parlor, and she jumped up pretty quick.
> INVESTIGATOR: Miss Anthony?
> BESSIE: Susan B. Anthony.

A reporter was instantly dispatched to Anthony's home, and the lady in question "threw the paper on the floor and burst into a fit of laughter, saying, 'That's too absurd to answer.'" *Nearly two months later, another reporter tried again, and under the tantalizing headline* WHY SHOULD SHE NOT SIT ON MR. TILTON'S KNEE? *Susan B. Anthony had some fun with the intrigue. Smiling at the young man, she said coyly,*

> Well, that was my only lapse from rigorous virtue. All the men had declared that Susan was so sour she couldn't get a husband, and I thought I would show them I could sit on a young man's knee just like any foolish girl.

The reporter went back at it one more time:

> Here I made a digression; Miss Anthony was looking into the future of her sex with calm complacency when I attacked her with a question, so artfully put, as I believed, as to allow of no evasion. The gist of it was:
> "Did you, Miss Anthony, sleep with Mrs. Tilton one night and did she tell you all about Mr. Beecher?"

How little I know the strategy of that wise General. She looked at me with mild reproach in her expressive gray eyes.

"Yes, I did sleep with Mrs. Tilton at different times, but I shall not tell the world what I know or do not know. If I am summoned before the courts, and examined legally as a witness, it will be my duty to go; but I don't think I can remember all the things that have been told me in confidence during all my journeyings. The fact is, if a woman gives herself to a man, either in marriage or out of marriage, he will trample her into the dirt to serve his own ends. Women sell themselves too cheap. They sacrifice themselves on the spot, and it does not matter whether the man has any brains or not; it is the creation over again. Old Adam said, 'The woman tempted me and I did eat.' Beecher says, 'The woman tempted me and I did *not* eat.' In both cases, she gets the blame."

Earlier that summer she had said, "in this case men proved themselves the champion gossips of the world."

The Character Issue

Today's political candidates who are exasperated with the pressure to disclose so much of their personal lives had an ally in Susan B. Anthony. During the 1872 presidential campaign, she expressed horror at the idea of the candidacy of Horace Greeley, calling him "utterly unfitted, by his credulity and lack of judgment, either for a successful statesman or wise President. In all questions where principle is involved he is fluctuating and unreliable." But she still pronounced him morally fit, saying his "private character is above reproach."

REPORTER—Do you mean to assert that public professions of fine theories are more desirable than honest practice?

MISS A.—Precisely. If a man's public record be a clear one, if he has kept his pledges before the world, I do not inquire what his private life may have been. I judge a man by his convictions of right, for a man's principles are the result of his better judgment, whilst his practice is influenced by his associations.

19. GET MONEY—
GET WEALTH

*T*he Susan B. Anthony dollar, issued in 1979, represents her entire weekly salary as a schoolteacher just over a century earlier. Male teachers were customarily paid four times that amount. "I think the first seed for thought was planted during my early days as a teacher. I saw the injustice of paying stupid men double and treble women's wages for teaching merely because they were men," she told reporter Nellie Bly. Independence, Anthony realized, was possible only with money. That meant not only married women—whose cause she took up first—but single workingwomen, as well. She called for equal pay, equal access to jobs, and—perhaps most radical of all—for women not only to earn but also to manage their own money. And that evolved quite naturally into goading women to give their money lavishly to the only campaign she believed would help them win all those rights: the suffrage treasury.

In her own career as a workingwoman, Anthony was always underpaid—but not for the usual reasons. Once she quit teaching, she never held a full-time salaried position again, existing instead on the fees she earned as a lecturer or writer. In describing her income, the word "modest" comes to mind. While she did spend some financially rewarding seasons on the road for commercial agents, most of her speeches were uncompensated. She never *took a salary from the national suffrage association but frequently covered her own expenses and then donated all of her time and most of her meager earnings to getting the vote for all women. When forced to miss two of her beloved suffrage conventions due to lecture engagements, she promptly donated a week's salary to The Cause. At the same time, she bemoaned the extravagance of the unenlightened. One trip to Chicago led to a typical entry in her diary: ". . . there in my lovely tapestried room was the new Louis the 14th $5,200 bed-stead & bureau for me to christen!! My how much good suffrage work could have been done for that money!"*

Susan B. Anthony understood the essential need for cash in politics. At early suffrage conventions, it was she who passed the hat (or bonnet), begged for subscriptions to women's journals, identified potential contributors, and implored delegates to open their purses. Anthony was an immensely successful fund-raiser, in part because her personal commitment convinced so many newcomers of their own duty. The rest she converted with pure charm. Cornelia C. Hussey, a successful realtor from East Orange, New Jersey, donated $10,000 to The Cause at her death in 1902:

> She has indeed been a generous giver to it and to me personally for nearly twenty years. The dear woman came home [from Europe] on the same steamer with me nineteen years ago and we walked on the deck and talked for hours on the woman question. She then declared that every penny of her surplus profits she should give towards suffrage and she has kept her word all these years.

One can only imagine the conversation unleashed on the unsuspecting Mrs. Hussey.

Financially, the movement was sustained by a wide variety of donors. Day laborers—seamstresses and laundresses—sent in pennies; professional women contributed dollars. A description of the 1896 California campaign from Harper touches the heart.

> Often when there was not enough money on hand at headquarters to buy a postage stamp, there would come a knock at the door and a poorly dressed woman would enter with a quarter or half-dollar, saying, "I have done without tea this week to bring you this money;" or a poor little clerk would say, "I made a piece of fancy work evenings and sold it for this dollar." Many a woman who worked hard ten hours a day to earn her bread,

would come to headquarters and carry home a great armload of circulars to fold and address after night. And there were teachers and stenographers and other workingwomen who went without a winter cloak in order to give the money to this movement for freedom.

There were other big donors, too. In 1881 Eliza Eddy, whose philan-thropist father had earlier donated $5,000 to the movement, left nearly $25,000 to Susan B. Anthony (and an equal amount to her Boston coun-terpart, Lucy Stone) "for the advancement of the women's cause." It was called the first instance "where a woman has bequeathed a large amount of money to the cause of equal rights . . . to secure freedom for those of their own sex."

It took nearly three years to retrieve the inheritance from legal tangles, an event that gave the usually intrepid Anthony a major trauma. On the sleeper train home from Boston, with the treasured stocks and bonds of the legacy sewed into her clothing, she awoke screaming from a nightmare that someone was stealing her money at knifepoint. She sat up for the rest of the trip and then spent every penny efficiently to promote The Cause. We know because Anthony prided herself on keeping careful records and insisted that the suffrage organizations do the same. Every dollar she ever earned seems to be registered in her handwritten diaries. One admiring newspaper re-porter wrote, "she has carried on more campaigns upon less capital than ever did Napoleon or any other commander of whom record has been pre-served."

Ironically, despite her advice to other women, Anthony's money rarely landed in her own purse. She was just too busy working for everyone else. Whenever she received cash presents on her birthday (a common gift), she gave them to The Cause. When, at her seventy-eighth birthday celebration, she was given a huge cake—four feet across—by her admirers in Washing-ton, D.C., she had it sliced up and auctioned off as souvenirs—then con-tributed all $130 to the NAWSA treasury.

Her brother D.R. had warned of the consequences as early as 1870:

You have put in your all and all you can borrow, and all is swallowed up. You are making no provision for the future, and you wrong yourself by so doing. . . . Although you are now fifty years old and have worked like a slave all your life, you have not a dollar to show for it. This is not right. Do make a change.

Of course she would not. There was no room on her agenda to care for herself when there was a greater cause to sustain.

Dear Emma

Independent bread gives independent morals:—while pecuniary dependence makes moral subserviency;—So get money—get wealth—

> Susan B. Anthony
> Rochester N.Y.

—*Autograph message, 1874*

If women had *money* they might move the world. But they are making this fight with hands tied, financially, as well as politically.

—*Letter, 1877*

It is continually forced on my attention that women have excessive demands made upon them. How many times it is the case that when there's one smart woman in the family all the rest sit down and fold their hands and seem to think there is no end to her pocketbook. The woman is generous and proud to be able to do for them. She has little of that prudence that prepares for old age, and continues to work and work till the crash comes. You look about and see how many women you can count who are just getting to that point. Women must learn to have prudence and thrift as well as ability to earn.

—*Remarks, 1891*

To one of her favorite friends, the very wealthy widow Jane L. Stanford, Anthony wrote a characteristic sermon on the evils of giving up control.

I trust your university is prospering even beyond your highest expectation. I have seen items lately that you have put out of your hands the control of nearly your entire estate. I hope that this is not true, for your power over the university and over various incorporated associations in which you are stockholder depends very largely on your holding the helm tightly in your own right hand. Nearly all women and very many men make the mistake of ceding or deeding away control of their property during their lifetime. You will remember how happy it made me when you told me about exhibiting the contents of the box of bonds and securities to the university trustees, then putting them back, locking the box and saying, "No one but myself will clip these coupons as long as I have the ability to do it."

You will pardon me for this unasked advice; but, as you know, I feel this strong interest in your management of your millions because the world will credit the whole sex with your success or charge it with your failure. Thus far it seems to me that no man could have conducted his business with better judgment than you have yours ever since your dear husband left you all of his great responsibilities, so remembering all your good words and works, I am very lovingly and trustingly yours.

— *Letter, 1900*

Anthony herself hated being out of control of her finances — so much so that she was deeply mortified the only documented time she missed a payment. In her letter to a Boston colleague, which verges on the neurotic, she also fears that the rival suffrage group led by Lucy Stone ("the Pharisees") will make political hay out of her forgetfulness:

I was awfully embarrassed last Saturday A.M. to leave my bill unpaid at the Parker House—so afraid it would get out among the Pharisees of Boston—Do please write me at once—to Rochester NY that you have been there and paid it—I mailed the bill to you that morning—it was $11.75—perfectly awful—& yet I kept as close on the line of economy as I honestly could—but expected to *pay it myself*—leaving you only the R.R. fare to & from—which was $29 . . . & that was awful—what little I helped you wasn't worth the round sum of $40—If you will send me the Parker house bill *receipted* so that I may [know] it is settled—you need not worry about the $29—but credit me with that sum as a contribution and put the same sum into your expenses—Don't send it back only do *tell me* the *hotel bill is paid*!! . . . I am so *"mad"* at myself that I should have taken out of my jacket so much money & put into the safe here—for fear I might go down in the New York bay—taking all with me—as not to leave enough to cover my expenses there & back & while there—I have fretted over the senseless act more than enough to pay the whole $40— Twice over—I never did such an unbusiness thing before—I am continually ashamed of myself—

— *Letter, 1885*

Anthony always championed the less fortunate workingwoman, and while publishing The Revolution, *she organized several Working Woman's Associations to agitate for better pay and conditions. One session at a New York City tenement housing several hundred female laborers produced a graphic report of their conditions:*

A PLEASANT, LADY-LIKE GIRL, IN A LOW VOICE: I get $2 a piece for making ladies' cloth cloaks.

MISS ANTHONY: How long does it take you to make one?

YOUNG GIRL: Less than a day. It is partly machine and partly hand work.

MISS ANTHONY: Well, go on, girls.

A GIRL IN A DARK DRESS, LOOKING VERY PALE FROM OVER-WORK: I make lace collars for twenty-two cents a dozen. I can make three dozen in a day, twelve hours' work, that's sixty-six cents.

ANOTHER GIRL: There are several machine operators here. Some of them can make $6 a week by working ten or fourteen hours a day. Others not $5 a week.

A FUR-SEWER: I make fur collars and muffs, and earn seventy-five cents a day by hard work.

ANOTHER GIRL: Why, I know some girls who make $1 a day fur-sewing, and sometimes, by bringing their work home, they make as much as $2 a day.

FIRST FUR-SEWER: No, I don't think that's so. She must work very hard.

A SEAMSTRESS: I can make two dozen of men's flannel shirts a day. I get sixty cents a dozen for them.

A DRESSMAKER, VERY PRETTY: I can make $7 a week by working from six o'clock in the morning until eight in the evening.

MISS ANTHONY: That's hard work, indeed.

A SILK HAT MAKER: I can make $1 to $2 dollars a day by working long hours at men's silk hats.

A TAILORESS: I can make $11 a week by working constantly from 7 until 6, on men's overcoats.

HOOP-SKIRT MAKER: I can make $7 to $8 a week at hoop-skirts, working from 7 in the morning until 6 in the evening.

A BRIGHT-EYED GIRL: I make $6 a week feeding a press in a printing-office, ten hours a day, plenty of work.

MISS ANTHONY: That's pretty rich.

A VEST-MAKER: I work at home, from early morning until night, on vests. I get fifty cents a piece for making them. I make $5 a week.

A SEAMSTRESS: I am a sewing finisher and make $3 to $4 a week, working moderately ten hours a day. If I work very hard, and bring home night work, finishing on the machine, I can make $5 a week at the most.

ANOTHER SEAMSTRESS: I make men's striped, white and blue shirts, fifteen cents a dozen, and by bringing home night work I can finish two dozen a day.

[*Cries of "shame," and "that's not so," and laughter.*]

MISS ANTHONY: I am here to find out your wants, and to help you make more money. Pray do not make it any worse than it is. Heaven knows, it is bad enough. . . .

A GIRL LOOKING VERY ILL, AND WEAK IN VOICE: I am a carpet-sewer. I work for one of the largest carpet-houses in the Bowery. The Brussels carpets are very stiff sometimes, and I blister my hands very badly [*showing her blistered fingers*]. I worked nearly three days, and I sewed fifty yards of carpet, and when I asked him to pay me for sewing the borders, which is additional work, he laughed and said it was "chucked in."

[*Sensation and cries of what's his name?*]

MISS ANTHONY: Reporters, don't give the name, it is the crime of a system not of an individual. The individual slaveholder was not a criminal—his system was a crime. So it is with these poor white slave girls. . . .

AN UMBRELLA-MAKER, A FAIR AND DELICATE YOUNG GIRL: By working from daylight until dark I can make $6 a week. It's very hard work. . . .

PAPER COLLAR MAKER: I make paper collars and paste little pieces of cloth where the button-holes are. I get eight cents a hundred. By hard work until my eyes get dim, from 7 until 6 in the evening, I can make $6 to $8 a week. I have to make 1,250 collars for one dollar.

[*And so it went on . . . with a metal burnisher, corset maker, straw hat sewer.*]

MISS ANTHONY: I believe that you girls live here on the restaurant plan, and I think you live cheaper than we can down town at restaurants. If you didn't I don't see how you could get along at all at your wages.

[*There is a pitch by an organizer.*]

MISS ANTHONY: Have a spirit of independence among you, a

wholesome discontent, as Ralph Waldo Emerson has said, and you will get better wages for yourselves. Get together and discuss, and meet again and again to discuss this question, and all the time have a wholesome discontent, or you will never achieve your rights. You must not work for these starving prices any longer. Talk to one another, and I will come and talk to you, and the press will support you, for the reporters put everything down . . . and by and by we will have an immense mass meeting of women, where all can talk if they choose, and all the good men and women of America, listening to your appeal will come forward and stand by you. Get the ballot, and then if you strike the men of the Trade Unions will sustain you with money and assistance.
—*Meeting, 1868*

Yes, and another thing, make up your mind to take the "lean" with the "fat," and be early and late at the case precisely as men are. If you allow yourselves to be "petted," you must content yourselves with half pay. I do not demand *equal pay* for any women save those who do equal work in value. *Scorn to be "petted" by your employers; make* them understand you are in their service AS WORKERS not as WOMEN; and that you will ask and will accept nothing less nor more because of your sex.
—*Remarks, 1869*

What we want in the world of work is not that women be allowed to do this or to do that, but that they may get the same pay that men get for doing the same work. The trades and professions are practically open to women now. Medicine and law both have women practitioners. Elizabeth Blackwell was the first woman doctor in this country. She graduated at the head of her class in Geneva college, yet on the day after her graduation the faculty voted to admit no more women. Now, all over the country women are practicing medicine and doing the work of killing or curing, as the case may be. There has been the same change in the trades, in official employment and in the departments at Washington.

But as a rule women receive only two-thirds of men's salaries. When I was in Kansas I found a woman superintendent of schools with a man assistant. The woman received $1,000 and the man $600. I wept for joy. But that was a rare exception.

When men elect women superintendent of schools, as the law allows them to do, they do it from a selfish motive. By electing women they can get better talent for less money.
—*Speech, 1889*

We now have nearly equality of rights everywhere. They let us work everywhere, but only give us half pay.
—*Interview, 1898*

The battle now is the same as fifty years ago—to get equal pay for equal work and equal eligibility to the highest salaried positions. Even in states where the law requires that there shall be no discrimination against women, men are appointed to the highest places as a rule. It is woman's necessity to earn a living that causes her to take less wages than a man receives. This is an appeal to the parsimony of the employer, for it is a law of economics to get as much work done as possible and as good as possible for the least amount of pay. Women must take what they are offered or nothing. I do not see any hope of a change in this matter until women are enfranchised and until they combine and control their work and wages as do men.
—*Letter, 1903*

We certainly are very heartily in favor of organized labor. But you'll never get what you are after until you get the ballot.
—*Interview with member of striking laundry workers' union, 1903*

I think the girl who is able to earn her own living and pay her way should be as happy as anybody on earth. The sense of independence and security, as long as she retains her health, is very sweet to such a woman. Wealth to a woman does not always bring happiness unless she tries to help others with it. A woman who has nothing but her selfish personal interests to occupy her thoughts is never happy. It is a good thing for a woman to be brave enough to go into business and hold her own with the men. The woman who can work for herself does not snap at the first chance to get married simply to obtain a home. She can afford to wait a little and make a good selection.
—*Interview, 1905*

Optimistic? Of course I'm optimistic and I am assuredly not one of those who believe that the United States is going to—well, going to what men call the bow-wows. Because a train runs into an open switch when traveling at seventy-five miles an hour—is that any argument against fast trains? Would not a train going at forty miles have run into it just the same?

I don't think Americans are living too fast. The eager, ambitious, keen, striving life of the United States is but an indication of the youth and virility of the country. We wanted to beat England in running fast trains—well, we've done it. . . .

Do I deplore the fact that so many women are being forced into the stress of industrial life? Certainly not. I hope that a constantly increasing number of women will earn their own living instead of marrying men with whom it is impossible to live. It is true, of course, that the uneducated women of the country are not getting as good wages as they should get or as they will get, but they are vastly better off than the same class fifty years ago.

The cry that women did not work then is absurd—they did the hardest kind of menial labor on farms, and they toiled at the loom. The difference is this—that fifty years ago these women were not paid for their labor, while to-day they are.

To-morrow the factory operatives, shop girls and other workers of this country are going to be much better paid than they are now, and they're going to get that better pay through organization.

When the women workers of the United States realize their power and the strength that lies in union, they will form a huge national woman's organization which will, by its sheer bulk and force, wring from the employers more pay, shorter hours, improved working conditions.

— *Interview, 1905*

Anthony's constant preoccupation with money—as a means to independence, as a requirement to support herself—also served her political views. In 1869 she was notified that she owed the Internal Revenue Service taxes on her newspaper. Her response was a model of political protest:

THE REVOLUTION, you are aware, is a journal, the main object of which is to apply to these degenerate times the great principles on which our ancestors fought the battles of the Revolution, and whereon they intended to base our Republican government, viz., that "Taxation and representation should go together;" and that to inflict taxation upon any class of the people, without at the same time conferring upon them the right of representation, is tyranny.

I am not represented in the United States government, and yet that government taxes me; and it taxes me, too, for publishing a paper the chief purpose of which is to point out and rebuke the glaring and oppressive inconsistency between its professions and its practices.

Under the circumstances, the Federal government ought to be ashamed to exact this tax of me. However, as there is such pressing need of money to supply a treasury which is so sadly depleted by extravagant expenditures and clandestine abstractions by its own officials, I consent to contribute to its necessities this large sum ($14.10), assuring you that when the women get the ballot and become their own representatives, as they surely will and that very soon, they will conduct themselves more generously and equitably toward the men than men now do toward them; for we shall then not only *permit* you to pay taxes, but *compel* you to vote also. I had thought of resisting the payment of this tax on high moral grounds, as an unjustifiable exaction, but learning that the courts do not take cognizance of moral questions, I have decided to send you the sum ($14.10) enclosed.
—*Letter, 1869*

Her reluctance to part with what little money she had was aimed only at what she considered unjust causes. Suffrage was something else. She noted with joy the progress in women's benevolence.

The Mischief is those women who can *make money* out talking on women's rights, *don't give themselves* nor any of their money to help carry on *the movement.*
—*Letter, 1876*

Today's mail brought a $100 check to our National treasury from a New York woman. Oh! that a thousand of our good women who *wish* success to our cause would be moved thus to send in their checks! Only a very few women can go abroad to lecture, organize, agitate and educate, but very many can contribute money to help pay the expenses of those who, to help, must leave all, their home, friends, comforts and luxuries! Oh, if the many who stay at home and wish, could only believe for a moment that we who go out not knowing where our heads will rest when night comes, really love our homes as they love theirs, they would each vie with the other to throw in their mite to make smooth the way for the wayfarers. But we, every one of us who can speak acceptably to the people, must do all in our power to persuade the men of these States to vote for the amendment, and they who can't go, and can't speak, must help, each and everyone in every possible way, with their hope, their faith, their money.

... Who will send the next $100? Oh, that we had $10,000 to start with! Can't we have it, is the question?
—*Letter, 1893*

One effect of our suffrage movement is that women are learning to do more for women. Hitherto when a rich woman died leaving a large legacy to some institution, it was usually one for men that derived the benefit. Women are now understanding that their own sex has the first claim. Women throughout the land are quickly recognizing their duties as citizens; that as members of a great nation they have the same rights as all other members according to the fundamental principles of our Government. They object to being considered simply in the light of wife and mother.
—*Interview, 1905*

An American in Europe

Susan B. Anthony's very democratic views on money and status did not always translate across the seas. She never could get royal English titles quite right, and therefore substituted plain old "Mr." or "Mrs." for "your grace" or "your ladyship." Once she horrified passengers on a transatlantic steamer by turning to an English lord and, placing her hand on his shoulder, announcing, "I want to vote for the same reason that this fellow does." It is reported that his "lordship fairly gasped, his eyeglass fell out and his eyes almost did the same." And then there was the time in Rome when she startled her companions, ladies of noble lineage. Gazing on a grand old palace, Anthony announced, "What a magnificent orphan asylum that would make. . . . I think about 700 of these little ragamuffins could be put in there. . . . I don't see a better use to which these old palaces could be put."

20. PERPETUAL MOTION

The word "workaholic" had not been coined in the mid-1800s, but no one told that to Susan B. Anthony. A close colleague, abolitionist Parker Pillsbury, jokingly wrote her friend Lydia Mott about Anthony's schedule:

> Is there work down there among you for Susan to do? Any shirt-making, cooking, clerking, preaching or teaching, indeed any honest work, just to keep her out of idleness! She seems strangely unemployed—almost expiring for something to do, and I could not resist the inclination to appeal to you, *as a person of particular leisure,* that an effort be made in her behalf. At present she has only the Anti-Slavery cause for New York, the "Woman's Rights Movement" for the world, the Sunday evening lectures for Rochester and other lecturing on her own from Lake Erie to the "Old Man of Franconia mountains;" private cares and home affairs and the various et ceteras of *womanity.* These are about all so far as appears, to occupy her seven days of twenty-four hours each, as the weeks rain down to her

ANTHONY *(FIFTH WOMAN FROM LEFT)* ASTRIDE
HER MULE, MOSES, AT YOSEMITE, 1895

from Eternal Skies. Do pity and procure work for her if it be possible!

Elizabeth Cady Stanton saw it another way. Anthony, she wrote, was, next to Theodore Roosevelt, "the nearest example of perpetual motion" she knew.

Blessed with a robust body and enviable health, she maintained her punishing schedule by following a regime that might meet with modern approval: up early, simple meals, plenty of outdoor walking, no late dinner, absolutely no alcohol, and in bed by 9 or 10 P.M. Her one concession to a "health fad" was the water cure, a then-popular system of baths and cold packs that anticipated today's spas. The process seems to have restored Anthony during her rare bouts of fatigue or pain. Her personal physician practiced homeopathy, but Anthony consulted her infrequently until she was in her eighties.

For Anthony, the best cure of all was work, and it never occurred to her that other people might have other physical needs. Reverend Anna Howard Shaw, her treasured associate, wrote of Anthony's stamina one night in Chicago after an evening meeting. Shaw, then forty-one, was in bed, nearly asleep, when Anthony, approaching seventy, slipped into the room.

"Aunt Susan" . . . was still as fresh and as full of enthusiasm as a young girl. She had a great deal to say, she declared, and she proceeded to say it—sitting in a big easy-chair near the bed, with a rug around her knees, while I propped myself up with pillows and listened.

Hours passed and the dawn peered wanly through the windows, but still Miss Anthony talked of the Cause—always of the Cause—and of what we two must do for it. The previous evening she had been too busy to eat any dinner, and I greatly doubt whether she had eaten any luncheon at noon. She had been on her feet for hours at a time, and she had held numerous discussions with other women she wished to inspire to special effort. Yet, after it all, here she was laying out our campaigns for years ahead, foreseeing everything, forgetting nothing, and sweeping me with her in her flight toward our common goal, until I, who am not easily carried off my feet, experienced an almost dizzy sense of exhilaration.

Suddenly she stopped, looked at the gas-jets paling in the morning light that filled the room, and for a fleeting instant seemed surprised. In the next she had dismissed from her mind the realization that we had talked all night. Why should we not talk all night? It was part of our work. She threw off the enveloping rug and rose.

"I must dress now," she said, briskly. "I've called a committee meeting before the morning session."

On her way to the door nature smote her with a rare reminder, but even then she did not realize that it was personal. "Perhaps," she remarked, tentatively, "you ought to have a cup of coffee."

That was "Aunt Susan."

Anthony's incredible vitality persisted well into her later years. At seventy-four she noted in her diary that she had walked across New York's Central Park (from her cousin's at Sixty-eighth Street and Madison Avenue to Stanton's apartment at Sixty-first and Broadway, a distance of nearly a mile) in twenty minutes. At seventy-five, she showed off the recent photograph taken of herself astride a mule in California's Yosemite Valley (and confessed that she was "decidedly in favor" of the bloomers she'd donned for the occasion). At eighty, one of the birthday presents she received from the huge NAWSA celebration in Washington, D.C., was a spoon, which was designated "for your oatmeal, I guess; it is about the size." A reporter pointed out that "Miss Anthony . . . was generally one of the first down to breakfast in the hotel dining room, and, although there were all sorts of rich dishes on the bill of fare, she never failed to call instead, for oatmeal, cracked wheat, or something of that kind."

When she was eighty-five another reporter noted that she was "youthful looking and graceful still." But by then Susan B. Anthony was freely acknowledging her own limitations. In 1904 the proprietor of Washington's Shoreham Hotel hesitated about inviting Anthony to see the view from the top floor because they had to take a flight of stairs to get there. When a colleague noted that the famed suffrage leader regularly ran up and down stairs, Anthony replied, "No, I do not do that any longer because I don't think it wise, but I never walked up stairs till after I was eighty!"

How do I keep so energetic? By always being busy, by never having time to think of myself, and never indulging in any form of self-absorption.

— *Interview, 1895*

I attribute the secret of my good health to the fact that I never abused it. I have always made it a rule of my life to be regular in my habits. I have a time for everything. I live on simple, muscle and brain-giving food. I have not broken down in my campaign life simply because I never would indulge in dissipation, or late suppers after a lecture. I do not eat a hearty dinner before speaking in public; on the contrary, I eat very lightly. After my lecture, I do not accept invitations to swell suppers. I go straight to my rooms, take a bath and drink a cup of hot milk and eat a cracker. I think if I lived down in New Orleans I would merely eat an orange and a cracker before retiring, after a heavy evening's work.

Another thing, human nature demands a certain amount of sleep. Women need at least nine hours' sleep out of the twenty-four. If you go to bed and wake up in the morning without feeling refreshed, then the human machinery is out of gear, and the equilibrium must be restored or nervous prostration and a general break-down is the result. This is inevitable. Nature won't be cheated. Women try to do too much. The overdrawn drafts on nature must be paid. When there is tearing down, there must be upbuilding at the same time, or the structure falls. This upbuilding in the human wear and tear is accomplished by food and sufficient amount of rest, recreation and sleep. This has been my rule of life. Any woman may build up a strong, healthy constitution by following it.
—*Interview, 1895*

The salvation of the race depends, in a great measure, upon rescuing women from their hothouse existence. Whether in kitchen, nursery or parlor, all alike are shut away from God's sunshine. Why ... do not all of our wealthy women leave money for industrial and agricultural schools for girls, instead of ever and always providing for boys alone?
—*Letter, 1857*

My *back* has been wretched and good for nothing, all summer—but—I, now, am much better—The Teachers Convention seemed to bring me to life again.
—*Letter, 1858*

I get very weary in body, but not in mind. I do not long for the rest of inactivity. I glory in my work. I think it's a grand thing to

live. I enjoy life and friendship and good people's company more
and more, every year.
—*Interview, 1879*

BUT MISS ANTHONY, YOU HAVE GROWN YOUNG-LOOKING
AND HANDSOME WITHIN THE LAST TWO YEARS.

Well, why shouldn't I? The good cause is moving on and I am
contented to grow fat. I have gained more than ten pounds
within the past two years and the seams of my dresses have all
been altered to accommodate the new size. I shall be 78 years old
in February, but I feel young and buoyant and I have no concern
but that when I am done working for the suffrage cause thousands of other women will go right on with the work.
—*Interview, 1897*

I put a penny in the slot yesterday, and in no skirts and
the lightest possible grenadine dress, I pulled down one hundred and sixty pounds avoirdupois, so you see I am not being
reduced to either a shadow or a grease-spot by the work on the
biography.
—*Letter, 1898*

I never call myself old because I shall be young until the crack
of doom.
—*Remarks, 1892*

PRAY TELL, MISS ANTHONY, FOR THE BENEFIT OF EVERY
OTHER WOMAN IN THE COUNTRY, HOW YOU HAVE MANAGED
TO BE A YOUNG WOMAN AT EIGHTY?

Every other woman wouldn't follow my recipe. In the first
place, I have never tasted any alcoholic drink; why, I would as
soon touch arsenic. I was trained that way. In the second place, I
have abstained in the matter of food. In campaigns where I have
had to make as many speeches as any of the men who were speaking at the same time I would be the last to give out. That was because they would all refresh themselves after a hard evening by a
supper. Meanwhile I would be soundly asleep. So I have never
had any indigestion in my life, and do not intend to.

I suppose a share of my health is due to my activity, my constant exercise and so on; but after all I am firmly convinced that it
is mainly due to abstinence.
—*Interview, 1899*

Work is my gospel. I am seldom idle. In my younger days I used to make work for myself simply to have something to do. Now the work comes to me.
—*Interview, 1905*

HOW HAVE YOU BEEN ABLE TO RETAIN YOUR HEALTH IN SPITE OF ALL THE WORK YOU HAVE DONE TO SECURE EQUAL SUFFRAGE?

By working for women, and not for myself. Nobody could retain her health who was working for her own aggrandizement.
—*Interview, 1900*

Anthony recorded the very few instances of serious illness in her life with her usual precise observation. These diary entries of a fainting episode, a stroke, and heart problems also illustrate her extraordinary calm in the face of circumstances she cannot control.

Became faint & full of pain when lecture was half done—& stopped & was taken to Mrs. Williams's—Brandy & Doctor—seemed to [*sic*] total suppression of action—
—*Diary, 1873*

Went to church—had a sleepy time—had a sleepy time—seems as if something the matter with my tongue—had a feeling of strangeness—could not think of what I wanted to say—a queer sensation—all the afternoon—Mary asked me if my teeth were out—shall be better or worse tomorrow!!
—*Diary entry after what was diagnosed as a stroke, September 9, 1900*

Monday—felt queer. But went to the Williams affair [appointment to ensure that University of Rochester would become coeducational].
—*Diary, the next day, September 10, 1900*

The Dr. came this morning & again & again for a whole *month everyday*—
—*Diary, the next day, September 11, 1900*

I wish you could come and see me, or I could go and see you; but I cannot see my way clear to do anything but stay at home. I would tell you, if I dared to speak of it, that Richard is not quite himself again, but perhaps if I tough it through this winter as lazy as I have been for the last three months, I may feel like myself

again. My doctor, a homeopathic woman, thinks that it is simply overwork, but my rest will prove whether there is not something else at the bottom of it all. I eat and sleep and go round doing nothing, looking just as well as ever, but I suppose at eighty-one we must naturally begin to feel a change come over us.
—*Letter, December 28, 1900*

I had the *Dr.* [Marcena Sherman] *Ricker* yesterday P.M; She gave me medicine—something for my heart which acts all the time as if I had been running to the top of my speed—...It is very annoying in the nights—I cannot lay on my left side with any comfort—indeed I hear the beating awake or asleep—
—*Diary, 1903*

Even before her body became vulnerable and her energy started to flag, Anthony herself understood that she just couldn't do everything anymore.

Dear Friend
I did partly promise...I would be at your Church Sunday night—but the divisions & subdivisions of myself—utterly forbid my going—So I have to tell you how very much I regret that I cannot be in a half-dozen places at the same hour—not only tomorrow evening—but nearly every hour of every day of my crowded—life—
—*Letter, 1892*

Toward the end of her life, reviewing her experiences for her forthcoming biography, Anthony amazed even herself with her exploits.

Rochester, 4/9/97
My Dear Cousin:—
it just makes my head whirl to think of the way I rushed from one thing to another in those days
—*Letter, 1897*

Susan B. Anthony Not Dead

That was the headline in the Philadelphia *Record* on July 27, 1895, a day after the formerly invincible Anthony fainted at the close of a speech in Lakeside, Ohio. "All turned black," she wrote in her diary, "...next I knew there was a crowd around me; blanched & speechless." The news flashed across the nation that the seventy-five-year-old leader had expired. When Anthony recovered—almost immediately—she was particularly amused by the Associated Press dispatch to its Ohio correspondent: "Send us five thousand words if she is alive, unlimited if she is dead." The story was a short one.

21. DIVINE DISCONTENT

"$\mathcal{T}$*don't know what religion is," Susan B. Anthony confessed to a meeting of a liberal offshoot of the Friends when she was sixty-five years old. "I only know what work is, and that is all I can speak on, this side of Jordan." In many ways, work was her religion. The call, or invitation, to the twenty fifth annual NAWSA convention in Washington — which she, as president, signed and likely wrote — sounds almost like a holy tract. It aimed to "arouse that divine discontent" of women, since until "women are enfranchised, they cannot be considered free moral agents." There are references to NAWSA's "mission" and "public morality."*

Her best friend, Elizabeth Cady Stanton, said she was an agnostic.

Every energy of her soul is centered on the needs of this world.... She has not stood aside, shivering in the cold shadows of uncertainty, but has moved on with the whirling world, has done the good given her to do, and thus, in darkest hours, has been sustained by an unfaltering faith in the final perfection of all things. Her belief is not orthodox, but it is religious. In ancient Greece she would have been a Stoic; in the era of the Refor-

ANTHONY STAINED GLASS WINDOW,
MEMORIAL A.M.E. ZION CHURCH,
ROCHESTER, NEW YORK

mation, a Calvinist; in King Charles' time, a Puritan; but in this nineteenth century, by the very laws of her being, she is a *Reformer.*

Anthony believed unequivocally in religious freedom but had no tolerance for what she saw as the hypocrisy of most organized sects. It is significant that two of her dearest friends came from the most liberal traditions of religious thought: Lucretia Mott, a Quaker preacher, and Ernestine Rose, a Polish-born reformer who had abandoned her Jewish roots to become an atheist. Anthony took pride in her own Quaker background and always identified herself as a Friend, even though her family had switched to the Unitarian church when the Rochester Quakers did not support the Anthony position against slavery. While presiding over suffrage conventions, she generally had to be reminded to call for the opening prayer—and then preferred the Quaker way of giving thanks in silence. But when she was home in Rochester, she rarely missed services. "Sunday up-lifts," she called them, where "my spirit was born anew . . . and what feasts of soul those hours were to my over hurried life." One preacher "perpetually stirs us up to vigorous thought and self-requirement."

Her life was informed by various aspects of religion. Many of her friends and colleagues were ministers. She took an interest in spiritualism, one of the more popular "isms" of the day, and was curious about its attempts to communicate with the dead. In fact, she wondered often about death, writing to her friends and in her diary about "crossing over to the other side" with an ambivalent blend of skepticism and awe.

Unlike Stanton, whose irreverent—some might say blasphemous— attitude toward religion alienated many of her more conservative coworkers, Anthony found room for everyone in the suffrage tent. She counted Christians, Mormons, Jews, and nonbelievers among her staunch supporters, as long as they agreed on Anthony's own holy of holies: the vote.

Sometimes her tolerance was contagious. At a Woman's Christian Temperance Union convention in Washington, D.C., in 1881, she was introduced to the delegates—a somewhat more conservative crowd than showed up at the suffrage meetings—by WCTU President Frances Willard. One woman in the audience sniffed that Willard had insulted them all because Susan B. Anthony did not recognize God. "Well, I don't know about that," replied a woman from Indianapolis, "but I do know that God has recognized her and her work for the last thirty years."

DO YOU PRAY?

I pray every single second of my life; not on my knees but with my work. My prayer is to lift women to equality with men. Work and worship are one with me. I know there is no God of the universe made happy by my getting down on my knees and calling him "great."
—*Interview, 1896*

It is plain to me now that it is not sitting under preaching that I dislike, but the fact that most of it is not of a stamp that my soul can respond to.
—*Diary, after hearing a good sermon, 1855*

God is not responsible for our human ills and we should not believe or disbelieve in Him on account of our aches and pains. It surely is not the good people who escape bodily ailments. Certain fixed laws govern all, and those who come nearest to obeying these laws will suffer least; but even then we must suffer for the failures of our ancestors.
—*Letter, 1897*

Our hotel here is an old monastery, and on one side of its court is the cathedral, with its grotesque paintings. One gets awfully sickened with the ghastly spectacle of the *dead* Christ. It is amazing how little they make of the *living* Christ.
—*Letter from Amalfi, Italy, 1883*

"Let your women keep silence in the churches." That was the text they always hurled at our heads. Before giving a lecture I have known every minister in the town to denounce us from the pulpit beforehand, calling us infidels, because they said our speaking in public was in direct opposition to St. Paul's teaching. As a rule, on the night of the lecture, the ministers arranged prayer-meetings at the same hour, and made the women understand that their soul's salvation depended on attending the meeting.
—*Interview, 1895*

Anthony's distrust of many clergymen stemmed from an early temperance speaking tour. In 1852, while on the road, she discovered she was barred from lecturing in many churches, and thus reaching many people, because of the gentlemen who regularly preached there.

The power of the clergy over the minds of the people, particularly the women, is truly alarming. I am every day, more and more made to feel the importance of woman's being educated to *"lean not upon man but upon her own understanding."* The question now, with the masses of the women, is not whether they may be instrumental in doing good to society by engaging in the temperance work we propose to them, but will the minister approve of the plan of action. . . .

The connexion of the churches with the liquor traffic is truly fearful. We can hardly find one but is in some way connected with it. It is my solemn duty to speak against this monster vice of rum drinking wherever it may be found. The place that is not too holy to give shelter to this abomination is not too exalted to be attacked by both man and woman. I hope the day not far distant when those professing to be the light of the world shall absolve all connexion with the liquor traffic and all who sanction or sustain it.

Yours for Temperance,
SB Anthony
—*Letter to Editor, 1852*

It was dangerous to discuss religion with Susan B. Anthony if you did not know her attitude beforehand. Those who assumed she was as devout as they were rudely awakened. For instance, the cousin who sent her a biblical gift:

Your little birthday present, the Book of Proverbs, came duly. Solomon's wise sayings, however, don't help me very much in my work of trying to persuade men to do justice to women. These men and their progenitors for generations back have read Solomon over and over again, and learned nothing therefrom of fair play for woman, and I fear generations to come will continue to read to as little purpose. At any rate, I propose to peg away in accordance with my own sense of wisdom rather than Solomon's. All those old fellows were very good for their time, but their wisdom needs to be newly interpreted in order to apply to people of today.
—*Letter, 1896*

Then there was a relative who wrote from California that "God would punish the people in that State who worked aginst the woman suffrage amendment."

It is hardly worth while for you or anybody to talk about "God's punishing people." If He does, He has been a long time

about it in a good many cases and not succeeded in doing it very thoroughly. He certainly didn't punish the liquor dealers of San Francisco; instead of that, He let them rejoice over us women because of their power to cheat us out of right and justice. I think it is quite time, at least for anybody who has Anthony blood in her, to see that God allows the wheat and the tares to grow up together, and that the tares frequently get the start of the wheat and kill it out.
—*Letter, 1896*

And imagine the horror of the organizers when they heard this speech delivered at the World's Columbian Exposition, Public and Religious Press Congresses:

I am asked to speak upon "The Moral Leadership of the Religious Press." For one who has for fifty years been ridiculed by both press and pulpit, denounced as infidel by both, it is, to say the least, very funny. Nevertheless I am glad to stand here today as an object lesson of the survival of the fittest, from ridicule and contempt. I was born into this earth right into the midst of the division of the Society of Friends, as it was called, on the great question which has divided all the religious peoples of Christendom, and my grandfather and grandmother and my father, all Quakers, took the radical side, the Unitarian, which has been denounced as infidel.

I passed through the experience of three great reforms, not only with the secular press but with the religious press. The first one was that of temperance . . .

I went as a delegate of the New York State Woman's Temperance Association to Syracuse . . . When the committee reported it was adversely, that it was very well for women to belong to the temperance society, but wholly out of the way for them to be accepted as delegates or to speak or to take any part in the meetings, and I want to say to you that the majority of the men of that convention were ministers. . . . I want to say . . . that the most terrible Billingsgate, the most fearful denunciation, and the most opprobrious epithets that I ever had laid on my head were spoken that day by those ministers; and when there was time to report the proceedings the whole religious press of the country, the liberal, the Unitarian, as well as the orthodox, came down on my head for obtruding myself there, claiming that St. Paul had said: "Let your women keep silence in the churches," and no one but an infidel would attempt to speak there. I submit that was not leadership in the right direction.

Then next came the anti-slavery movement. And nobody can say for a moment that either the religious pulpit or the religious press was a leader in the great work of breaking the chains of the millions of slaves in this country; but on the other hand, church after church was rent in twain; the press . . . used to make my hair stand straight for fear I might go to the bottomless pit because I was an abolitionist.

The next great question has been this woman question. When we started out on that the whole religious world was turned upside down with fright. We women were disobeying St. Paul; we women were getting out of sphere and would be no good anywhere, here or hereafter; and the way that I was scarified! I don't know, somehow or other the press both secular and religious, always took special pride in scarifying Miss Anthony. I used to tell them it was because I hadn't a husband or a son who would shoot the men down who abused me. Well, now they take special pains to praise. [*Applause.*] It is a wonderful revolution of the press.

. . . The religious press, instead of being a leader in the great moral reform, is usually a little behind. [*Applause.*]
—*Speech, 1893*

That same event, a world's fair to celebrate Columbus' discovery of America, gave Anthony another chance to go against the grain of orthodox religion. In an era when the Christian Sabbath was a religious day, a burning national question was, Should the Exposition be open on Sundays? Anthony, as usual, disagreed with the clergymen:

It seems to me the common sense thing that all public places of art, science and learning should be open to suit the convenience of all classes of people; the ten hours of each week-day for such as have leisure, the evenings and Sundays for those whose bread-winning employments occupy every one of those ten hours of each of the six week-days.

And if this rule is but fair play with the permanent institutions of our cities, great and small—our libraries, art galleries, museums, etc., etc., how vastly more imperative is its application to the Columbian Exposition at Chicago . . .

Indeed I can think of nothing profane, nothing not worshipful—likely to be inside those gates—either Sundays or week-days—unless "powers that be" should permit the entrance of intoxicating liquors with their concomitant train of gamblers, blacklegs, thieves, libertines, prostitutes—which, may the civilization of these closing days of the 19th century forbid!!

Think for a moment of the million, or half a million of visitors . . . Only the smallest fraction of this vast visiting army could, if it would, get into the churches; all of Chicago's places of useful instruction and innocent amusement are closed; its libraries, and art galleries, its museums and gymnasiums, and, now that the Exposition has possessed them and locked the gates—its magnificent southern parks and its long and delightful lake front!—all are closed!! Hence for the vast majority of the vast multitude there is left absolutely no decent or comfortable place for them to go or stay. . . .

I am as earnest a Quaker as my friend Miss [Frances] Willard is a Methodist; and I would not only pull out the sheep fallen into the ditch on Sunday, but would also devise all possible ways and means to entice the loiterers away from the pitfalls on that day.
—*Letter to Editor, 1892*

Anthony tried hard to keep Church and State separate at the suffrage conventions. She had to temper both extremes: the traditionalists, who wanted to add God to every resolution, and the Stanton-led faction, who wanted their platform to reject every single form of organized religion. Anthony opposed both.

[T]he woman suffrage platform must be kept free from all theological bias, so that unbelievers as well as evangelical Christians can stand upon it.
—*Remarks, 1889*

If it is necesssary, I will fight forty years more to make our platform free for the Christian to stand upon, whether she be a Catholic and counts her beads, or a Protestant of the straightest orthodox sect, just as I have fought for the rights of the "infidels" the last forty years. These are the principles I want to maintain— that our platform may be kept as broad as the universe, that upon it may stand the representatives of all creeds and of no creeds— Jew and Christian, Protestant and Catholic, Gentile and Mormon, believer and atheist.
—*Speech, 1890*

Ironically, her bitterest battle was with Stanton, who criticized Anthony for extending a hand to all women—including those who still fol-

lowed orthodox religion — in her effort to broaden the base of suffrage support. In 1888 she wrote her friend Frances Willard about the flap, angry that Stanton had teamed up with Matilda Joslyn Gage and sent her criticism of Anthony to Clara Colby's Woman's Tribune.

I am more vexed than I can tell you—that Mrs. Stanton should send that wretched scribble of Mrs. Gage's to her—to the Woman's Tribune—and I am chagrined that Mrs. Colby should publish it—even if Mrs. S. did send it to her—It is too *idiotic* for anything—it is *complimentary* to *you*—in comparison to its fling at *"Susan"*—the *vulgar way* in which it calls me *"Susan"* and jibes my *lack* of fight & insight!! Well you & I can stand it!—But the National W.S.A. *platform* is not agnostic—any more than it is Roman Catholic or Methodistic—women of *all* beliefs have *perfectly equal rights upon it*—and it [is] on this point that both Mrs. G. & Mrs. S. are at fault—it seems to me.

They, *to my face*—charge me with having *become weak & truckling* not only to the *Church Women*—but also to *society women!*—they say I am eaten up with desire to make our movement *popular* &c—So you see—each & all of us who think & act for ourselves—have to be judged—& mis-judged by our associates—and as I have stood it 40 years—I shall hope to be able to endure it unto the end.

Of one thing I feel pretty sure—and that is that I shall not allow myself to act the *bigot* and persecute women who don't believe about God, or Christ, or heaven or earth as I do—The trouble with so many is that they can't see that so called Liberals are likely to become as bigoted and narrow as are the bigots of the various religions of the past or present—Lets [sic] you & I—my dear—stick together on this point—

—*Letter, 1888*

But that was nothing compared to the controversy over The Woman's Bible. *Stanton had been working on it for years — rewriting the Holy Scriptures from a purely feminist perspective. Anthony found it a major distraction.*

No—I don't want my name on that Bible Committee—You fight that battle—and leave me to fight the secular—the political fellows— . . . know your [sic] doing good because you are making Rome Howl,—So go ahead—but do at least have the members of your committee of those who have even read the Bible once through—consecutively—in their lives—I simply don't want the enemy to be diverted from *my* practical ballot fight—to that of scoring me for belief one way or the other about the bible—The religious *part* has *never been mine*—you know and I won't take it up—so long as the men who hold me in durance vile—won't care a dime what the Bible says—all they care for is what the *Saloon* says—So go ahead—in your own way—and let me stick to my own—

—*Letter, 1895*

Still, loyalty prevailed; when the controversy erupted into a floor fight at the 1896 NAWSA convention, Anthony returned to her colleague's side. Some delegates wanted to censure Stanton and offered a resolution to distance themselves from the work. Despite her distaste for The Woman's Bible, *Anthony, unwilling to let the organization be threatened by such a divisive issue, supported her old friend.*

The one distinct feature of our association has been the right of individual opinion for every member. We have been beset at each step with the cry that somebody was injuring the cause by the expression of sentiments which differed from those held by the majority. The religious persecution of the ages has been carried on under what was claimed to be the command of God. I distrust those people who know so well what God wants them to do, because I notice it always coincides with their own desires. All the way along the history of our movement there has been this same contest on account of religious theories. Forty years ago one of our noblest men said to me: "You would better never hold another convention than allow Ernestine L. Rose on your platform;" because that eloquent woman, who ever stood for justice and freedom, did not believe in the plenary inspiration of the Bible. Did we banish Mrs. Rose? No, indeed!

Every new generation of converts threshes over the same old straw. The point is whether you will sit in judgment on one who questions the divine inspiration of certain passages in the Bible derogatory to women. If Mrs. Stanton had written approvingly of these passages you would not have brought in this resolution for fear the cause might be injured among the *liberals* in religion. In other words, if she had written *your* views, you would not have considered a resolution necessary. To pass this one is to set back the hands on the dial of reform.

What you should say to outsiders is that a Christian has neither more nor less rights in our association than an atheist. When our platform becomes too narrow for people of all creeds and of no creeds, I myself cannot stand upon it. Many things have been said and done by our *orthodox* friends which I have felt to be extremely harmful to our cause; but I should no more consent to a resolution denouncing them than I shall consent to this. Who is to draw the line? Who can tell now whether these commentaries may not prove a great help to woman's emancipation from old superstitions which have barred its way?

Lucretia Mott at first thought Mrs. Stanton had injured the cause of all woman's other rights by insisting upon the demand for suffrage, but she had sense enough not to bring in a resolution against it. In 1860 when Mrs. Stanton made a speech before the New York Legislature in favor of a bill making drunkenness a ground for divorce, there was a general cry among the friends that she had killed the woman's cause. I shall be pained beyond expression if the delegates here are so narrow and illiberal as to adopt this resolution. You would better not begin resolving against individual action or you will find no limit. This year it is Mrs. Stanton; next year it may be I or one of yourselves who will be the victim.

If we do not inspire in women a broad and catholic spirit, they will fail, when enfranchised, to constitute that power for better government which we have always claimed for them. Ten women educated into the practice of liberal principles would be a stronger force than 10,000 organized on a platform of intolerance and bigotry. I pray you vote for religious liberty, without censorship or inquisition. This resolution adopted will be a vote of censure upon a woman who is without a peer in intellectual and statesmanlike ability; one who has stood for half a century the acknowledged leader of progressive thought and demand in regard to all matters pertaining to the absolute freedom of women.
—*Speech, 1896*

The resolution passed anyway. Anthony continued trying to act the mediator, publicly defending Stanton's right to present the Bible, privately chewing her out.

DID YOU HAVE ANYTHING TO DO WITH THE NEW BIBLE, MISS ANTHONY?

No, I did not contribute to it, though I knew of its preparation. My own relations to or ideas of the Bible always have been peculiar, owing to my Quaker training. The Friends consider the book as historical, made up of traditions, but not as a plenary inspiration. Of course people say these women are impious and presumptuous for daring to interpret the Scriptures as they understand them, but I think women have just as good a right to interpret and twist the Bible to their own advantage as men have always twisted it and turned it to theirs.

—*Interview, 1896*

You say "women must be emancipated from their superstitions before enfranchisement will be of any benefit," and I say just the reverse, that women must be enfranchised before they can be emancipated from their superstitions. Women would be no more superstitious today than men, if they had been men's political and business equals and gone outside the four walls of home and the other four of the church into the great world, and come in contact with and discussed men and measures on the plane of this mundane sphere, instead of living in the air with Jesus and the angels. So you will have to keep pegging away, saying, "Get rid of religious bigotry and then get political rights;" while I shall keep pegging away, saying, "Get political rights first and religious bigotry will melt like dew before the morning sun;" and each will continue still to believe in and defend the other.

Now, especially in this California campaign, I shall no more thrust into the discussions the question of the Bible than the manufacture of wine. What I want is for the men to vote "yes" on the suffrage amendment, and I don't ask whether they make wine on the ranches in California or believe Christ made it at the wedding feast. . . . I shall not circulate your "Bible" literature a particle more than Frances Willard's prohibition literature. . . .

I have been pleading with Miss Willard for the last three months to withdraw her threatened W.C.T.U. invasion of California this year, and at last she has done it; now, for heaven's sake, don't you propose a "Bible invasion." It is not because I hate religious bigotry less than you do, or because I love prohibition less than Frances Willard does, but because I consider suffrage more important just now.

—*Letter to Elizabeth Cady Stanton, 1896*

Susan B. Anthony's relationship with Mormon women was a source of constant surprise and frequent headlines. How could a women's rights leader befriend polygamists? The answer was twofold. One, she actually liked *most of the women and applauded their enterprise and early political freedom. Two, she believed that many were simply victims, and she wanted to help. Given such appalling circumstances, she reasoned, couldn't some-one make a difference? On her first trip out west, she attended a meeting of a group that had split off from Brigham Young.*

Salt Lake City, July 5, 1871

To the Editor of the Revolution:

If I were a believer in special providences, I should say that my being in Salt Lake City at the dedication of the new Liberal Institute was one. On Sunday A.M., July 2nd, this beautiful hall of the Liberal Party—*apostate party,* the saints call it—was well filled. . . . and as they sang their songs of freedom, and poured out their rejoicings over their emancipation from the thrall of the theocracy of Brigham . . . my soul was dipped into the deepest sympathy with the women around me; and, rising at an opportune pause, I asked if a woman and a stranger might be permitted a word. At once the circle of the men on the platform arose and beckoned me forward; and with a Quaker inspiration not to be repeated, much less put on paper, I asked those men around me, so bubbling over with the divine spirit of freedom, if they had thought whether the women in their households (many of them still in polygamy) were to-day rejoicing in like manner. I cannot tell what I said, only this I know—that beautiful women wept; old, wrinkled women wept, and men said "I wanted to get out of doors where I could scream." The transition of these people into the new life is complicated—is heart-rending. . . .

To illustrate: one man, a noble, loving, beautiful spirit, nothing of the tyrant, nothing of the sensualist, with four *lovely wives,* three of whom I have seen, and in the homes of them I have broken bread, with thirteen loved and loving children in three of these houses, wakes up to the new idea; four women's hearts breaking, three mothers and three sets of children must leave father and husband, that the *one wife system* may be realized. And I can assure you that my heart aches for the man, the women, and the children, and cries God help them one and all! Where man is a brutal tyrant that problem is comparatively easy.

What we have tried to do is to show them that the principle of the *subjection of woman* to man, whether it be that of one, four, or sixteen, is the point of attack. Woman's work in monogamy and polygamy is essentially one and the same—that of planting her feet on the solid ground of self-support; that there is and can be no salvation for womanhood but in the possession of *power over her own subsistence.*

The saddest feature here is that there really is nothing by which these women can earn an independent livelihood for themselves and children. No manufacturing establishments; no *free schools* to teach. Women here as everywhere, must be able to live honestly and honorably *without men,* and before it can be possible to save the masses of them from entering into polygamy or prostitution, legal or illegal. Whichever way I turn, whatever phase of social life presents itself, the same conclusion comes—*independent bread alone can redeem woman from her curse of subjection to man.*

. . . Here is missionary ground. Not for any "thus saith the Lord," divine rights, canting priests, or echoing priestesses of any sect whatsover; but for great, god-like, humanitarian men and women, who "feel for them in bonds as bound with them." No holy hands, no shouts of puritanic horror, no standing afar off to lift with "forty-foot pole"; but a simple, loving, sisterly clasp of hands with these struggling women, and an earnest work with them. Not to modify nor ameliorate, but to ABOLISH *the whole system of woman's subjection to man in both polygamy and monogamy.*
—*Letter to Editor, 1871*

At least one Mormon woman subscribed on the spot to The Revolution, *and Anthony wrote her friends back at the newspaper that she had "thrown into this polygamic camp the bombshell of woman's individual sovereignty, and direct inspiration from the heart of God equally with that of man." A later letter home indicates that the going was not always so smooth:*

Our afternoon meeting of women alone was a sad spectacle. There was scarcely a sunny, joyous countenance in the whole 300, but a vast number of deep-lined, careworn, long-suffering faces —more so, even, than those of our own pioneer farmers' and settlers' wives, as I have many times looked into them. Their life of dependence on men is even more dreadful than that of monogamy, for here it is two, six, a dozen women and their great broods of children each and all dependent on the one man. Think of fifteen, twenty, thirty pairs of shoes at one strike, or as many hats and dresses! . . .

But when I look back into the States, what sorrow, what broken hearts are there because of husbands taking to themselves new friendships, just as really wives as are these, and the legal wife feeling even more wronged and neglected. I have not the least doubt but the suffering there equals that here—the difference is that here it is a religious duty for the man to commit the crime against the first wife, and for her to accept the new-comer into the family with a cheerful face; while there the wrong is done against law and public sentiment. But even the most devoted Mormon women say it takes a great deal of grace to accept the other wives, and be just as happy when the husband devotes himself to any of them as to herself, yet the faithful Saint attains to such angelic heights and finds her glory and the Lord's in so doing. The system of the subjection of women here finds its limit, and she touches the lowest depths of her degradation.

The empire totters and Brigham feels the ground sliding from under his feet. . . . One man came to me relating a new vision, direct from Christ himself . . . and I said: "Away with your man-visions! Women propose to reject them all, and begin to dream dreams for themselves."
—*Letter, 1871*

Some years later, when Anthony spoke out against those in Congress who refused to seat a Mormon representative, Brigham Henry Roberts, she was accused of being propolygamy. Once again, she had to explain her very simple credo on hypocrisy:

No woman could abhor polygamy more than myself, but I detest even more the license taken by men under the loose morals existing in what the Mormons call the Gentile world. It is not that I uphold polygamy or any of its exponents, but I do feel more charity for a Mormon who has been taught from his birth that it is not only his right but his duty to God to enter into plural marriages, and that the man who has the greatest number of wives stands highest in God's favor, than I do for the man who has been taught from his cradle that the unpardonable sin is the desecration of womanhood; whose religious training and the moral code of civilization in which he is reared both make it a crime to violate the Seventh Commandment and the established law of monogamy. Yet, judging from the testimony we see all about us . . . the married or single man who lives a pure life is rare. I have more respect for the Mormon polygamist, who follows his teachings and lives up to the traditions of his religious sect by marrying

the different women with whom he cohabits and supporting
them and their children, than I have for the man who defies public opinion and in the light of our advanced civilization and religious moral teachings gives his name and support to one woman
openly while secretly desecrating the lives of others, thus committing a crime against his lawful wife as well as the other women
whom he wrongs. . . .

Therefore, while abhorring the principles of polygamy I think
the wives and mothers of the country might better enter into a
crusade against the licentiousness existing all around us and pol-
luting our manhood, and leave it to our lawmakers to settle the
matter of Roberts' fitness to be their associate in Congress.
—*Article, 1899*

*It turns out she had to be even more forceful. She welcomed Susa
Young Gates, one of Brigham Young's daughters, into her home for dinner
but had to send her a stern letter when Gates wanted to include her in a
book as a friend of Mormon women.*

I cannot let you use my name in any way in your book. You fail
to comprehend that I am among those who hate polygamy and all
the subjection of women in the Mormon faith.

The situation is indeed bad enough as we have it in what you
call "the Gentile world," but in that when a man and woman con-
sort outside of the monogamic marriage they do so against the
law of the State, the law of religion and the law of society. They,
(and especially the woman), who are guilty of such a partnership
are shunned by all decent people. When you justify polygamy as a
requirement of religious faith you make it entirely too re-
spectable. I recognize no excuse for it.
—*Letter, 1905*

*Anthony's very practical approach to religion extended to her views on
death. She wrote and talked about it frequently—sometimes with humor,
sometimes with resignation, always with great curiosity. In 1854 she participated in a discussion on whether there is life after death.*

The negative had reason on their side; not an argument could
one of us bring, except an intuitive feeling that we should not
cease to exist. If it be true that we die like the flower, what a delu-
sion has the race suffered, what a vain dream is life!
—*Remarks, 1854*

Just three years ago this day was our dear Hannah's [Susan's next younger sister's] last on earth, and I can see her now sitting by the window and can hear her say, "Talk, Susan." I know she wanted me to talk of the future meetings in the great beyond, all of them, as she often said, so certain and so beautiful to her; but they were not to me, and I could not dash her faith with my doubts, nor could I pretend a faith I had not; so I was silent in the dread presence of death. Three years—and yet what a living presence has she been in my thoughts all the days! There has been scarcely one waking hour that I have not felt the loss of her. We can not help trying to peer through the veil to find the certainty of things over there, but nothing comes to our eyes unless we accept the Spiritualistic testimony, which we can not wholly do.

Well, only you and I are left of mother's four girls, and when and how we also shall pass on is among the unknown problems of the future.

— *Letter to her sister Mary, 1880*

The pain over the death of her sixteen-year-old niece Susie B. was still raw just four weeks after the fatal skating accident, when Anthony wrote to her friend the Reverend Olympia Brown. The horrible tragedy had made Anthony reflect again on the hereafter—but it did not alter her views.

My Dear Olympia
. . . She is no more here—She looked at rest when we last saw the blanched-cold face—it was & is too cruel—but it is one of the inevitable things that must be submitted to—She was 16 years & five months old—and five feet six inches tall—she didn't *walk*— she *skipped & danced*—My hopes were set on her making a splendid womanly woman of great independence & power—But they are dashed to the earth—No my dear—I know of no change in my ideas of the present or future life—Instinctively I feel that the *vital thing—the heart—the spirit—the something that thinks & feels—enjoys & suffers—must survive the part that decays*—before our eyes—But how or where it exists—I know not—and none of the various theses have ever made me feel that I *knew*!! So I have always been—& still am—content to trust—as my dear & noble & good father said on his dying bed—that "the same farmer that orders all things well for the children of this life—will do the same for them in the next"—whatever is the next—will be right—will be the inevitable—be it what & how it may—But I cannot—like our dear Isabella [Beecher Hooker]—see & know—as it were face

to face—the *spirits* of my departed loved ones—I shall have to await *certain knowledge* until I go hence—as I fear all others will have to—No, No! My dear Olympia—I have not changed my views—and I do not know as I should be any happier & better if I had or could change them—I am content to do all I can to make the conditions of this life better for the next generation to live in—assured that right-living here is not only the best thing for me & the world here—but the best possible fitting for whatever is to come in the hereafter—I suppose your feeling of my change—is the same as that of Mrs. Gage & Mrs. Stanton—that is because I am not as *in*tolerant of the so called *Christian women*—as are they—that therefore I have gone—or am about to go over to the popular church—I do not approve of their system of fighting the religious dogmas of the people I am trying to convert to my doctrine of equal rights to women—But if they can afford to distrust my religious integrity—I can afford to let them—But what matters it—our funny notions of things don't—can't—make or change one fact of the universe—I believe *absolutely* in *law*—and that there is no mortal of us that can escape the penalty of any violation of law!!

—*Letter, 1889*

[W]omen must shake off conventional thraldom in many ways. Do you know, I think a widow's shrouding herself in black and secluding herself from the world is scarcely less barbarous than casting herself upon the funeral pyre? A crape veil makes me shudder. Who can rightly face the world through a crape veil—and who has the right to shirk the facing of the world?

This ostentatious advertising of one's grief is wrong. I have lost almost all my dear ones—father, mother, sisters, brothers, all—but I never put on black. One's duty is to the living. Sorrow should not be flaunted.

—*Interview, 1895*

Annie Besant, the English spiritualist and freethinker, with her theories of reincarnation, provided grist for plenty of conversations and at least one characteristically down-to-earth letter to Anthony's good friend the Reverend Anna Howard Shaw:

I wondered how you felt about Mrs. Besant's lecture. I had quite a little talk with her about it on Friday morning, and then her lecture Friday night on "The Brotherhood of Man" . . . I told her the humiliating part of her theory was that, after a soul had been developed and lived in the heavenly kingdom for fifteen thousand years in glory, in order to get back here to help us poor creatures, it had to resort to the doubtful process of getting born and going through mumps, measles and teething after the same old style, over and over again. I think it is the least attractive speculation of any of them, and it does not matter whether it is Calvinism, Unitarianism, Spiritualism, Christian Science, or Theosophy, they are all mere speculations. So I think you and I had better hang on to this mundane sphere and keep tugging away to make the conditions better for the next generation of women.

—*Letter, 1897*

Brother Anthony

During her first trip to Europe, Susan B. Anthony refused to let the traditions of the Old World stifle her hopes for the New. On a visit to a monastery in Florence, Italy, she saw the open visitors' register with its nearby pen and ink as an opportunity to promote The Cause. Elizabeth Cady Stanton describes the unlikely results: "[S]he made the rebellious pen inscribe, 'Perfect equality for women, civil, political, religious. Susan B. Anthony, U.S.A.' Friends, who visited the monastery the next day, reported that lines had been drawn through this heretical sentiment."

The President and Mrs. Roosevelt
request the pleasure of the company of

Miss Anthony

at a reception to be held at the
White House
Thursday, evening, February the eleventh,
nineteen hundred and four,
from nine to half after ten o'clock

22. THE PLEASURE OF HER COMPANY

*S*he knew everyone who was anyone in public life. Or figured out a way to meet them if she thought they could help The Cause. Susan B. Anthony was so famous herself, it was not always clear who sought out whom.

Most of the best-known women — and many of the men — were simply her friends: the suffragists, of course, including authors Harriet Beecher Stowe, Julia Ward Howe, Louisa May Alcott (to whom she sent a copy of her own work, History of Woman Suffrage), and the very popular and witty Cary Sisters (Phoebe and Alice); the reformers, including Frederick Douglass, William Lloyd Garrison, Wendell Phillips, and Booker T. Washington (who hosted Anthony's visit to his new center for black studies, Tuskegee Institute, in 1895). And the esteemed Clara Barton, with whom Anthony enjoyed a relationship that was both professional and girlish. In one 1902 letter to "My dear friend," Anthony thanks the Red Cross founder for sending along a copy of her new report from the war front in St. Petersburg, then dives right into the gossip:

What a row they are making about the Czar getting a divorce from the Czarina because she bears him *only daughters*. Why cant he see that he had better cling to his first love and *get the laws changed* so that the woman can succeed to the throne. It is too cruel to read the gossip. He had better remember Napoleon. To put Josephine away was the most wicked thing done by him. I wish you would write to the Czar. The little family of four daughters looks so beautiful, and the mother so sad. It is quite as likely that he is at fault as that she is. . . .

Barton answers by return mail, confessing to having "heard little or nothing in Russia concerning the so-called divorce of the Czar," but eagerly weighing in. "The thought of divorce at their age seems absolutely preposterous. Can they not wait?"

It is probably not coincidental that their letters talked about Czar Nicholas, since Anthony spent a good deal of her time courting, criticizing, or working with world leaders. On each of her three trips to Europe, she was received and entertained by some of the most prominent members of political and royal life. At the International Council of Women in Berlin in 1904, the Empress Augusta Victoria (wife of Kaiser Wilhelm) greeted her as "an honored guest" and acknowledged in a bond of sisterhood that "The gentlemen are very slow to comprehend this movement." In England in 1899, Anthony and the Council took tea at Windsor Castle, although Anthony's only encounter with its imperial inhabitant was limited to watching Queen Victoria wave as she rode by in her carriage. Anthony did, however, spend considerable time with the English suffrage leaders, then in the midst of their own campaigns. And Emmeline Pankhurst, whose advocacy of such militant tactics as hunger strikes probably hastened passage of the British women's vote, claims in her memoirs to have met Anthony and been greatly influenced by hearing her speak.

Back home, besides the hundreds of senators, representatives, governors, and mayors who fell under her spell, she knew every President of the United States after Lincoln—and treated them all with a decided lack of awe. When crowds rushed out to catch a glimpse of President Martin Van Buren in Saratoga Springs, the nineteen-year-old schoolteacher indignantly wrote her family.

[O]ne would have thought an angelic being had descended from heaven to have heard and seen the commotion . . . large crowds of people called to look at him as if he were a puppet-show. . . . I regret to hear that the people of Battenville are possessed of so little sound sense as to go 20 miles to shake hands with the President, merely to look at a *human being*, one who is possessed of nothing more than ordinary men & therefore should not be *worshipped* any more than any *mortal being.*

Celebrity just didn't impress this very egalitarian Quaker, and while she was always courteous, she was never cowed in the company of the renowned. Long before security concerns made Chief Executives so hard to approach, she was introduced to President Ulysses S. Grant while taking a stroll in Washington, D.C. When he expressed his greetings and asked what he could do for her, Anthony replied, without missing a beat, "I have only one wish, Mr. President, and that is to see women vote." "Ah, I can't do quite as much as that for you," he said, laughing. "I can't put votes into the hands of you women, but it may comfort you to know that I have just appointed more than five thousand postmistresses." On another occasion, she again ran into him on Pennsylvania Avenue. This time, with an opening for chief justice of the Supreme Court still pending, Anthony boldly suggested that he nominate Henry R. Selden, the lawyer who had defended her at her trial. The President did not acquiesce.

Over time, Anthony was a regular visitor at the White House for both social and business functions. She felt comfortable enough to drop a note to President and Mrs. Grover Cleveland inviting herself and the entire International Council of Women for an "audience" in 1888. (It was accepted.) And her delightful irreverence was evident one administration earlier, when she paid a visit to President Chester A. Arthur. Accompanied by a hundred women from the National Woman Suffrage Association convention across town, Anthony told the President at a reception in the Blue Room that he would have a better chance of reelection if he would throw his support to the proposed suffrage amendment. According to a newspaper report,

This little speech of Miss Anthony rather nonplussed the President, who, after some hesitation, made a reply, which was of a non-committal character. He, however, in a pleasant manner, formally welcomed the ladies, and said he felt certain that, as the ladies were earnest and determined, they would secure what they ought to have. Not to be outwitted by this flank movement, Miss Anthony persisted in asking, "Ought women not to have full equality and political rights?" To this Mr. Arthur replied, "We should probably differ upon the details of that question."

[Back at the suffrage convention], Miss Anthony opened the afternoon session, with the hall two-thirds full of ladies, by telling something of what had happened . . . "I asked him," said Miss Anthony, "if he did not think women ought to have the same rights and privileges as men. He answered—well; I don't think anybody could tell which way it was he answered, but it was very polite."

Miss Anthony's clever way of expressing the President's non-committal responses excited much laughter in the audience.

The newspaper headline read: MISS ANTHONY'S ENCOUNTER WITH THE POLITE BUT NON-COMMITTAL PRESIDENT. *The official convention proceedings appended a sigh of resignation to her afternoon's work:*

Miss Anthony then told how many times similar calls and appeals had been made upon the different occupants of the White-House during the past sixteen year[s], and that they always had been received courteously—but never had a President recommended equality of rights for women in his inaugural address or message to Congress.

Although Anthony never actually met Queen Victoria, she spent enough time in England and got a close enough look to form a very diplomatic opinion. Here is how she described her in an interview:

I thought Her Majesty was a very human looking woman—a good, motherly woman. . . . The Queen is a most conspicuous example to refute the oft repeated assertion that public life destroys the feminine instincts and unfits women for home duties. As the mother of nine children and head of the largest household in the world, she always has been distinguished for her wifely and maternal devotion and for her thrift and ability in managing her domestic affairs. . . .

However much I appreciate her splendid record I cannot but remember that in all matters connected with women she has been very conservative, never wholly yielding her assent to any innovation until it was already practically established. I have no recollection of her ever giving her influence for any improvement in the laws relating to women.

—*Interview, 1899*

She first visited James A. Garfield in 1880, right after he was nomi-
nated by the Republicans as their candidate, and wrote him about his posi-
tion on the suffrage amendment. Their initial exchange of letters
demonstrates Anthony's easy manner with the powerful.

Dear Miss Anthony:

. . . in view of the fact that the Chicago convention has not discussed your question do you not think it would be a violation of
the trust they have imposed in me to speak . . . as their nominee
and add to the present contest an issue which they have not
raised? . . . while I am open to the freest discussion and fairest
consideration of your question I have not yet reached the conclusion that it would be best for the women of the country that she
should have the suffrage. I may reach it but whatever time may
do to me that fruit is not yet ripe on my tree. I ask you therefore
for the sake of your own questions do you think it wise to pick
my apples now. Please answer me in the frankness of personal
friendship. With kindest regards I am Very Truly Yours
     J A Garfield
—*Letter, 1880*

Hon. James A. Garfield
Dear Sir
Yours of the 25th ult. has waited these many days, simply be-
cause I didn't know what to say to you in reply.

. . . For the candidate of a party to *add* to the discussions of the
contest an issue unauthorized or unnoted in its platform, when
that issue was one vital to its very life,—would, it seems to me be
the grandest act imaginable. . . .

As to picking fruit before it ripens!!—Allow me to remind you
that very much fruit is *never picked.*—some gets worm-eaten and
falls to the ground . . .

But really, Mr. Garfield, if, after passing through the war of the
rebellion and your sixteen years of service in Congress,—if, after
seeing and hearing, and repeating . . . that no class ever got justice
and equality at the hands of any government, except it had the
power, the ballot, to clutch them for itself,—if, after all your opportunities for growth and development, you cannot yet see the
truth of the great principle of *individual self-government,*—if you
have only reached the idea of *class-government,* and that, too, of the
most hateful and cruel form,—bounded by sex,—there must be
some radical defect in the tree or fruit. And the more is the pity,

because in the Democratic Party and its nominee there is *no hope whatever*—the root itself being defective, if not altogether *rotten*.—

With great respect for your frank and candid talk with one of the disfranchised, I am very sincerely yours,

Susan B. Anthony

—*Letter, 1880*

Not all the presidential candidates she knew went on to the White House. In 1880 she met Eugene V. Debs, the perennial Labor and Socialist candidate, who later wrote that Anthony impressed him "as being a wonderfully strong character, self-reliant, thoroughly in earnest, and utterly indifferent to criticism." Debs' observations of her trip to Terre Haute, Indiana, provide a bleak picture of the hostility still evident in the late 1800s.

I can still see the aversion so unfeelingly expressed for this magnificent woman. Even my personal friends were disgusted with me for piloting such an "undesirable citizen" into the community. It is hard to understand, after all these years, how bitter and implacable the people were, especially the women, toward the leaders of this movement.

As we walked along the street I was painfully aware that Miss Anthony was an object of derision and contempt, and in my heart I resented it and later I had often to defend my position, which, of course, I was ever ready to do. . . .

To all of this Miss Anthony, to all appearance, was entirely oblivious. She could not have helped noticing it for there were those who thrust their insults upon her, but she gave no sign and bore no resentment.

I can see her still as she walked along, neatly but carelessly attired, her bonnet somewhat carelessly awry, mere trifles which were scarcely noticed, if at all, in the presence of her splendid womanhood. She seemed absorbed completely in her mission.

Theodore Roosevelt was the last President she would know and the one to whom she was closest in personality, according to her best friend. "The fact is, he is vain of seeming so strong and active and I am afraid there is a touch of the same feeling in Susan," Elizabeth Cady Stanton wrote in 1902. Later that year, just after Stanton's death, Anthony wrote the President on behalf of her latest concern: removing the barriers against woman suffrage in the new territories of Hawaii and the Philippines. Once again, she dangled the hope of reelection to a sitting politician.

A word from you, President Roosevelt, on any phase of the woman suffrage question would be of inestimable benefit and would give it a prestige and a sanction which would carry it immeasurably forward. This much you can do now, and two years hence it will be within your power to send it to assured victory.

I may not be here, then, as I should be nearly eighty-five years old, and so I take this opportunity to urge, by all that is just and sacred, that before you leave your high office you will recommend to Congress the submission of an Amendment to enfranchise women. It would be as noble an act as the Emancipation Proclamation of Abraham Lincoln, and would render you immortal. . . .

How eagerly they are looking to you—the only President who ever has offered them the slightest ground for hope—cannot be put into words. Thousands of men also are waiting for you to give the sign. Dear Mr. Roosevelt, let us not watch and wait in vain.

   Respectfully and sincerely yours,
   Susan B. Anthony
—*Letter, 1902*

A handwritten note at the bottom, by Ida Husted Harper, says of the letter: "No attention ever was paid to it except a formal receipt from [Commerce and Labor] Sec'y [George Bruce] Cortelyou."

It should not have surprised them. Before he lived in the White House, Roosevelt had made his position clear to Anthony:

I have always favored allowing women to vote, but I will say frankly, that I do not attach the importance to it that you do. I want to fight for what there is the most need of and the most chance of getting, at the moment. I think that, under the present laws, women can get all the rights she will take; while she is in many cases oppressed, the trouble is in her own attitude, which laws cannot alter.

—*Letter from Theodore Roosevelt, 1898*

Two years later, in 1904, Anthony again confronted President Roosevelt, this time at an Army and Navy reception at the White House. It is not clear which of them was the bigger star. The President's irrepressible daughter, Alice, had slipped away from a party of her own to attend, telling friends, "I must speak to Miss Anthony, she is my father's special guest." Here is how another guest, Governor Alva Adams of Colorado, described the scene:

I was at her side in the line that was being received by President and Mrs. Roosevelt. As we approached the President, he grasped Miss Anthony by the hand and arm, and with enthusiastic greeting pulled her to his side, there to remain during the reception. I passed on, and as I looked back upon these two dominant characters, there flashed into my mind the thought that, when this great woman and this great man are weighed in the scales of God, the woman will not be found to be the lesser figure.

Anthony was very well behaved that evening. She told him, "Now, Mr. President, we don't intend to trouble you during the campaign, but after you are elected, then look out for us!" Mr. Roosevelt and his wife were heard to laugh heartily. Sure enough, as he was preparing to be sworn in for his second term, Anthony contacted him again.

In your Inaugural Address I beg of you to speak of Woman as you do of the Negro—speak of her as a human being, as a citizen of the United States, as a half of the people in whose hands lies the destiny of this Nation. Woman is entitled to that share in the political life of the country which is warranted by her individual ability and integrity and the position she has won for herself, just as the negro is. I could not have such confident faith as you have in the destiny of this mighty people if I had it in but one-half of them. For weal or for woe we are knit together and we shall go up or down together, and I believe that we shall go up and not down, that we shall go forward instead of halting and falling back, because I have an abiding faith in all my countrymen and countrywomen. And for their full development it is necessary that women, just as much as negro men, shall be granted perfect equality of rights.
—*Letter, 1905*

Several months later, Anthony showed up again. At 11 A.M. on November 15, 1905, she had a private meeting with President Roosevelt in the Cabinet Room at the White House, along with Ida Husted Harper and Harriet Taylor Upton, another suffrage lieutenant. Anthony ran the session, entreating him for half an hour ("while eminent and impatient men waited on the outside") to aid their campaign in a number of ways, including mentioning woman suffrage in his speeches. When Roosevelt pointed out that he almost always mentioned women in his speeches, Anthony responded, "Yes, as wives, as mothers, as wage-earners, but never with any reference to their political rights." She ended with this plea:

> Mr. Roosevelt, this is my principal request—it is almost the last request I shall ever make of anybody. Before you leave the presidential chair, recommend Congress to submit to the Legislatures a Constitutional Amendment which will enfranchise women, and thus take your place in history with Lincoln, the great emancipator. I beg of you not to close your term of office without doing this.

Then, laying her hand on his arm, the ever-blunt suffragist said, "And I hope you will not be a candidate for the office again!" Although he was, he lost, and never did comply with a single one of her requests.

Miss Anthony Goes to the Rodeo

Fame had its rewards. In 1893, while attending the World's Columbian Exposition in Chicago, Susan B. Anthony offended a number of clergymen by proclaiming that the fair ought to remain open on Sunday. When one of the churchmen asked if she would approve of her own son's attending Buffalo Bill's Wild West Show on the Sabbath, Anthony answered, "Of course I would. In fact, I think he would learn more there than from the sermons preached in some churches." Colonel William F. (Buffalo Bill) Cody was so enthralled, he invited Anthony to his show, and the lively leader showed up with a dozen suffrage friends. One of them described the scene as Colonel Cody entered the arena on horseback. "He rode directly to our boxes, reined his horse in front of Miss Anthony, rose in his stirrups, and with his characteristic gesture swept his slouch-hat to his saddle-bow in salutation. 'Aunt Susan' immediately rose, bowed in her turn, and, for the moment as enthusiastic as a girl, waved her handkerchief at him, while the big audience, catching the spirit of the scene, wildly applauded."

23. SPARROWS, SPOONS, AND SURNAMES

In 1893, when Anthony was seventy-three, a woman who had heard one of her lectures sent her a letter from California. She said she knew about the damage caused by English sparrows and enclosed a description and sketch of a device she had invented to snare the birds and keep them from disfiguring buildings. Could Miss Anthony help her to get it produced? She went on, "and if anything can be made of it I should be glad to share it equally with you for your trouble." Susan B. Anthony passed the letter on to someone who presumably could help, with the handwritten note, "I enclose this — hoping that you can give aid & comfort to the writer. S.B.A." It was emblematic of the many odd and occasionally outrageous requests that came to her desk at the house on Madison Street.

Another letter that has survived grants Millie Burtis Logan "the exclusive right to use the representation of my features and my name upon souvenir goods or as a Trade Mark." Specifically, Mrs. Logan sent along an engraving of a spoon bearing Anthony's face and name and the phrase "Political Equality."

Thus, the price of fame.

She was regularly asked for autographs. That was fine—as long as they were for personal use.

> Oh yes My dear Little boy—
> I do like to correspond with the likes of you—or should like to—if I only had the time—I hope when you are grown up—and as you are growing up—you will always speak & act toward your Mother and sisters—as if their opinion were of equal value with those of your father & brothers—and when you are twenty-one— I hope you will work & vote for their enfranchisement—that they may stand equal with you & your father before the law—
> > Sincerely yours
> > Susan B. Anthony
> —*Letter, 1890*

But Anthony drew the line at commercial ventures, unlike her pal Elizabeth Cady Stanton, who let Lewis Union Suits, the underwear people, use her name and picture in a magazine advertisement. In other words, no celebrity endorsements for Susan B. Anthony.

> I will *not* give you a recommendation for the Fairy soap or anything of the sort. I might be willing to go out and lecture, if I could, and earn $20 to *give you,* but I cannot lend my name to your soap business any more than I could to that Chicago woman's insurance business, at Washington last winter. I consider the whole scheme of *buying up people's names* to recommendations for all sorts of truck villainous, and do not wish to be one to encourage it, even to help you to some money—as much as I could wish you might be able to get. . . .
> Now, my dear, you needn't think I have thrown you altogether overboard because I won't go into trying to humbug people through advertisements. When I was at Geneva Mrs. Stanton told me she was going to give you another recommendation for some underwear, and I told her if she wanted to be bruited about on all the advertising pages of the world, she could; that I shouldn't follow her in that.
> —*Letter, 1899*

On the other hand, she was always happy to talk up a new trend if it was good for women. One of her favorite innovations was the bicycle.

I think it has done a great deal to emancipate women. I stand and rejoice every time I see a woman ride by on a wheel. It gives her a feeling of freedom, self-reliance and independence. The moment she takes her seat she knows she can't get into harm while she is on her bicycle, and away she goes, the picture of free, untrammeled womanhood. . . .

The bicycle also teaches practical dress reform, gives women fresh air and exercise, and helps to make them equal with men in work and pleasure; and anything that does that has my good word. What is better yet, the bicycle preaches the necessity for woman suffrage. When bicyclists want a bit of special legislation, such as side-paths and laws to protect them, or to compel railroads to check bicycles as baggage, the women are likely to be made to see that their petitions would be more respected by the law-makers if they had votes, and the men that they are losing a source of strength because so many riders of the machine are women. From such small practical lessons a seed is sown that may ripen into the demand for full suffrage, by which alone women can ever make and control their own conditions in society and state.

—Letter to Editor, 1898

When Lucy Stone married Henry Blackwell in 1855, she made a public issue out of retaining her own name—a deed that for years led other such independent wives to be known as "Lucy Stoners." Once Anthony got used to the idea of Lucy's being married at all, she heartily approved of the practice and said so in a letter referring to some British women who failed to comply.

I am more and more rejoiced that you have declared by the actual doing, that a woman has a name and may retain [it] through all her life—Articles on Madame Bodishon [sic], *she that was*— and on Madam _____ she that was Meriton White of England, have freshly reminded me of the ridiculousness of the present custom.

—Letter, 1858

A reporter queried Anthony on the same issue:

I SUPPOSE YOU WILL DO AWAY WITH THE GRAMMATICAL DISTINCTIONS WHICH EXPRESS THE GENDERS OF THE SEXES . . . AND WE SHALL NOT KNOW WHETHER IT IS A MASCULINE OR FEMININE WHO IS IN OFFICE UNLESS THE NAME IS SPECIFIED?

To be sure we shall; we shall do away with such words as editress, poetess, doctress and other such expressions which are absurdities. We do not call Rosa Bonheur a paintress, though no man can equal her in painting cattle; we call her an artist.

HOW WILL YOU DISTINGUISH BETWEEN THE CHRISTIAN NAMES OF MARRIED MEN AND WOMEN; WILL THE WIFE CALL HERSELF AFTER THE CHRISTIAN NAME OF THE HUSBAND?

No; a woman is as much entitled to her first name as a man, and she should retain it; and for that, her surname also. Hereafter, instead of calling a married woman Mrs. John Smith or Mrs. Thomas Jones, she will be known as Mrs. Abigail Smith or Mrs. Susan Jones.

DO THE WOMEN WHO SIGNED THE RECENT CONSTITUTION BELIEVE IN THAT MODE?

Of course they do; did you not see that they signed their Christian names?

I SAW ONE OR TWO EXCEPTIONS, WHERE I THOUGHT A LITTLE VANITY WAS DISPLAYED; INSTEAD OF MERCY, OR PATIENCE, OR SUSAN MARIA SAXTON, I SAW ONE NAME CALLED MRS. GENERAL SAXTON; I SUPPOSE MILITARY TITLES ARE EXCEPTIONS TO THE GENERAL RULE, AND THAT MRS. SERGEANT RAMROD AND MRS. CORPORAL O'CASEY WILL BE THE PROPER MODE OF SIGNATURE FOR THE SPOUSES OF THE FOLLOWERS OF MARS?

Not at all; that mistake was made, but the cause of it was that her Christian name was not known. She was appointed a delegate to act in conjunction with me at the National Convention, to be held in Washington, in January.

AND THEY THOUGHT THE NAME WOULD ADD DIGNITY TO HER CONSTITUENTS?

[T]here is no necessity for that cloak. Woman has an individuality as well as man, and she should preserve it. It is the fashion now . . . to keep their maiden name after marriage, as for instance, Mrs. Cady Stanton—Cady was her maiden name; don't you know that is the fashion now?

LIVING HERE [OREGON], I AM, OF COURSE, UNABLE TO

KEEP PACE WITH ALL THE TRANSFORMATIONS OCCURRING IN
THE EAST. . . .

Why, you are behind the age. You don't know what is going on
in the world. Do you suppose that a woman who makes a reputation under her maiden name is going to lose that name by marriage, and adopt that of an unknown creature of a husband. Who
knows Goldsmith, the husband of Jenny Lind? Nobody; but she
is known throughout the world. If Anna Dickinson should marry
a Smith, and adopt his name, she would have to make another
reputation in the world, which would be unjust to her, as but few
were so great as to make two reputations in an ordinary life time.
— *Interview, 1871*

I am glad you like your name without the prefix either of Miss
or Mrs—So do I—
— *Letter, 1888*

For if *Catt* it must be then I insist, she should keep her own father's name—Lane—and not her first husband's name—Chapman.
— *Letter regarding the appellation of Carrie Lane Chapman Catt,
Anthony's successor as president of NAWSA, 1894*

*Anthony's advice to her cohorts ran the gamut—from the very serious
to the truly frivolous. She had an opinion on everything:*

Don't be afraid of saying *I.* Our women need not be ashamed
of saying or writing, "I did,"—for each one knows but very little
beyond what she herself did!
— *Letter, 1884*

To My Suffrage Nieces:—Now that you have voted me your
president, and every one will be writing me about your work, I
have just one earnest request to make of one and all, and that is
that you do not write with any of the pale, fluid ink, but with a jet
black ink, to start with, then you'll be sure it is black; I use
Stafford's, but if any of you can tell me of a blacker ink as it flows
from the pen, I shall be glad to use it. The pale fluids of to-day,
whether for hand or type written letters, are simply atrocious.
And I protest against our suffrage girls using them for their own
eyes' sake as well as for those of their older sister and co-worker.
— *Letter to suffrage newspaper, 1892*

Women in public life can never escape the kitchen. Think of Hillary Clinton's chocolate chip cookies. Or the southern state official who stunned the entire press corps following Geraldine Ferraro in 1984, by asking the nation's first female vice-presidential candidate whether she could make blueberry muffins. ("Sure can, can you?" Ferraro shot back. Jim Buck Ross could not. "Down here in Mississippi, the men don't cook," he explained.) Susan B. Anthony may have started that great tradition.

"Miss Anthony, can you make a loaf of bread, cook a pot of potatoes or bake a cake?"

This was the startling query that greeted the scribe's ears yesterday afternoon as he silently joined a little circle gathered about Miss Susan B. Anthony at No. 79 Winder Street, where the famous expounder of woman suffrage was being entertained during her brief stay in Detroit.

Abashed at the intrepidity of the fair devotee, who had thus openly impugned the domestic abilities of the able platform advocate, the reporter, impressed with the grave significance of the moment, eagerly pricked up his ears to await Miss Anthony's revelation.

For four distinct seconds by the little marble clock over the mantel, a death-like silence fell upon the startled auditors. A handsome young lady on the lecturer's right blushed furiously, and cast down her eyes, mechanically counting the red roses that figured in the pattern of the carpet; while the elderly woman in the corner coughed asthmatically and glanced out of the window at the flying snowflakes. As for Miss Susan B. Anthony herself, this estimable lady inclined her bright-blue eyes toward the crackling grate fire, rubbed her soft, white hands meditatively, then threw back her snow-crowned head, a youthful smile lighting her face, said very softly:

"Well, I used to be considered—the—the—the best cook in our family of four girls! Why, bless you, I remember now how brother . . . stood by my cooking. He used to work in a little place a number of miles from where we lived. Whenever he came home he used to insist on it that Susan should do the cooking."

"Strange how some people imagine that the domestic arts are inseparably divorced from the higher education," put in a matronly woman in black silk.

"Yes," said Miss Anthony, carefully whisking a speck off her rich black satin and letting her fingers move softly through a bit of bright yellow ribbon that she wore upon her breast. "I have al-

ways held that the girl who had brains enough to understand philosophy or Latin can very easily master the art of cookery. I am decidedly in favor of both these kinds of education."
—*Newspaper article, 1889*

Ten years later, she received a request from some college girls for her favorite cake recipe. This was her first draft, with the blanks meant to be filled in:

Dear Junior Girls:

My favorite cake is the old-fashioned sponge, made of ＿＿＿ eggs, the whites lashed to a stiff froth, the yolks beaten thoroughly with ＿＿＿ cups of pulverized sugar, a pinch of salt, a slight flavor of almond. Into these stir ＿＿＿ cups of flour—first a little flour, then a little of the white froth—and pour the foaming batter into a dish with a bit of white buttered paper in the bottom. Clap into a rightly tempered oven as quickly as possible and take out exactly at the proper minute, when it is baked just enough to hold itself up to its highest and best estate. Then don't cut, but break it carefully, and the golden sponge is fit for the gods. . . .

Well, the dickens is to pay—I can not find the old cook book—so just put in any good sponge cake recipe for me, and then add, "It matters not how good the recipe or the ingredients may be, the cake will not be good unless there is a lot of common sense mixed in with the stir of the spoon!"

Lovingly yours.

—*Letter, 1898*

In the pre-Freudian era there were several popular means of analysis, including phrenology (the study of the bumps on the head) and palmistry (the study of the lines in the hand). Susan B. Anthony adventurously submitted to both. She was only thirty-three and barely known when the phrenologist, blindfolded, made his examination. Either he made some very good guesses or we should take another look at the practice.

You have a finely organized constitution and a good degree of compactness and power. There is such a balance between the brain and the body that you are enabled to sustain mental effort with less exhaustion than most persons. You have an intensity of emotion and thought which makes your mind terse, sharp, spicy and clear. You always work with a will, a purpose and a straight-

forwardness of mental action. You seldom accomplish ends by in-
direct means or circuitous routes, but unfurl your banner, take
your position and give fair warning of the course you intend to
pursue. You are not naturally fond of combat, but when once
fairly enlisted in a cause that has the sanction of your conscience
and intellect, your firmness and ambition are such, combined with
thoroughness and efficiency of disposition, that all you are in energy and talent is enlisted and concentrated in the one end in view.

. . . I judge that in the main you have your father's character
and talents and your mother's temperament. . . . You have large
benevolence, not only in the direction of sympathy but of gratitude. You have frankness of character, even to sharpness, and you
are obliged to bridle your tongue lest you speak more than is
meet. You have mechanical ingenuity, the planning talent, and
the minds of others are apt to be used as instruments to accomplish your objects. . . . At fifteen your mind was devoted to facts
and phenomena; of late years you have been thinking of principles and ideas.
—*Phrenology report, 1853*

*Her palm was read by Stella, a Gypsy queen who showed up at the
Anthony house in Rochester in 1899. Queen Stella, decked out in a fantastic
costume, sat at the feet of Susan B. Anthony, who was dressed in her plain
black gown relieved by a bit of white lace. A newspaper reporter described
the unlikely exchange:*

"No business capacity," declared the seeress, "at least, not for
yourself; for others, yes. You never think of your own affairs; it is
always for others you think. You have a sensuous nature—mind,
I do not say sensual—but you have a sensuous love of the beautiful. Beautiful music, beautiful pictures, birds and flowers, they all
attract you and you love them.

"Oh, but you have a fighting thumb! People who have that
thumb go through life sleeping on the ground, if need be."

"Fighting thumb! I like that," said Miss Anthony, laughing.

"Then the poetry of life. That is as strong within you now as it
was when you were a little child, for you have never grown old,
but you have no logic. Oh, no! The world says you have, but you
have wisdom, and not logic. Why, if you had logic, no one could
live with you. But you have tenacity of purpose; when you think
you are right no one can stop you; you go ahead, no matter what
the consequences. . . .

"The finger of Apollo says you love melody and the beautiful colors, only you have no time for them. You cannot keep money. It comes and goes, and others enjoy it more than you. . . .

"The Mercury finger says you have great ability of expression, conquering through ability and daring expressing. No matter what it is, if you think you are right, you say it. . . .

"The line of the heart shows that the brain dictates one thing, and the heart another. It is strange, the great capacity you have for being loved, and then stopped single all your life," said the gypsy looking wonderingly into Miss Anthony's face, as if unable to comprehend.

"Would she have been happy with a husband and children," here interposed the reporter.

"With children, yes; with husband, I don't know. If the husband had been a companion, yes; but with hand like hers, the man would have had to look up, and the woman drag him along."

—*Newspaper report of palm reading, 1899*

The First Time

Susan B. Anthony was sixty-three when she had her first breakfast in bed ("What would my mother say?"); sixty-seven when she first went to the seashore ("It seems very odd to be one of the giddy summer resort people!"); seventy-five when she tasted her first truffles ("Truffles, why what are truffles?"); and seventy-eight when she went to her first football game. It was 1898, and from her seat near the fifty-yard line in the Chicago stadium she wondered aloud, "Why don't they kick the ball?" Later she reported spending a most pleasurable afternoon. Her opinion of the game? "There is no game to it. At least I can't see any. They just take the ball and then fall down in heaps. It's ridiculous. The boys who play the game don't look like human beings at all. At first I thought they resembled apes, but after they got to plowing about in the mud they reminded me more of the seals I saw in the Pacific when last in California. They dove just as the seals did. Is it brutal? I don't think so. I failed to see anyone hurt and do not see why mothers should be afraid of the game. It's silly, but not brutal."

24. FOREMOTHERS

*S*usan B. Anthony called them Foremothers—the women who had paved the way for the movement she now led. She was deeply conscious of the legacy she had inherited and always paid tribute to other women. But she was also aware that somewhere along the line, she had become a Foremother herself, with an obligation to pass on the heritage to the next generation.

It was always her dream to get the history into some kind of permanent form—yet another inheritance from her father, who had first suggested she keep a scrapbook of clippings and notable items. That dream started to take shape in 1876. She and Elizabeth Cady Stanton, with help from feminist writer Matilda Joslyn Gage and journalist Ida Husted Harper, compiled an amazingly complete record of nearly three quarters of a century of the national campaign to win the vote for women. It was called History of Woman Suffrage. The single book they'd proposed expanded to a six-volume series (almost 1,000 pages per volume); the two original authors were supplemented by two more. The project was so massive, so overwhelming, that sorting through the letters, documents, bills, and minutes for the first three volumes alone finally took ten years.

Anthony and Stanton had modestly thought they could put it all together in a year.

HISTORY OF WOMAN SUFFRAGE AND
LIFE AND WORK OF SUSAN B. ANTHONY

Today, despite a powerful but forgivable bias, History of Woman Suffrage *remains the primary source for understanding what happened on the road to the Nineteenth Amendment. It is also a lively, funny, very instructive lesson in fighting for credibility. And it was produced despite great obstacles. Lucy Stone, leader of the American Woman Suffrage Association (rival of Stanton and Anthony's National for more than twenty years), was indignant: "In regard to the History of the Woman's Rights Movement, I do not think it can be written by any one who is alive today," she wrote to Stanton. But the authors knew it could be, knew they were not being overly optimistic in starting their project nearly half a century before women actually got the vote.*

Some object to the title of our work; they say you can not write the "History of Woman Suffrage" until the fact is accomplished. We feel that already enough has been achieved to make the final victory certain.

Which is not to say that they always enjoyed the work. Anthony in particular loathed the job—begrudged every moment away from the field and in the study. One of Stanton's daughters, Margaret, has painted a tender picture of the two historians on the job at the Stanton home in Tenafly, New Jersey:

In the centre of a large room, 20 by 22, with an immense bay window, hard wood floor and open fire, beside a substantial office desk with innumerable drawers and doors, filled with documents,—there sit our historians, surrounded with manuscripts and letters from Maine to Louisiana . . . in the centre of their desk are two ink stands and two bottles of mucilage, to say nothing of divers pens, pencils, scissors, knives, etc., etc. As these famous women grow intense in working up some glowing sentence, or pasting some thrilling quotation from John Stuart Mill, Dumas or Secretan, I have seen them again and again dip their pens in the mucilage and their brushes in the ink . . . it is as good as a comedy to watch these souls from day to day. They start off pretty well in the morning, fresh and amiable. They write page after page with alacrity, they laugh and talk, poke the fire by turn, and admire the flowers I place on their desk each morning. Everything is harmonious for a season, but after straining their eyes over the most illegible, disorderly manuscripts I ever beheld, suddenly the sky is overspread with dark and threatening clouds, and from the adjoining room I hear a hot dispute about something. The dictionary, the encyclopedia . . . are overhauled, tossed about in an emphatic manner for some date, fact, or some point of law or constitution. Susan is punctilious on dates, mother on philosophy, but each contends as stoutly in the other's domain as if equally strong on all points. Sometimes these disputes run so high that down go the pens, one sails out of one door and one out of the other, walking in opposite directions around the estate, and just as I have made up my mind that this beautiful friendship of forty years has at last terminated, I see them walking down the hill, arm in arm . . . to watch the sun go down in all his glory. When they return they go straight to work where they left off, as if nothing happened.

This was not a profitable enterprise. Publishers were not interested in such a massive venture that had little prospect of being on the best-seller list. Thanks to one sympathetic firm and Anthony's willingness to invest her own money, along with a large bequest, they got the books into print. Then Anthony gave away hundreds of copies to be sure libraries and important personages would have it for reference.

But it wasn't just the movement she wanted down on paper. In 1897 she contracted with Harper to write the authorized Anthony biography. Once again she found herself mired in old manuscripts and letters—and was so eager to get the story down right, she placed ads in women's journals to borrow back letters she'd written. The months spent in the attic going over facts led the two women to refer to the ponderous biography as "the bog." Finally, two volumes of Harper's Life and Work of Susan B. Anthony *were published in 1899; the third came out posthumously in 1908. They, too, are the primary source for much of the story of Anthony's life, but not only because of their insight. Eager to retain her status as the first—and most authoritative—Anthony biographer, Harper, when she had finished, destroyed untold numbers of priceless letters and documents in a raging fire that burned for weeks. Anthony was distraught at the loss. Modern historians share her grief.*

At least we have her scrapbooks. Several dozen oversize volumes, stuffed with clippings, posters, photographs, and odd sorts of memorabilia, now rest in the Library of Congress, a remarkable work on their own. When she donated them in 1902, Anthony assigned the scrapbooks, with both an obvious sigh of relief and a pioneer's sense of responsibility, to the inheritors of her life's work.

I now leave the *History writing*—as well as *making,* to my younger friends & coworkers—Mrs. Carrie Chapman Catt—Rev.

Anna H. Shaw & others—They are the *fruit* of the *early seed-sow-ing*—may they not have to work to the end of their days to secure the right to *represent* themselves—as have so many who began this public movement! But that future generations of women may see & learn of the struggles that the pioneers went through— I give these *Scrap-Books* and all they contain that is *false*—as well as true—to
The Library of Congress
Washington—D.C.

———

Her concern about pioneers extended beyond her own work. When the Kentucky branch of the Daughters of the American Revolution wrote to her about marking historic spots, Anthony—a DAR member herself— made sure they included foremothers:

I hope in your selections you will be exceedingly careful to dis-tinguish those actions in which our Revolutionary mothers took part. Men have been faithful in noting every heroic act of their half of the race, and now it should be the duty, as well as the plea-sure, of women to make for future generations a record of the heroic deeds of the other half . . . however heroic our pioneer fa-thers may have been, our pioneer mothers, in the very nature of things, must have braved all the hardships of the men by their side with the added one of bearing and rearing children when de-prived of even the vital necessities of maternity.
—Letter, 1897

In time Anthony acknowledged that the founders of the movement were aging. On her first speaking trip without Stanton in 1882, she started to face up to the changing of the guard.

Only think, I shall not have a white-haired woman on the plat-form with me, and shall be alone there of all the pioneer workers. Always with the "old guard" I had perfect confidence that the wise and right thing would be said. What a platform ours then

was of self-reliant, strong women! I felt sure of you all, and since you earliest ones have not been with us, Mrs. Stanton's presence has ever made me feel that we should get the true and brave word spoken. Now that she is not to be there, I can not quite feel certain that our younger sisters will be equal to the emergency, yet they are each and all valiant, earnest and talented, and will soon be left to manage the ship without even me.
—*Letter, 1882*

Yes My Dear—
I know I ought to be in Washington—but you young people will have to pull the oar sometime—and this is a good time to begin—You are doing splendidly— ...
—*Letter, 1891*

My dear, what we older ones all have to learn is that these young and active women now doing the drudgery in each of the forty-five States, must be consulted and must have a vote on all questions pertaining to the association, and we must abide by the decision of the majority. This is what I am trying to learn. No one or two can manage now, but all must have a voice.
—*Letter, 1895/6*

Girls,—yes, I call you girls, as you are all girls compared with me—you have expressed your joy and thankfulness that you have had an opportunity to be present at this Congress. What do you think I feel, I, who remember the time when woman's cause had no friends outside a little group of pioneers? What do you think I feel when I . . . have experienced, that there is now a whole generation of women able to lead the work when the old pioneers will be away?
—*Speech, 1899*

Her complaints about working on History of Woman Suffrage *form an almost farcical counterpoint to her far more satisfying campaigns in the field—especially when you realize the book was her own idea.*

[T]his attempt to write our history is simply appalling—It resigns me down to the bout of blue—
—*Diary, 1876*

I am just sick to death of the whole of it—I had rather wash or whitewash or any possible hard work than sit here & go through

digging into the dirty records of the past—that is rather *make* history than *write* it—
—*Letter, 1880*

I hope to be freed from this awful slavery by the first of June—& I shall feel like a long caged lion let loose—
—*Letter, 1882*

All the work of today put aside to grope into the old past. . . . here Mrs. Stanton and I are, scratching, scratching every hour . . . I am a fish out of water. . . . It makes me feel growly all the time. . . . I can not get away from my ball and chain. . . . Now here is the publisher's screech for money. . . . O, to get out of this History prison!
—*Letters, 1884*

My Dear Cousin Jessie
I am now deep in the mysteries of old letters, old scrap books, and diaries of everybody's that have fallen into my hands. It's a musty, dirty old job too.
—*Letter, 1897*

I wish I were footloose—I would love to go over the mountains and be with you for a few weeks—but I am chained here now with Mrs. Ida H. Harper—mousing through old letters, papers & memories of the past.
—*Letter, 1897*

I never started out to gain honor or notoriety for myself. This much, though, I have wanted—I have always longed to stand well on the page of history.
—*Interview, 1900*

As someone else said in regard to a very different situation, writing the history wasn't even over when it was over. After they had turned in their chapters, the authors waited impatiently to be published. Anthony was especially tough on the indexer, the man who had to pore through all the "pentracks" to make it easier on readers. If you have ever written a book, you will recognize her frustration in these letters posted during her summer of anxiety.

My Dear Sir
Before leaving Rochester I mailed to you last chapters of Vol.

III—leaving nothing but the few pages of the Appendix to be sent, when you would have the complete book in hand—I trust you have the appendix and all before this—and that you will soon be able to report the whole job done from page one Vol. 1. to page 1,000 and something Vol. III!

You will of course correct the proof of your work—so that every line of it will be right—all is now waiting your finishing of the index—and I meanwhile am visiting my two brothers in Kansas—go to Fort Scott—in two days, where I can be addressed for the next three weeks—and where I shall hope by that time to hear from you that you are ready for the remainder of the cash for indexing the three volumes—

Very sincerely yours
Susan B. Anthony
—*Letter, 1886*

Dear Mr. Weinheimer

I fear you are ill—Since I have not had a line from you this summer—and I now hear that my printer has not heard from you since he sent you the last of the plate proofs of Vol. III of W.S. History—I shall be at home by the 15th inst.—and shall be greatly disappointed if your part of the job is not done—It is now two months since you had all the book in hand—and you told me *one* month would be all the time you would need!!

I pray you let me know the exact facts in the matter—

If you are too ill to finish up the job—what am I to do? I am in great anxiety about it—

Hoping to hear that the job is done—I am

Very respectfully yours
Susan B. Anthony
—*Letter to indexer, 1886*

At the end of 1900, a newspaper asked a number of noted people to contribute to an article on the Best Books of the Year. Predictably, Anthony chose her own, which, the article's author noted, left her "open to the charge of narrowness."

The book that I think most important to be read by the people of the United States is the *History of Woman Suffrage,* the 4th volume of which will soon be issued, bringing the records down to the close of the 19th century. There is no history about which

there is so much ignorance as of this great movement for the establishment of equal political rights for women. I hope the twentieth Century will see the triumph of our cause—
—*Article, 1900*

These records will tell future generations of the heroic struggle made by the few for the masses of the unthinking, unphilosophical women of the past and the present.
—*Remarks, date unknown*

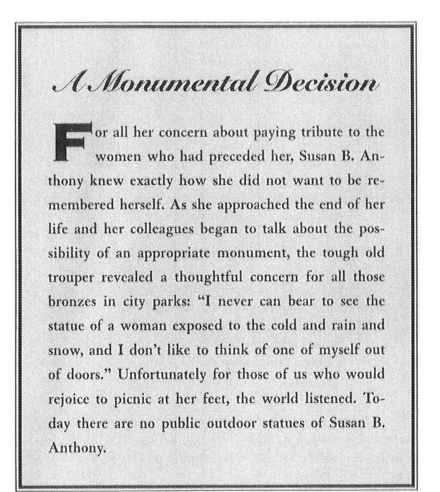

A Monumental Decision

For all her concern about paying tribute to the women who had preceded her, Susan B. Anthony knew exactly how she did not want to be remembered herself. As she approached the end of her life and her colleagues began to talk about the possibility of an appropriate monument, the tough old trouper revealed a thoughtful concern for all those bronzes in city parks: "I never can bear to see the statue of a woman exposed to the cold and rain and snow, and I don't like to think of one of myself out of doors." Unfortunately for those of us who would rejoice to picnic at her feet, the world listened. Today there are no public outdoor statues of Susan B. Anthony.

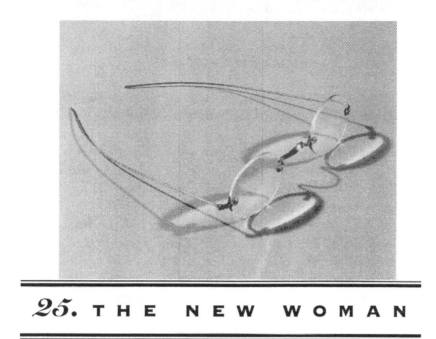

25. THE NEW WOMAN

Susan B. Anthony's vision of the woman of the future was grounded in her belief that women were the keepers of the nation's morals. At an 1851 Daughters of Temperance meeting she ran, one gentleman made this toast:

> The Daughters:
> Our characters they elevate,
> Our manners refine;
> Without them we should degenerate
> To the level of the swine.

Anthony the reformer took that notion and expanded upon it, while Anthony the General used it to inspire her troops and change the world.

It is generally acceded that it is our sex that fashions the social and moral state of society. We do not presume that females possess unbounded power in abolishing the evil customs of the day, but we do believe that were they en masse to discountenance the use of wine and brandy as beverages at both their public and private parties, not one of the opposite Sex, who has any claim to the title of gentleman, would so insult them as to come into their presence after having quaffed of that foul destroyer of all true delicacy and refinement.

Although she soon abandoned her crusade for temperance to redirect her energies towards the single cause of suffrage, she never stopped seeing woman as the moral compass. Thus, she often insisted that women alone would close down the saloons, that they could persuade Congress to abolish slavery, and that, given the vote, they would clean up politics, end all forms of sex discrimination, abolish prostitution, and proceed into perfect marriages with newly enlightened men.

At least, that's what she said publicly. But on other occasions she viewed the possibilities with her usual clear-eyed practicality and seems to have realized things wouldn't work out quite that neatly. She knew that slavery had been ended for political, not moral, reasons; that saloons would not close as long as powerful liquor companies made money; and she figured out with some exasperation that once women got the vote, they would use it exactly as men had—which meant they might also neglect to use it. A full century before political analysts bemoaned the huge numbers of nonvoters in America, Susan B. Anthony cautioned a group of women in Leavenworth, Kansas—the first state to grant women the right to vote in municipal elections—that their new right entailed a new duty.

The women of the east are looking to the women of Kansas. Much rests upon you and I appeal to you to vote whether you want to vote or not. Vote because it is your right as a citizen. Did you ever think what it is to vote? The law which gave you that right said to each of you that your judgment was sound and your opinion worthy to be counted.

I live where disfranchisement is my portion, where the law says to me, "your judgment is not sound and your opinion is not worthy to be counted." I wish every woman could feel the crown of glory which is upon you by virtue of possessing this right. . . .

When women in every state are working with might and main, willing to make any sacrifice, to secure this right, to establish this fundamental principle; when the legislature has granted half what has been asked for, do you not think it would be a gracious act for you to go solidly to the ballot box? Can you not encourage us who live where there is less hope than here and hold up our hands and help us to refuse the argument used against us that women will not vote when they have the right?

It is often pointed out that Susan B. Anthony lived to see many of the changes she was advocating—except the vote—a satisfaction granted few reformers. The results confirmed many of her predictions about the benefits to women—and society—when women were not shackled by unjust laws and practices. And she understood that the changes she was advocating would not affect women alone. That while the process and the transition might be painful and uncomfortable—at least, at first—the economic and political independence of women would, in the long run, free men from the stereotypes of society as well. Today's new, sensitive man wouldn't surprise Susan B. Anthony at all. She was waiting for him all along.

I do not assume that woman is better than man. I do assume that she has a different way of looking at things. She is often called more angelic and so on, but I don't know that woman would be and maybe she would not be more than what man is, if they both had the same code of morals. If a man were required to be just as refined as a woman you could not tell how refined that man would be. The man has made a code of morals for himself, but does not let the woman have the same code. There is no incentive for a man to be good as long as he can get an angel, even if he isn't one himself. In the days of slavery the master made a code of morals for himself and another for his slaves. His slave was flogged, punished, and killed for the same crimes the master was allowed to commit and nothing was thought of it. The one who makes, shapes and controls the conditions, and who makes the social and moral code does not care to live up to it himself. The moment that woman has any voice in the matter it will mean that she will insist that man must be her equal, and then she will demand of him what she is herself and must be her highest ideal, what he wants her to be. Man is enabled to compel her to to be his ideal, but a woman is not enabled to do the same with him. Just the moment that she is empowered with this then woman will demand that man come up to her ideal.
—Interview, 1893

I am a full and firm believer in the revelation that it is through *woman the race is to be redeemed.* And it is because of this faith that I ask for her immediate and unconditional emancipation from all political, industrial, social and religious subjection. As the fountain can rise no higher than the spring that feeds it, so a legislative body will enact or enforce no law above the average sentiment of the people who created it. Any and every reform work is sure to lead women to the ballot-box. It is idle for them to hope to battle successfully against the monster evils of society until they shall be armed with weapons equal to those of the enemy, votes and money.

Archimedes said "Give me a fulcrum on which to plant my lever, and I will move the world."

And I say, give to woman the ballot, the political fulcrum, on which to plant her moral lever, and she will lift the world into a nobler and purer atmosphere.

—*Speech, 1898*

It is said, "Men are what their mothers made them," but I say that to hold mothers responsible for the character of their sons, while denying to them any control over the surroundings of the sons' lives, is worse than mockery, it is cruelty. Responsibilities grow out of rights and powers. Therefore before mothers can rightfully be held responsible for the vices and crimes, for the general demoralization of society, they must possess all possible rights and powers to control the conditions and circumstances of their own and their children's lives.

—*Speech, 1901*

Anthony often addressed the notion of the New Woman, or True Woman, terms very much in vogue as the world looked ahead to the twentieth century. The first excerpt below is from a letter to an Alabama judge she had met at a lecture in New York State.

I hope you and your daughters arrived home safe. Say to the elder I shall be most happy to hear from her when she shall have fairly inaugurated some noble life work. I trust each will take to her soul a strong purpose and that on her tombstone shall be engraved her own name and her own noble deeds instead of merely the daughter of Judge Ormond, or the relict of some Honorable or D.D. When true womanhood shall be attained it will be spoken of and remembered for itself alone. My kindest regards to them, accompanied with the most earnest desire that they shall make truth and freedom the polar star of their lives.

—*Letter, 1859*

The true woman will not be exponent of another, or allow another to be such for her.—She will be her own individual self,—do her own individual work,—stand or fall by her own individual wisdom and strength. . . . The old idea that *man* was made for himself, and woman for him, that he is the oak, she the vine, he the head, she the heart,—he the great conservator of wisdom principle, she of love, will be reverently laid aside with other long since exploded philosophies of the ignorant past.—She will proclaim the "glad tidings of good news" to all women, that women equally with man was made for her own individual happiness,—to develop every power of her three-fold nature, to use, worthily, every talent given her by God, in the great work of life, to the best advantage of herself and the race.
—*Speech, 1859*

The woman of the future will far surpass her of the present, even as the man of the future will surpass him of to-day. The ages are progressive, and I look for a far higher manhood and womanhood than we have now. I think this is to be obtained somewhat by making the sexes coequal. When women associate with men in serious matters, as they do now in frivolous society ones, both will grow better and the world's work will be better done than it is now. I look for the day when the woman who has a political or judicial brain will have as much right to sit on the Supreme Bench or in the Senate as you men have now; when women all over this country will have equal property rights, equal business rights, and equal political rights with men; when the only criterion of excellence or position shall be the ability, honor, and character of the individual without regard to whether he or she be male or female. And this time will come. . . . The woman of the future will be a better mother, a better wife, and a better citizen than the woman of to-day.
—*Interview, 1883*

The term [New Woman] has become a cant phrase, carrying almost as much opprobrium as the term "woman's rights woman" used to imply. The "new woman," as the phrase goes, may mean a loud, mannish woman affecting the boisterous conduct of men, with none of the saving graces of her own sex. If that be the new woman I do not welcome her coming. If by the new woman is meant a woman earnest, thoughtful, lofty of purpose, self-reliant and equally well educated with man, why, then, she has come. We have got her in our homes, where she stands side by

side with her husband, welcoming his friends on the common
ground of intellectual equality, joining in their discussions—a
college-bred woman who can do something more than pour tea
when her husband entertains his friends. We have got the new
woman in everything except the counting of her vote at the ballot
box. And that's coming. It's coming sooner than most people
think.
—*Interview, 1895*

*Anthony even learned the politics of language. Once branded a
"manly woman" by her enemies, she co-opted the term to describe her own
vision of the future.*

We are all familiar with the ideal woman in vogue when I was
young. Her portrait still exists in the family albums, and her pro-
totype is faithfully reproduced in the pages of the harrowing novels on which she was wont to feed her intellect. Pale, delicate,
sentimental, with the wasp-like waist and a tendency to faint, she
was the pet and plaything or the menial of man, typifying in her
life and her attitude toward her husband, whom she ever regarded as a superior being, the ivy and the oak. And in this subjection she believed as religiously and unquestioningly as she did
in her Bible. She was a good woman, did her work, and served
her purpose in the world according to her light.

But evolution and woman herself have wrought a mighty
change in the status of the sex, and now, at the dawning of the
twentieth century, we have that product of modern civilization
and progress known as the new woman, or the manly woman.
She is not yet a perfect or a fully-developed creature, nor is her
type so common that she has ceased to be the subject of the
satirist, or the peg on which the humorist hangs his jokes. But she
is here, and she has come to stay, and another generation will not
only see her at her best, but vastly in the majority. Then, indeed,
will civilization have reached a height and greatness as yet unknown to history. For a people is only as great, as free, as lofty, as
advanced, as its women are free, noble and progressive. It is the
mothers who shape the destiny of the race.

The manly woman of the new century will be an all-around
being, with heart, mind, body, soul and brain fully developed. She
will be educated with her brother from the cradle till they have
finished their college course, and she steps out from the halls of
their alma mater equally equipped with him to fight the battle of

life and bring a practical, trained mind in a healthy body to bear upon the problems of the society and the commonwealth of which she is a part.

The manly woman will not be sequestered through the most vital years of her life behind the walls of a "female" boarding-school or a woman's college, those hotbeds in which an absurd sentimentality and an abnormal femininity are fostered and ripened. Here she "sees through a glass darkly," and beholds her brother man as an exaggerated, gigantic figure of the demigod type, or a wickedly-fascinating, mysterious being who must be rigidly excluded from her school-life.

On the contrary, her constant association with him from childhood to maturity, from kindergarten to college, where she competes with him for prizes in mathematics, physics, and even athletics, will develop in her the manly attributes of strength, self-reliance, independence, perception, and energy. And this training, side by side with him, will also help her brother to develop such feminine traits of gentleness, culture, sympathy, and affection as will round out his character, and so establish that equilibrium of the sexes which makes for perfect harmony.

Nor will their life long comradeship be sundered at the ballot-box. The women of the twentieth-century will possess, unchallenged, "the citizen's right to vote," and with it the power to make, shape, and control the conditions surrounding her in the home, the church, and the state. The manly woman of this new century will preside in her home with grace and dignity as the intellectual peer of any guest, whether that home be hers alone or in association with father, husband, or son. If occasion demand, or the cook should leave without warning, she can also prepare the dinner, bringing both skill and science to her task: and she will have the backbone and the independence even to do the family washing in an emergency.

Whatever career she may adopt, she will recognize that it is a high and sacred destiny to be a wife and mother, but she will choose with wise deliberation the father of her children, bearing well in mind the influence of heredity, and will bequeath to them right moral and physical qualities. In selecting her husband she will hold love founded on respect above expediency . . . and integrity of character above mammon. Her equal and enlarged opportunities in the world will make this possible. Marriage will not decrease, but it will be on an infinitely higher plane, thereby striking directly at the root of evil of divorce; and this blight of society, following the natural law of cause and effect, will be greatly diminished.

The twentieth-century woman will know man for what he is—neither a monster of iniquity to be shunned, nor a superior creature to be worshiped as an idol, nor a lord and master to be cringingly obeyed; but a human being like herself, full of imperfections, but striving withal to make the world better for having lived in it. She will be his equal partner in marriage, sharing fully in his joys as in his sorrows, in his prosperity as in his adversity, and, whether much or little, the half of what he has will be unquestioningly hers. . . .

From the cradle the children of the manly woman and the womanly man of the twentieth century will be trained in the principles of good government. They will be taught that might is not right, either in the home or the state; that arbitration rather than human slaughter should settle all international difficulties, precisely as an individual should appeal to the justice of the courts instead of resorting to a brutal attack upon an enemy; and that the disfranchisement of one-half the people is a relic of barbarism not to be tolerated.

The son of the manly woman will learn courage and tolerance from her precept and example, and will respect her opinions, both political and social. When just turned twenty-one he will not take precedence over his mother, holding his immature judgment as superior to her years of experience; but, instead, he will escort her to the polls, and rejoice in being lifted to the high plane of legal equality on which she stands.

I may not be here to witness the full fruition of this balancing of the sexes, but already we see the promise of its coming, and future generations will reap its blessings.

—*Article, 1900*

The modern girl sees the dawn of a new day. Women at the editor's desk, women teaching in the colleges, women healing the sick, women practicing in the courts, women preaching from the pulpit and lecturing from the platform—call them new women or what you please—they are the women the world welcomes today.

—*Interview, 1905*

WHEN WOMEN GET THE BALLOT, WHAT USE WILL THEY MAKE OF IT, WHAT GOOD DO THEY PROPOSE TO ACCOMPLISH?

They propose to do away with vice and immorality, to prevent the social evil by giving women remunerative employment; to forbid the sale of spiritous liquors and tobacco, and to teach men a higher and nobler life than the one they now follow. . . .

I UNDERSTAND ONE OF THE FOLLIES WHICH THE WOMEN CLAMORING FOR RIGHTS INTEND TO DO AWAY WITH, IS THE POWER VESTED IN MAN TO MAKE THE PROPOSITION OF MARRIAGE; YOU INTEND, I BELIEVE, TO STIMULATE THE COURAGE OF THE GIRLS TO MAKE PROPOSITIONS ALSO.

I believe a girl has more right to make a proposition of marriage than a man, and when she becomes independent of him she will do it. Now she is a pauper, dependent on man, but when she earns a good salary, and maybe a better one than her lover, she can approach him without shame and ask him to unite with her for life. At present she cannot do it, as she is a pauper on his bounty; and no person can be independent unless he or she has pecuniary means. . . .

I would have a woman marry for love alone; I would place her in a position to be able to earn a competent livelihood, and live independent of man until she finds someone who she thinks would increase her happiness. When woman gets the ballot she can receive positions under Government the same as men now do, then they can become arbiters of their own destiny.

PERHAPS [WOMEN] CAN BECOME CONGRESSWOMEN AND SENATORESSES.

Exactly; women should go to Congress, and they would have a higher ambition than to be the wife of some Congressman or Senator. They would be the ideal women, and fulfill their mission to do away with immorality, which would give us a more moral and intellectual race of people. Then asylums, penitentiaries, jails and policemen would be done away with, and we should reach the highest happiness. . . .

—*Interview, 1871*

DO YOU THINK THE POSSESSION OF THE FRANCHISE WILL CURE EVERY EVIL?

No, indeed; but it will place us in a position to say what remedies shall be adopted.

—*Interview, 1889*

What we are struggling for is not the supremacy of one party or the overturning of another, but the establishment of a principle. We demand that woman shall be given the means to assert herself, regardless of whether she ever uses it or not. I think more of the self-respect a woman would feel with the ballot in her hand, than of the mere privilege she would enjoy of casting it. She would realize that she is a responsible being. The young woman of the future, instead of devoting all her thoughts to frivology, spending hours in reading trashy novels, or flirting with beaux, or posing before the glass, or trying to match two pieces of colored ribbon to adorn a gown, would feel the necessity of improving her mind and putting herself abreast of the world by the study of subjects of public moment.

WOULD YOU, THEN, ROB SOCIETY OF A MARKED ELEMENT OF BEAUTY?

By no means. The girl need not be the less beautiful because she knows something; and I can't help thinking that the average man would find more to attract him to his wife or his sweetheart if, instead of talking mere empty twaddle, she could discuss the tariff, or the finances, or the state of the crops, or the President's message, or the latest struggle in Congress, and do it intelligently.

IN SPITE OF THEIR EMANCIPATION, THOUGH, MISS ANTHONY, WOULD NOT THE WOMEN IN A THOROUGHLY HAPPY HOME BE LIKELY TO FOLLOW THE BENT OF THE HEAD OF THE FAMILY IN POLITICAL MATTERS?

No more than the men in the same family. A man who has made himself truly loved and respected as husband, father or brother would be very likely to set the fashion in politics for the household. His wife, his daughters and his sisters would defer to his judgment as to how they should vote—that is natural enough. But is not the same thing true now of the sons and the father? In how many families of your own acquaintance do you find, for instance, the father a Democrat, the elder son a Republican and the younger son a Prohibitionist? They incline to flock together rather than to divide. But, mark you—it is the one among them who possesses the strongest character and the best intelligence, who sets the style for the others. The fact that you so often see the sons following the father is not because he is older than they or bears the relation to them of parent to offspring, but because they have learned to look up to him as wiser and better than they. Now, suppose—as you must admit we not unseldom find it— that the real head of the family is the mother. The father himself, though perhaps a worthy enough person, has not the force of will or the clearness of vision that the mother has, but goes to the mother for advice at every turn. Under the existing system, that father, who does not know his own mind too well, has a vote; while that mother, who knows just what she wants and why she wants it, has none. Under the system I advocate, it is the mother who would cast the deciding vote for the family, the sons as well as the daughters following her lead. The difference is that, under the one system, the politics of the family is a question of sex; under the other, a question of brains. And I think my plan is the more logical of the two.

—*Interview, 1890*

There was a time when white men said that it was of no use to argue with a negro; his skull was so thick. But that was before he was given the franchise. Since he has been a voter there has been no trouble about his skull. Politicians think it worth their while to argue with him all night if necessary. It will be so with women after they are given the franchise. Now, when some question comes up in the family and the man and the woman differ on it, and the woman argues the man down to his last resource, when the poor fellow can make no other answer, he will say, "Oh well; it's no use. You can't argue with a woman."

—*Speech, 1894*

The strong point in favor of ballot for women is in this: that it will compel both political parties to nominate candidates of the highest character. A woman would no more vote for a low-down man than a good man for a degraded woman. The high ideals entertained by each sex for the other here becomes [*sic*] a great influence. Herein the ballot for women will promote the cause of temperance. The convention will not nominate the barroom aspirant for office, because the leaders will at once comprehend that the better class of women will not vote for the saloon rounder. It is in the order of politics that each party will nominate the candidate who has the best chance of obtaining a large vote. To get the ballot for women, both parties must join. . . .

To some extent she will be influenced by the church. But, admitting this, is it not a better influence than the saloon, which controls the votes of so many men?

—*Article, 1895*

BUT, EXCUSE MY EVEN SUGGESTING A DOUBT, DO YOU THINK THE SUFFRAGE WILL DO SO VERY MUCH FOR WOMEN? IT SEEMS TO ME THAT THE ENTRANCE OF WOMEN INTO THE PROFESSIONS, THEIR IMPROVED EDUCATION, MORE ASSIMI-LATED AS IT IS NOW TO THAT OF MEN, THEIR BETTER STA-

TUS, ARE INFINITELY MORE IMPORTANT THAN ALL THE BAL-
LOTS TOGETHER.

You can't separate our intricately interwoven social life into
compartments. The ballot must come with these things. And
mind, as women go on, they find invidious distinctions made between them and men—disparity of treatment. I can trust them to
discover the cause. The ballot will do very little for the individual
woman, but it will do much for the sex.

HAS IT DONE MUCH FOR HER IN AMERICA?

Yes, a great deal. In Colorado women have the ballot. The
Mayor of Denver, the chief city, declared that a revolution had
thereby been effected. The saloon had been lifted out of politics;
saloon men could not have the women's votes.

The candidates for Congress used to be nominated in the saloons; they had only got to suit the men who assembled there. But
now neither Democrats nor Republicans can afford just to please
saloon men. Candidates who please other than saloon frequenters
must be chosen, and thus the women's vote affects the balance of
power, and elevates society.

—*Interview, 1899*

Miss Anthony believes that women should be eligible to every
administrative office. At the same time she is candid enough to
admit that it would be difficult to manage a home and children
and to be a good Governor or President.

"But," she explained, "that isn't a real difficulty. You see, a man
isn't chosen for such an office as President until he is fifty. The
same custom would apply to a woman. By that time her children
would be grown up and the house ought to be able to take care of
itself. Her knowledge of politics and government would have
been part of her earliest training, and she would have broadened
it every year. Of course it wouldn't be exactly dignified to have a
woman in the office of Mayor if she had a family of babies. But as
a matter of fact she would not be elected. Consult the records of
the States that have suffrage and you will see it does not happen."

All of which sounded plausible as Miss Anthony said it.

I tried to get Miss Anthony's estimate of the time that must
elapse before women, with babies or without, are likely to become Governors and Presidents.

"Ah," she said, a little sadly, "it may not be until long after my
work is done. But it is sure to come."

—*Interview, 1899*

What women want to learn is political sagacity, and to philosophize on the effect of their votes. To study what the effect of voting for a certain man was, and to vote differently the next time if this man fails. Men haven't learned to philosophize on the effect of their votes yet. Women will come to the ballot trained and will vote intelligently and carefully. Women in politics will purify society and women on the bench will stand for an equal moral code.
— *Interview, 1899*

The woman of the Twentieth Century will be the peer of man. In education, in art, in science, in literature; in the home, the church, the state; everywhere she will be his acknowledged equal, though not identical with him. We cannot begin to see the good of this recognition.

It is impossible to foretell the exact conditions that will exist in the home; but we may be sure they will be more in accord with enlightened manhood and womanhood than any now known. The children will be better fed and clothed and schooled when the father, together with the mother, remains at home and takes part in their training.

The transition period from absolute subjection inevitably has many crudities, and many mistakes will be made; but we must have faith to believe that the final working out of the great principles of justice and equality into woman's perfect freedom with man will result in something vastly superior to the present. Man himself will be greatly improved when he finds at his own fireside an equal in the person he calls wife.

And this cannot be until she holds in her hand that right preservative of all other rights—the ballot. So the sooner man takes the adjective "male" from all of his creeds, codes and constitutions, and leaves woman to feel her responsibility equally with himself in making and executing all the laws that govern society, the sooner will he begin to reap the harvest of the seed sown in the woman's rights agitation of the nineteenth century.

The Twentieth Century will see man and woman working together to make the world the better for their having lived. All hail to the Twentieth Century!
—*Article, 1900*

DO YOU BELIEVE WOMEN WILL EVER HAVE FULL SUFFRAGE IN THIS COUNTRY?

Do I? Do I believe women will ever take their rightful place at the ballot-box, and record their wishes as to the affairs of govern-

ment, and that the injustice of "taxation without representation," that has so long applied to one-half of our citizens, will be abolished? I firmly believed at one time that I should live to see that day, and, thank heaven it is already realized in four states of our great country. But universal woman suffrage in United States? Assuredly; I have never for one moment lost faith. It will come, but I shall never see it. Probably you will. It is inevitable. We can no more deny forever the right of self-government to one-half our people than we could keep the negro in bondage. It will not be wrought by the same disrupting forces that freed the slave, but come it will, and I believe within a generation.
— *Interview, 1902*

It may be delayed longer than we think, it may be here sooner than we expect, but the day will come when man will recognize woman as his peer, not only at the fireside, but in the councils of the nation. Then, and not until then, will there be the perfect comradeship, the ideal union between the sexes, that shall result in the highest development of the race. What this shall be we may not attempt to define, but this we know, that only good can come to the individual or to the nation through the rendering of exact justice.
— *Newspaper article, 1904*

Men who say in sage sarcasm that it is utterly impossible to tell what a woman would do under any given circumstances have no hesitation whatever in predicting precisely what she would do with her ballot. It is not by any means an assured thing that she would vote as her husband does. Husbands and wives do not generally agree on politics if the woman does any thinking on her own account. In the West husbands and wives vote rival political tickets without breaking up their happy homes.
— *Interview, 1905*

I have known nothing for the last thirty years save the struggle for human rights on this continent. If it had been a class of men who had been disfranchised and denied their legal rights, I believe I would have devoted my life to them precisely as I have devoted it to the fight against the wrongs of my sex. To feel that you have worked as earnestly for another's rights as you would have done for your own or for those of your own class, is the true test of the reformer.
— *Interview, 1883*

I firmly believe that some day a woman will be elected President of the United States.
— *Interview, 1905*

Women Voters? You Must Be Crazy!

The problem with predicting the effect of the women's vote was that there was no database. But Susan B. Anthony knew a scam when she heard one. In 1899, when someone claimed that woman suffrage in Colorado had led to a rise in the number of female insanity cases, she laughed and said, "How absurd. Why, Colorado has had woman suffrage for only six years, and therefore it is hardly to be supposed that in that time all of the women have gone insane . . . The idea that reliable statistics can be compiled . . . in six years is absurd. It would be as reasonable to expect that women should revolutionize the whole body politic in that short space of time." She also pointed to Wyoming, where women had had the right to vote for thirty years: "Statistics show there is just one insane person in the state, and that one is a man."

26. SAINT SUSAN

By the time she was in her eighties, Susan B. Anthony was a certified saint. At least, that's the message in the 1901 Anthony Home Calendar, *an illustrated collection of pithy sayings from the venerable leader that sold for fifty cents, proceeds earmarked for you-know-where. Next to her birthday is the endearing notation "February 15 — St. Susan's Day."*

May Wright Sewall, the loyal lieutenant who had early recognized Anthony's genius for leadership, also hailed her new state of grace. After reading all one thousand pages of the just-published Life and Work of Susan B. Anthony, *Sewall dispatched a telegram that said:*

> Biography finished, more than history, greater than literature, it is a religion. Dear general, accept renewed allegiance.

The great respect Anthony now enjoyed was unmistakable the following summer. At a session of the International Council of Women in England in 1899, her speech at Westminster Hall was greeted with a spontaneous, emotional gesture that has completely disappeared from modern use. Instead of applauding, the audience waved white handkerchiefs, a symbol of approval called the Chautauqua salute. As a newspaper reporter in London explained, "it is, after all, the prettiest way a woman can show her applause, by the fluttering of handkerchiefs. It is so much more dignified than handclapping and stamping."

The picturesque practice — "a token of special honor" that originated at the Chautauqua Institution, an educational movement in New York State — welcomed Susan B. Anthony with regularity, along with standing ovations, both abroad and at home. She had, in the words of one longtime supporter, become "not only our Susan but everybody's." She was, to quote her introduction at the International Council of Women in Berlin in 1904, "Miss Anthony of the world."

Ironically, she had stayed away from a session on suffrage before the Berlin meeting, in deference to those who thought it might be unwise to impose American suffrage politics on the new international organization. The Reverend Anna Howard Shaw, Anthony's devoted aide and another member of the American delegation, described the dramatic turnaround:

When the meeting was opened the first words of the presiding officer were, "Where is Susan B. Anthony?" and the demonstration that followed the question was the most unexpected and overwhelming incident of the gathering. The entire audience rose, men jumped on their chairs, and the cheering continued without a break for ten minutes. Every second of that time I seemed to see Miss Anthony, alone in her hotel room, longing with all her big heart to be with us, as we longed to have her. I prayed that the loss of a tribute which would have meant so much might be made up to her, and it was. Afterward, when we burst in upon her and told her of the great demonstration the mere mention of her name had caused, her lips quivered and her brave old eyes filled with tears. As we looked at her I think we all realized anew that what the world called stoicism in Susan B. Anthony throughout the years of her long struggle had been, instead, the splendid courage of an indomitable soul—while all the time the woman's heart had longed for affection and recognition.

She hid her feelings well. That same year, at the suffrage convention in Washington, D.C., the now-retired president slipped quietly into a morning meeting already in progress. It happened to be her eighty-fourth birthday. Instantly the delegates arose and turned the hall into a field of white handkerchiefs. As Anthony modestly made her way onto the platform, she smiled, turned to the audience, and, waving off the tribute, said, "There now, girls, that's enough."

The "girls" had always admired her; now they revered her, a transfor-

mation built on half a century of awe and appreciation. They knew exactly how much had been accomplished under her splendid command: most states—there were now forty-five—had passed laws giving married women their legal rights. Coeducation was growing, with some 36,000 women in state universities and private colleges by 1906. Women were accepted in the workplace. At her fiftieth birthday, in 1870, she had been warmly feted in New York City by a crowd consisting mostly of women. But when she turned seventy, she was the guest of honor at a national event in Washington, D.C., with toasts and gifts from two hundred guests, including prominent members of the House and Senate, along with congratulatory editorials and telegrams from around the country. Anthony's eternal collaborator, Elizabeth Cady Stanton, wrote an amusing poem that captured the new tolerance of the aging spinster:

> Better than to be any man's wife,
> She says: To "the cause" devote your life;
> Because husbands may die, or run away.
> But the suffrage movement is here to stay.

The movement had not yet succeeded, but in converting a good number of the enemy, Anthony had made considerable progress and a world of constant friends and admirers. Her appearance in England led to one breathless headline reading MISS ANTHONY THE LONDON SENSATION with the correspondent noting:

> London papers are going wild over Miss Anthony, declaring her to be the most unaggressive woman suffragist they ever saw. They are accustomed to the bifurcated, loud-voiced, strident women of the stump, and therefore, Miss Anthony's slim figure, severe face and smoothly banded hair was an innovation.

The object of their affection had already commented with wry satisfaction on the new appreciation of these dedicated women who had once been branded "women unsexed":

> It was not because the early advocates were not attractive, but because the public mind was benighted and not ripe. People regarded the idea of woman suffrage as so monstrous that they thought everybody who advocated it must be a monster. Now they think we are all lovely. It is only because the times are better. . . .

I don't think it probable that we are any sweeter-faced or that our voices are any more melodious than they were thirty years ago. It is only that the whole matter was regarded with such horror and aversion then that any one connected with it was looked upon in the same light; it is very different now. . . .

Oh, no! It isn't the women, it's the attitude of the world that has changed. The world has grown to believe in the principle, and so the women who work for it seem all right. People say to me that I remind them of their aunt, who died at the age of 90, or of their grandmother. And I know that if I remind them of their grandmother I cannot seem altogether homely.

She hadn't convinced everyone, but she had gotten their attention and earned their respect. Her name was given to newborns; her advice was sought by strangers; her opinions counted in the columns. For a woman who had been scorned outright when she first tried to speak publicly at a teachers' convention in 1853; who had been assailed and assaulted by mobs for refusing to compromise on slavery; who had been humiliated and shunned and then actually convicted for the crime of being a woman, it must have been heavenly justice, indeed. Better yet, it was an earthly esteem, one she could savor in this life.

———

She is one of the remarkable women of the world. In appearance she has not grown a day older in the past ten years. Her manner has none of the excitement of an enthusiast; never discouraged by disappointment, she keeps calmly at work, and she could give points in political organization and management to some of the best male politicians in the land. Her features have become familiar throughout the country. . . . It is a strong and intellectual face, but full of womanly gentleness. . . . Her gold spectacles give her a motherly rather than a severe expression, and a stranger would see nothing incongruous in her doing knitting or fancy-work. In no sense does she correspond with the distorted idea of a woman's rights agitator. In conversation, her manner is that of perfect repose, and her speech denotes strong intellectuality and thought-

fulness. She is always entertaining, and the most romantic idealizer of women would not expect frivolity in one of her age and would not charge it to strong-mindedness that she is sedate.
— *Washington* Star, *1889*

Of all the eminent women who are here, no one is such a favorite with a Boston audience as Susan B. Anthony. Her courage and strength and the patient devotion of a life consecrated to the advancement and the elevation of womanhood, her invincible honor, her logic and her power to touch and sway all hearts, are felt and reverently recognized. The young women of the day may well feel that it is she who *has made life possible* to them; who has trodden the thorny paths and, by her unwearied devotion, has opened to them the professions and higher applied industries; nor is this detracting from those who now share with her the labor and the glory. Each and all recognize the individual devotion, the purity and singleness of purpose that so eminently distinguish Miss Anthony.
— *Boston* Globe, *1881*

Some one wishes to know which of the advocates of woman's rights we think the ablest. Why, Susan B., of course. Without her, the organization would have been utterly broken to pieces and scattered. She is the guiding spirit, the executive power that leads the forlorn hope and brings order out of chaos. Others seek to promote their own interests, but Susan, earnest, honest, self-sacrificing, much-enduring, thinks only of the work she has in hand, and speculates solely on the chances of living long enough to accomplish it. She has given up home, friends, her profession of teacher and the modest competence acquired by her labor; has been caricatured, ridiculed, maligned and persecuted, but has never turned aside or faltered in the work to which she has given her life. Whatever may be the opinion of the conservative or fogy world with regard to Susan B. Anthony, those who know her well and have watched her career most attentively, know her to be rich in all the best and most tender of womanly virtues, and possessed of as brave and noble a spirit and as great integrity of character as ever fell to the lot of mortal woman.
— *Philadelphia* Sunday Republic, *1877*

Susan B. Anthony . . . goes abroad a republican queen—uncrowned to be sure, but none the less of the blood royal.
— *Kansas City* Journal, *1883*

In 1895 Anthony headed west to attend the Congress of Women in San Francisco—a California-based group. Her appearance at Golden Gate Hall—amid flowers and banners and sublime feelings—was the high point of the meeting. The president, Sarah B. Cooper, introduced her with the words, "I have the very great honor and pleasure of introducing to this assembly one who has done more towards lifting up women than any other one woman . . . Miss Susan B. Anthony." And then 2,500 women in the audience went wild:

> They clapped and cheered and waved, and some of the gray-haired women wiped their eyes because it is so seldom that people live to be appreciated. Very erect of head and clear of voice she began her little speech.
> —*San Francisco* Chronicle, *1895*

> The path blazed by Miss Anthony nearly sixty years ago is now an easy one to follow. There are few dangers to be encountered now in the wilderness of woman's rights; in fact it is not a wilderness any more but a land of promise well settled by many citizens. Today to proclaim one's self an advocate of equal suffrage is to own fellowship with the cleverest, noblest women of the country. The women who assembled around the thirty tables at this luncheon represented nearly every profession, to all of which women have been admitted since Susan B. Anthony knocked on the closed doors and presented her card.
> —*New York* World, *1906*

Newspapers may have been the last to come around, but they were not alone in adoring Susan B. Anthony. Here are just a handful of testimonials from her friends and coworkers:

> I wish to inquire what has become of Susan? You know she is my North Star. I take all my bearings from her, and when I lose sight of her I wander helplessly, uncertain of my course.
> —*Letter from Olympia Brown, 1886*

> I have been intending for several days to tell you that however your sister may have been regarded forty years ago, she is today the most popular woman in the United States. The federation [General Federation of Women's Clubs, meeting in Chicago] closed . . . on Friday night. During the meetings she was several times asked to come forward on the platform, which she did to the manifest gratification of the people, saying something each

time which "brought down the house." On the last night a note was sent to the president asking that "Susan B.," Julia Ward Howe and Ednah D. Cheney |a writer and reformer| would please step forward. They came, but only your sister spoke, and what she said was vociferously cheered over and over again.
—*Letter to Mary Anthony, 1892*

A Washington and a Lincoln have come in our great century, and between their birthdays was born a Susan B. Anthony, whose grand life has been given to a noble cause; once the target for the cruel and bitter shafts of ridicule; now deemed the noblest among women. The task of Washington and Lincoln could not be complete till the crown was placed on the brow of woman as well as man; and when the angels shall call Susan B. Anthony to the life immortal, her name, her memory on earth should and will take its place among the martyrs and saints of liberty, not for man alone, but for woman and child.
—*Sermon by Dr. H. W. Thomas, of Chicago, 1896*

Amidst all the eulogy which has surrounded Miss Anthony this afternoon, her brother said to me, "Don't you think this will turn Susan's head?" I answered, "No, she has had so many years of misrepresentation and abuse that if they keep on eulogizing her as long as she lives, it won't balance the other side."
—*Anna Howard Shaw, 1897*

We do not hail you, love you, as one who has made woman's life easier, strewn it with more rose leaves of idleness, shielded it from more stress and storm, but as one who has taken the grander, truer view, that by equally sharing stress and storm, by equal effort and work, by equality in rights, privileges, powers and opportunities with man—her other self—woman will evolve and will reach her loftiest, loveliest development. Not as an apostle of ease, shrinking fear and parasitism do we regard you, but as the apostle, the incarnation of work, of high courage, of deathless endeavor.
—*Ellen Powell Thompson, 1900*

|Women| needed a leader to rally them, to give them the courage of their convictions, and such a leader Miss Anthony has been. She spoke to the world in tones which rang out so clear and true that they will echo down the centuries. Some who had been protected and petted were slow to rally; others who had broader views accepted sooner the doctrine of rights—not privileges—of

rights for all women. Miss Anthony taught us the sisterhood of women, and that the privileges of one class could not offset the wrongs of another. . . .
—*Fannie Humphreys Gaffney, 1900*

As we sat at her feet day after day between sessions of the convention, listening to what she wanted us to do to help women and asking her questions, I realized that she was the *greatest person I had ever met.* She seemed to me everything that a human being could be—a leader to die for or to live for and follow wherever she led.
—*M. Carey Thomas, 1935*

A few days ago some one said to me that every woman should stand with bared head before Susan B. Anthony. "Yes," I answered, "and every man as well." I would not retract these words. I believe that man has benefited by her work as much as woman. For ages he has been trying to carry the burden of life's responsibilities alone and when he has the efficient help of woman he will be grateful. Just now it is new and strange and men cannot comprehend what it would mean but the change is not far away. The nation is soon to have woman suffrage and it will be a glad and proud day when it comes.
—*Clara Barton, 1906*

Miss Anthony has lived to see the work of her hands established in the gaining of educational and social rights for women which might well be called revolutionary, so momentous have been the changes. In temperance work, on school and health boards, in prison reform, in peace conferences, in factory and shop inspection, in civil service reform, in attempts to solve social and industrial problems, women are not only a factor but in many cases the chief workers. It seems almost inexplicable that changes, surely as radical as giving women the opportunity to vote, should be accepted today as perfectly natural, while the political right is still viewed somewhat askance. . . .

Some movements in history have been brought about by a stroke of the pen or a sudden uprising of the people, like a great tidal wave sweeping everything before it; others have come slowly as the result of the cumulative force of years of effort and represent the gradual growth of conviction. The time will come when some of us will look back upon the arguments against the granting of the suffrage to women with as much incredulity as

that with which we now read those against their education. Then shall it be said of the woman who, with gentleness and strength, courage and patience, has been unswerving in her allegiance to the aim she had set before her: "Give her of the fruit of her hands, and let her own works praise her in the gates."
— *Mary E. Woolley, 1906*

For a larger outlook on life we are all indebted to Miss Anthony, to Mrs. [Julia Ward] Howe, and to their colleagues. We are indebted to them in large measure for the educational opportunities of today. We are indebted to them for the theory, and in some places for the reality, of equal pay for men and women when the labor performed is the same. We are indebted to them for making it possible for us to spend our lives in fruitful work rather than in idle tears. We are indebted to these pioneer women for the substitution of a positive creed for inertia and indifference. And from them we also inherit the weighty responsibility of passing on to others in degree, if not in kind, all that we have received from them.
— *Lucy M. Salmon, 1906*

The women of today may well feel that it is Miss Anthony who has made life possible to them; she has trodden the rough paths and by her unwearied devotion has opened to them the professions and higher applied industries. Through her life's work they enjoy a hundred privileges denied them fifty years ago; from her devotion has grown a new order; her hand has helped to open every line of business to women.

She has spoken at times to thousands of girls on the public duties of women. . . . Her life story, when written, must epitomize the victorious struggle of women for larger intellectual freedom in the last century. . . . The world does move. . . .
— *Eva Perry Moore, 1906*

I suppose it is true that all through history individual women have been able, sometimes by cajolery, sometimes by personal charm, sometimes by force of character, to get for themselves privileges far greater than any that the most radical advocates of woman's rights have yet demanded. But in the case of Miss Anthony and the other early suffragists all that force of character was turned not to individual ends, not to getting great things for themselves, but to getting little gains, step by step, for the great

mass of other women; not for the service of themselves, but for the service of the sex, and so of the whole human race . . .
— *Maude Wood Park, 1906*

Saint Susan herself was often overwhelmed by the accolades, telling one reporter before her eightieth birthday party, "I dread all the fuss and ceremony. . . . Somehow the whole thing seems like going to my own funeral." But in the interest of The Cause, she took it all in good, Quaker stride.

During those days people who did not know me thought I was a witch with horns. That has all passed now and I am accorded nearly the same privileges as men in my country. The first quarter century of my career was a stormy one—so tempestuous, in fact, that I have often asked myself how I have managed to retain that equable temperament and sweet disposition with which God has endowed womanhood. I did it through philosophy. When I started on this career I realized that the task I had assumed was a stupendous one, and I trained my mind to cool, philosophical reflection. I have been a profound student of sociology, and what I have accomplished has been done by patient and persistent effort which few men could sustain.

I have had but one object before me all my life. As soon as my mind began to unfold I saw the injustice of the system which deprives woman of the natural rights of the human being. I did not shrink from this like other women. I consecrated myself to the work of reforming this system. I have lived to see what few reformers have been spared to enjoy —a realization in large part of the reformation which I inaugurated. I expect to live to see a still fuller realization.
— *Interview, 1894*

I wish you could be here and see the honors I receive, it would make you happy and be something for you to remember. It is very pleasant to be so kindly spoken to, but—all are telling of my *past* service, all knowing that my work-days are no more. Yes, it is pleasant—but sad to feel it is true. If only I can go the rest of the time allotted and not undo the things I have done—not make my friends wish I had died long before—that is all I ask.
— *Letter, 1902*

The Making of a Saint

The seeds of beatification were planted early. In 1886, at a rally in Lincoln, Kansas, according to Anthony's diary, a mother brought her four-week-old daughter "twenty-five miles in a carriage, so she might tell it, when grown, that Susan B. Anthony had taken it in her arms." In 1903, in New Orleans, older women brought their teenage daughters from school, "that she may imbibe your spirit." One eyewitness wrote: "And then the blushing girl comes forward, while Miss Anthony takes her by the hand with a cordiality of greeting that goes right to the heart."

National-American
Woman Suffrage Association.

Honorary Presidents:
ELIZABETH CADY STANTON.   LUCY STONE.

President, SUSAN B. ANTHONY.
17 MADISON STREET, ROCHESTER, N. Y.

Vice-President-at-Large, REV. ANNA H. SHAW,
SOMERTON, PHILADELPHIA, PA.

Cor. Sec., RACHEL FOSTER AVERY,
SOMERTON, PHILADELPHIA, PA.

Rec. Sec., ALICE STONE BLACKWELL,
3 PARK STREET, BOSTON, MASS.

Treasurer, JANE H. SPOFFORD,
1412 Q STREET N. W., WASHINGTON, D. C.

Auditors: HARRIET TAYLOR UPTON.
HON. WM. DUDLEY FOULKE.

Rochester, N. Y., _____ 189_

---

27. FAILURE IS
IMPOSSIBLE!

---

ike any sensible executive concerned about the future of the com-
pany, Susan B. Anthony understood that the time had come to retire.
This was not a rash decision: she was eighty. But it was neither failing
health nor fading ambition nor professional restlessness that convinced her
to relinquish control of the organization she'd created with Elizabeth Cady
Stanton three decades earlier. Rather, it was the wisdom of a concerned
leader that only with an orderly transfer of power could the goal be met. She
spelled it out:

> I am not retiring now because I feel unable, mentally or physi-
> cally, to do the necessary work, but because I wish to see the orga-
> nization in the hands of those who are to have its management in
> the future. I want to see you all at work, while I am alive, so I can
> scold if you do not do it well.

> *She made it clear to her "girls" that while she would pursue other av-*
> *enues in the direction of suffrage, she would never stray far from the center*
> *of power — nor lose her good humor.*

NAWSA LETTERHEAD

I wish you could realize with what joy and relief I retire from the presidency. I want to say this to you while I am still alive— and I am good yet for another decade—don't be afraid. As long as my name stands at the head, I am Yankee enough to feel that I must watch every potato which goes into the dinner-pot and supervise every detail of the work. For the four years since I fixed my date to retire, I have constantly been saying to myself, "Let go, let go, let go!" I am now going to let go of the machinery but not of the spiritual part. I expect to do more work for woman suffrage in the next decade than ever before.

And so in 1900 she presided over her last NAWSA convention, pounding the gavel during three sessions a day for nearly a full week in a gorgeous, grand exit. As usual, the stage of the church in Washington was decorated in ladies' living room style, with tulips, carnations, and bowls of white and purple violets. As usual, Anthony's matter-of-fact way dispensed with ceremony. The palms lining the front of the platform would have to be moved elsewhere, she ordered, explaining: "Of course, palms are very fine; I admire them; but I cannot talk to an audience over the tops of a lot of trees."

The balloting for the new president came at the end of the week. Carrie Chapman Catt, at forty-one about half Anthony's age, was easily elected, 254–24. When the results were announced, the delegates and others burst into applause. Then, as the realization sank in that the woman who had guided and inspired them for half a century would no longer be in charge, a profound silence blanketed the hall. Against the background of a few muffled sobs in the audience, the business of the convention proceeded. Eyewitnesses were in awe:

Miss Anthony was made a committee of one to present Mrs. Catt to the convention. The women went wild as Miss Anthony, erect and alert, with her snowy white hair banded smoothly about her face, walked to the front of the platform, holding the hand of her young co-worker, of whom she is extremely fond and of whom she expects great things. Miss Anthony's eyes were tear-dimmed, and her tones were uneven, as she presented to the convention its choice of a leader, and paid her tribute of praise to the woman who had been her "right-hand man" for so many years. It was such a tribute as most people get only after the sun of another world dawns upon them. It was a tribute freighted with love and tender solicitude, rich with reminiscences of the past, and full of hope for the future of Mrs. Catt and her work.

"Suffrage is no longer a theory, but an actual condition," she said, "and new conditions bring new duties. These new duties, these changed conditions, demand stronger hands, younger heads and fresher hearts. In Mrs. Catt you have my ideal leader. I present to you my successor."

By this time half the women were using their handkerchiefs on their eyes and the other half were waving them in the air. Mrs. Catt said quickly: "Your president, if you please, but Miss Anthony's successor never! There is but one Miss Anthony, and she could not have a successor."

Anthony's own brief farewell closed the convention. The mood was captured by a very understanding reporter:

Last night as she stood before a vast audience in the Church of Our Father, the lights gleaming on her silvery hair, her strong, true face so framed by it that it appeared almost like a halo; as she awaited the silence that it seemed never would come from the shouting multitude; as she saw the waving handkerchiefs, heard the cheers and felt the enthusiasm that her very presence inspired—there must have come back to her the memory of those awful days when she stood before the howling mobs and when her gently-bred senses were stunned by the imprecations of the jeering populace, for she raised her thin, white hand, with delicate lace falling around it, and in the strong clear voice which age has not touched and time only softened, said:

"There is, after all, compensation. Good friends, I have been reviled most of my life; I have been scoffed and jeered at; I have heard myself called dreadful names and have been the target for every kind of discourtesy—but tonight I am ready to believe that there are people who love and respect me. I am indeed grateful."

Over and over again the audience cheered the white-haired woman who stood there like a statue, and on her high brow, but little lined with the weight of years, one could almost see the word "vindicated."

In retirement, she was not idle. Over the next six years she traveled to eighteen states (including Oregon, where she dedicated a statue of the Indian guide Sacajawea); to Europe (where she made her triumphal appearance in Berlin, then toured England and France); finished the fourth volume of History of Woman Suffrage; *privately interviewed President Theodore Roosevelt and publicly scolded ex-President Cleveland; attended six more suffrage meetings and four congressional hearings. And as hon-*

orary president of NAWSA, she kept a close eye on its new leadership. With great skill she had closed the circle: the torch had been passed. The lieutenants she'd trained were now generals themselves. The suffrage group that had begun in 1869 with a handful of loyalists was now a great national organization with influence far beyond its thousands of members. Congress regularly held hearings on the subject. And while she still was not rich (she had teasingly commented at the 1900 ceremony, "Not one of our officers has a salary. I retire on full pay."), she was existing modestly but comfortably on the $800-a-year income from a $5,000 annuity raised by her friends and presented to her on her seventy-fifth birthday. But there was still no vote.

And time was running out. In 1902 Elizabeth Cady Stanton died, leaving Anthony as the only link to the pioneering days. In 1904 she lost her brother, D.R. In 1905 Anthony's own body sent her an unmistakable message. It happened one morning in November outside Philadelphia, after she had spent the day at Bryn Mawr College with her friend, its president, M. Carey Thomas. As Anthony later described it, "I fainted away and was nothing; it seemed as if the hold-together muscles just let go."

She had held together so long and defied so many rules, it was clear only nature could subdue her. Her health plummeted; her heart weakened. She rallied briefly but would never be the same.

Anthony was determined to attend the NAWSA convention of 1906, in Baltimore, celebrating nearly four decades of the organization she had nurtured and led. Her close friends said she knew it would be her last. Her hair was white, her body frail, and she required a full-time nurse (disguised as a housekeeper to protect the proud pioneer from the gravity of her condition). But she climbed out of her sickbed to attend a session filled with testimonials from women teaching at colleges across the country. Bryn Mawr's Thomas ended the toasts:

"Other women reformers, like other men reformers, have given part of their time and energy. She has given to the cause of women every year, every month, every day, every hour, every moment of her whole life, and every dollar she could beg or earn . . .

"To most women it is given to have returned them in double measure the love of the children they have nurtured. To you, Miss Anthony, belongs by right, as to no other woman in the world's history, the love and gratitude of all women in every country of the civilized globe. We, your daughters in the spirit, rise up today and call you blessed. . . .

"Two generations of men lie between the time when in the early fifties you and Mrs. Cady Stanton sat together in New York

State, writing over the cradles of her babies those trumpet calls to freedom that began and carried forward the emancipation of women, and the day, eighteen months ago, when that great audience in Berlin rose to do you honor—thousands of women, from every country in the civilized world, silent, with full eyes and lumps in their throats, because of what they owed you. Of such as you were the lines of the poet Yeats written:

> They shall be remembered forever,
> They shall be alive forever,
> They shall be speaking forever,
> The people shall hear them forever.

After the applause had ended there was a moment of intense silence, and then, as Miss Anthony came forward, the entire audience arose and greeted her with waving handkerchiefs, while tears rolled down the cheeks of many who felt that she would never be present at another convention. "If any proof were needed of the progress of the cause for which I have worked," she said, in clear, even tones, distinctly heard by all, "it is here tonight. The presence on the stage of these college women, and in the audience of all those college girls who will some day be the nation's greatest strength, tell their own story to the world. They give the highest joy and encouragement to me—I am not going to make a long speech but only to say thank you and good-night."

It was all she had the strength to say but she never would publicly confess it.

Once more she boarded a train, this time headed for Washington, D.C. There would be one final celebration, one final birthday. With superhuman effort she sat through the program on an easy chair upon the stage of the Church of our Fathers at Thirteenth and L Streets, the same stage where she'd resigned six years earlier. There was still some fight left. After effusive praise from numerous elected officials, a letter was read from the President himself.

Pray let me join with you in congratulating Miss Anthony upon her eighty-sixth birthday and in extending to her the most hearty good wishes for the continuation of her useful and honorable life.

Sincerely yours,
Theodore Roosevelt.

Anthony was incensed. Rising from her chair and proceeding to center stage, the feisty old leader fumed:

I wish the men would do something besides extend congratulations. I have asked President Roosevelt to push the matter of a constitutional amendment allowing suffrage to women by a recommendation to Congress. I would rather have him say a word to Congress for the cause than to praise me endlessly.

Her indignation was infectious. The crowd, jammed into seats on the floor and in the galleries, responded with cheers. But her definitive words were yet to come. At the end of the evening, her heart full from the love around her, her head plainly aware of the finality of the moment, the eighty-six-year-old legend took her place at the podium and, leaning on Reverend Shaw, thanked all her colleagues for their loyal support. The Speakeress who had spent her life at the lectern with passionate two-hour talks on the need for the vote now condensed her message into a crisp, inspiring prophecy:

There have been others also just as true and devoted to the cause—I wish I could name every one—but with such women consecrating their lives, failure is impossible!

It was her final public utterance. The next day she was bundled back on the train to her home in Rochester, and not until the following afternoon did she have strength enough to climb the stairs to her bedroom. She would never leave it. Pneumonia set in, and her heart was failing. As she slid from this life that she had devoted to others, her sister, Mary, combed her hair and her friend Anna Howard Shaw clasped her hand. On March 13, 1906, at forty minutes past midnight, Susan B. Anthony died in her own bed.

We should all try to live so as to make people feel that there is a vacancy when we go; but, dear friends, do not let there be a vacancy long. Our battle has just reached the place where it can win, and if we do our work in the spirit of those who have gone before, it will soon be over.

—Remarks, 1896

She was as principled in death as she had been in life. In accord with her Quaker distaste for ceremonial mourning, no shades were drawn, no black crepe hung. Sunlight streamed into the house, and a wreath of violets decorated the front door. Flowers from NAWSA sat on the round mahogany table where the Declaration of Rights had been written for the Seneca Falls Convention in 1848. For two days, close friends and family came to call. The next day, the world said good-bye at an immense funeral held in Central Presbyterian Church, chosen over her own Unitarian church, a Baptist church, and a Jewish temple because of size. Amid a raging blizzard as severe as those that had challenged her own forays for The Cause, some ten thousand mourners passed by her flag-draped coffin, patrolled by an honor guard of female students from the University of Rochester — the school she'd helped open up to them. Two special banners attended her: floating over her head, a silk suffrage flag with four gold stars representing the only states where women could vote; pinned on her breast, a jeweled flag pin with four diamond stars, a gift from women of Wyoming, the first in the world to be enfranchised.

Rochester made no secret of its personal grief. There must have been people of every creed, political party, nationality and plane of life in those lines that kept filing through the aisles of Central Church. The youth and the age of the land were represented. Every type was there to bow in reverence, respect and grief. Professional men, working men, financiers came to offer homage. Women brought little children to see the face of her who had aimed at being the emancipator of her sex, but whose work had ended just as victory seemed within reach.

Priests, ministers of the Protestant faiths, rabbis of the Jewish congregations, came to look upon her who had more than once given them inspiration in dark moments. . . .

A noticeable feature was the many negroes who passed the bier. . . . One old, white-haired man, limped down the aisle, stood for a moment at the casket, and plucking a leaf from a wreath said, "I'll keep this to 'member Miss Anthony by."
—Newspaper article, 1906

The eulogies were delivered by a representative chorus of lives she had touched. From the ministers, thanks for her presence and prayers for her soul; from William Lloyd Garrison, Jr., whose father had inspired Anthony's abolitionist work, a memoir of her "undaunted courage" on the antislavery trail; from an African-American woman leader, gratitude to "our friend for many years — our champion," who looked "to better and brighter days that would surely come to us as a race"; from Carrie Chapman Catt, her successor at NAWSA, marvel at the unshakable optimism of "her self-appointed task of uplifting the world to a more just order of things." Anna Howard Shaw, at Anthony's request, delivered the final farewell.

There is no death for such as she. There are no last words of love. The ages to come will revere her name. . . . Her words, her work and her character will go on to brighten the pathway and bless the lives of all peoples. . . .

Hers was the most harmoniously developed character I have ever known—a living soul whose individuality was blended into oneness with all humanity. She lived, yet not she; humanity lived in her. Fighting the battle for individual freedom, she was so lost to the consciousness of her own personality that she was unconscious of existence apart from all mankind.

Her quenchless passion for her cause was that it was yours and mine, the cause of the whole world. She knew that where freedom is, there is the center of power. In it she saw potentially all that humanity might attain when possessed by its spirit. Hence her cause, perfect equality of rights, of opportunity, of privilege for all, civil and political—was to her the bed-rock upon which all true progress must rest. Therefore *she* was nothing, her *cause* was everything. She knew no existence apart from it. In it she lived and moved and had her being. It was the first and last thought of each day. It was the last word upon her faltering lips . . .

She instinctively grasped the truth underlying all the great movements which have helped the progress of the ages, and did not wait for an individual or a cause to win popularity before freely extending to its struggling life a hand of helpful comradeship. She was never found in the cheering crowd that follows an already victorious standard. She left that to the time-servers who divide the spoil after they have crucified their Savior. She was truly great: great in her humility and utter lack of pretension. . . .

The world is profoundly stirred by the loss of our great General, and in consequence the lukewarm are becoming zealous, the prejudiced are disarming and the suffragists are renewing their vows of fidelity to the cause for which Miss Anthony lived and died. Her talismanic words, the last she ever uttered before a public audience, "Failure is impossible," shall be inscribed on our banner and engraved on our hearts.

—Anna Howard Shaw, 1906

The fierce snowstorm kept all but the most intimate friends and rela-
tives from the cemetery. There, beneath a simple white stone engraved only
with her name and dates, she was laid to rest. Some years earlier, during a
family reunion at her birthplace in Adams, Massachusetts, Susan B. An-
thony had written her own epitaph. As the family gathered out in the yard
on a glorious summer day, amid the horse-drawn carriages of those who had
come to call, someone remarked that the scene looked like a funeral. An-
thony spoke out:

When it is a funeral, remember that I want there should be no
tears. Pass on, and go on with the work.

**ANTHONY'S GRAVESTONE, MOUNT HOPE CEMETERY,
ROCHESTER, NEW YORK**

EPILOGUE

Febuary 15, 1907: The second day of the thirty-ninth annual NAWSA convention, in Chicago, is devoted to Susan B. Anthony's memory. Onstage, a bust of the deceased leader watches over the proceedings, a flag draped around its pedestal. According to her will, all her money—$4500—goes to the suffrage treasury. And, as she would have wished, the work of The Cause goes on.

1910–1919: Eleven more states give their women full suffrage; a number of others grant limited suffrage.

January 10, 1918: The U.S. House of Representatives passes the amendment giving all American women the vote. The Senate surrenders a year and a half later. Now it goes to the states.

August 26, 1920: Just days after Tennessee becomes the thirty-sixth (and last-needed) state to ratify, the U.S. secretary of state signs the proclamation, and what had been proposed as the Sixteenth Amendment in 1878 becomes the Nineteenth Amendment to the U.S. Constitution. The National American Woman Suffrage Association, transformed into the League of Women Voters, helps women learn how to use their new privilege. That November, for the first time ever, 26 million American women are eligible to vote. By a coincidence of luck and drama, it comes during the one hundredth anniversary of the birth of Susan B. Anthony.

THE ANTHONY MOTTO, ON A BANNER CARRIED IN
A SUFFRAGE MARCH AFTER HER DEATH

WELL, MISS ANTHONY, WHAT MESSAGE HAVE YOU FOR THE NEW CENTURY?

We women must be up and doing. I can hardly sit still when I think of the great work waiting to be done. Above all, women must be in earnest, we must be thorough, and fit ourselves for every emergency; we must be trained, and carefully prepare ourselves for the place we wish to hold in the world. . . . I shall not be here to see it, but the twentieth century will see as great a change in the position and progress of woman in the world as has been accomplished in this century, but it will have ceased to cause comment, and will be accepted as a matter of course. There will be nothing in the realm of ethics in which woman will not have her own recognized place, and all political questions, and all the laws which govern us will have a feminine side, for woman and her influence, in making and shaping of affairs, will have to be reckoned with. . . .

I am filled with sadness at this passing of the nineteenth century. I feel as if I had buried my dearest friend, but then, this new century will be just as good.
— *Interview, 1901*

If I could only live another century! I do so want to see the fruition of the work for women in the past century. There is so much yet to be done, I see so many things I would like to do and say, but I must leave it for the younger generation. We old fighters have prepared the way, and it is easier than it was fifty years ago when I first got into the harness. The young blood, fresh with enthusiasm and with all the enlightment of the twentieth century, must carry on the work.
— *Interview, 1902*

Defeats? There have been none in my life and work. All our defeats have been glorious victories, in that the cause of woman has never been presented to the voters of the country without winning very many of them. We never lose. We are always progressing.
— *Interview, 1905*

It isn't Susan B. Anthony they applaud, it is her principles. They know now that she had principles, that she had a message for the world, and that she has trodden a narrow path that she might deliver that message. It is a message they all want to hear now, and there are so many teachers. I am so glad, so happy to know that they at last understand why I have been in public life all these years.

I am letting go a little now, because younger women are taking up the work for women. Such a great work, such a magnificent one. Oh, yes; I helped to give it a little impetus.

Can you blame the pioneers . . . Elizabeth Cady Stanton, Lucy Stone, and all those others, when we all saw with clear eyes the future spread out before us with all its grand possibilities for women? We were not seers, but we did see that something must be done for women, and Quaker though I was, I had to do my part. That is all.

—Interview, 1905

In 1895, while in California for the campaign to add the vote to the state constitution, Susan B. Anthony was interviewed yet again. The skeptical reporter, Miriam Michelson, was quickly won over by the dignified leader, and affixed an unusual personal paragraph to her very enthusiastic story.

I wish I were a Susan B. Anthony. Not that I want to be seventy-five years old, and not that I regret that I married. But I should like to feel that I was really of as much consequence in the world as Miss Anthony feels herself to be—and she is not a bit conceited, either. It must be a fine thing to believe that you are leading in a great movement that will triumph and prove to the immense benefit of the world. To have the conviction that you are preaching a gospel that will save womankind, and that nothing else can do it, is explanation enough of Miss Anthony's comparatively youthful appearance at her age. . . . [T]here is something lovable in Miss Anthony's face and voice. I do not wonder that she has made converts to her cause; the wonder is that she has not made more. She is beautiful in her plainness, and her smile is not to be forgotten. There is—and that's what I'm trying to say—a very feminine side to this old maid of seventy-five, this crusader, this platform speaker and aggressive champion of her sex's "rights." Almost thou persuadest me to be a suffragist.

—Interview, 1895

Miriam Michelson wanted to be Susan B. Anthony. One hundred years later, I think I'd be satisifed just to meet her. Simply so I could say thank you—at the very least, every February 15.

ACKNOWLEDGMENTS

esearch can be progressively frustrating, challenging, thrilling, and enlightening. In the course of writing this book, I have experienced all those emotions.

I am indebted first, of course, to Susan B. Anthony herself, whose passionate commitment to history ensured that records were kept and proper sources credited. She was primarily responsible for the preservation of many letters, speeches, and newspaper articles, although anyone in search of her own words must lament the vast numbers of pages destroyed by the bonfires of Ida Husted Harper and the normal negligence of countless correspondents. Still, I am thankful that Anthony lived long before the computer. While e-mail and fax modems might have facilitated the General's command and hastened the accomplishment of her goal, it is stunning to realize the body of work that would thus have been lost in cyberspace.

Which leads me to another revelation. One of the pleasures of digging into her life was the sheer joy of holding in my hand actual letters she wrote more than a century ago. The penmanship mutates from fine schoolgirl tracings to the hurried scrawl of a busy executive; the NAWSA letterhead reflects different presidents, different headquarters; the stationery is yellowed, or stained, or barely legible. No matter: they stirred my imagination and linked me to her in a way that I never dreamed possible. Although I personally combed through files in only two places—the Huntington Library in San Marino, California, and the New York Public Library—I am

*greatly appreciative that dozens of such repositories all across the country
maintain similar collections.*

*The reason I didn't visit more libraries is because of yet another dis-
covery I made—the one for which I am most grateful of all. In 1991, in ac-
knowledgment of the difficulty of gaining ready access to the diaries,
manuscripts, letters, newspaper articles, and other material relating to Anthony and her colleague Elizabeth Cady Stanton—papers that are scattered
in several hundred libraries—a microfilm edition was published.* The Papers of Elizabeth Cady Stanton and Susan B. Anthony, *with accompanying* Guide and Index, *is an extraordinary work: forty-five reels of
microfilm detailing the lives, careers, and relationships of these outspoken
and well-traveled women. To the editors, Patricia G. Holland and Ann D.
Gordon, should go the thanks and support of every woman in America. The
compilation is so complete, only rarely did I have to go to another source for
information. I particularly want to thank Ann Gordon, now at Rutgers
University, who took time out from her own book project to answer all my
questions and rejoice over my own little discoveries. Her generosity was
overwhelming. And she's probably right that we may be the only people
alive who refer to Susan B. Anthony in the present tense.*

*I am also grateful to the authors of the five principal biographies. Ida
Husted Harper came first, writing the initial two volumes of the authorized*
Life and Work of Susan B. Anthony *with Anthony's cooperation. A third
volume was published after Anthony's death. Although she appears to have
been a good reporter and did quote Anthony accurately on a number of occasions, I have found too many rewrites of Anthony's own words to make
me trust Harper implicitly. Still, she remains the only source for myriad incidents and quotes. As a result, I cite her with respect for her enterprise and
admiration for her craftsmanship, tempered by exasperation over her tendency to polish Anthony's own perfectly acceptable language. The two other
early biographers were Rheta Childe Dorr, who became a suffragist at age
twelve, when she sneaked off to hear Anthony lecture in Nebraska; and
Katharine Anthony (no known relation), who was equally devoted. In the
modern era, Alma Lutz helped popularize Susan B. Anthony, and Kathleen
Barry took a more sociological approach. More comprehensive for the period is the fascinating six-volume* History of Woman Suffrage, *the massive chronicle of the entire movement. Susan B. Anthony served as coauthor
of the first four volumes.*

*There were others who helped me put all this together. Once again,
my friend and agent Esther Newberg was both supportive and successful.
Ann Godoff at Random House supplied editorial enthusiasm and insight.
Thanks, too, to several members of the growing Susan B. Anthony network:
Lorie Barnum, director of the Susan B. Anthony House in Rochester, New*

York, provided me unusual access to the site; Mary Huth, at the Department of Rare Books and Special Collections, University of Rochester Library, patiently dug out photographs and files. I was also assisted by Gail K. Malmgreen at the Wagner Labor Archives, New York University; Karen E. Kearns at the Huntington Library; Edith Mayo at the Smithsonian Institution, and a number of individuals at the Library of Congress, the Sophia Smith Collection (Smith College), the Arthur and Elizabeth Schlesinger Library (Radcliffe College) and the New York Public Library. In New York, Joanna Samuels again helped with research, as did Kathleen Hendry. All the assistance I received was invaluable as I tried to record Anthony's words and awkward grammar as accurately as possible. If there are mistakes in transcription or questions of meaning, they are mine alone. While Anthony's syntax may be odd, and her apostrophes frequently missing, her ideas were and are solid. They remain the inspiration —and reward—for this entire project.

NOTES

*M*ost of the documents I used for research are included in the microfilm edition of The Papers of Elizabeth Cady Stanton and Susan B. Anthony. *Since the microfilm is organized chronologically, I have not given reel and page numbers.*

Susan B. Anthony's diaries are a frequent source on the Stanton-Anthony microfilm. Most are located in the Library of Congress, Susan B. Anthony Papers. Diaries for 1837–38, 1839, and 1853–54 are in the Schlesinger Library of Radcliffe College, Susan B. Anthony Papers. If a diary entry is followed by a reference to Harper, it means the original is not available and is cited only in her biography.

The same is true of the newspaper articles. If followed by a reference to Harper, it means I did not locate them elsewhere. Some articles were found only in Susan B. Anthony's scrapbooks, which are in the Library of Congress (volumes 1–34 in the Susan B. Anthony Papers, Rare Books Division; volumes 1876–1903, 1902–04, and 1905–06 in the Susan B. Anthony Papers, Manuscript Division).

In addition, items from publications not on the microfilm edition are fully sourced; items from books often cited are referred to by author only (Katharine Anthony, Barry, Catt, Edwards, Harper, Lutz, Shaw, Stanton, Stanton and Blatch) and fully referenced in the bibliography. Likewise HWS, *which is* History of Woman Suffrage.

I have tried to keep abbreviations to a minimum. SBA is Susan B. Anthony; ECS, Elizabeth Cady Stanton. And there are these organizations:

AERA—American Equal Rights Association
NAWSA—National American Woman Suffrage Association
NCW—National Council of Women
NWSA—National Woman Suffrage Association
WLNL—Women's Loyal National League
WSA—Woman Suffrage Association

Finally, I have used Library of Congress abbreviations for sites of the original papers.

CSmH—Henry E. Huntington Library, San Marino, California
CtHSD—Stowe-Day Memorial Library and Historical Foundation, Hartford, Connecticut
CU-BANC—University of California, Berkeley, Bancroft Library, Berkeley, California
DLC—Library of Congress, Washington, D.C.
ICU—University of Chicago Library, Chicago, Illinois
IEWT—National Woman's Christian Temperance Union, Evanston, Illinois
KHi—Kansas State Historical Society, Topeka, Kansas
KU-S—University of Kansas, Kenneth Spencer Research Library, University Archives, Lawrence, Kansas
KyBgW-K—Western Kentucky University, Department of Library Special Collections, Bowling Green
MCR-S—Radcliffe College, Arthur and Elizabeth Schlesinger Library on the History of Women in America, Cambridge, Massachusetts
MdHi—Maryland Historical Society Library, Manuscripts Division, Baltimore, Maryland
MHi—Massachusetts Historical Society, Boston, Massachusetts
MnHi—Minnesota Historical Society, St. Paul, Minnesota
MNS-S—Smith College, Sophia Smith Collection, Northampton, Massachusetts
MoSHi—Missouri Historical Society, St. Louis
NB—Brooklyn Public Library, Brooklyn, New York
NcU—University of North Carolina at Chapel Hill, Southern Historical Collection, Chapel Hill, North Carolina
NIC—Cornell University Library, Ithaca, New York
NjGbS—Glassboro State College, Savitz Library, Glassboro, New Jersey
NjR—Rutgers University Libraries, New Brunswick, New Jersey
NN—New York Public Library, Astor, Lenox and Tilden Foundations, New York, New York
NPV—Vassar College Library, Poughkeepsie, New York
NR—Rochester Public Library, Rochester, New York
NRU—University of Rochester, Rochester, New York
NSyU—Syracuse University, George Arents Research Library, Syracuse, NY
OClWHi—Western Reserve Historical Society, Cleveland, Ohio
OFH—Rutherford B. Hayes Presidential Center, Fremont, Ohio
OkU—University of Oklahoma at Norman, Oklahoma
WHi—State Historical Society of Wisconsin, Madison, Wisconsin

INTRODUCTION

p. xi. "We shall some": *HWS* 4, p. 223.

xii. "[S]o many of": *HWS* 4, p. 204.

xiii. "I waited and": Harper 3, pp. 1240–41.

xiii. "I told him": Diary, September 19, 1901.

xiv. "dominant mind that": Rochester *Evening Times,* March 13, 1906, SBA Scrapbook 1905–06.

xiv. "throughout civilized lands" . . . "of her sex": *Proceedings of the Twenty-Eighth Annual Convention of NAWSA,* January 23–28, 1896, Rachel Foster Avery, ed., Philadelphia, n.d., pp. 13–14.

xv. "not to speak": Harper 1, p. 65.

xvi. "had the courage": New York *Sun,* reprinted in *The Revolution,* 8 (February 24, 1870), p. 117.

xvi. "She has perpetrated": New York *World,* February 16, 1870, SBA Scrapbook 3.

xvi. "Fiftieth birthday! One": Diary, Harper 1, p. 344.

xvi. "She is an": Portland *Oregonian,* September 1 and 2, 1871; August 2, 1871; in Edwards, p. 31.

xvi. "Height, 5 ft.": Medical certificate, December 18, 1855, by Dr. Edward M. Moore, for New York Life Insurance Company policy, Harper 1, p. 136.

xvii. "Sentiment never was": *Woman's Journal,* March 31, 1906.

xvii. "no puffs—just": SBA to Laura de Force Gordon, May 15, 1876, CU-BANC, Laura D. Gordon Collection.

xvii. "With an ocean": *Woman's Tribune,* February 22, 1890, report on ECS speech "The Friendships of Women," from SBA's 70th birthday party.

xviii. "We hear it": Adrian (Mich.) *Times & Expositor,* October 21, 1874, SBA Scrapbook 8.

xviii. "There was never": Unidentified clipping, July 14, 1901, from McClure Syndicate, "Why Some Marriages Are Failures," by SBA, CSmH, Rare Books Dept., SBA Memorial Library Collection, Clippings Scrapbook 1.

xviii. "The women of": SBA to Isabella Beecher Hooker, September 29, 1875, CtHSD, Isabella Hooker Collection.

xviii. "the earth was": Carrie Chapman Catt at Anthony family reunion, 1897, Harper 2, p. 943.

xviii. "Abraham Lincoln was" . . . "Stanton was four": Lilian Whiting in Boston *Traveller* reporting on SBA's 70th birthday party, 1890, Harper 2, p. 672.

xix. "I had all": Baltimore *Sun,* February 17, 1900.

xix. "Never again ask": Harper 1, p. 223.

xix. "never asked me": SBA to Rachel Foster, May 1880, Harper 1, p. 513.

xx. "In 1875 Anthony": SBA speech "Social Purity," Harper 2, p. 1004.

xx. "My fancy for": SBA to family, June 1847, Harper 1, p. 51.

xx. ". . . and at the": Los Angeles *Times,* June 13, 1895, SBA Scrapbook 24.

xxi. "I did read": *Report of the International Council of Women, Assembled by the National Woman Suffrage Association,* Washington, D.C., March 25–April 1, 1888, p. 47.

xxii. "probably not one": Daniel Anthony to SBA, April (probably) 1853, Harper 1, p. 85.

xxii. "I remember once": Washington *Evening Star,* January 23, 24, 27, and 29, 1896; NRU, E. B. Sweet Papers.

xxii. "I wish you": Frances D. Gage to *Woman's Advocate,* January 26, 1856, reporting on SBA's January 4–10 speaking tour.

p. xxiii. "The Committee is": Albany *Register,* March 1856, *HWS* 1, p. 629, and Harper 1, pp. 140–1.

xxiv. "She does not": Washington *Evening Star,* February 8, 1900, reporting on Anna Howard Shaw's speech at NAWSA.

xxv. "219 women coal": Unidentified clipping, n.d., probably March 4, 1900, "Women and the Century," by SBA, DLC, NAWSA papers, Ida Boyer Scrapbooks.

xxv. "I do not": *North American Review* 175 (December 1902), p. 809, "Woman's Half-Century of Evolution," by SBA.

xxv. "Because granting to": *Englishwoman's Review of Social and Industrial Questions* 14 (July 14, 1883), pp. 294–5, SBA Speech to Central Committee of the National Society for Women's Suffrage, London, England, June 25, 1883.

xxvi. "The world never": New York *Sun,* February 21, 1904.

xxvi. "How long must": *Independent* 52 (February 15, 1900), p. 417.

xxvi. "To get the": Catt, pp. 107–8.

xxvii. "It has been": Diary, June 3, 1883.

xxvii. "Verb or substantive": Stanton, p. 174.

xxviii. "Her career illustrates": New York *Globe,* cited in unidentified, undated clip, SBA Scrapbook 1905–06.

CHAPTER 1: MISS ANTHONY

3. "All say the": SBA to "Dear Friends at the Cottage," August 12, 1846, MCR-S, SBA Papers.

3. "A slab-sided spinster": Edwards, p. 81.

4. "grim Old Gal" Harper 1, p. 397.

4. "Get a good": Antoinette Brown Blackwell to SBA, March 12, 1856, MCR-S, Blackwell Family Papers.

4. "Now, Nette, *not*": SBA to Antoinette Brown Blackwell, April 22, 1858, MCR-S, Blackwell Family Papers.

4. "*I say stop*": SBA to Antoinette Brown Blackwell, May 2, 1858, MCR-S, Blackwell Family Papers.

4. "baby tender" . . . "work": SBA to Antoinette Brown Blackwell, April 22, 1858, MCR-S, Blackwell Family Papers.

4. "Lucy, *neither* of": SBA to Lucy Stone, August 11, 1857, DLC, Blackwell Family Papers.

4. "I only *scold*": SBA to Antoinette Brown Blackwell, September 4, 1858, MCR-S, Blackwell Family Papers.

5. "*Be sure* you": SBA to Lucy Stone, May 23, 1854, DLC, Blackwell Family Papers; transcript prepared by Alice Stone Blackwell.

5. "If it is": SBA to ECS, September 29, 1857, DLC, ECS papers.

5. "Oh Anna—I": SBA to Anna Dickinson, February 22, 1870, DLC, Anna Dickinson Papers.

5. "seemed to lessen": See Ruth Freeman and Patricia Klaus, "Blessed or Not? The New Spinster in England and the United States in the Late Nineteenth and Early Twentieth Centuries," *Journal of Family History* 9 (Winter 1984), pp. 394–414.

5. "I have been": *North American,* March 15, 1903.

5. "Had Miss Anthony": Harper 3, p. 1304.

p. 6. "I'm sure no": San Francisco *Chronicle,* June 28, 1896.

6. "These old Bachelors": SBA to Guelma Penn Anthony, June 15, 1839, MCR-S, SBA Papers.

6. "It is almost": Diary, 1874, Harper 1, p. 463.

6. "Joseph had a": SBA to Lucy Read Anthony, March 1849, Harper 1, p. 52.

6. "For a woman": New York *World,* February 2, 1896.

7. "I think any": Diary, February 26, 1838.

7. "This idea that": *North American,* March 15, 1903.

7. "I would not": SBA to unknown, probably November 1888, Harper 2, p. 644. Anthony wrote this after learning that Rachel Foster, her invaluable aide, was going to marry Cyrus Miller Avery of Chicago, son of a noted suffrage worker. Harper points out that Anthony sent cordial congratulations and that Rachel Foster Avery "has proved an exception to the rule," working tirelessly for The Cause and contributing thousands of dollars.

7. "Those of you": SBA to ECS, June 5, 1856, DLC, ECS Papers.

7. "Courage, Susan, this": ECS to SBA, August 20, 1857, NPV, ECS Papers.

7. "I feel *discouraged*": SBA to Martha Coffin Wright, June 6, 1856, MNS-S, Garrison Family Papers.

8. "Where are the": SBA to Amy Kirby Post, August 1, 1857, NRU, Post Family Papers.

8. "There is not": SBA to Lydia Mott, Fall 1858(?), Harper 1, p. 171.

8. "Mrs. Stanton is": SBA to Isabella Beecher Hooker, December 12, 1878, CtHSD, Isabella Hooker Collection.

8. "But so it": Fall 1853, Harper 1, p. 134, notes that Anthony wrote this after missing the Cincinnati Women's Rights convention; she was sad "because her married sisters never have time to write her."

8. "Nette, I don't": SBA to Antoinette Brown Blackwell, April 22, 1858, MCR-S, Blackwell Family Papers.

8. "Nette, Institutions, among": SBA to Antoinette Brown Blackwell, likely November 1858, MCR-S, Blackwell Family Papers.

9. "Oh this babydom": SBA to ECS, probably March or April 1861, Harper 1, p. 213.

9. "The dear little": SBA unidentified remarks, ca. 1861, Harper 1, p. 214. In April of 1862, Anthony took Stanton's four boys from Seneca Falls to New York to care for them while the Stanton family moved to the city.

9. "[T]o be a": SBA to ECS, September 29, 1857, DLC, ECS Papers.

10. "In the true": Diary, 1855.

10. "May your independence": Harper 2, p. 923.

10. "My Dear Friends": SBA to Dexter Chamberlain Bloomer and Amelia Jenks Bloomer, April 9, 1890, cited in D.C. Bloomer, *Life and Writings of Amelia Bloomer* (1895; reprint, New York: Schocken, 1975), pp. 312–3.

10. "TOAST—: Why don't": *The Revolution* 3(12) (March 25, 1869), p. 186.

11. "Men want for": San Francisco *Examiner,* October 11, 1896.

11. "The ideal husband": Cleveland *Leader,* June 23, 1901, "The Ideal Husband," by SBA, for McClure Syndicate; in CSmH, Rare Books Dept., SBA Memorial Library Collection, Clippings Scrapbook 1.

13. "I never cared": New York *World,* November 5, 1899, NRU, E. B. Sweet Papers.

13. "It always happened": *Woman's Column,* August 14, 1897.

13. "There were all": San Francisco *Chronicle,* June 28, 1896.

13. "[T]he man who": Ibid.

p. 14. "I have not": New York *Recorder,* February 16, 1895, SBA Scrapbook 23.

14. "[I]n those days": Chicago *Union Signal,* November 8, 1894.

14. "I never felt": New York *World,* February 2, 1896.

14. "He said: 'Miss": *Woman's Tribune,* April 4, 1891, reporting on Sorosis Banquet speech in New York.

15. "At home—Riggs": Diary, January 24, 1890

15. "As to her": SBA to Frances Willard, April 8, 1897, IEWT, in microfilm edition of *Temperance and Prohibition Papers,* R. C. Jimerson et al., eds. (Ann Arbor, Mich., 1977).

16. Box: Harper 1, p. 196.

CHAPTER 2: SCHOOL DAYS

17. "listened in vain . . . assigned them": SBA to editor of *Carson League,* August 18, 1853, regarding August 2–4 teachers' meeting.

17. "I probably shall": Diary, March 11, 1839.

18. "Dr. Dewitt Rile": SBA to Lucy Read Anthony, February 7, 1849, MCR-S, SBA Papers.

18. "the exclusion of": Boston *Liberator,* August 21, 1857, report on August 1857 teachers' convention at Binghamton.

18. "not a proper": *National Anti-Slavery Standard,* August 15, 1857.

18. "Is there any": SBA to Kate Stephens, July 7, 1888, KU-S University Archives, Kate Stephens Papers.

18. "Oct 4—In": Diary, October 4, 1883.

19. "Not a trustee": Diary, November 10, 1900.

19. "same way all": Rochester *Democrat and Chronicle,* September 21, 1899, SBA Scrapbook 20.

19. "If all the": *HWS* 1, pp. 513–5.

19. "It seems to": Ibid.

20. "Eyewitness accounts report": Ibid.

20. "In this State": *Proceedings of the Woman's Rights Convention, Held at the Broadway Tabernacle, in the City of New York, Tuesday and Wednesday, Sept. 6th and 7th, 1853* (New York, 1853), p. 82.

20. "Miss Anthony moved": New York *Teacher* 7 (September 1858), pp. 533–48 reporting on August 3–5 meeting.

21. "Teachers should not": Philadelphia *Press,* November 6, 1903.

22. "Oh, that I": SBA to ECS, May 26, 1856, NPV, ECS Papers, Scrapbook 1.

22. "And Mrs. Stanton": SBA to ECS, June 5–[6], 1856, DLC, ECS Papers.

22. "Why the Sexes": SBA to ECS, enclosed in letter of June 5–[6], 1856, DLC, ECS Papers.

23. "Both sexes eat": Springfield (Mass.) *Republican,* August 22, 1856, report on August 5–7 speech at New York State Teachers' Association 11th Annual Meeting, Troy, N.Y.

23. "The Colleges of": SBA handwritten speech, "Educating the Sexes Together," New York State Teachers' Association 11th Annual Meeting, August 5–7, 1856, Troy, N.Y., DLC, SBA Papers.

23. "*Resolved,* That since": Harper 1, pp. 155–6; also Binghamton *Daily Republican,* August 6, 1857, SBA Scrapbook 1.

23. "a vast social": Ibid.

p. 24. "Do you mean": Ibid.

24. "I did indeed": ECS to SBA, August 20, 1857, NPV, ECS Papers.

24. "[T]he women's colleges": New York *World,* November 5, 1899, NRU, E. B. Sweet Papers.

24. "The husband of": Los Angeles *Times* Sunday Magazine, July 7, 1901, "Educating Husbands," by SBA, McClure Syndicate; CSmH, Rare Books Department, SBA Memorial Library Collection, Clippings Scrapbook 1.

24. " 'But,' I said": SBA to Mary Anthony, Fall 1901, Harper 3, pp. 1242–3.

25. "Yes, we women": Rochester *Democrat and Chronicle,* June 29, 1902, SBA Scrapbook 1902–04.

25. "If there is": Autograph message, September 16, 1902, NN, Manuscript Division, Alfred W. Anthony Collection.

25. "The real reason": Rochester *Post Express,* October 16, 1891, SBA Scrapbook 17.

25. "Before sailing I": SBA to Jane Stanford, June 13, 1899, Harper 3, pp. 1133–4.

27. "I am still": SBA to ECS, September 1862, Harper 1, p. 221.

27. "I am glad": SBA to Dr. Sarah R. Dolley of Rochester, 1900, Harper 3, p. 1204.

27. "well they let": Diary, September 10, 1900.

28. Box: Clipping from unidentified Philadelphia newspaper, April 1902, SBA Scrapbook 1902–04.

CHAPTER 3: OH SLAVERY, HATEFUL THING

29. "The people around". SBA to Guelma Penn Anthony, June 15, 1839, MCR-S, SBA Papers.

30. "I feel that": SBA to Lucy Stone, March 12, 1854, DLC, Blackwell Family Papers.

30. "The Winter of": Handwritten heading in SBA Scrapbook 1.

30. "Miss Susan B." Albany *Argus,* undated, reporting on her January 3–4, 1861, appearance in Buffalo, SBA Scrapbook 1.

31. "We women are": *Proceedings, 31st Annual Convention of the NAWSA, Grand Rapids, Michigan,* April 27–May 3, 1899, Rachel Foster Avery, ed., (Warren, Ohio, n.d.), p. 161.

31. "it *has no*": SBA to ECS, January 27 and 29, 1884, NRU, SBA Papers.

31. "Sojourner [Truth] combined": *HWS* 1, p. 567.

31. "bowed most graciously": Diary, February 20, 1895.

32. "It is the": Speech, date not certain, "What Is American Slavery?," DLC, SBA Papers.

32. "[T]he mark of": Diary, March 29, 1854.

32. "This noon I": Diary, March 30, 1854.

33. "[S]uperintended the plowing": Diary, 1861, Harper 1, p. 216.

33. "Object of meeting": Notes of Winter 1857 speaking tour, Harper 1, p. 153.

33. "Can the thousands": Lecture, probably October 1862, "Civil War and Slaves," for gubernatorial campaign of James S. Wadsworth; MCR-S, SBA Papers.

34. "[T]here is great": *Proceedings of the Meeting of the Loyal Women of the Republic,* New York, May 14, 1863.

p. 36. "Resolved, That a": New York *Herald,* May 15, 1864, report on business meeting of the WLNL, SBA Scrapbook 1.

37. "Was there ever": SBA to ECS, April 19, 1865, DLC, ECS Papers.

37. "I was reading": Leavenworth *Evening Bulletin,* April 24, 1865, report on April 23 speech at Memorial Service for Lincoln.

37. "In this city": SBA to ECS, February 14, 1865, DLC, ECS papers.

38. "With the above": Inscription, June 25, 1891, at John Brown Farm.

38. "This is a": *HWS* 2, p. 270.

38. "The real fact": SBA to Caroline Dall, January 30, 1866, MHi, C. H. Dall Collection.

39. "Dear Anna": SBA to Anna Dickinson, November 28, 1867, DLC, Anna Dickinson Papers.

39. "My Dear Olympia": SBA to Olympia Brown, July 20, 1868, MCR-S, Olympia Brown Papers.

39. "MR. DOUGLASS—I": Remarks at AERA, May 12, 1869, from phonographic report in SBA Scrapbook 2; also *HWS* 2, pp. 392 and 379–83.

42. "The color line": Chicago *Times-Herald,* June 25, 1900.

42. "It was splendid": Diary, September 19, 1901.

42. "[I will tell": Rochester *Herald,* April 8, 1895, SBA Scrapbook 1876–1903; also Harper 2, p. 815.

43. "Ida B. Wells": Diary, April 8, 1895.

43. "To refuse to": Rochester *Union and Advertiser,* February 20, 1903, reporting on letter of SBA read at mass meeting at Cooper Union in New York to protest disfranchisement of blacks in the South.

44. "[T]he only way": Diary, probably March 1905, Harper 3, p. 1356.

44. Box: Rochester *Union and Advertiser,* August 31, 1865.

CHAPTER 4: WHAT DO WOMEN WANT?

45. "Wo´man's Rights, a": Johnson's *New Universal Cyclopaedia,* vol. 4, "S-Appendix" (New York, 1878), p. 1477.

45. "delicately flavored soup": SBA to Amelia Bloomer, *The Lily,* August 26, 1852, p. 73.

45. "shiftless, drunken, precarious": Unidentified clipping, probably around January 1, 1897, SBA Scrapbook 26.

46. "the brothers will": SBA to Lucy Stone, May 1, 1853, DLC, Blackwell Family Papers.

46. "First day—Crowding": New York *Tribune,* September 1853, Harper 1, p. 102.

46. "We stopped at": SBA to family, January 14, 1856, Harper 1, pp. 138–9. Although this letter describes a later trip, the situation was the same.

47. "Hurrah Susan! Last": Lucy Stone to SBA, March 25, 1856, DLC, Blackwell Family Papers.

47. "Well, well; while": SBA to Lydia Mott, Spring 1862, *HWS* 1, pp. 748–9.

48. "I am tired": SBA to Lucy Read Anthony, October 15, 1848, MCR-S, SBA Papers. This quote has been edited for legibility. The actual letter—written in typical Anthony haste—reads "much" for "must" and "depen" for "depend."

48. "Cautious, careful people": Harper 1, p. 197.

48. ". . . it is only": SBA to Mary Anthony, August 27, 1883, Harper 2, p. 572.

p. 48. "In those early": New York *Mail and Express,* January 12, 1895, SBA Scrapbook 23.

49. "I want to": Emporia (Kans.) *Daily Republican,* October 8, 1887, reporting on October 6–8, 1887, Fourth Congressional District Equal Suffrage Convention, Emporia, Kansas, SBA Scrapbook 12.

49. "Thus as I": Diary, 1853.

50. "Friends, when we": Lecture, 1854, "Rights and Wrongs of Woman," manuscript in MCR-S, SBA Papers.

51. "Men may prate": SBA to Amelia Bloomer, *The Lily,* September 1852, p. 74, reprinting SBA's August 26, 1852, letter.

51. "I have thought": SBA to Lucy Stone, July 18, 1857, SLC, Blackwell Family Papers.

51. "Lucy, I want": SBA to Lucy Stone, June 16, 1857, DLC, Blackwell Family Papers; transcript prepared by Alice Stone Blackwell.

51. "Marriage has ever": *HWS* 1, p. 735.

52. "I do not": Washington *Post,* April 15, 1905, reporting on Triennial NCW meeting, April 9–14, 1905.

52. "U.S. Representative": *HWS* 2, pp. 455–6.

52. "A married woman": Speech, 1873, *HWS* 2, p. 643.

53. "Don't trust to": Minneapolis *Tribune,* October 24, 1889, reporting on annual Minnesota WSA meeting. The article notes that Anthony was frequently applauded.

53. "Primarily I want": Topeka *Journal,* May 9, 1894.

54. "The Men, even": SBA to Lucy Stone, October 27, 1856, DLC, Blackwell Family Papers; transcript prepared by I. P. Boyer.

54. ". . . he set forth": SBA to ECS, September 29, 1857, DLC, ECS Papers.

55. "You blunder on": SBA to Daniel Read Anthony, Winter 1859, Harper 1, pp. 169–70. In one of the only existing letters from Daniel to Susan, he writes that he "can't say how much I can help the cause—we have enough to attend to besides *Woman's Rights* just now——"; KHi, Manuscript Department, Daniel Read Anthony Letters.

55. "We want to": Chicago *Daily Tribune,* May 16, 1893, SBA statement on World's Columbian Exposition to World's Congress of Representative Women.

56. "The best of": SBA to ECS, October 26, 1883, NjR, Douglass Library, T. Stanton Collection, ECS Papers; transcript prepared for T. Stanton and H. S. Blatch.

56. "That women are": SBA to Jane Grey Swisshelm, February 5, 1883, MnHi, William Bell Mitchell and Family Papers.

56. "What every woman": New York *World,* November 5, 1899, NRU, E. B. Sweet Papers.

56. "In the first": Chicago *Union Signal,* November 8, 1894, reporting SBA speech at Dr. Strong's Sanitarium on September 19 in Saratoga Springs.

57. "From time immemorial": San Francisco *Examiner,* May 17, 1896, "The Necessity of Woman Suffrage," by SBA.

57. "The tap-root of": Unidentified clipping, undated, SBA Scrapbook 27. This statement earlier appears in her 1875 "Social Purity" speech.

58. "We women have": New York *Times,* August 31, 1889, reporting speech to Seidl Society, Brooklyn.

59. Box: Recollections of Antoinette Brown Blackwell, Harper 1, pp. 176–7.

CHAPTER 5: THE CAUSE

p. 60. "individuals, not echoes": Unidentified clipping, probably November 25, 1892, SBA Scrapbook 18.

60. "march to the": *North American Review* 175 (December 1902), p. 806, "Woman's Half-Century of Evolution," by SBA, talking about her May 1852 activities.

61. "their own conditions": Harper 2, p. 844.

61. "the home, the": Diary, May 14, 1899.

61. "jewels": SBA to Olympia Brown, January 15, 1900, MCR-S, Olympia Brown Papers.

61. "I am weary": SBA to Jane Spofford, May 20, 1883, Harper 2, p. 562.

61. "It is my": San Francisco *Examiner,* May 20, 1895.

61. "dark, discouraging road": SBA to woman from Illinois, Harper 2, pp. 897–8.

61. "Not necessarily. It": Nebraska *State Journal,* undated article, SBA Scrapbook 12.

61. "It was that": SBA speech to Grand Rapids Trades Assembly, October 4, 1874, unidentified clipping, n.d., SBA Scrapbook.

62. "Disfranchisement means inability": SBA speech "Woman Wants Bread, Not the Ballot," Harper 2, pp. 996–1003.

62. "Disfranchisement in a": *HWS* 2, p. 154, on resolutions presented to Woman's Rights Convention, New York, May 6, 1866.

62. "The Chairman of": George William Curtis at 1867 New York Constitution Convention debate, *HWS* 2, pp. 292–3.

63. "answered with much": Portland *Daily Oregonian,* September 12, 1871.

63. "Women already have": Composite of questions and answers from SBA's September 11, 1871, appearance at Portland's Oro Fino Hall; sources: *New Northwest,* September 15, 1871; Portland (Ore.) *Herald,* September 12, 1871, SBA Scrapbook 4; Portland *Daily Oregonian,* September 12, 1871.

64. "A dear and": *Report of the Sixteenth Annual Washington Convention,* NWSA, March 4–7, 1884 (Rochester, N.Y., 1884).

64. "Yesterday's paper brings": Rochester *Union and Advertiser,* June 4, 1897, SBA signed column.

64. "What is this": *Woman's Journal,* June 9, 1888, reporting on May 30 speech to New England Woman Suffrage Festival in Boston.

65. "Politically her opinion": *Woman's Journal,* March 3, 1900, SBA remarks during 1900 NAWSA meeting.

65. "It does seem": SBA to DAR, 1900, Harper 3, pp. 1199–1200.

66. "[U]ntil women are": SBA to Thomas Bowman, September 7, 1894, CSmH, Anthony Family Collection, AF 23.

66. "Women, we might": Cleveland *Leader,* November 19, 1894, report on SBA address to WCTU, November 17, 1894; also Harper 2, p. 801.

66. "Women's progress has": St. Louis *Post Dispatch,* not dated, on May 2, 1895, interview, SBA Scrapbook 24.

67. "If there is": Chicago *Tribune,* November 20, 1897.

67. "The chief danger": New York *World,* December 30, 1900, response to question "What is the chief danger, social or political, that confronts the new century?" Another respondent answered, "Deterioration of the press and the sacrifice of its sense of responsibility to the demands of sensationalism"; the president of Yale said, "Legislation based on self-interest."

p. 67. "You may pet": Rochester *Herald,* February 16, 1905.

67. "I care very": London *Times,* July 16, 1899, CSmH, Rare Books Dept, SBA Memorial Library Collection, Clippings Scrapbook 1.

68. "Now, I appeal": SBA to Senate Select Committee on Woman Suffrage, in *Hearing Before the U.S. Senate Committee on Woman Suffrage, Held in the Marble Room of the U.S. Senate on the 13th Day of February, 1900.*

68. "We are utterly": Brooklyn *Daily Eagle,* November 16, 1893, on SBA speech to New York State Woman Suffrage Association meeting.

69. Box: *HWS* 2, p. 284; also Harper 1, pp. 279–80.

CHAPTER 6: GENERAL ANTHONY

70. "I was elected": SBA at 1900 NAWSA meeting, Washington *Post,* Harper 3, p. 1170.

71. "My dear general": May Wright Sewall to SBA, June 9, 1897, NRU, Anthony-Avery Papers.

71. "subsoil plowing": New York *Tribune,* February 16, 1870, reporting on SBA's 50th birthday party.

71. "All we can": *Kate Field's Washington* 1 (February 12, 1890), pp. 108–9.

72. "The one work": SBA to *Woman's Tribune,* December 7, 1889.

72. "I am glad": San Francisco *Bulletin,* May 27, 1895, report on meeting of California Suffrage Constitutional Amendment Campaign Association, SBA Scrapbook 24.

72. "First, your local": SBA to North Dakota Woman Suffrage Association Annual Meeting, Grand Forks, November 14–15, 1895, *HWS* 4, p. 547.

73. "The spring campaign": San Francisco *Examiner,* June 28, 1896, "One Campaign Ended, Now for the Next," by SBA.

74. "Whereas, 17,000 Kansas": Topeka (Kans.) *Daily Capital,* July 12, 1895.

74. "startling": Unidentified newspaper clipping, n.d., probably July 1895, SBA Scrapbook 23.

74. "unworthy": Unidentified newspaper clipping from Shelbyville, Ky., July 25, 1895, SBA Scrapbook 23.

74. "spiteful": Rochester *Democrat and Chronicle,* July 22, 1895, SBA Scrapbook 23.

74. "I must just": SBA to unidentified Topeka suffrage leader, unidentified newspaper clipping of July 1895 citing Topeka *Press* account, SBA Scrapbook 23.

75. "But be careful": SBA to Clara Colby, January 14, 1895, CSmH, Clara (Bewick) Colby Collection.

75. "My Dear Friend": SBA to Clara Colby, January 24, 1900, CSmH, Clara (Bewick) Colby Collection.

75. "Mrs. Colby writes": SBA to Harriet Taylor Upton, March 14, 1892, NRU, SBA Papers.

76. "February 1—Received": Diary, February 1, 2, 3, and 14, 1888.

77. "Better lose me": May Seymour Howell's account of the 1890 South Dakota campaign, Harper 2, p. 692.

77. "[N]ow comes Colorado": SBA to *Women's Tribune,* April 22, 1893.

77. "My Dear Mrs.": SBA to Lucy Ware Webb Hayes, February 9, 1879, OFH, Lucy Webb Hayes Collection.

78. "Dear Sir": SBA to Dear Sir, January 12, 1875, NPV, SBA Papers.

p. 79. Box: Harper 2, p. 570, and San Francisco *Examiner,* April 26, 1896, "Susan B. Anthony Argues for a Vote," by SBA.

CHAPTER 7: ONE MORE SCREECH FOR FREEDOM

80. "What are you": Chicago *Daily Tribune,* October 13, 1874, interview before large suffrage meeting.
81. "Miss Anthony is": Atlanta *Constitution,* February 1, 1895.
81. "[T]he woman suffragists": Baltimore *Sun,* 1888, report on her March appearance at International Council of Women Meeting, Harper, p. 637.
81. "If ever there": New York *World,* 1888, report on March 25 ICW meeting, Harper, p. 638.
82. "is not a" . . . "first in order": SBA to Rachel Foster Avery, September 8, 1897, NRU, Anthony-Avery Papers.
82. "My dear Rachel": SBA to Rachel Foster Avery, September 20, 1897, NRU, Anthony-Avery Papers.
83. "Taxation without Representation" . . . "barbarism to civilization": Washington *Evening Star,* January 21, 1880.
83. "woman suffrage follows": *Woman's Journal,* February 9, 1895.
83. "seven thousand": SBA speech at World's Columbian Exposition, World's Congress of Representative Women, May 20, 1893, "Organization Among Women as an Instrument in Promoting the Interests of Political Liberty," cited in May Wright Sewall, ed., *World's Congress of Representative Women* (Chicago and New York: Rand, McNally, 1894), pp. 463–6.
84. "A resolution was": Washington *Chronicle,* January 28, 1883, MCR-S, Robinson-Shattuck Papers, Scrapbook 54, and DLC, Rare Books Division, SBA Scrapbook 10.
84. "The speeches of": *National Republican,* February 18, 1886.
84. "Miss Anthony presented": *Woman's Tribune,* March 7, 1891.
85. "If you don't": National American Woman Suffrage Association, *Proceedings of the Twenty-Fifth Annual Convention of the National American Woman Suffrage Association,* Washington, D.C., January 16–19, 1893, Harriet Taylor Upton, ed. (Washington, D.C., 1893), p. 14.
85. "Washington, D.C., had" . . . "expect the invasion": *HWS* 4, p. 188.
85. "MISS ANTHONY: I": *Proceedings of the Twenty-Fifth Annual Convention of the National American Woman Suffrage Association,* op. cit., pp. 49–51.
87. "The badges worn": This quote is compiled from reports in the Atlanta *Constitution,* February 1, 1895, and the Atlanta *Journal,* January 31, 1895.
87. "I hope the": Atlanta *Constitution,* February 1, 1895.
87. "MISS ANTHONY Now": Compiled from reports in the *Woman's Journal,* February 9, 1895, and the Atlanta *Constitution,* February 1 and 2, 1895.
89. "Each convention takes": Washington *Evening Star,* January 25, 1887. This is SBA's response to reporter's assertion that nothing had been accomplished by eighteen national conventions held in D.C.
89. "I think the": *Proceedings of the Twenty-Sixth Annual Convention of the National American Woman Suffrage Association,* Washington, D.C., February 15–20, 1894, Harriet Taylor Upton, ed. (Washington, D.C., 1894), pp. 52–3.
90. Box: Shaw, p. 208.

CHAPTER 8: THE YEARS OF THE WOMEN

p. 91. "Our Congressmen are": Daniel Anthony to Lucy Anthony, September 11, 1837, Harper 1, p. 33.

92. "I thought just": Henry Blair to SBA, Harper 2, p. 606.

92. "a lobbyist without": Katharine Anthony, pp. 378–9.

92. "The memorial of": Ibid.

93. " 'woman suffrage' in": Washington *Evening Star,* February 15, 1890.

93. "Miss Anthony, bearing": Catt, p. 232.

93. "She found the": Washington *Evening Star,* January 24, 1896.

93. "and she was": SBA to New York Senate Judiciary Committee, Albany, March 1897, Harper 2, p. 914.

94. "Sec. 1—The": *HWS* 2, p. 75.

94. "There is no": Leavenworth *Times,* September 11, 1900, "Political Women," by SBA, SBA Scrapbook 1892–1901.

94. "Governments never do": *Transactions of the National Council of Women of the United States,* Washington, D.C., February 22–25, 1891, Rachel Foster Avery, ed., p. 229.

94. "My answer is": March 7, 1884, *U.S. Congress, Senate, Committee on Woman Suffrage, Report to Accompany S.R. 19, 48th Cong., 1st sess., Sen. Report 399, P.1, Serial 2175,* pp. 13–14.

95. "One reason why": *HWS* 4, p. 365, reporting 1900 NAWSA speech. A foot-note on page 366 notes that "all but one of the favorable reports from congressional committees were made during the years when Miss Anthony had a winter home at the Riggs House, through the courtesy of its proprietors, Mr. and Mrs. C. W. Spofford, and was able to secure them through personal attention and influence . . . excellent reports of 1879, 1882, 1883, 1884, 1886, 1890."

96. "Dear Sir": SBA to Rep. James Brooks, January 20, 1866, reprinted in *Congressional Globe,* 39th Cong., 1st Session, January 23, 1866, p. 380.

96. "My dear friend": SBA to Sidney Clark, January 21, 1866, OkU, Western History Collections, Carl Albert Center Archives, Sidney Clarke Collection.

97. "No one shrinks": SBA to Hon. William D. Kelley, January 6, 1884, Harper 2, p. 584.

97. "This is a . . . I deserved that": Florence Kelley, *The Autobiography of Florence Kelley,* Kathryn Kish Sklar, ed. (Chicago: Charles H. Kerr, 1986), p. 62.

98. "Dear Sir": SBA to Matt Whitaker Ransom, February 3, 1892, NcU, Southern Historical Collection, Matt Whitaker Ransom Papers; similar to John Sherman, courtesy Mrs. George J. Gibson, Salt Lake City, Utah.

98. "I want to": SBA to Mrs. William E. Chandler, Harper 3, p. 1209.

99. "I never come": February 16, 1904, Hearing, Senate Select Committee on Woman Suffrage.

99. "great quadrennial bluster": San Francisco *Examiner,* July 19, 1896, "If Hysteria Bar, Then Who Will Vote?" by SBA.

99. "You mean to": Unidentified newspaper, February 28, 1884, SBA Scrapbook 10.

100. "THE CHAIRMAN—I": New York *Sun,* July 7, 1868, reprinted in *The Revolution* 2(2) (July 16, 1868), p. 18.

100. "You see our": SBA interview, ca. May 1, 1872, on upcoming Liberal Re-

publican Party, National Convention in Cincinnati; in unidentified clipping, n.d., SBA Scrapbook 4.

p. 100. "Gentlemen": SBA to Republicans, June 5, 1872, SBA Scrapbook 4.

101. "The Republican party": *Harper* 1, p. 416

101. "blood was at" . . . "trifling reward": Philadelphia *Press,* June 7, 1872, report on Radical Club of Philadelphia meeting of June 5–6.

101. "I am sure": SBA to Martha Coffin Wright, June 13, 1872 (in hand of MCW); MNS-S, Garrison Family Papers.

101. "Women of the": Address sent out July 19, 1872, by SBA and Matilda Joslyn Gage; from *HWS* 2, pp. 517–8.

101. "I think about": SBA to Elizabeth Boynton Harbert, October 12, 1879, CSmH, Elizabeth Morrison (Boynton) Harbert Collection.

102. "WHERE DO YOU": Chicago *Daily Tribune,* December 10, 1879.

102. "Our next movement": Cincinnati *Daily Gazette,* June 25, 1880.

103. "We shall ask": Topeka *Daily State Journal,* June 13, 1894, report on June 12–13 Kansas People's Party State Convention, SBA Scrapbook 22.

104. "Lots of the": *Woman's Tribune,* June 30, 1894.

104. "BUT IT ALWAYS": Rochester *Democrat and Chronicle,* June 22, 1894.

104. "At home—Reporter": Diary, June 24, 1894.

104. "I was born": *Woman's Tribune,* September 22, 1894.

105. "Women can belong": SBA to Mary Keith, March 20, 1896, CSmH, Anthony Family Collection, AF26(1); transcript prepared by unidentified person.

106. Box: Unidentified clipping from November 10, 1895, response to question by Frank George Carpenter, "If women came to Congress, what would be the result?"; others asked included Clara Barton, Oregon Sen. John H. Mitchell; New Jersey Rep. Thomas Dun English; CSmH, Rare Books Department, SBA Memorial Library Collection, Clippings Scrapbook 4.

CHAPTER 9: A FINE AGITATION

107. "Now Register! To-day": Rochester newspaper, November 1, 1872, *HWS* 2, p. 627.

108. "Any person" . . . "of the law": Rochester *Union and Advertiser,* November 11, 1872, Connecticut Archives, History, and Genealogy Unit.

108. "in the days": *HWS* 2, p. 629.

109. "On the bench": *HWS* 2, p. 647.

109. "The greatest outrage": Diary, June 18, 1873.

110. "Dear Mrs. Stanton": SBA to ECS, November 5, 1872, CSmH, Ida (Husted) Harper Collection, HM10549.

110. "My dear Mrs. Wright": SBA to Martha Coffin Wright, January 1, 1873, MNS-S, Garrison Family Papers.

110. "Friends and fellow-citizens": SBA speech to twenty-nine districts in Monroe County and twenty-one of Ontario County before her June 1873 trial; in *HWS* 2, pp. 630–647.

113. "THE UNITED STATES": *HWS* 2, pp. 648–89.

117. "If it is": Washington Co. (N.Y.) *County Post,* June 27, 1873, in *HWS* 2, p. 944.

118. Box: *HWS* 3, pp. 944–5.

CHAPTER 10: THE ORIGINAL FREQUENT FLIER

p. 119. "Men, women and": SBA to Carson League from Syracuse, N.Y., September 30, 1852.

120. "I had been": SBA to Lucy Stone, March 22, 1858, DLC, Blackwell Family Papers.

120. "delivered sixty speeches": Edwards, p. 9.

120. "The train trip" . . . "in 1873": Diary, 1873.

120. "mountains and through": SBA to editor of Toledo (Ohio) *Ballot Box,* September 21, 1877.

120. "hardest part of": Shaw, p. 201.

121. "I have been": SBA to Duniway family, 1871, cited in Helen Krebs Smith, *Presumptuous Dreamers,* vol. I (1834–71) (Lake Oswego, Ore.: Smith, Smith and Smith Publishing Company, 1974), p. 165.

121. "Bloomington, Ind.": Diary, June 18, 1870.

121. "sat on the": Diary, June 22, 1894.

121. "For the first": Ibid.

121. "[T]hey say that": Rochester *Democrat and Chronicle,* April 30, 1894.

122. "Slept in my": Diary, November 16, 1894.

122. "My trips from": Diary, May–June 1867, Harper 1, p. 278.

122. "He explained the": Diary, August 11, 1871.

122. "Ship Idaho": Diary, August 25, 1871.

122. "I am now": SBA to Lucy Read Anthony, November 24, 1871, Harper 1, p. 403.

123. "Recently to reach": Matilda Joslyn Gage in Syracuse (N.Y.) *National Citizen and Ballot Box,* May 1879, reporting on SBA's pre–May 1879 trip.

123. "December 28—Eastern": Diary, December 1871–January 1872.

124. "On Union Pacific": SBA to cousin Frank Anthony, January 2, 1872, from transcripts prepared for Mrs. Albert E. Sheppard, Houston, Tex., copy not located.

125. "old fogies of": Aberdeen (S.D.) *Saturday Pioneer,* May 10, 1890.

125. "and would attract": T. A. Larson, "Woman Suffrage," in *The Reader's Encyclopedia of the American West,* Howard R. Lamar, ed. (New York: Crowell, 1977), pp. 1282–5.

125. "The reporter inquired": Unidentified clipping, n.d., probably November 18–22, 1884, SBA Scrapbook 10.

126. "WHERE ARE YOU": *Kate Field's Washington* 1, (February 12, 1890), pp. 108–9.

126. "I don't see": Philadelphia *Evening News,* February 22, 1883, SBA Scrapbook 10.

126. "By this time": SBA to Lucy Read Anthony, July 31, 1871, Harper 1, pp. 392–4.

127. "On Board the": SBA to Mary Anthony, March 5, 1883, Harper 2, p. 552.

128. "Rome, April 1": SBA to D. R. Anthony, Harper 2, p. 557.

128. "Heidelberg, May 11": SBA to D. R. Anthony, May 11, 1883, unidentified clipping, n.d., SBA Scrapbook 10.

128. "Sept 11—In": Diary, September 11 and 29 and October 3, 1883, Harper 2, p. 576.

129. "a dreary cloudy": Diary, October 20, 1883.

129. "October 27—It": SBA to Mary Anthony, October 27, 1883, Harper 2, p. 576.

p. 129. "I am sorry": SBA to a West Coast friend, Harper 2, p. 1360.

130. Box: Unidentified newspaper clipping, probably August 1871, citing Grass Valley (Calif.) *Republican* of August 10, SBA Scrapbook 3.

CHAPTER 11: THE SPEAKERESS

131. "It always requires": Indianapolis *Saturday Herald,* December 21, 1878, SBA Scrapbook 8.

131. "In debate she": Stanton, p. 170.

131. "At the beginning": Daniel R. Anthony, Jr., to his parents, 1889, Harper 2, p. 658.

131. "Miss Anthony deals": Indianapolis *Saturday Herald,* December 21, 1878, SBA Scrapbook 8.

132. "Miss Anthony evidently": Pittsburgh *Commercial,* cited in *The Revolution* 5(10), (March 10, 1870), p. 153.

132. "In your meetings": ECS to SBA, April 2, 1852, Stanton and Blatch, 2, p. 38.

132. "Why do you": Lucy Stone to SBA, July 22, 1856, DLC, Blackwell Family Papers.

132. "The speakeress rattled": Detroit *Free Press,* December 10, 1869.

132. "Was happy in": Diary, October 13, 1871.

132. "estimated 42,000 people": Syracuse (N.Y.) *National Citizen and Ballot Box,* June 1878 (SBA letter of May 29).

132. "Two decades later" . . . "State Legislature": SBA to unknown correspondent, probably 1897, Harper 2, p. 925.

132. "all converted": Diary, February 25, 1876.

132. "dreadfully fagged" . . . "speeches": Diary, March 2, 1876.

133. "up to $150": Lutz, p. 178.

133. "Dear Mrs. Bloomer": SBA to Amelia Bloomer, *The Lily,* September 1852, printing SBA's August 26, 1852, letter.

134. "No advanced step": *Independent* 52 (February 15, 1900), pp. 414–17, "Fifty Years of Work for Woman," by SBA.

135. "I haven't gotten": Kentucky *Leader,* January 10, 1895, KyBgW-K, Dept. of Library Special Collections, Calvert-Obenchain-Younglove MSS Collection.

135. "I have learned": SBA to Frances Willard, as recalled by Willard in Chicago *Union Signal,* January 28, 1897.

135. "So difficult to": Katharine Anthony, p. 339.

135. "A novel spectacle": SBA to Marius Racine Robinson, Salem (Ohio) *Antislavery Bugle,* November 11, 1857.

135. "Had a fine": Diary, June 9, 1894.

135. "Mrs. President, I": New York *Daily Tribune,* September 14, 1852, and Harper 1, p. 75, quoting SBA at her first Woman's Rights Convention, Syracuse, September 8–10, 1852.

136. "Now—don't stop": SBA to Harriet Taylor Upton, July 24, 1892, NRU, SBA Papers.

136. "But I declare": SBA to Elizabeth Boynton Harbert, October 12, 1879, CSmH, Elizabeth Morrison (Boynton) Harbert Papers.

137. "I should vastly": SBA to Elizabeth Boynton Harbert, December 1, 1886, CSmH, Elizabeth Morrison (Boynton) Harbert Collection Box 2.

p. 137. "I am here": Cleveland *Herald,* November 11, 1884, SBA Scrapbook 10.

137. "My purpose tonight": Speech, "Bread, Not the Ballot," as compiled in Harper 2, pp. 996–1003.

138. "You say that": Milwaukee *Sentinel,* March 20, 1876.

138. "The question with": Harper 2, pp. 996–1003.

141. Box: Harper 2, p. 693, quoting Anna Howard Shaw.

CHAPTER 12: THE ENEMY

142. "To those of": Grover Cleveland, "Woman's Mission and Woman's Clubs," *Ladies Home Journal,* May 1905, pp. 3–4.

142. "The restlessness and": Ibid.

143. "harmful in a": Ibid.

143. "Ridiculous! Pure fol-de-rol!": Rochester *Evening Times,* April 25, 1905, SBA Scrapbook 1906.

144. "Susan B. / Anthony": Harper 3, p. 1359.

145. "Our Philadelphia ladies": Philadelphia *Public Ledger and Daily Transcript,* reporting on 1848 Seneca Falls and Rochester conventions, *HWS* 1, p. 804.

145. "We received a": Utica (N.Y.) *Evening Telegraph,* April 28, 1853, SBA Scrapbook 1.

146. "We saw, in": New York *Herald,* September 7, 1853, *HWS* 1, p. 556.

147. "The farce at": New York *Herald,* September 12, 1852, *HWS* 1, pp. 853–4.

147. "Susan is lean": New York *World,* reporting on response to November 21, 1866, meeting re upcoming Constitutional Convention, Harper 1, p. 264.

147. "In appearance, Miss": Adrian (Mich.) *Times and Expositor,* April 9, 1870, SBA Scrapbook 3.

148. "People went there": Detroit *Free Press,* December 10, 1869.

148. "Some were tall": Portland (Ore.) *Herald,* September 10, 1871, cited in Edwards, p. 47.

148. "We could not": Oregon City (Ore.) *Weekly Enterprise,* September 15, 1871, Edwards, p. 56.

148. "To any who": Portland (Ore.) *Bulletin,* September 17, 1871, Edwards, p. 54.

149. "To untaught minds": Mercer (Pa.) *Western Press,* May 2, 1873, SBA Scrapbook 4.

149. "gabble [of] the": *Daily Star,* September 11, 1852, *HWS* 1, p. 852.

149. "[T]he right of": Washington, D.C., suffrage debate, December 11, 1866, *HWS* 2, pp. 108–9.

150. "I think I": Washington, D.C., suffrage debate, December 11, 1866, *HWS* 2, pp. 134–5.

150. "Voting is no": Suffrage debate, 1874, *HWS* 2, pp. 576–7.

150. "Now it is": *HWS* 3, p. 209.

151. "Society can not": January 25, 1887, suffrage debate in Senate, *HWS* 4, p. 95.

151. "When woman becomes": January 25, 1887, suffrage debate in Senate, *HWS* 4, p. 99.

151. "I am not": January 25, 1887, suffrage debate in Senate, *HWS* 4, pp. 106–7.

152. "I have always": Senator Lodge to SBA, October 10, 1902, NN, Manuscript Division, NAWSA records.

p. 152. "Kindly do not": Nicholas Murray Butler to SBA, October 13, 1902, NN, Manuscript Division, NAWSA records.

153. "We oppose woman": Unidentified clipping, n.d., reporting on July 1894 Democratic Convention, SBA Scrapbook 22.

153. "I honor all": Grace Greenwood (pen name of Sara Jane Clarke Lippincott), journalist, speech, in *Report of the International Council of Women,* assembled by the National Woman Suffrage Association, Washington, D.C., March 25–April 1, 1888, pp. 353–4.

154. Box: Harper 2, p. 874, footnote, reporting on 1896 California event.

CHAPTER 13: GENTLEMEN, TAKE NOTICE

155. "so that it": Philadelphia *Press,* January 24, 1870, reporting on Washington, D.C., Hearing, House and Senate Committees, DLC, Rare Books Division, M. J. Gage Scrapbooks and SBA Scrapbook 3.

155. "Miss Susan B.": *The Revolution,* 4(14) October 7, 1869), p. 219.

155. "It has become": Indianapolis *Herald,* December 21, 1878, SBA Scrapbook 8.

156. "Here is a": SBA introducing Henry Blackwell at 1900 NAWSA meeting, *HWS* 4, p. 357.

156. "Laurel wreaths and": *HWS* 4, p. 201.

157. "[W]e once induced": *Kate Field's Washington* 1 (February 12, 1890), pp. 108–9.

157. "the federal government": Washington *Post,* January 11, 1891.

157. "I tell you": SBA to ECS, September 29, 1857.

157. "I went to": Diary, April 29, 1874. SBA actually wrote, "man makes & break laws—& woman . . . soften [*sic*]"

158. "Oh, if men": Diary, 1883, Harper 2, p. 583.

158. "Right here I": Philadelphia *North American,* March 15, 1903.

158. "That is quite": Unidentified clipping, n.d., February 13, 1903, SBA Scrapbook 1902–04.

158. "[M]en are afraid": International Council of Women, *Women in Politics, Being the Political Section of the International Congress of Women,* London, July 1899, Vol. 5 of *Report of Transactions of Second Quinquennial Meeting of the International Congress of Women,* Countess of Aberdeen, ed., (London, 1900), p. 129.

158. "every whiskey maker": Diary, November 4, 1874.

158. "In South Dakota": Rochester *Morning Herald,* December 15, 1890.

159. "The opposition has": San Francisco *Call,* July 12, 1896, SBA signed letter/article.

159. "It was indeed": Harper 2, p. 1208.

159. "At the close": *Woman's Tribune,* March 1886.

160. "As to *men*": SBA to Elizabeth Boynton Harbert, July 7, 1880, CSmH, Elizabeth Morrison (Boynton) Harbert Collection, Box 2.

160. "Women are too": SBA to Laura de Force Gordon, November 17, 1870, CU-BANC, Laura D. Gordon Collection.

160. "The interests of": Henry Blackwell speech at Women's Rights Convention in Cleveland, Ohio, October 6–8, 1853, responding to a letter from Horace Greeley, quoted in *HWS* 1, p. 126.

161. "was in process": *HWS* 4, p. 554.

p. 161. "Like life insurance": *HWS* 4, pp. 62–9.
163. "I think one": San Francisco *Examiner,* May 28, 1895, report on SBA after-dinner address to San Francisco Unitarian Club meeting.
164. Box: SBA speech at NAWSA, Grand Rapids, Mich., April 27–May 4, 1899, in *Woman's Tribune,* May 20, 1899.

CHAPTER 14: SISTERHOOD IS POWERFUL

165. "in silent, reverential": SBA to unknown, 1862, Harper 1, p. 219.
166. "I wish he": Lucy Stone to SBA, March 25, 1856, DLC, Blackwell Family Papers.
166. "As a mother's": Leavenworth (Kans.) *Times,* February 15, 1889, SBA Scrapbook 14.
166. "My Dear Chicky": SBA to Anna Dickinson, February 13, 1868, DLC, Anna Dickinson Papers.
166. "They valued one": Carroll Smith-Rosenberg, *Disorderly Conduct, Visions of Gender in Victorian America* (New York: Alfred A. Knopf, 1985), p. 644.
167. "my oldest and": SBA to Isabella Beecher Hooker, April 22, 1871, CtHSD, Isabella Hooker Collection.
167. "There she stood": ECS "Reminiscences," *HWS* 1, p. 457.
167. "looking earnestly at": ECS to SBA, May 4, 1879, NjR, Douglass Library, T. Stanton Collection, ECS Papers; transcript prepared for T. Stanton and H. S. Blatch.
167. "I am willing" . . . "they are crossed": ECS to SBA, possibly February 25, 1860, Harper 1, p. 187.
168. "Thus, whenever I": Stanton, pp. 164–6.
168. "You stir up": ECS to SBA, probably August 20, 1857, NPV, ECS Papers.
168. "I shall not" ECS to SBA, June 27, 1870, Stanton and Blatch 2, pp. 27–8.
168. "To secure 'equality'": SBA to Elizabeth Boynton Harbert, September 24, 1903, CSmH, Elizabeth Morrison (Boynton) Harbert Collection, Box 2.
169. "Dear Clara Barton": SBA to Clara Barton, December 14, 1889, DLC, Clara Barton Papers.
169. "The time is": SBA to ECS, January 8, 1897, CSmH, Anthony Family Collection, AF24(4).
169. "No *one* woman": SBA to Elizabeth Boynton Harbert, September 12, 1885, CSmH, Elizabeth Morrison (Boynton) Harbert Collection, Box 2.
170. "We women are": Council Bluffs (Iowa) *Daily NonPareil,* June 25, 1905.
170. "It is not": *Woman's Tribune,* August 7, 1897, reporting on SBA speech at family reunion.
170. "Every woman presiding": *Woman's Tribune,* February 22, 1890, reporting on SBA's 70th birthday celebration.
171. "Dear Miriam Alice": SBA to Rachel G. Foster, June 22, 1887, NRU, Anthony-Avery Papers.
171. "The sunniest of": Anna Dickinson to SBA, 1862, Harper 1, p. 220.
171. "Dear Chick a" . . . "awful long squeeze": SBA to Anna Dickinson, July 12, 1867, and March 31, 1868, DLC, Anna Dickinson Papers.
171. "My Dear Chicky": SBA to Anna Dickinson, February 13, 1868, DLC, Anna Dickinson Papers.
172. "Dear Dicky Darling": SBA to Anna Dickinson, March 18, 1868, DLC, Anna Dickinson Papers.

p. 172. "real mother yearnings": SBA to Anna Dickinson, likely January 1869, DLC, Anna Dickinson Papers.

172. "My Darling Anna": SBA to Anna Dickinson, November 5, 1895, DLC, Anna Dickinson Papers.

172. "Dear Mrs. Stanton": SBA to ECS, September 29, 1857, DLC, ECS Papers.

173. "I miss Mrs.": SBA to Lucy Read Anthony, September 1, 1871, Harper 1, pp. 395–6.

173. "If there is": *Woman's Tribune,* February 22, 1890.

174. "The one thought": Ibid.

174. "My Dear Mrs.": SBA to ECS, September 8, 1896, CSmH, Anthony Family Collection.

175. "It is too": SBA to Elizabeth Smith Miller, February 15, 1892, NN, Manuscript Division, Smith Family Papers.

175. "My Dear Mrs.": SBA to ECS, October 1902, *Pearson's Magazine* (American Edition) 14 (December 1902), unpaginated.

175. "Mother passed away": Harriot Stanton Blatch to SBA, October 26, 1902, DLC, ECS Papers.

176. "To see poor": Genevieve Lel Hawley to her Aunt Eliza H. Hawley, October 26 and 27, 1902, University of Rochester, Department of Rare Books, Special Collection.

176. "ANTHONY LEFT BEHIND": New York *Sun,* October 29, 1902.

176. "Well, it is": SBA to Ida Husted Harper, October 28, 1902, CSmH, IHH collection, HM 10692.

176. "Dear me! how": SBA to Theodore Stanton, May 18, 1903, DLC, ECS Papers.

177. Box: Harper 1, p. 122, and Lutz, pp. 44–5; See also *HWS* 1, p. 411, for ECS' description of a typical Mott dinner party.

CHAPTER 15: WITH FRIENDS LIKE THESE...

178. "In the autumn" ... "become very disagreeable": San Francisco *Bulletin,* November 27, 1898, SBA Scrapbook 28.

178. "What is the": Ibid.

179. "Nature puts certain": Ibid.

180. "have dwelt since": *HWS* 4, p. xxv.

180. "answer was No": New York *Times,* January 3, 1897.

180. "We feel that": Cleveland *Leader and Morning Herald,* January 22, 1886.

180. "I never could": Mrs. Jennett Blakesley Frost, a New Yorker who challenged SBA on Oregon trip in 1871, Edwards, p. 74.

181. "[Susan B. Anthony is]": Victoria (B.C.) *Colonist,* 1871, Harper 1, p. 402.

181. "A large majority": Catharine Beecher, *Woman Suffrage and Woman's Profession* (Hartford: Brown and Gross, 1871), p. 5, cited in Jeanne Howard, "Our Own Worst Enemies: Women Opposed to Woman Suffrage," *Journal of Sociology and Social Welfare,* 1984, p. 466.

181. *"To the Congress":* Presentation to Senate, January 1871, SBA Scrapbook 3.

182. "Why has the": SBA Scrapbook 16.

182. "Large mail sacks": Ibid.

182. "We assert that": *Why Women Do Not Want the Ballot* (Boston: Massachusetts Association Opposed to the Further Extension of Suffrage to

Women, 1896), pp. 2–3, cited in Jeanne Howard, "Our Own Worst Enemies: Women Opposed to Woman Suffrage," *Journal of Sociology and Social Welfare* (1984), pp. 469, 471.

p. 183. "Women vote! Never!": New York *Herald,* May 6, 1894, SBA Scrapbook 20.

184. "[T]he glory of": "Attitude of Southern Women on the Suffrage Question," *The Arena* 11 (February 1895), p. 366, cited in Mariam Darce Frenier, "American Anti-Feminist Women: Comparing the Rhetoric of Opponents of the Equal Rights Amendment with That of Opponents of Women's Suffrage," *Women's Studies International Forum* 7(6) (1984), p. 457.

184. "And the suffrage": Harper 2, p. 770.

184. "This opposition movement": Rochester *Democrat and Chronicle,* April 30, 1894.

184. "All women who": New York *Daily News,* December 10, 1894, SBA response to question "Should women vote?"

185. "Our worst enemies": Chicago *Daily Tribune,* April 12, 1885, reporting on SBA speech to Cook County WSA, April 11.

185. "They forget, too": Chicago *Daily Tribune,* June 25, 1900.

185. "I wonder if": SBA to Clara Colby, December 17, 1898.

186. "While I do": SBA to friend in England, Summer 1870, Harper 1, p. 366.

186. "I have very": SBA to Mathilde Anneke, September 27, 1875, WHi, Archives Division, M. F. Anneke Papers.

186. "[T]his great national": SBA speech at World's Columbian Exposition, World's Congress of Representative Women, May 20, 1893, "Organization Among Women as an Instrument in Promoting the Interests of Political Liberty," cited in May Wright Sewall, ed., *World's Congress of Representative Women* (Chicago and New York: Rand McNally, 1894), p. 464.

187. "Oh, if I": Harper 3, p. 1165, reporting on SBA's 1900 remark to IHH before upcoming convention.

187. "It is the": SBA to Clara Colby, March 12, 1894, CSmH, Clara (Bewick) Colby Collection.

187. Box: SBA to House Committee on the Judiciary, Hearing; January 28, 1896; DLC, Susan B. Anthony Foundation Records; typed manuscript, with editorial comments by Clara Colby.

CHAPTER 16: DRESSING FOR SUCCESS

188. "First you lace" . . . "your side-laced shoes": Interview with Shelly Foote, Smithsonian Institution, Museum Specialist.

189. "I admit that": Amelia Bloomer, unpublished letter, ca. 1852–54, Harper 1, p. 114.

189. "The boys followed": *Proceedings of the Twenty-Fifth Annual Convention of the National American Woman Suffrage Association,* Washington, D.C., January 16, 17, 18, 19, 1893, Harriet Taylor Upton, ed. (Washington, D.C., 1893), p. 34.

189. "to don bloomers": Harper 1, p. 113.

189. "What think you": SBA to Lucy Stone, December 19, 1852, DLC, Blackwell Family Papers.

189. "her ungainly form": New York *Sun,* 1853, Harper 1, p. 90.

p. 189. "Queen Victoria's palace": Katharine Anthony, p. 361.

189. "I want to": SBA to ECS, 1871, Harper 1, pp. 396–7.

189. "Please tell the": SBA to Jane Spofford, December 1886, Harper 2, p. 612.

190. "Why cannot these": *New Era* 1 (February 1885), pp. 53–60, reporting on NWSA convention.

190. "silk crepe of" . . . "Anthony's red shawl": Harper 3, p. 1113.

190. "her clothes-prison &": Gerrit Smith to ECS, November 6, 1856, NPV, ECS Papers, Scrapbook 1.

191. "Dearest Lucy": SBA to Lucy Stone, February 9, 1854, DLC, Blackwell Family Papers, transcript prepared by I. P. Boyer.

191. "Dear Susan": Lucy Stone to SBA, February 13, 1854, DLC, Blackwell Family Papers, transcript prepared by I. P. Boyer.

192. "Dearest Lucy": SBA and ECS to Lucy Stone, February 16, 1854, DLC, Blackwell Family Papers, transcript prepared by I. P. Boyer, first version.

193. "Dear Susan": ECS to SBA, February 19, 1854, DLC, ECS Papers, transcript prepared for T. Stanton and H. S. Blatch.

193. "Here I am": SBA to Lucy Stone, February 1854, Harper 1, p. 116.

193. "Dear Susan": Lucy Stone to SBA, March 3, 1854, DLC, Blackwell Family Papers, transcript prepared by I. P. Boyer.

194. "Lucy is not": SBA to Lucy Stone, March 7, 1854, DLC, Blackwell Family Papers, transcript prepared by I. P. Boyer.

194. "The dress question": SBA to Lucy Stone, DLC, Blackwell Family Papers, transcript prepared by I. P. Boyer.

194. "I stand alone": SBA to Gerrit Smith, December 25, 1855, NSyU, George Arents Research Library, Gerrit Smith Papers.

194. "If you are": Chicago *Inter-Ocean,* July 16, 1895, SBA Scrapbook 23.

195. "I felt the": Harper 1, p. 117.

195. "while Miss Anthony": St. Louis *Republic,* May 5, 1895, SBA Scrapbook 24.

195. "I am glad": Ibid.

197. "I wear corsets": Unidentified clipping, April 25, 1899, MCR-S, A. L. T. Blake Papers.

197. "The men are": Chicago *Herald,* July 16, 1895.

197. "Dear Friend": SBA to Olivia Bigelow Hall, January 7, 1904, DLC, Olivia Bigelow Hall Papers.

197. "Somehow I feel": SBA to Olivia Bigelow Hall, October 28, 1904, DLC, Olivia Bigelow Hall Papers.

198. "I want the": New York *World,* November 5, 1899, NRU, E. B. Sweet Papers.

198. Box: Harper 2, p. 1113.

CHAPTER 17: PUBLISH OR PERISH

200. "Educated Suffrage, irrespective": *The Revolution* 1(1) (January 8, 1868), p. 1.

200. "Johnson stood at": *The Revolution* 1(1) (January 8, 1868), p. 4.

201. "None but the": SBA to unidentified friend, 1870, Harper 1, p. 362.

201. "The Examiner will": San Francisco *Examiner* to SBA, May 5, 1896, SBA Scrapbook 25.

201. "gaining access to": Patricia G. Holland and Ann D. Gordon, eds., *The Papers of Elizabeth Cady Stanton and Susan B. Anthony, Guide and Index to*

the Microfilm Edition (Wilmington, Del.: Scholarly Resources, Inc., 1992), p. 16.

p. 202. "If the great": Portland *Sunday Oregonian,* July 2, 1905, reporting on panel at 1905 NAWSA meeting, SBA Scrapbook 1905–06.

202. "Our movement depends": *HWS* 4, p. 254, reporting on 1896 NAWSA meeting.

202. "My friends, what": SBA at ICW in Berlin, 1904, Harper 3, pp. 1325–6.

202. "I remember well": Chicago *Daily Tribune,* May 24, 1893, reporting on SBA's May 23 speech to Woman's Auxiliary Press Congress at World's Columbian Exposition, Public Press Congress.

203. "The press was": Ibid.

203. "I had an": report on 1893 NAWSA meeting, *HWS* 4, p. 216; also in *Proceedings of the Twenty-Fifth Annual Convention of the National American Woman Suffrage Association,* Washington, D.C., January 16–19, 1893, Harriet Taylor Upton, ed. (Washington, D.C., 1893).

203. "Women's papers are": report on 1905 NAWSA meeting, Portland *Sunday Oregonian,* July 2, 1905, SBA Scrapbook 1905–06.

203. "The time has": Chicago *Daily Tribune,* May 24, 1893, reporting on SBA's May 23 speech to Woman's Auxiliary Press Congress at World's Columbian Exposition, Public Press Congress.

204. "WHAT IS YOUR": Chicago *Tribune,* May 28, 1893.

206. *"CHAMPION OF HER SEX":* New York *World,* February 2, 1896.

211. Box: Unidentified clipping, January 14, 1887, SBA Scrapbook 12.

CHAPTER 18: CURRENT AFFAIRS

213. "Phoebe Harris Phelps": Boston *Globe,* April 1902, obituary of Charles Abner Phelps.

213. "a very easy": Harper 1, pp. 200–5; also *Fitzgerald's Coy Item,* December 7, 1861, SBA Scrapbook 1.

214. "I can not": SBA to William Lloyd Garrison, January 1861, Harper 1, pp. 203–4.

214. "DON'T YOU KNOW": Harper 1, p. 204.

215. "wife and children": Unidentified article, likely New York *Tribune,* September 1871, SBA Scrapbook 4.

215. "Before twelve hundred" . . . "a few tears": San Francisco *Morning Call,* July 13, 1871, SBA Scrapbook 4.

215. "You women who": San Francisco *Daily Evening Bulletin,* July 13, 1871, SBA Scrapbook 4.

216. "S.B.A spoke Platts": Diary, July 12, 1871.

216. "Every paper came": Diary, July 13, 1871.

216. "The shadow of": Diary, July 15, 1871.

216. "at the announcement": New York *Times,* October 1, 1872, p. 1.

217. "But alas—alas—": SBA to Dear Friends, August 20, 1869, NPV, SBA Papers.

217. "I should gladly": Washington, D.C. *Daily Patriot,* January 12, 1872, SBA Scrapbook 4.

217. "Man is the": Portland (Ore.) *Herald,* November 18, 1871, Edwards, pp. 118–20.

217. "Now comes the": Diary, August 20, 1874.

p. 218. "Hester Vaughan, a" . . . "both were discovered": Harper 1, pp. 309–10.

218. "Miss Anthony wanted": New York *World,* December 2, 1868, reporting on December 1 Working Woman's Association meeting to protest conviction of Hester Vaughan.

218. "in the miserable": New York *Herald,* July 28, 1895, SBA Scrapbook 23.

219. "My opinion is": SBA statement to New York *Herald,* July 28, 1895, on trial of Maria Barberi, SBA Scrapbook 23.

219. "the world is": New York *Herald,* July 28, 1895, SBA Scrapbook 23.

219. "would be a": Ibid.

220. "In December 1896" . . . "reason of insanity": New York *Times,* December 13, 1896, p. 12.

220. "Not until we": SBA to Isabella Beecher Hooker, March 21, 1871, CtHSD, Isabella Hooker Collection.

221. "When we women": SBA to Martha Coffin Wright, March 21, 1871, CtHSD, Isabella Hooker Collection.

221. "When I heard": Washington, D.C. *Daily Patriot,* January 12, 1872, SBA Scrapbook 4.

222. "If she were": SBA to ECS and Isabella Beecher Hooker, March 13, 1872, Harper 1, p. 413.

223. "*this kissing* &": SBA to ECS, May 29, 1872, CtHSD, Isabella Hooker Collection.

223. "BESSIE: I saw": Rochester *Union and Advertiser,* August 24, 1874.

223. "That's too absurd": Rochester *Union and Advertiser,* August 24, 1874.

223. "Well, that was": Chicago *Daily Tribune,* October 13, 1874.

223. "Here I made": Ibid.

224. "in this case": Harper 1, p. 461.

225. Box: Unidentified clipping (possibly Philadelphia *Inquirer*), n.d., ca. June 7, 1872, SBA Scrapbook 4.

CHAPTER 19: GET MONEY—GET WEALTH

226. "I think the": New York *World,* February 2, 1896.

227. ". . . there in my": Diary, January 21, 1897.

227. "She has indeed": Diary, 1902, obituary of Mrs. Hussey, Harper 2, p. 1271.

227. "Often when there": Harper 2, pp. 889–90.

228. "for the advancement": Harper 2, p. 539.

228. "where a woman": Harper 2, p. 598, footnote.

228. "On the sleeper" . . . "of the trip": Diary, April 1884, Harper 2, pp. 598–9.

228. "she has carried": New York *World,* February 12, 1870, SBA Scrapbook 3.

228. "When, at her" . . . "the NAWSA treasury": Washington, D.C. *Evening Star,* February 19, 1898.

228. "You have put": Daniel Read Anthony to SBA, 1870, Harper 1, pp. 355–6.

229. "Dear Emma": SBA autograph message to Emma, November 18, 1874, OClWHi, Manuscript Collection.

229. "If women had": SBA to Abigail Scott Duniway, in *New Northwest,* September 7, 1877.

229. "It is continually": Unidentified statement in Washington *Post,* April 5, 1891.

p. 229. "I trust your": SBA to Jane L. Stanford, 1900, Harper 3, p. 1207.

230. "I was awfully": SBA to Harriet Jane Hanson Robinson, February 26, 1885, MCR-S, Robinson-Shattuck Papers.

231. "A PLEASANT, LADY-LIKE": *The Revolution* 2(13) (October 1, 1868), pp. 197–8, reprinting New York *World* account of meeting.

233. "Yes, and another": *The Revolution* 3(6) (February 11, 1869), p. 90.

233. "What we want": Minneapolis *Tribune,* October 24, 1889.

234. "We now have": Springfield (Ill.) *State Register,* November 16, 1898, SBA Scrapbook 28.

234. "The battle now": SBA to Margaret A. Haley of Chicago, president of National Federation of Teachers, June 27, 1903, CSmH, Elizabeth Morrison (Boynton) Harbert Collection, Box 2.

234. "We certainly are": Unidentified clipping, July 31, 1903, SBA Scrapbook 1905–06.

234. "I think the": New York *Press,* February 26, 1905, SBA Scrapbook 1905–06.

234. "Optimistic? Of course": Unidentified clipping, June 23, 1905, SBA Scrapbook 1905–06.

235. "THE REVOLUTION, you": *The Revolution* 1(24) (June 17, 1869) p. 369.

236. "The Mischief is": SBA to Elizabeth Boynton Harbert, December 23, 1876, CSmH, Elizabeth Morrison (Boynton) Harbert Collection, Box 2.

236. "Today's mail brought": SBA to Laura Clay, April 13, 1893, printed in *Woman's Tribune,* April 22, 1893, Harper 2, p. 742.

237. "One effect of": New York *Press,* February 26, 1905, SBA Scrapbook 1905–06.

238. Box: Harper 2, p. 943; Harper 3, pp. 1145, 1335.

CHAPTER 20: PERPETUAL MOTION

239. "Is there work": Parker Pillsbury to Lydia Mott, probably end of 1853—early 1854, Harper 1, p. 105.

240. "the nearest example": ECS to Ida Husted Harper, September 30, 1902, CSmH, Ida (Husted) Harper Collection, HM 10691.

240. "in her eighties": Harper 2, pp. 931–2.

240. " 'Aunt Susan' . . . was": Shaw, pp. 189–91.

241. "At seventy-four, she" . . . "in twenty minutes": Diary, December 4, 1894.

241. "At seventy-five, she" . . . "for the occasion": Troy (N.Y.) *Times,* July 23, 1895, SBA Scrapbook 23.

241. "At eighty, one" . . . "about the size": *Woman's Journal,* March 3, 1900, reporting on February NAWSA meeting.

241. "Miss Anthony . . . was": Ibid.

241. "youthful looking and": Omaha *World-Herald,* June 24, 1905.

241. "No, I do": Harper 2, p. 1306.

241. "How do I": San Francisco *Examiner,* May 20, 1895.

242. "I attribute the": New Orleans *Daily Picayune,* January 23, 1895.

242. "The salvation of": SBA to Theodore Higginson, 1857, Harper 1, p. 160.

242. "My *back* has": SBA to Lucy Stone and Antoinette Brown Blackwell, August 22, 1858, MCR-S, Blackwell Family Papers.

242. "I get very": Unidentified clipping, December 12, 1879, SBA Scrapbook 8.

p. 243. "BUT MISS ANTHONY": Grand Rapids (Mich.) *Democrat,* November 23, 1897, NN, Manuscript Division, M. G. Hay Scrapbook.

243. "I put a": SBA to Clara Colby, July 22, 1898, CSmH, Clara (Bewick) Colby Collection.

243. "I never call": SBA introducing Isabella Beecher Hooker during 1892 Senate hearings, *HWS* 4, p. 194.

243. "PRAY TELL, MISS": New York *World,* November 5, 1899, interview with Olivia Howard Dunbar, NRU, E. B. Sweet Papers.

244. "Work is my": New York *Press,* February 26, 1905, SBA Scrapbook 1905–06.

244. "HOW HAVE YOU": Baltimore *Sun,* February 17, 1900.

244. "Became faint &": Diary, February 25, 1873.

244. "Went to church": Diary, September 9, 1900.

244. "Monday—felt queer": Diary, September 10, 1900. Harper 2, p. 1225, says Anthony went to her room, where Mary found her unconscious. She was later diagnosed as having had a slight apoplexy (stroke).

244. "The Dr. came": Diary, September 11, 1900.

244. "I wish you": SBA to Jane H. Snow Spofford, December 28, 1900, NR, SBA Collection.

245. "I had the": Diary, January 5, 1903.

245. "Dear Friend": SBA to Jenkin Lloyd Jones, May 14, 1892, ICU, Jenkin Lloyd Jones Papers.

245. "My Dear Cousin": SBA to Jessie Anthony, April 9, 1897, CSmH, Anthony Family Collection, AF 18(19).

246. Box: Rochester *Democrat and Chronicle,* July 28, 1895; also Diary, July 26, 1895.

CHAPTER 21: DIVINE DISCONTENT

247. "I don't know" . . . "side of Jordan": SBA's June 4–6 address on suffrage to Pennsylvania Yearly Meeting of Progressive Friends, Longwood, Pa., in *Proceedings of the Pennsylvania Yearly Meeting of Progressive Friends,* 1885 (Kennett Square, Pa., 1885).

247. "The call, or" . . . "and 'public morality' ": *Proceedings of the 25th Annual Convention of the National American Woman Suffrage Association,* Washington, D.C., January 16–19, 1893, Harriet Taylor Upton, ed. (Washington, D.C., 1893).

247. "Every energy of": Stanton, p. 161.

248. "perpetually stirs us": SBA to Fiftieth Birthday Celebration of the Rochester Unitarian Church, May 1–2, 1892, NRU, Unitarian Church Papers.

248. "Well, I don't": Harper 2, p. 537.

249. "DO YOU PRAY?": SBA interview with Nellie Bly, New York *World,* February 2, 1896.

249. "It is plain": Diary, 1855, Harper 1, p. 133.

249. "God is not": SBA to Prohibition speaker, 1897, Harper 2, p. 922.

249. "Our hotel here": SBA to Daniel Read Anthony, April 1, 1883, Leavenworth (Kans.) *Times,* n.d., SBA Scrapbook 10.

249. "Let your women": San Francisco *Call,* May 20, 1895.

249. "the power of": SBA to John Thomas, September 20, 1852, in Syracuse (N.Y.) *Carson League,* September 30, 1852.

p. 250. "Your little birthday": SBA to her cousin, likely Semantha Lapham (?), possibly February 1896, Harper 2, p. 897.

250. "It is hardly": SBA to family member, 1896 or 1897, Harper 2, p. 921.

251. "I am asked": *Woman's Tribune,* June 17, 1893, report on SBA's May 27 speech.

252. "It seems to": Rochester *Union and Advertiser,* April 23, 1892, NR, SBA Collection.

253. "[T]he woman suffrage": Harper 2, p. 655, on SBA at Kansas state convention in October 1889.

253. "If it is": *HWS* 4, p. 169, on 1890 NAWSA meeting.

254. "I am more": SBA to Frances Willard, August 23, 1888, IEWT, in microfilm edition of *Temperance and Prohibition Papers,* R. C. Jimerson et al., eds. (Ann Arbor, Mich., 1977).

254. "No—I don't": SBA to ECS, July 24, 1895, CSmH, Anthony Family Collection, AF 24(2).

255. "The one distinct": *HWS* 4, pp. 263–4.

256. "DID YOU HAVE": Rochester *Democrat and Chronicle,* possibly 1896, Harper 2, p. 856.

257. "You say 'women": SBA to ECS, probably April 1896, Harper 2, p. 857.

258. "To the Editor": *The Revolution* 8(3) (July 20, 1871) (not paginated).

259. "thrown into this": *The Revolution* 8(4) (July 27, 1871) (not paginated).

259. "Our afternoon meeting": SBA to family, July 1871, Harper 1, p. 390.

260. "No woman could": New York *World,* November 20, 1899.

261. "I cannot let": SBA to Susa Young Gates, December 31, 1905, Harper 3, p. 1153; also see Joan Iversen, "The Mormon Suffrage Relationship: Personal and Political Quandaries," *Frontiers* 11(2/3) (1990), pp. 8–16.

261. "The negative had": Unidentified remarks, 1854, Harper 1, p. 119.

262. "Just three years": SBA to Mary Anthony, May 12, 1880, Harper 2, p. 516.

262. "My dear Olympia": SBA to Olympia Brown, March 11, 1889, MCR-S, Olympia Brown Papers.

263. "[W]omen must shake": Lexington (Ky.) *Leader,* January 10, 1895, KyBgW-K, Dept. of Library Special Collections, Calvert-Obenchain-Younglove MSS Collection.

263. "I wondered how": SBA to Anna Howard Shaw, September 8, 1897, MCR-S, SBA Papers.

264. Box: Stanton, pp. 175–6.

CHAPTER 22: THE PLEASURE OF HER COMPANY

265. "What a row": SBA to Clara Barton, November 25, 1902, DLC, Clara Barton Papers.

266. "The thought of": CB to SBA, November 28, 1902, DLC, Clara Barton Papers.

266. "The gentlemen are": SBA interview with Ida Husted Harper, *Woman's Journal,* July 9, 1904.

266. "And Emmeline Pankhurst" . . . "hearing her speak": In her biography, *My Own Story* (New York: Hearst's International Library Co., 1914, p. 37), Emmeline Pankhurst says Anthony's visit to Manchester "was one of the contributory causes that led to the founding of our mili-

tant suffrage organisation.... After her departure Christabel [Emmeline's daughter] spoke often of her, and always with sorrow and indignation that such a splendid worker for humanity was destined to die without seeing the hopes of her lifetime realised." Unfortunately, Pankhurst got the date wrong: she claims Anthony spoke in 1902; it was actually 1904.

p. 266. "[O]ne would have": SBA to Aaron M. McLean, August 10, 1839, MCR-S, SBA Papers; also Harper 1, p. 41.

267. "I have only" . . . "five thousand postmistresses": New York *World,* November 5, 1899, NRU, E. B. Sweet Papers.

267. "did not acquiesce": *HWS* 2, p. 544.

267. "She felt comfortable" . . . " 'audience' in 1888": SBA to President and Mrs. Grover Cleveland, March 27, 1888, NPV, SBA Papers.

267. "This little speech": Boston *Daily Advertiser,* March 7, 1894, MCR-S, Robinson-Shattuck Papers, Scrapbook 33.

267. "[Back at the": *National Republican,* March 7, 1884.

268. "Miss Anthony then": *Report of the Sixteenth Annual Washington Convention,* NWSA, March 4–7, 1884 (Rochester, N.Y., 1884).

268. "I thought Her": Harper 3, pp. 1156–7, citing her own articles for McClure Syndicate.

269. "Dear Miss Anthony": James A. Garfield to SBA, draft dated August 24, 1880, DLC, James A. Garfield Papers; letter sent August 25, 1880, in *HWS* 3, pp. 185–6.

269. "Hon. James A. Garfield": SBA to James A. Garfield, September 9, 1880, DLC, James A. Garfield Papers.

270. "I can still": Eugene V. Debs, "Susan B. Anthony: A Reminiscence," *The Socialist Woman* (January 1909), p. 3.

270. "The fact is": ECS to Ida Husted Harper, September 30, 1902, CSmH, Ida (Husted) Harper Collection, HM 10691.

271. "A word from": SBA to President Theodore Roosevelt, November 28, 1902, DLC, Rare Books Division, IHH Woman Suffrage Scrapbook 6.

271. "I have always": Theodore Roosevelt to SBA, December 12, 1898, CSmH, IHH collection, HM 10654.

272. "I was at": Katharine Anthony, p. 490.

272. "Now, Mr. President": *HWS* 5, p. 88; also, Rochester (N.Y.) *Herald,* February 14, 1904, SBA Scrapbook 1902–04.

272. "In your inaugural": SBA to Theodore Roosevelt, Harper 3, p. 1345.

272. "while eminent and": Harper 3, p. 1375.

273. "And I hope": Harper 3, pp. 1375–8.

274. Box: Shaw, pp. 206–7.

CHAPTER 23: SPARROWS, SPOONS, AND SURNAMES

275. "and if anything": Irene Strong to SBA, May 22, 1893, NIC, Department of Manuscripts and University Archives, Sarah B. Cooper Papers No. 1273.

275. "the exclusive right": SBA to Millie Burtis Logan, September 15, 1891, NRU, E. B. Sweet Papers.

p. 276. "Oh yes My": SBA to unknown correspondent, February 7, 1890, NjGbS, Special Collections.

276. "I will *not*": SBA to Clara Colby, September 14, 1899, CSmH, Clara (Bewick) Colby Collection.

277. "I think it": Letter to Editor of *Sidepaths,* probably 1898, SBA Scrapbook 27.

277. "I am more": SBA to Lucy Stone, June 8, 1858, DLC, Blackwell Family Papers.

278. "I SUPPOSE YOU": Portland (Ore.) *Herald,* November 18, 1871; this is partly adapted from the interview.

279. "I am glad": SBA to Laura Carter Holloway, February 10, 1888, NB, Laura C. Holloway Collection.

279. "For if *Catt*": SBA to Clara Colby, March 1, 1894, CSmH, Clara (Bewick) Colby Collection.

279. "Don't be afraid": SBA to Elizabeth Buffum Chace, August 30, 1884, cited in Lillie B. C. Wyman and Arthur C. Wyman, *Elizabeth Buffum Chace, 1806–99* (Boston, 1914), vol. 2, p. 185.

279. *"To My Suffrage Nieces"*: *Woman's Tribune,* February 20, 1892.

280. "Miss Anthony, can": Detroit *Free Press,* November 30, 1889.

281. "Dear Junior Girls": SBA to college girls, 1899, Harper 3, pp. 1117–8.

281. "You have a": Phrenology report, 1853, Harper 1, pp. 85–6.

282. "No business capacity": Rochester *Democrat and Chronicle,* January 29, 1899.

284. Box: Harper 2, pp. 561, 624; New Orleans *Daily Picayune,* January 22, 1895; Chicago *Chronicle,* November 13, 1898.

CHAPTER 24: FOREMOTHERS

285 "her father, who" . . . "and notable items": SBA's father had suggested she keep clippings since 1855.

286. "In regard to": Lucy Stone to ECS, August 3, 1876, DLC, Blackwell Family Papers.

286. "Some object to": *HWS* 2, Introduction, p. iv.

286. "In the centre": Margaret Stanton Lawrence, letter to *The Arena,* November, 1885, p. 323.

287. "burned for weeks": Harper 3, pp. 1296–7.

287. "I now leave": Inscription in SBA Scrapbook 33.

288. "I hope in": SBA to Kentucky DAR, 1897, Harper 2, p. 919.

288. "Only think, I": SBA to Clarina Howard Nichols, September 1882, Harper 2, p. 544.

289. "Yes My Dear—": SBA to Harriet Taylor Upton, December 10, 1891, NRU, SBA Papers.

289. "My dear, what": SBA to friend, late 1895 or early 1896, Harper 2, pp. 805–6.

289. "Girls,—yes, I": SBA speech, July 5, 1899, in International Council of Women, *Report of the Transactions of Second Quinquennial Meeting of the International Congress of Women,* Countess of Aberdeen, ed. (London, 1899), p. 195.

289. "[T]his attempt to": Diary, September 22, 1876.

p. 289. "I am just": SBA to Rachel Foster, December 15, 1880, DLC, SBA Papers.
290. "I hope to": SBA to Lillie Devereux Blake, probably March, 1882, MoSHi, Lillie Devereux Blake Papers.
290. "All the work": SBA to various correspondents, Fall 1884, Harper 2, p. 602.
290. "My Dear Cousin Jessie": SBA to Jessie Anthony, March 5, 1897, CLCM California Collection.
290. "I wish I": SBA to Jessie Anthony, March 17, 1897, CSmH, Anthony Family Collection, AF 18(17).
290. "I never started": Baltimore *Sun,* February 17, 1900.
290. "My Dear Sir": SBA to John L. Weinheimer (indexer), May 22, 1886, Author's collection.
291. "Dear Mr. Weinheimer": SBA to John L. Weinheimer (indexer), July 9, 1886, Author's collection.
291. "The book that": Chicago *Daily Tribune,* December 30, 1900, "Best Books of the Year."
292. "These records will": SBA unidentified writings, Harper 3, p. 1282.
292. Box: Harper 3, p. 1470.

CHAPTER 25: THE NEW WOMAN

293. The Daughters": Toast by a man at a February 21, 1851, temperance meeting SBA organized and ran in Rochester, unidentified newspaper clipping, n.d., SBA Scrapbook 1.
293. "It is generally": Speech, March 2, 1849, Daughters of Temperance, Canajoharie Union Meeting, DLC, SBA Papers. SBA calls this her first public address.
294. "The women of": Leavenworth (Kans.) *Times,* March 14, 1889, reporting on SBA's March 13 speech.
295. "I do not": Chicago *Daily Tribune,* May 28, 1893.
295. "I am a": Unidentified clipping, n.d., probably 1898, SBA Scrapbook 27.
296. "It is said": SBA speech at NAWSA meeting, May 30–June 4, 1901, Minneapolis, *HWS* 5, pp. 5–6.
296. "I hope you": SBA to Judge John J. Ormond, October 1859, Harper 1, p. 183.
297. "The true woman": Speech, "True Womanhood," 1859 and later, autographed manuscript, MCR-S, SBA Papers.
297. "The woman of": Cleveland *Leader,* December 17, 1883.
297. "The term [New": Chicago *Herald,* May 2, 1895.
298. "We are all": *Leslie's Weekly,* March 3, 1900, "The New Century's Manly Woman," by SBA.
300. "The modern girl": New York *Press,* February 26, 1905, SBA Scrapbook 1905–06.
300. "WHEN WOMEN GET": Portland (Ore.) *Herald,* November 18, 1871, Edwards, pp. 118–20.
301. "DO YOU THINK": Toronto *Empire,* December 7, 1889, SBA Scrapbook 14.
301. "What we are": *Kate Field's Washington* 1 (February 12, 1890), pp. 108–9.
303. "There was a": Watertown (Conn.) *Daily Times,* April 24, 1894, report on public meeting for New York State Constitutional Convention, SBA Scrapbook 21.

p. 303. "The strong point": San Francisco *Call,* May 20, 1895.

303. "BUT, EXCUSE MY": London *Times,* July 16, 1899, CSmH, Rare Books Dept., SBA Memorial Library Collection, Clippings Scrapbook 1.

304. "Miss Anthony believes": New York *World,* November 5, 1899, NRU, E. B. Sweet Papers.

305. "What women want": Indianapolis *Sentinel,* December 7, 1899.

305. "The woman of": Brooklyn *Daily Eagle,* December 30, 1900, Twentieth Century Supplement, "Woman to Have the Ballot," by SBA.

305. "DO YOU BELIEVE.": Rochester *Democrat and Chronicle,* August 28, 1902.

306. "It may be": Waterloo (Ia.) *Woman's Standard,* June 1904.

306. "Men who say": New York *Press,* February 26, 1905, SBA Scrapbook 1905–06.

306. "I have known": Philadelphia *Press,* February 20, 1883.

307. "I firmly believe": New York *Press,* February 26, 1905, SBA Scrapbook 1905–06.

307. Box: Boston *Morning Journal,* November 27, 1899, SBA Scrapbook 31.

CHAPTER 26: SAINT SUSAN

308. "Biography finished, more": May Wright Sewall to SBA, November 28, 1898, DLC, Rare Books Division, Ida Husted Harper Woman Suffrage Scrapbook 3.

308. "it is, after": Rochester *Post Express,* July 7, 1899, SBA Scrapbook 30.

309. "a token of": Jesse L. Hurlbut, *The Story of Chautauqua* (New York: George P. Putnam's Sons; London: the Knickerbocker Press, 1921), p. 111–2.

309. "not only *our*": Frances Willard to SBA, 1893, Harper 2, p. 747.

309. "Miss Anthony of": Harper 3, p. 1321.

309. "When the meeting": Shaw, p. 210.

309. "There now, girls": HWS 5, p. 99, footnote; also, Washington *Post,* February 16, 1904, reporting on February 15 NAWSA meeting.

310. "Better than to": *Woman's Tribune,* February 22, 1890, reporting on SBA's 70th birthday party; ECS poem, "Susan Wedding."

310. "London papers are": Rochester *Post Express,* July 7, 1899, SBA Scrapbook 30.

310. "It was not": *Woman's Journal,* February 22, 1896, report on January 23–28 NAWSA meeting.

311. "I don't think": Unidentified clipping, November 1892, SBA Scrapbook 18.

311. "Oh, no! It": New York *Sun,* November 16, 1893.

311. "She is one": Washington *Evening Star,* December 1889, reprinted in Leavenworth (Kans.) *Times,* January 2, 1890, KHi, Manuscript Department, Kansas Scrap-Book Biography.

312. "Of all the": Boston *Globe* report on Boston convention of May 1881, Harper 2, p. 534.

312. "Some one wishes": Philadelphia *Sunday Republic,* possibly September 1877, Harper 1, p. 489.

312. "Susan B. Anthony": Kansas City *Journal,* January 14, 1883, SBA Scrapbook 10.

313. "I have the": San Francisco *Chronicle,* May 21, 1895, report on SBA speech

and introduction by Mrs. Sarah B. Cooper at Golden Gate Hall, San Francisco Congress of Women.

p. 313. "They clapped and": Ibid.

313. "The path blazed": New York *World,* February 1906, also Harper 3, p. 1410, reporting on SBA birthday party at New York's Astor Hotel on February 20, 1906. Although she was too ill to attend, the luncheon proceeded anyhow, complete with guests, speeches, and yellow jonquils.

313. "I wish to": Olympia Brown to ECS, probably 1886, Harper 2, p. 608.

313. "I have been": Lydia Avery Coonley's mother to Mary Anthony, May 1892 (she hosted SBA at General Federation of Women's Clubs meeting in Chicago), Harper 2, pp. 720–1.

314. "A Washington and": Sermon by Dr. H. W. Thomas, "Progressive Greatness," at Vicker's Theater, Chicago, 1896, Harper 2, p. 900.

314. "Amidst all the": Berkshire County *Eagle* (Pittsfield, Mass.), July 30, 1897, and *Woman's Tribune,* August 7, 1897, paraphrase these remarks; Harper attended the Anthony family reunion and reports on it in Harper 2, p. 945.

314. "We do not": Ellen Powell Thompson, District Equal Suffrage Association (Washington, D.C.), at SBA's 80th birthday party, Harper 3, p. 1184.

314. "[Women] needed a": Fannie Humphreys Gaffney, president of National Council of Women, at SBA's 80th birthday party, in *Woman's Tribune,* Harper 3, p. 1181, and *HWS* 4, p. 397.

315. "As we sat": Reminiscences of M. Carey Thomas, referring to SBA during 1906 NAWSA convention. Lutz, p. 307, cites Una Winter Collection, 1935. Barry, p. 352, cites Sophia Smith Collection. I was unable to locate the original at either source.

315. "A few days": Clara Barton at 1906 NAWSA meeting, *HWS* 5, pp. 154–5.

315. "Miss Anthony has": College Night, 1906 NAWSA meeting, Rochester (N.Y.) *Union and Advertiser,* March 14, 1904, SBA Scrapbook 1905–06.

316. "For a larger": College Night, 1906 NAWSA meeting, Harper 3, p. 1391.

316. "The women of": Ibid., pp. 1392–3.

316. "I suppose it": Ibid., p. 1393.

317. "I dread all": Rochester *Democrat and Chronicle,* January 15, 1900.

317. "During those days": Topeka *State Journal,* May 9, 1894.

317. "I wish you": SBA to Ida Husted Harper, January–February 1902, Harper 3, p. 1248.

318. Box: New Orleans *Daily Picayune,* March 19, 1903; also Diary, October 8–9, 1886, Harper 2, p. 610.

CHAPTER 27: FAILURE IS IMPOSSIBLE!

319. "I am not": Washington *Post,* February 8, 1900, reporting on resignation speech at NAWSA, in *HWS* 4, pp. 385–6, also Harper 3, p. 1170.

320. "I wish you": *HWS* 4, pp. 386–7.

320. "Of course, palms": Washington *Evening Star,* February 9, 1900.

320. "Miss Anthony was": Washington Evening *Star,* February 14, 1900.

321. "Last night as": Isabel Worrell Ball in Washington *Evening Star,* Harper 2, p. 1175.

322. "Not one of": *Woman's Journal,* March 3, 1900.

322. "I fainted away": SBA to Ida Husted Harper, Harper 3, p. 1378.

p. 322. "Other women reformers": Harper 3, pp. 1395–6; also Baltimore *American,* February 9, 1906, DLC, NAWSA Papers, Ida Boyer Scrapbooks.

323. "Pray let me": President Theodore Roosevelt to Anna Howard Shaw, February 6, 1906, DLC, TR papers.

324. "I wish the": Washington *Post,* February 16, 1906.

324. "There have been": SBA speech at 1906 NAWSA meeting, Harper 3, p. 1409. There is another version of this statement that appeared in a variety of newspapers right after Anthony died. It reads: "Most of those who have worked with me in the early years of the task have gone on. I am here for a little time only, but my place must be filled as theirs were filled. The fight must not cease; you must see that it does not. Failure is impossible." It is not clear which of her colleagues gave out the quote to the papers, but the various clips appear in SBA Scrapbook 1905–06.

324. "We should all": *HWS* 4, p. 260, SBA statement at 1896 NAWSA meeting.

325. "Rochester made no": Rochester *Post Express,* Harper 3, pp. 1430–1.

325. "undaunted courage": William Lloyd Garrison, Jr., eulogy at funeral, Rochester *Democrat and Chronicle,* March 16, 1906.

325. "our friend for": Hester C. Jeffrey, eulogy at funeral, Rochester *Democrat and Chronicle,* March 16, 1906.

326. "her self-appointed task": Carrie Chapman Catt eulogy at funeral, Harper 3, p. 1438.

326. "There is no": Anna Howard Shaw, eulogy at funeral, Rochester *Democrat and Chronicle,* March 16, 1906; also Harper 3, pp. 1440–2.

327. "When it is": Alice Stone Blackwell in *Woman's Column,* August 14, 1897, reporting on reunion of July 25–30, 1897.

EPILOGUE

329. "WELL, MISS ANTHONY": Rochester *Democrat and Chronicle,* January 2, 1901.

329. "If I could": Rochester *Democrat and Chronicle,* August 28, 1902.

329. "Defeats? There have": San Francisco *Examiner,* July 22, 1905.

329. "It isn't Susan": Washington *Evening Star,* April 10, 1905.

330. "I wish I": *Arthur McEwen's Letter* (San Francisco), May 1895, SBA Scrapbook 24.

BIBLIOGRAPHY

$\mathcal{I}$ consulted a number of books in my research, relying most heavily on the biographies of Anthony and the first-person accounts of her contemporaries. What follows is a selected listing of mostly original sources.

Anthony, Katharine. *Susan B. Anthony: Her Personal History and Her Era.* New York: Doubleday, 1954.

Barry, Kathleen. *Susan B. Anthony: A Biography of a Singular Feminist.* New York: Ballantine, 1988.

Bloomer, D. C. *Life and Writings of Amelia Bloomer.* New York: Schocken, 1975. Reprinted from the Arena Press edition of 1895.

Catt, Carrie Chapman, and Nettie Rogers Shuler. *Woman Suffrage and Politics: The Inner Story of the Suffrage Movement.* Seattle and London: University of Washington Press, 1970.

Cromwell, Otelia. *Lucretia Mott.* Cambridge, Mass.: Harvard University Press, 1958.

Dorr, Rheta Childe. *Susan B. Anthony, The Woman Who Changed the Mind of a Nation.* New York: Frederick A. Stokes, 1928.

DuBois, Ellen Carol, ed. *The Elizabeth Cady Stanton–Susan B. Anthony Reader: Correspondence, Writings, Speeches* (rev. ed.). Boston: Northeastern University Press, 1992. (Parts One through Three copyright 1981 by Schocken Books, Inc.)

Duniway, Abigail Scott. *Pathbreaking: An Autobiographical History of the Equal Suffrage Movement in Pacific Coast States.* New York: Schocken, 1971. Reprinted from the James, Kerns & Abbott edition of 1914.

Edwards, G. Thomas. *Sowing Good Seeds: The Northwest Suffrage Campaigns of Susan B. Anthony.* Portland: Oregon Historical Society Press, 1990.

Flexner, Eleanor. *Century of Struggle: The Woman's Rights Movement in the United States.* New York: Atheneum, 1970.

Griffith, Elisabeth. *In Her Own Right: The Life of Elizabeth Cady Stanton.* New York: Oxford University Press, 1984.

Harper, Ida Husted. *Life and Work of Susan B. Anthony.* Salem, New Hampshire: Ayer, 1983. Volumes 1–2 reprinted from the Hollenbeck Press edition of 1898. Volume 3 reprinted from a copy in the Columbia University Libraries.

History of Woman Suffrage. Volumes 1–3, edited by Elizabeth Cady Stanton, Susan B. Anthony, and Matilda Joslyn Gage and first published in New York: Fowler & Wells, 1881. Volume 4, edited by Susan B. Anthony and Ida Husted Harper, first published 1902. Volumes 5–6, edited by Ida Husted Harper, published 1922. All six volumes have been reprinted in New York: Arno & The New York Times, 1969.

Holland, Patricia G., and Ann D. Gordon, eds. *The Papers of Elizabeth Cady Stanton and Susan B. Anthony.* Wilmington, Delaware: Scholarly Resources, 1991, microfilm.

Holland, Patricia G., and Ann D. Gordon, eds. *Guide and Index to the Microfilm Edition.* Wilmington, Delaware: Scholarly Resources, 1992.

Lutz, Alma. *Susan B. Anthony: Rebel, Crusader, Humanitarian.* Boston: Beacon Press, 1959.

Shaw, Anna Howard. *The Story of a Pioneer.* New York and London: Harper & Brothers, 1915.

Smith, Helen Krebs. *Presumptuous Dreamers,* vol. I (1834–71). Lake Oswego, Oregon: Smith, Smith and Smith Publishing Company, 1974.

Stanton, Elizabeth Cady. *Eighty Years and More.* New York: Schocken, 1971. Reprinted from the T. Fisher Unwin edition of 1898.

Stanton, Theodore, and Harriot Stanton Blatch. *Elizabeth Cady Stanton as Revealed in Her Letters, Diary and Reminiscences.* New York: Harper & Brothers, 1922.

PHOTO CREDITS

Cover. Photograph by C. M. Hayes, Detroit, Mich., 1899; courtesy University of Rochester Library, Department of Rare Books and Special Collections

Frontispiece. Elizabeth McDade

Title Page. Illustration from Atlanta Constitution: January 28, 1895, in SBA Scrapbook 23

Chapter 1. University of Rochester Library, Department of Rare Books and Special Collections

Chapter 2. Susan B. Anthony House

Chapter 3. Library of Congress

Chapter 4. Library of Congress

Chapter 5. Schlesinger Library, Radcliffe College

Chapter 6. Smithsonian Institution

Chapter 7. Susan B. Anthony House; Robert Clinger

Chapter 8. Library of Congress, SBA Scrapbook 21

Chapter 9. National Archives, Northeast Region, RG 21, Records of the District Courts of the U.S.; Lois Sherr Dubin

Chapter 10. Susan B. Anthony House

Chapter 11. Library of Congress, SBA Scrapbook 8

Chapter 12. Library of Congress; Cartoon by Charles Lewis Bartholomew

Chapter 13. Library of Congress, The Daily Graphic, June 5, 1873

Chapter 14. Photo by Frances Benjamin Johnston; Library of Congress

Chapter 15. Women Oppose Women: February 11, 1900, Washington Post; Illinois Women Fiercely Attack Woman Suffrage: January 18, 1900, Philadelphia North American, SBA Scrapbook 32; Women Against Women: New York News, January 17, 1900, SBA Scrapbook 32; Mrs. Crannell: San Francisco Bulletin, November 27, 1898, SBA Scrapbook 28

Chapter 16. Smithsonian Institution

Chapter 17. Rochester Public Library, Local History Division

Chapter 18. Headlines: Tilton's Knee: Chicago *Daily Tribune,* October 13, 1874; Murderess and Her Champion: New York *Herald,* August 4, 1895, SBA Scrapbook 23; also, *Daily Patriot,* January 12, 1872, SBA Scrapbook 4

Chapter 19. U.S. Mint

Chapter 20. Schlesinger Library, Radcliffe College

Chapter 21. Elizabeth McDade

Chapter 22. Library of Congress, SBA Papers

Chapter 23. University of Rochester Library, Department of Rare Books and Special Collections; from Emma B. Sweet Papers

Chapter 24. Susan B. Anthony House

Chapter 25. Susan B. Anthony House

Chapter 26. Illustration from Rochester *Post Express,* July 7, 1894, SBA Scrapbook 30

Chapter 27. Letterhead: University of Rochester Library, Department of Rare Books and Special Collections; Grave: Elizabeth McDade

Epilogue. Library of Congress

INDEX

A B O U T   T H E   A U T H O R

LYNN SHERR, correspondent with the ABC newsmagazine *20/20,* has chronicled the women's movement and its history for many years, both on television and in print. She is co-author (with Jurate Kazickas) of *Susan B. Anthony Slept Here: A Guide to American Women's Landmarks* (1994), and *The Woman's Calendar* (1971–1980). She lives in New York City.

CPSIA information can be obtained
at www.ICGtesting.com
Printed in the USA
LVHW091455031019
633100LV00001B/35/P